MAIN STREET, U.S.S.R.

IRVING R. LEVINE

MAIN STREET,

U.S.S.R.

1959 DOUBLEDAY & COMPANY, INC., GARDEN CITY, NEW YORK

CONTENTS

6

ILLUSTRATIONS

MAIN STREET, U.S.S.R.

CHAPTER 1

A MYSTERY INSIDE AN ENIGMA

The sun seldom sets on the Soviet Union.

When a man in Kaliningrad on the Baltic Sea is rising to the count of *ras, dva, tree, chitiri* of setting-up exercises on the government radio his fellow citizen in Petropavlovsk on the Pacific is getting home from work on a crowded bus.

So vast is the territory of this largest country on earth that eleven of the world's twenty-four time zones are included in it. When it's midnight at one end of the U.S.S.R. it's almost noon at the other.

A country is bound to be complicated when it covers almost one sixth of the globe's surface and combines, by or against their wills, peoples speaking sixty different languages.

The Soviet Union is twice as big as the forty-nine states and Hawaii; its area is greater than Canada and the Chinese People's Republic combined. It has natural resources with unknown limits, and claims to store within its earth 90 per cent of the world's manganese, 57 per cent of mankind's coal, and 25 per cent of all iron ore deposits.

It's claimed that anything you say about Russia can be proved true.

You can say that Russia is a police state and show examples. A man sidled up as I was conducting sidewalk interviews with Russians and whispered: "I'd like to tell you some things, but I'm afraid to speak freely." I asked a young Russian why she was not with her husband on a vacation cruise around Europe aboard the Soviet ship *Georgia,* and she replied: "Don't you know that they don't ordinarily allow husbands and wives to leave the country at the same time? They're afraid we won't come back." The leaders who succeeded Stalin themselves admit that millions have been jailed or executed without justice.

But examples can also be offered of a contemptuous attitude toward police that contradicts the concept of a police state. Whatever other inhibitions they endure, Russians show an utter disregard for authority in crossing the streets. Pedestrians surge back and forth in total defiance of traffic lights and of policemen, who seem powerless to stop them even though they have authority to impose fines on the spot. It came as a shock the first time I heard a taxi driver talk back to a policeman who had ordered him into another lane of slow-moving traffic. "Nothing doing," snarled the driver through his open window. And it seems most unauthoritarian, too, to see Soviet policemen smoke on duty as they are permitted to do.

An interpreter named Vladimir assigned by Intourist, the Soviet agency for care and feeding of foreign travelers, confides that Intourist interpreters have instructions never to go to the room of an American correspondent. An interpreter named Victor eagerly agrees to stay for lunch and speaks quite freely, even criticizing Soviet newspapers for containing too much propaganda and too little news.

This dichotomy in almost every aspect of life in Russia soon endows a reporter with a respect for the saying attributed to onetime U. S. Ambassador George Kennan that "there are no experts on the Soviet Union; only varying degrees of ignorance."

It's not uncommon for visitors to Russia to express surprise that "it's better than we expected." Part of the reason is that they expected so little. During Stalin's time the concept grew abroad of Russia as a land of people in chains; figuratively this was the case, and in some respects still is. A visitor who, on his first night in Moscow, hears the voices of Russians singing in the street as they make their late way home and the next day sees children playing jump rope may feel he has been cheated. Even though he may notice an inordinate number of policemen around, the sights and sounds—people hurrying on their errands, a boy and girl holding hands on a park bench, a mother comforting a crying baby—look and listen very much like home in an unfamiliar setting.

The brief visitor sees and is impressed by imposing façades of apartment houses lining thirteen-lane Gorki Street. He is conducted on a whirl of sight-seeing of museums, parks of culture and rest, theaters, and there is seldom opportunity to wander behind the façades to slums where a whole family lives in a single basement room and where an outdoor pump is the only source of water.

The contradictions become apparent only with time. Add to the complexity of the Soviet Union the aura of mystery of hermit isolation. It was Winston Churchill who declared: "I cannot forecast to you the action of Russia. It is a riddle wrapped in a mystery inside an enigma." Even with Russia's emergence, to a degree, from isolation since Stalin's death, much of the mystery and secrecy persists. Apparently the Russians prefer this. Or so it would seem from the actions of the Soviet censors when the Soviet leaders were planning a trip to Czechoslovakia. It was impossible to obtain an official date for their departure. I wrote, in a script for radio broadcast, that the "indecision and secrecy" of the leaders made it difficult for correspondents to make plans. The censors crossed out the word "indecision" but left in the word "secrecy." Soviet authorities would never admit to indecision but they seem to take pride in secrecy. Although some statistics on the Soviet economy and society are now being published, it still is impossible to obtain data which by its very nature might be considered derogatory to Russia—the auto-accident rate, the suicide rate, the incidence of homosexuality.

Even as the veil of mystery gradually clears, misinformation persists about the most mundane matters. A visitor from England called on me with a letter of introduction and a request which he hesitated to put into words for some minutes. "I hear," he finally said, "that you have a map of Moscow. I wonder if you could entrust it to me for a few days." For a decade the Russians treated ordinary street maps as confidental documents, so it was understandable that my visitor looked skeptical when I told him that maps of the city could be bought at almost any newsstand.

When I arrived in Moscow I was told by Americans that it was next to impossible to get telephone numbers, especially of prominent Russians. It often *is* difficult. But on an impulse I dialed Information and asked for the home number of Galina Ulanova, one of the most prominent of Russians, star of the Bolshoi Theatre Ballet troupe. To my surprise, the operator gave her number: B-7 44 47.

There are other cases, insignificant in themselves to be sure, but indicative of the self-perpetuating misinformation that isolation, secrecy, and persistent rumor create. Americans in Moscow assured me when I arrived that there are no dry cleaners in Russia. Certainly the soiled, unpressed appearance of clothes worn by Russians would give that impression. But a limp and stained suit which a chambermaid removed from my room was returned a week later as perfectly dry-cleaned as one could wish.

It must be added that on later occasions my experience with the cleaners was less satisfactory. Another suit was brought back nicely cleaned, but I noticed that the lining and buttons were missing. The chambermaid offered apologies and explanations. Linings are removed because they shrink in Soviet garments. Buttons are taken off to prevent cracking. The cleaning establishment was able to find the lining, but the buttons were lost, and it took several days to find a new set.

In the succeeding chapters I have tried to bear in mind the hazards in writing about Russia—the contradictions, the complexities, the ever present exceptions to every generality.

For example, Russia and the Soviet Union are actually different places. The Soviet Union or, more correctly, the Union of Soviet Socialist Republics (the U.S.S.R.) is the proper name for the whole country. Russia or, more correctly, the Russian Socialist Federated Soviet Republic, is only *one* of the fifteen republics that now comprise the Soviet Union. Russia is the largest and most populous of the republics, and it has become common foreign practice to refer loosely to the whole country as Russia. That practice is followed in these pages.

A problem arises when comparing Soviet currency with dollars. The only meaningful way to equate prices in Russia with those in the outside world is to reckon the hours a man in Russia would have to work to earn enough money to buy a certain product. However, a rough yardstick is 10 rubles to the dollar. This is the rate of exchange at which most transactions are carried out by the Soviet bank for foreign trade: tourists and resident foreigners in Moscow receive ten rubles for each dollar. However, in overseas commerce the Soviet Government prescribes four rubles to the dollar—an arbitrary and unrealistic figure. Here I use the figure of 10 rubles to the dollar in making comparisons.

The idea for this book grew out of a weekly radio program in which I replied from Moscow to listeners' questions about Russia. The questions caused me to look into aspects of life that I might otherwise have ignored in day-by-day news coverage. "Are there chiropractors in the U.S.S.R.?" asked a postcard from a woman in Des Moines. (Chiropractic techniques are used, but there are no chiropractors as specialists.) A man in Houma, Louisiana wrote: "I have a trained monkey who plays a drum. Would he need a union card in Moscow?" (No, he wouldn't, but his trainer would belong to a union.) What's on Russian television? Do Russians buy goverment bonds? How do Russians vote? Are there public telephones? Do Russians have pets? Are there savings banks? Is there a stock exchange? How much does a set of false teeth cost? "Are your broadcasts from Moscow censored?" was a frequent question. (Usually they were, but the manuscript for this book, although most of it was written in Russia, was carried out of the country without submission to censors.)

This book seeks to convey some basic information about an engrossing, fascinating, and important country. It pretends neither to be encyclopedic in its content nor definitive in its treatment. Many things are changing in Russia, particularly since the death of Stalin. It is a country showing signs of emerging from absolute, centralized dictatorship: efforts are being made at a sort of justice; control of industry is transferred from Moscow ministries to regional councils. It is a country emerging from a shell of isolation: tourists are admitted and selected Soviet delegations of ballet dancers, scientists, and tourists are permitted to travel abroad. It is a land bursting suddenly from the age of the sickle into the era of the sputnik.

There are a succession of minor changes too. Sixteen Soviet republics are reduced to fifteen; for convenience in administration the Karelo-Finnish Republic is merged with the Russian Republic by a vote of the Supreme Soviet parliament. The price for airmailing a letter abroad is increased from one ruble 40 kopecks (14 cents) to one ruble 60 kopecks (16 cents). Horn blowing is outlawed in Moscow and other major cities. With the purge of V. M. Molotov the map of Russia goes through one of its periodic revisions with the renaming of factories, schools, towns, and districts like that in the Central Asian republic of Kazakhstan. Its name is changed to Balkash. The city of Molotov, east of Moscow, reassumes its original name of Perm.

In most respects, though, Russia is not likely soon to change.

The clock in the Spasky (Savior's) tower of the Kremlin's wall strikes chimes for each quarter hour and its plangent tones mark the hours. Built in 1491, a year before the discovery of America, the red brick tower with its crenelations and conelike spire has seen czars and boyars, Napoleon and Stalin pass under its archway.

On winter nights the snow sweeps purposefully across Red Square, and Russians, hunched in deep fur collars and fur hats, their legs formless in traditional peasant *valenki* (high boots), seem like ageless shadows.

As spring approaches, the Moscow River, flowing at the foot of one segment of the Kremlin's wall, bears on its unruffled surface great sheets of ice in odd and grotesque configurations, from the ancient steppes to the ancient seas.

Like many of Russia's other churches, St. Basil's Cathedral, constructed at the south end of the cobblestone expanse of Red Square in 1560 to commemorate a military triumph of Ivan the Terrible, is now a state museum. But Russians, who change no easier than other peoples, still worship, and even the Soviet leaders themselves slip into such expressions as "God willing" when talking about the future.

CHAPTER 2

NO PLACE TO BE RUSSIAN

The story is told of a Russian scientist who returned from Copenhagen, his first trip abroad, and was asked by Westerners at a diplomatic function what he thought of Denmark.

The Russian replied that he had found economic conditions very bad. This surprised his listeners, who knew that there was great prosperity in Denmark, and one of them pursued the subject: "But didn't you notice that store windows are full of goods?"

"Oh yes," acknowledged the Russian, "but the Danish people have no money to buy. There were no *lines* in front of the stores."

Lines are so much a part of the Russian's everyday life that it was difficult even for the educated scientist to understand the absence of a long queue waiting to buy ordinarily scarce goods. Russians stand in line for almost everything. There are lines outside an electrical appliance store which has received a stock of electric heaters. People wait patiently for their turn to buy grapes at an outdoor stand. Russians queue up to buy tickets to the movies, to get on a bus, to enter the tomb in Red Square where V. I. Lenin and Joseph Stalin lie on ghoulish display.

Although the Russian respects a line and seldom tries to get ahead of his turn, he is completely undisciplined in unorganized crowds. In a crowd the Russian is rude, even brutal, mercilessly elbowing his or her way and never bothering to offer apologies. At least part of the rudeness may be attributed to peasant directness. A Russian woman explained it this way: "I had my arms full of bundles and was trying to climb aboard a crowded bus. Neither of my arms was free to help myself, but the people behind me practically lifted me off the ground and into the bus. It might have looked rough, but it was only their way of being helpful."

Russians, although rude to each other, are especially solicitous toward foreigners. Clerks in offices and stores display a shocking lack of civility toward their countrymen. Yet few people shed tears with greater profusion and emotion than do Russians at a death scene on stage. Russians almost never respond to a wrong number by apologizing, but rather by slamming down the telephone receiver without even bothering to tell the caller that it's a wrong number. Yet when my wife had a cough, the Russian waitress in our hotel solicitously refused to serve her ice cream, insisting that it would irritate her throat.

Approaches to Red Square are closed during the hours that the Lenin-Stalin mausoleum is receiving the orderly line of ticket-bearing visitors. Yet the cordon of police will open to admit any foreigner, and Russians, who have been waiting in line for hours, will graciously motion the foreigner to the head of the serpentine queue. Guides assigned by the Soviet government's "Intourist" organization will knife their way through a crowd at a counter selling *shapkas* (fur hats) with the magic words "foreign tourist," and Russians generously stand aside to make room for the visitor.

It's not uncommon for a Russian patiently to help a foreigner shop for an item or to remain on a bus past his intended stop in order to make sure that the stranger gets off at his destination. It's difficult for Russians to get tickets to the grand Bolshoi Theatre's ballet and opera, but a visiting foreigner can get the best seat in the house the day after his arrival. On trains it's the same. A young lady from West Germany found herself assigned to a compartment with a Russian army major; it's considered perfectly proper for a man and woman who have never seen each other before to share a compartment. When the girl protested, the porter rearranged the berth assignments of Russians in order to provide her privacy. A Russian may have to wait months to buy a television set or a refrigerator of his choice. I was able to buy a TV set in three weeks and a refrigerator in one by applying to the government bureau in charge of the needs of foreigners. Russians usually live three or four or even six persons to a single room, but foreigners living in Moscow are assigned two-room suites or apartments which are spacious by comparison. This precedence given to foreigners amid Soviet privations must persuade many a Russian that Russia is no place to be Russian.

From birth in a government hospital to the grave in a government cemetery the life of a Russian is intertwined with government regulations that reflect a curious intermixture of concern and contempt. Mothers are granted generous maternity leaves of 112 days with pay, and hospital care is free, but fathers are not permitted to see either their wife or baby during their nine days in the hospital. During pregnancy Russian women are seldom seen on the street; pregnancy garments are not available, so, without clothes to fit, women stay home.

Russians marry by registering their intention, paying a small fee, and returning a week later to confirm the marriage. No vows are exchanged. There is no ceremony. At one time the marriage was accomplished on the first visit, but the week-long "cooling-off" period was introduced to try to slow down the rate of divorce. The district bureau, a small, cheerless room with a potted rubber plant in one corner, is the same for registering marriages, births, and deaths. The government has tried to introduce a bit of cheer into the drab ritual by suggesting in the columns of a youth newspaper that the bride should wear a white or gaily flowered dress for the occasion and the groom should wear a necktie.

In the early days after the Revolution it was easy to obtain a divorce. During the years of World War II divorce requirements were tightened and the divorce act of July 8, 1944, provided that those seeking a divorce must submit to a court hearing and pay a divorce tax of about thirty dollars. Divorce in Russia is complicated by the housing shortage. It's not uncommon for a divorced couple to go on sharing the same room and even the same bed, because neither can find another place to live.

In Russia, too, taxes are as inevitable as death. Russians pay income taxes, penalty taxes for not marrying, and a tax, the amount of which is never indicated, is included in the price of almost every purchase. Russians make out wills and may leave property to their heirs. There is an inheritance tax of about 10 per cent. Income taxes are never more than 13 per cent, but for most people they are considerably less. It is in the form of the hidden purchase tax that the Soviet citizen pays his greatest monetary contribution to the State. This tax is known as the "turnover tax."

A Russian's funeral depends on his station in life. A farmer goes to his grave in an open casket drawn in a horse-drawn wagon or an open truck while mourners trudge behind in a sorrowful column. A prominent member of the Communist Party lies in state in Moscow's Hall of Columns amid banks of flowers. Cremation is common, and a large crematorium chimney rises in Moscow. The family of the deceased is expected to pay for the coffin, transportation, flowers, and other expenses at the government-operated funeral parlor. Usually the union helps its members bear funeral costs. Needy people can obtain assistance from government social welfare committees in their neighborhood. In a land of red tape and shortages it is natural that bribery should be common practice. The price of getting things done is often a bribe. This does not exclude burials, and there have been cases of cemetery caretakers extorting bribes to provide plots for graves. In a period of two years alone two Moscow cemetery directors were sentenced to jail, five were arrested and were undergoing trial, ten were subjected to trial by their co-workers (a peculiarly Soviet practice), and more than twenty were fired for graft.

Few societies have given rise to such a variety of swindles as does the Soviet society. Shortages cause people to grasp at opportunities to obtain scarce items. The work of swindlers is facilitated by the citizen's acceptance of government authority in every aspect of daily life. There are variations, for example, of a fraud by which a knock at the door brings a housewife the word that her husband has been arrested. The remarkable feature of those swindles which have been exposed is that the Russian usually accepts without question the tidings that a relative has been arrested. Sometimes the bearer of the news represents himself as a fellow worker. He warns the wife that the police, who have apprehended her husband, will arrive soon to confiscate their possessions. The "friends" offer to help the distressed wife carry their valuables to a hiding place. Once the possessions are loaded into a waiting car the swindlers drive off without the wife.

Another version used by two Russians was narrated during their trial in a Moscow people's court. E. M. Grafman and M. S. Khilko, the accused, knocked at the door of a sixty-year-old housewife and told her to prepare herself for bad news: her husband had been taken into custody. Grafman and Khilko represented themselves as policemen, explained to the bewildered woman that they must search the room but that out of respect for her age they would permit her to hand over valuables without the need of their ransacking the place. The frightened woman obediently handed the two men 11,000 rubles ($1100). Tucking the money into a brief case, the men assured the woman that because of her co-operation they would put in a good word for her husband at headquarters. No sooner had the swindlers departed than the husband arrived home from work.

Grafman and Khilko preferred old people for their victims, perhaps on the theory that Russians accustomed to the Stalin era of the midnight knock on the door and peremptory arrest would accept their pretense with greater gullibility. They were men of nerve. When a seventy-two-year-old woman, informed that her son had been arrested, protested against a search unless the apartment house caretaker were present, Grafman dispatched Khilko ostensibly to fetch the caretaker. This reassured the old woman, and she permitted Grafman to begin looking through drawers and shelves. When he had found 4800 rubles ($480) in cash and 11,800 rubles ($1180) in government bonds, Grafman expressed concern that it was taking so long for his assistant to return with the caretaker. Grafman went to find them, and that was the last the woman saw of them and of her valuables until the pair was finally caught and brought to trial.

The prevalence of swindles is just one of many inconsistencies in a state where the power of authority is constantly apparent. Sometimes it seems that more attention is paid to protecting pigeons than pedestrians. Knee-high blue fences in Moscow parks and several squares mark off pigeon preserves. Women in white coats sell bags of crumbs and grain to feed the birds. Blue trough-shaped feeding boxes bear the words, "Take care of pigeons." The streets leading to pigeon areas are marked by circular yellow traffic signs with two white pigeons painted on a black triangle. A driver who accidentally runs down a slow-footed pigeon may be fined 25 rubles ($2.50) on the spot by a policeman. If the driver is suspected of having run down the bird purposely he may be taken to court and prosecuted as a criminal.

This regard for the safety of pigeons may stem partly from the fact that the dove is a symbol of peace. Russians deeply hate war. Russia lost more than 30,000,000 soldiers and civilians in World War II. Another twenty-five million were left homeless. In cities like Leningrad which endured long siege by the Germans almost every family lost someone. Yet (or perhaps *because* of this) men often wear rows of service ribbons on the breast pocket of their business suit as a reminder of those days. Also, because of the high price of clothing, discharged servicemen continue to wear their uniforms, although shorn of braid and insignia, as civilians. This gives the impression that Moscow streets are populated with more men in military service than really is the case.

The terrible toll of war is reflected in Soviet population figures. The most recent Soviet census was held from January 15 to 22, 1959. About 210,000,000 inhabitants of the Soviet Union were counted. Earlier, in April 1956, on the basis of police registration and birth records, the Soviet population was announced officially as 200,200,000 people, with a birth rate of about 3,000,000 persons each year. Although the United States has a 20 per cent smaller population than Russia's, the U. S. birth rate is 25 per cent higher. Four million babies are born each year in the United States. The greatest brake on Soviet population growth is crowded housing conditions.

Although it took nearly two months to count American noses in the 1950 census, Soviet authorities tried to complete their census in eight days by employing a greater number of census takers. The January 1959 Soviet census was the first in 20 years, and the fourth since the Communists came to power in 1917. Actually, it may be considered the fifth, because the census taken in 1937 was considered to be inaccurate, the figures scrapped, and repeated in 1939. There were fifteen questions asked in the latest census, including name, age, sex, nationality, native language, education, and place of work.

In the interval after World War II many Western experts had overestimated Russia's population. They had not properly taken into account the nation's tremendous wartime casualties.

The fear of war, and especially the propaganda that tries to convince Russians that capitalistic nations have aggressive intentions, motivates Russians to ask Western visitors, "Why do you want war?" or "Are you for peace?" This same sort of suspicion finds expression in other instances too. With an intensity that varies periodically, Soviet authorities warn their citizens to beware of spies. I was taking moving pictures of a Moscow subway station when a youngster of no more than ten years of age approached and asked earnestly in Russian, "What are you doing, spying?"

In a similiar instance I had been taking photos on the bank of the Don River during a brief stop of the side-wheel steamer on which I was traveling with a delegation of American farm experts. In the foreground of the picture stood two small Russian boys pointing toward ships on the river. Later, aboard the steamer, one of the Soviet officials escorting our group chided me: "That was a very nice photo you took," he said with broad sarcasm, "your employers will be very happy to have such an anti-Soviet photograph." I was puzzled and asked what he meant. "You took that photo," he complained, "because one of those children was wearing a shirt that was torn."

The Soviet Union's more than 200 million comprise peoples of many and diverse racial and national stocks. Most numerous are the Russians. There are Byelorussians, Ukrainians, Latvians, Estonians, Lithuanians, Armenians, Azerbaidzhanis, Uzbeks, Tadzhiks, Kazakhs, Turkmans, Kirgizis, Georgians, Moldavians, Kalmyks, Balkars, Chechens, Ingushes, Crimean Tartars—most of them incorporated into the Soviet Union by force of Russian arms. There are many million Asians of yellow skin in Soviet Central Asia, but only a very few Negroes—most of whom came from the U.S. and stayed. Identification cards, known as passports, issued to all male inhabitants of the U.S.S.R. at the age of sixteen, name the bearer's nationality. (Only in urban areas do women require passports.) For example, Jews are considered a nationality, and their passports are inscribed with the word, Jew. Any ethnic group with common traits, customs, language is considered a nationality. There is sometimes confusion abroad about the Byelorussian, the nationality residing in the Byelorussian Republic with its capital at Minsk. "Byelo" means white, but the term "white Russian" is usually used abroad to describe a non-Red Russian, an *émigré* anti-Communist. Whatever white White Russians there are in Byelorussia, they presumably keep their politics to themselves.

The suspicion is tempered by skepticism. Skepticism runs deep in Russia. There is skepticism of government words and promises. People take little interest in changes in political personalities; they know that they are so far removed from influencing politics that they can only look on from afar. When Marshal Zhukov was purged as Defense Minister and as a member of the governing Communist Party Presidium, a Russian friend said: "What difference does it make to me? As far as I'm concerned, it's only a case of dog eat dog."

This cynicism was reflected, too, in the remark of a bent old woman sweeping a restaurant floor with a broom of stiff twigs. Russians are told by their theoreticians that the Soviet Union has now reached the stage of Socialism and is well on the way to Communism, when each man will be provided with goods according to his needs and without regard to money. Russians know that the Utopian day is a long way off, and this apparently crossed the sweeper's mind when a customer forgetfully walked out of the restaurant without paying. There were a few minutes of confusion as the cashier shouted at the waitress, who, in turn, followed in pursuit of the absent-minded customer. The old woman chuckled. "What does he think—that we've already reached Communism?"

Cynicism about Communism's special vocabulary is also indicated by the slang expression for a paunch. It is called "socialist accumulation"— a distortion of the Soviet economist's term for profit earned by a state enterprise.

The skepticism stems also from disappointment. Russians have long been promised a more bountiful life, and the lack of fulfillment leads to cynicism. Shortly after the launching of one of the Soviet earth satellites I visited the only automobile salesroom in Moscow, a poorly lighted room on Spartakovsky Ulitsa (street). Three Soviet-manufactured cars were on display: a Moskvitch (Little Moscow), with a price tag of 15,000 rubles ($1500); a Pobeda (Victory), priced at 20,000 rubles ($2000); and a Volga, named for the river, at 32,000 rubles ($3200). There was a bustle of buying of spare parts at long, seemingly well-stocked counters, and small knots of people were looking at the exhibition cars. The manager of the showroom told me that no more orders were being taken for cars because they then had a backlog of orders for cars that would take six years to satisfy. There were sputniks in the sky, but for Russians on the ground there were no cars to be bought, shortages of everyday goods, and cramped housing. Such disparity leads to disillusion. (Later the price of automobiles was raised from 20 to 50 per cent to discourage the growth of greater purchasing pressure for too few cars.)

Red tape is also partly responsible for Soviet cynicism. The Russian is entwined in it. It takes days of waiting and audiences at various government bureaus to obtain an identity card and to renew it periodically. Even the Government newspapers are aware of the economy-crippling red tape and, with varying degrees of success, try to cut through it. A story entitled "Snowstorm of Red Tape" in *Pravda* (meaning truth), the Communist Party paper, told of the construction of a railroad station in the city of Sverdlovsk. It was so poorly built that the untrained eye could count ninety-six faults. Nonetheless, the government commission which must approve all buildings before they are put into use affixed its stamp of approval. Complaints about the station's inconveniences poured into the Ministry of Railroads from indignant travelers. After several months the deputy minister of railroads signed the necessary papers to repair the station, but five years later the papers were still being shuffled and transferred from one bureaucratic desk to another. The appropriate authorities keep signing documents which are passed from department to department and the commuters of Sverdlovsk go on complaining. *Pravda* called to mind an old Russian fable, in which a cat ate all the butter and milk. Instead of whipping the cat the cook tried lecturing to it. This was *Pravda's* allegorical way of saying that it was time to stop talking about the station and to start whipping the bureaucratic cats.

The self-perpetuating quality of Soviet red tape was indicated in another *Pravda* piece entitled "Money Down the Drain." It seems that a custom started thirty-five years ago, when Soviet mails were less dependable than they are today, had lingered on although it had outlived its need. Accountants in factories and other enterprises are required to mail original *and* duplicate copies of accounts in separate envelopes to the state bank. Registered mail costs 1 ruble (10 cents) beyond the cost of postage so that the practice of mailing duplicates involved considerable expense. Attempts had been made from time to time to eliminate this needless red tape, but the bank insisted on clinging to the old tradition. Read *Pravda:* "The Soviet Union has solved many a problem, and among them the conquest of space. But the problem of the duplicate is still where it was. A trifle, one would think, a little slip of paper, but it has now acquired great importance from the point of principle. It shows the vast reserves we have for economy that even the most modest of rearrangements and abandonment of die-hard office tradition suggest."

Some of the simplest things in Russia can be complicated by red tape. Obtaining the arrival time of an airplane is an example. The first number I called responded that the flight from Helsinki would be on time, but the voice on the other end didn't know *what* time and suggested calling another number. That number said that the plane couldn't arrive on time because it hadn't even left Helsinki yet. A third number that was suggested for further information demanded, "Who are you? Why do you want to know?" This set me back momentarily, because it had seemed like a perfectly normal procedure to inquire about a plane's arrival time, but you can never be sure in Russia as to what is considered sensitive information. I politely responded that I had a friend arriving on the plane. Finally, the voice said the plane was due in an hour. Actually, when I got to the airport three quarters of an hour later, the plane had already arrived and my friend was waiting.

Sometimes persistence can wear down Soviet red tape. Such was the case when a package arrived from my New York office with typewriter ribbons, elastic bands, and other supplies. Ordinarily the Russians are very generous in their duty-free import allowances. A foreigner living in Russia can import 120 bottles of liquor a year without payment of duty, hundreds of cans of canned goods, and all personal items including clothes, cameras, radios, furniture, and books. The customs inspector pronounced duty amounting to 3 rubles (30 cents) for several boxes of elastic bands, 6 rubles (60 cents) for the typewriter ribbons, no duty for the carbon paper, and 650 rubles ($65) for a box of 1000 paper clips. This seemed excessive for a two dollar box of paper clips. The customs man, a friendly fellow, shrugged his shoulders and said he was sorry but there was nothing he could do about it. It was in the book of regulations under the paragraph headed "steel." No, the other items in the package could not be taken and the clips sent back. The package must be accepted and duty paid as a whole or not at all. I sent the package back. Some weeks later it was received in New York, $14 postage-due paid, and the mailroom clerk at my New York office, assuming it was an error at the Moscow end, mailed it right back out again. This second time around the customs man looked again at the contents, threw up his arms, and said, "All right, take the whole package for 50 rubles' ($5.00) duty." I did. Apparently the prospect of filling out the red-tape forms again to send the package back was more than the customs man could endure.

In spite of repression of individual liberties, material shortages, and frustrating red tape the Russians are a patriotic people. It is usually a mistake to interpret a seemingly irreverent comment by a Russian about the regime as a symptom of disloyalty. An attractive university graduate named Nina manifested an unusually avid interest in American publications, particularly fashion magazines, and confided her apparent disgruntlement with the lack of attractive clothes in Moscow stores and with the crowded conditions in which she lived. When I heard that Nina had been trusted to work in the Soviet tourist office in London I could not repress the thought that this might well be the last Moscow would see of her. I was completely mistaken. On a trip to London some months later I telephoned Nina, and she broke into tears. "I so miss Moscow," she sobbed. "I miss the streets, I miss the food, I miss my friends." My call was unexpected, and her reaction was so immediate and unprompted that it could not but be interpreted as sincere.

Certainly there are disloyal citizens of the U.S.S.R. This was demonstrated during World War II when thousands of people in the Ukrainian region of the country enthusiastically welcomed the Germans. Similarly in other of the so-called Republics appended to Russia there is evidence from time to time of unrest. Peoples such as the Georgians, who enjoyed independence for many centuries, and the Baltic Latvians, the Estonians, and the Lithuanians have in many cases never accepted their new status happily. Soviet newspapers carry brief items about individuals in these areas sentenced for concealing weapons, contrary to the law, in their homes. There is an official obsession about spies, real or imaginary, finding their way by foot, plane, and ship into the border states of the Middle Eastern and Asiatic U.S.S.R. This in itself reflects Kremlin anxiety that loyalty there may be less than 100 per cent. No one can fairly estimate how many Soviet citizens would leave the country if the opportunity to go elsewhere was theirs. A taxi driver from the Armenian Republic of the U.S.S.R. confided in the privacy of his cab one night that "I know America is a wonderful country. I only wish I could go there." But it is self-delusion to interpret these minute stirrings as sparks of revolution. When you get to know them, Russians will criticize their leaders and complain about their lack of freedom to speak freely, to travel abroad, to read what they wish. But Russians will rarely, if ever, suggest that they would like a return to the days of the Czar or that they would prefer intervention by a foreign country to liberate them from tyranny. The pressures seem to be in the direction of bringing about changes within the system rather than in overthrowing the system.

The elimination long ago of an opposition party in Russia has eliminated any apparent alternative to Communism. There is deep-seated dissatisfaction but little evidence of a spirit of overthrow. There are substantial potential pressures for change but few for revolution.

Russians are enormously earnest in their patriotism. They speak with tremendous pride of their accomplishments—the development of their country from illiteracy to a land where everyone reads: a taxi driver has an open book on the seat beside him; an elevator operator reads a manual on ham-radio operations; a cloakroom attendant at the Bolshoi Theatre reads a translation of Jack London while waiting for the rush at the final curtain. Unlike their propaganda newspapers and radio, individual Russians are modest; I heard no boasting, although there was much pride, when Russia won the Olympics and when the sputniks were sent into orbit.

Although education has become universal in Russia, it wears blinders and concentrates inwardly so much that it loses sight of much of the outside world. Isolation has made Russians provincial. A young, educated Russian with an all "five" (the mark for "excellent") record in secondary school and college claimed to have no knowledge of what I meant when I mentioned Charles Lindbergh and the Dionne quintuplets. But, like most educated Russians, he knows about William Shakespeare and Charles Dickens; he has read Upton Sinclair, William Faulkner, Howard Fast, and other authors whose works either are classics or who paint an unpleasant picture of some aspect of life in non-Communist societies. The *Pickwick Papers* are presented on the stage of the government's Moscow Art Theatre; children read *Oliver Twist* in school. Dickens' descriptions of exploitations of workers two centuries ago in England conform nicely with the concept of capitalism presented to Russians today.

Benjamin Franklin's birthday is sometimes observed by Soviet publications; he is described as a great educator and a man of the people. However, the Soviet censors take exception to the application of some of Franklin's writings to Soviet politics. In explaining the nature of the "committee government" that governed Russia immediately after Stalin's death, I wrote that the reason for the various leaders working together might be found in Franklin's words: "We must, indeed, all hang together, or, most assuredly, we shall all hang separately." The censor crossed this out.

Another American who is officially admired is Henry Wadsworth Longfellow. His *Hiawatha* (called *Giawatha* because of the absence of an "H" in the Russian alphabet; for the same reason Longfellow is called Genry) has been translated into Russian, and a special musical background has been composed for readings.

There is a reverse facet to the Soviet characteristic of earnestness. The Russians are a lusty, robust, warm, emotionally outgoing, generous people. They sacrifice for their children, pamper them, and almost never spank them. Russians love to sing, and their songs are the deep-throated, heart-tugging variety that only a people who have suffered can create. They eat enormous quantities of food, mostly starches and too few greens, so that short, stocky figures are characteristic; their appetites are those of a people who have known hunger. The men say they prefer women to have ample girth; a Russian friend, looking at an American fashion magazine, shook his head in sympathy at the sight of slim models. "They're frightfully thin. They all look so ill," he exclaimed. Russian woman stare blankly when you mention dieting, most work, and only a few are coy about giving their age.

The emotions of a Russian bubble quickly to the surface; when my wife and I left Russia on brief trips maids in the hotel wrung our hands and cried a bit at the separation. Men friends kiss each other squarely on the lips; it came as a shock the first time to see Soviet leaders, bald Nikita Khrushchev and bearded Nikolai Bulganin step from a plane on their return from India to be greeted by aged President Voroshilov with loud, moist kisses.

Russians seldom smile, but they do have a sense of humor. A Russian will explain that he must have something to smile about. Whereas to a Westerner a smile of greeting is as much a pleasantry as a cheerful "hello," the Russian considers a smile, without appropriate stimulus, to be foolish. Many Russian jokes seem pointless, but not all. Russians tell the story of a man who called Minister of Culture Mikhailov (the name varies with the teller) a fool and received a sentence of twenty years—five years for slander and fifteen years for revealing a state secret.

The annual page-a-day calendar published by a Soviet printing house carries a joke or riddle on those days when there is no anniversary to note. One Russian riddle asks: "What is it that's stronger than the sun, weaker than the wind; it can move without legs and weep without eyes?" The answer: a cloud. A calendar cartoon shows a young man, tilted back in his office chair, wasting government time, talking on the telephone to his girl friend. The caption reads: "It's time to hang up now, Klava, my working day is over." Russians like to punctuate their speech with proverbs. "The first pancake will be a lump," indicates that any first attempt may be expected to fail. There are jokes about mothers-in-law and baby-sitters and drunkenness. Russians often drink a great deal, mostly vodka, but many can hold great quantities without showing it.

Many Russians are superstitious. Monday and Friday, especially when they fall on the thirteenth, are considered unlucky days for undertaking a trip. Black cats crossing one's path are to be avoided, as is walking under ladders. Witches and fortunetellers persist despite official efforts to eliminate them. A dispatch from Soviet Azerbaidzhan told of the problem of police authorities in finding an appropriate law to prosecute a self-styled sorcerer known as the Unconquerable Zaynob. The lady had convinced great numbers of people that she could bring back wandering husbands, soften the hearts of unpleasant bosses, and generally brush away everyday cares. Seven was her magic number. She solicited seven pairs of stockings, seven bags of sugar, seven 100-ruble notes (totaling $70) to perform her magic.

Another fortuneteller in Soviet Estonia enjoyed great prosperity. She encountered trouble only when she tried to play both sides of the street at once. She plied her trade in a girls' dormitory at a factory, where she learned that the husband of one of the girls had left her. The troubled, gullible girl gave the fortuneteller money and clothes on her assurances that she would get the husband to return. Then the fortune-teller sought out the husband's new *amour* and received money from her for assurances that she would use her powers to persuade the errant husband not to return to his wife.

Russians love things to be big. This may be a consequence of being inhabitants of the largest country in the world; in some cases it may be a reflection of lack of taste. The Russian rule seems to be that if something is big it must be good. If it is twice as big it will be twice as good. A grocery store on Moscow's main Gorki Street takes pride in a window displaying a tank of gold fish. But these are not darting, slender flashes of sun—rather, the size of trout, the lazy, scaly Soviet versions float listlessly in murky gray water. There was great pride in a special outdoor production of the ballet "Swan Lake" with two hundred swans, seven or eight times more than usual. As a consequence, the airy, featherlike quality of the Tchaikovsky masterpiece became a Radio City-type "spectacular," devoid of daintiness and charm. Moscow has some of the biggest squares in the world where principal avenues converge, yet unlike those of Paris or London or Rome or Copenhagen they are ugly and totally out of proportion to the pea-size human beings who inhabit them. Restaurants are cavernous and without charm. The subway is grandiose in size but was excessively expensive to build. Apartment houses are enormous but so poorly constructed that it is often necessary to erect a canopy of netting to catch bricks that might fall on passersby.

Soviet public morals are prudish. The title of the play, *The Respectable Prostitute*, was changed to *Lizzie McKay,* because the word "prostitute" on the theater marquee or on a program would have been too shocking to Soviet morals. Although there are no religious considerations to govern the official attitude toward abortions, Soviet law does not consider that any child is "illegitimate" even if the father is unknown. A State allowance is provided an unmarried mother for her child's care, but the law cannot erase the stigma that many Russians still attribute to unwed motherhood.

There is a characteristic Soviet self-assurance, an attitude of presumptuousness, a certain bewildering "inexorable logic." This is composed in part of naïveté (born of prolonged national isolation) and in part of arrogance (born of constant official repetition that the Soviet way is the best of all possible ways).

It's displayed in everyday incidents. An American correspondent's wife was shocked to find on arrival in Moscow that the kitchen cupboards of their apartment, previously occupied by a bachelor correspondent for the newspaper, were dirty. When the maid who had served the previous correspondent came to work, the American woman started tentatively to reprimand her. "We were disappointed to find the kitchen cupboards so dirty." "I know," interjected the maid. "It was that way when I began working here."

No matter how far ahead airline tickets are requested, it is nearly impossible to obtain them until the night before departure. Theater tickets, even if reserved weeks previously, can be received only on the day of the performance. Sometimes it is just a few hours before curtain time that you learn that no tickets are available.

Soviet "logic" may sometimes work in your favor. An American correspondent walked into the barbershop of the Metropole Hotel just as a customer was arising from the barber's chair. A group of Russians sat awaiting their next turns. The barber detected the foreigner. He motioned him to the chair. The American protested, pointing to the Russians ahead of him. The barber insisted and as he flourished a white apron over the American, he said with solemn self-righteousness: "In this barbershop we take customers strictly by turn."

This attitude of officious self-righteousness doesn't always work to the foreigner's advantage. An English girl, sightseeing in Red Square on a summer's afternoon, wore a décolleté dress and a kerchief. She had not walked far when a robust woman stopped her. Chattering Russian, the woman pulled the kerchief off the English girl's head and arranged it over the startled girl's open neckline. The plunging décolleté was immodest in the Russian's eyes. Such incidents are not uncommon.

Although forthright in instructing *others* how to behave, Russians are usually timid in taking any initiative where their own routines are concerned. There is a persistent fear of "sticking out one's neck." This is an outgrowth of Stalin's rule, when fear had permeated every seam of Soviet existence. It was dangerous to do more than was prescribed. A lathe operator might think he could increase output by modifying a set procedure, but if his innovation failed, he might be accused of economic sabotage. Under these circumstances it was obviously preferable to stay in the old rut. This applied to every walk of life. Year after year a farm in the Ukraine would plant a field in wheat as once designated by argiculture officials even though barley or rye might flourish better. A Shostakovich criticized for incorrect "ideological" tendencies in his symphonies would devote himself to composing comparatively safe military marches. An artist was secure in painting portraits of Stalin. The nation's creative talent was stagnant. The economy was partially paralyzed. The country's administrative organization was slowly stifling from red tape. The toll in production, in scientific and artistic development, was immeasurable. There were countless minor annoyances, too, such as the time I learned that waitresses at the Metropole Hotel were being taught elementary English in anticipation of tourists from abroad, and I telephoned the manager to ask permission to take movies of a class. It took several days, but finally permission was granted. The waitresses were wearing their Sunday best when I arrived with camera and tape recorder. The manager objected. He had given permission for *pictures,* but not for a recording. I explained that the sound of the waitresses pronouncing English words would provide the sound track for the film. Argument and pleading would not persuade him. The tape recorder was a new factor and would require new permission. Finally, I took the pictures and left. A week later the manager phoned to say that he was now prepared to grant permission for the recording. The manager had obviously been unwilling to make a decision on his own on even so simple a request as mine.

It was in this atmosphere that Stalin's successors undertook a bold course of action that was to have profound and unforeseen consequences in the Soviet way of life.

CHAPTER 3

WAIT UNTIL THE LOBSTER LEARNS TO WHISTLE

A foreign diplomat was traveling through the Soviet countryside and struck up a conversation with a collective-farm member. He asked the Russian the name of his farm.

"Until *now*," replied the peasant, "it's *been* called the Stalin Collective Farm."

The farmer's tentativeness was the result of a Soviet development that struck deep into Russian souls and whose repercussions may be felt far into the future. This was the de-Stalinization program, a campaign of erratic speed and zigzag direction, that sought to create a new concept of Joseph Stalin in the public mind. Since Stalin was more than a man, rather a frame of mind, an attitude, an all-pervading influence in Soviet life, the program to devalue his importance caused reverberations in the Soviet system.

There were a number of reasons why Stalin's successors, led by Nikita Khrushchev, embarked on the revolutionary path of de-Stalinization. Above all was the need to restore the quality of initiative that had withered in Stalin's iron grip. Khrushchev, a man of energy and imagination, envisioned great new enterprises for Russia. He had already mobilized hundreds of thousands of Russians to break the ground of Siberia's "virgin lands." Yet to come was the massive reorientation of industry, the transfer of operational control of factories from Moscow to local managers. Yet to come, also, was the Khrushchev promise that Russia would soon produce as much meat, milk, and butter as the United States, although at the time the U.S. surpassed Russia by 50 to 300 per cent in these products. And yet to come too were the Soviet intercontinental ballistic missiles and the earth satellites.

In a country of still-limited basic resources everything was then being used to the limit. The new projects and goals conceived by Khrushchev could not be achieved simply by pouring in more resources; all resources were already fully committed. All the resources, that is, but the inner, *human* resources. Exploitation of human beings was the system used exclusively and successfully by Stalin for a long time, but Stalin was dead. Furthermore, methods appropriate for forcibly raising a nation from a backward, agrarian economy no longer achieved the same results once that nation became a technologically advanced industrial power. Khrushchev himself must have doubted, even if he *had* inherited Stalin's means of power, whether tightening the grip on the people could squeeze out the added human effort needed to accomplish his projects. Something more was now needed: human initiative, a partial freedom from paralyzing fear, a desire rather than a compulsion to work. The ingredient of incentive was to be added to the recipe of force.

This conversion-in-part from the club to the carrot manifested itself in many ways. Pensions were raised. Working hours were decreased. Slave-labor camps, which had ceased to be economic, were partially emptied. Workers were permitted to change jobs under certain conditions. Taxes were eliminated on the tiny plots of land that families on collectivized farms were permitted to cultivate privately. Arrest by the midnight knock gave way to more conventional legal methods. The general moderation in the Soviet way of life became known as de-Stalinization.

There were other reasons for undertaking de-Stalinization besides the need to evoke greater human initiative. It was a dramatic means of disassociation from past mistakes. It was also a convincing way to earn respectability abroad among nations whose distrust Stalin had earned. There was, of course, an element of revenge; Stalin had earned the personal hate of men around him. Too, in the politics of the Communist bloc, it was necessary to call Stalin wrong in order to placate Yugoslavia's Marshal Tito and to effect a reconciliation which, it was hoped, would achieve solidarity in the Communist camp.

For the new leadership to disassociate itself from certain features of Stalin in the eyes of the outside world it was necessary to denounce Stalin.

For the new leadership to destroy the paralyzing fear that Stalin had imposed on the land, it was necessary to destroy the aura of dread that surrounded the man. The de-emphasis of Stalin began soon after his death on March 5,1953, in a random manner by fewer mentions of his name in speeches and newspapers and by a decrease in the number of his portraits carried in holiday parades through Red Square. De-Stalinization got under way in a concerted fashion in February, 1956, when Khrushchev delivered a vicious secret (but not for long) speech before the twentieth congress of the Communist Party.

There have been few such classic examples of the denigration of a deceased dictator by a compatriot since the time Brutus denounced Caesar on the steps of the Roman Capitol. Khrushchev went even further than had the West in denunciation and accusation of Stalin. Khrushchev, who was once described as a combination of James Farley (politician), W. C. Fields (comedian), and Johnny Dio (gangster), read an indictment that accused Stalin of all manner of offenses from vanity to murder. Ironically, as a Stalin lieutenant, Khrushchev had punctuated speeches with adulation while Stalin lived. Four years earlier, at the previous Party congress, Khrushchev had spoken too. He concluded that address with the words, "Long live the wise leader of the Party and the people, the inspirer and organizer of all our victories, Comrade Stalin!"

The text of Khrushchev's de-Stalinization speech was not published in Russia. It was made public four months later by the State Department in Washington, which claimed to have obtained a copy prepared for the guidance of leaders of a Communist Party outside the Soviet Union. (In an interview months later Khrushchev was asked about the State Department's document. He refused to comment on it, dismissing it as a fabrication of the U. S. Central Intelligence Agency. In any event, the text made available in Washington conformed with what Russians were told about the Khrushchev report at meetings held in factories and other enterprises following the twentieth congress. It conformed, too, with derogatory material published about Stalin in Soviet newspapers as the de-Stalinization program gathered momentum.)

In this case, as in many other instances, Khrushchev sought posthumous endorsement of his point of view from V. I. Lenin. The writings of Lenin—speeches, letters, notes, and books—fill many volumes. At different times Lenin expressed differing views on the same subject. As in the case of proverbs or the Bible, Lenin can be quoted to support a variety of views. It's necessary only to select the passage carefully and to place it in the appropriate context. As the de-Stalinization program progressed, the Soviet leadership increasingly invoked the name of Lenin as the source of legality or legitimacy of their actions. Deprived by their own program of the inherited mantle of Stalin's authority, and lacking any sort of popular mandate, Stalin's successors sought justification for their acts in contrived blessings from Lenin's grave. As the leader of the Revolution, Lenin enjoyed the status of a veritable saint; now he was to be almost deified.

Khrushchev found the basic endorsement for his de-Stalinization speech in a document known as "Lenin's testament." Written on January 4, 1923, a year before Lenin's death, it was suppressed during Stalin's time, and understandably. In it Lenin pointed out to members of the Communist Party's Central Committee that "Stalin is too rude" for the office of Party chairman. "Therefore," wrote Lenin, "I propose to the comrades to find a way to remove Stalin from that position and appoint to it another man who in all regards differs from Stalin in these respects—namely, more patient, more loyal, more polite, and more attentive to comrades, less capriciousness, etc."

This long-dormant document provided Khrushchev with a springboard for denunciation. The great Lenin himself, declared Khrushchev, had "detected in Stalin in time those negative characteristics which resulted later in grave consequences. Fearing the future fate of the Party and of the Soviet nation, V. I. Lenin made a completely correct characterization of Stalin. . . ."

"Stalin," continued Khrushchev, "acted not through persuasion, explanation, and patient co-operation with people but by imposing his concepts and demanding absolute submission to his opinion. Whoever opposed this concept or tried to prove his viewpoint and the correctness of his position was doomed to removal from the leading collective and to subsequent moral and physical annihilation."

This description of a lack of tolerance toward any opposition could be applied to Khrushchev himself in his subsequent purges of V. M. Molotov, Lazar Kaganovich, Georgi Malenkov, Dimitri Shepilov, Mikhail Pervuhkin, Maxim Saburov, Georgi Zhukov, and Nikolai Bulganin.

Khrushchev's historic speech was a harrowing indictment of the Soviet system under Stalin. " 'Confessions' were acquired through physical pressures against the accused," declared Khrushchev. "Mass arrests and deportations of many thousands of people, execution without trial and without normal investigation created conditions of insecurity, fear, and even desperation."

Khrushchev recited grave crimes:

"It was determined that of the 139 members and candidates of the Party's Central Committee who were elected at the seventeenth congress, 98 persons, that is, 70 per cent, were arrested and shot."

"The same fate met not only the central committee members but also the majority of the delegates to the seventeenth Party congress. Of 1966 delegates with either voting or advisory rights, 1108 persons were arrested on charges of antirevolutionary crimes."

"Stalin put the Party and the N.K.V.D. (secret police) up to the use of mass terror when the exploiting classes had been liquidated in our country and when there were no serious reasons for the use of extraordinary mass terror.

"This terror was actually directed not at the remnants of the defeated exploiting classes but against the honest workers of the party and of the Soviet state; against them were made lying, slanderous, and absurd accusations concerning 'two-facedness,' 'espionage,' 'sabotage,' preparation of fictitious 'plots,' etc."

It's instructive that it was not terror as *such* that Khrushchev disapproved of. Rather, it was terror directed against the wrong elements.

Khrushchev's recital of the methods used during Stalin's rule might well have been taken from an Arthur Koestler novel; it was confirmation by a man who spoke for the Kremlin of the sort of brutality that anti-Communist *émigrés* had spoken for years. One example was the case of Robert I. Eikhe, an alternate member of the Party's governing Politburo (now called the Presidium), who was arrested in 1938 and executed in 1940:

"An example of vile provocation, of odious falsification and of criminal violation of revolutionary legality is the case of the former candidate (alternate) for the Central Committee Politburo, one of the most eminent workers of the Party and of the Soviet Government, Comrade Robert I. Eikhe was a party member since 1905.

"Comrade Eikhe was arrested April 29, 1938, on the basis of slanderous material without the sanction of the prosecutor of the U.S.S.R. which was finally received 15 months after the arrest.

"Investigation of Eikhe's case was made in a manner which most brutally violated Soviet legality and was accompanied by willfulness and falsification.

"Eikhe was forced under torture to sign ahead of time a protocol of his confession prepared by the investigative judges, in which he and several other eminent party workers were accused of anti-Soviet activity.

"On October 1, 1939, Eikhe sent his declaration to Stalin in which he categorically denied his guilt and asked for an examination of his case. In the declaration he wrote:

"'There is no more bitter misery than to sit in the jail of a government for which I have always fought.'

"A second declaration of Eikhe has been preserved which he sent to Stalin October 27, 1939. In it he cited facts very convincingly and countered the slanderous accusations made against him, arguing that this provocatory accusation was on the one hand the work of real Trotskyites whose arrests he had sanctioned as First Secretary of the West Siberian Krai Party committee and who conspired to take revenge on him, and, on the other hand, the result of the base falsification of materials by the investigative judges. Eikhe wrote in his declaration:

"'On October 25 of this year I was informed that the investigation in my case has been concluded and I was given access to the materials of this investigation. Had I been guilty of only one hundredth of the crimes with which I am charged, I would not have dared to send you this pre-execution declaration; however, I have not been guilty of even one of the things with which I am charged and my heart is clean of even the shadow of baseness. I have never in my life told you a word of falsehood and now, finding my two feet in the grave, I am also not lying. My whole case is a typical example of provocation, slander and violation of the elementary basis of revolutionary legality.

"'The confessions which were made part of my file are . . . only absurd' and 'not being able to endure the tortures to which I was submitted by Ushakov and Nikolayev—and especially by the first one —who utilized the knowledge that my broken ribs have not properly mended and have caused me great pain—I have been forced to accuse myself and others.

"'The majority of my confession has been suggested or dictated by Ushakov. . . . If some part of the story which I signed did not properly hang together, I was forced to sign another variation. . . .

"'I am asking and begging you that you again examine my case and this not for the purpose of sparing me but in order to unmask the vile provocation which like a snake wound itself around many persons in a great degree due to my meanness and criminal slander. I have never betrayed you or the Party. I know that I perish because of vile and mean work of the enemies of the Party and of the people, who fabricated the provocation against me.'

"It would appear," said Khrushchev, "that such an important declaration was worth an examination by the Central Committee. This, however, was not done, and the declaration was transmitted to Lavrenti Beria (Stalin's secret-police chief who was executed shortly after Stalin's death by Khrushchev and his colleagues) while the terrible maltreatment of the Politburo candidate member, Comrade Eikhe, continued.

"On February 2, 1940, Eikhe was brought before the court. Here he did not confess any guilt and said as follows:

" 'In all the so-called confessions of mine there is not one letter written by me with the exception of my signatures under the protocols which were forced from me. I have made my confession under pressure from the investigative judge who from the time of my arrest tormented me. After that I began to write all this nonsense. The most important thing for me is to tell the court, the Party, and Stalin that I am not guilty. I have never been guilty of any conspiracy. I will die believing in the truth of Party policy as I have believed in it during my whole life.'

"On February 4," recounted Khrushchev, "Eikhe was shot. It has been definitely established now that Eikhe's case was fabricated; he has been posthumously rehabilitated."

The Soviet secret-police method for preparing a victim for trial was described by Khrushchev in the case of another candidate member of the Politburo, Comrade Jan E. Rudzutak, member of the Party since 1905, who had spent ten years in a Czarist hard-labor camp. According to Khrushchev, Rudzutak had been told by the Communist secret-police inquisitor:

" 'You, yourself will not need to invent anything. The N.K.V.D. will prepare for you a ready outline. . . . You will have to study it carefully and to remember well all questions and answers which the court might ask. This case will be ready in four to five months or perhaps a half year. During all this time you will be preparing yourself so that you will not compromise the investigation and yourself. Your future will depend on how the trial goes and on its results. If you begin to lie and to testify falsely, blame yourself. If you manage to endure it, you will save your head, and we will feed and clothe you at the government's cost until your death.'

"This is the kind of vile things which were then practiced," admitted Khrushchev. During the years 1937–38 alone, 383 lists "containing the names of many thousands of Party, government, Komsomol (Communist Youth League), army, and economic workers were sent to Stalin" by the N.K.V.D. The sentences of these accused persons were set in advance and awaited only Stalin's signature, which he readily affixed.

"Mass arrests of Party, government, economic, and military workers," said Khrushchev, "caused tremendous harm to our country and to the cause of our Socialist advancement.

"Mass repressions had a negative influence on the moral-political condition of the Party, created a situation of uncertainty, contributed to the spreading of unhealthy suspicion, and sowed distrust among Communists. All sorts of slanderers and careerists were active."

For all of this was Stalin to blame, asserted Khrushchev, and for more.

"Stalin was a very distrustful man, sickly suspicious; we knew this from our work with him. He could look at a man and say: 'Why are your eyes so shifty today?' or 'Why are you turning so much today and avoiding looking me directly in the eyes?' The sickly suspicion created in him a general distrust even toward eminent Party workers whom he had known for years. Everywhere and in everything he saw 'enemies,' 'two-facers,' 'spies.'

"Possessing unlimited power, he indulged in great willfulness and choked a person morally and physically. A situation was created where one could not express one's own will.

"When Stalin said that one or another should be arrested, it was necessary to accept on faith that he was an 'enemy of the people.'"

"And how," asked Khrushchev, "is it possible that a person confesses to crimes which he has not committed?

"Only in one way—because of application of physical methods of pressuring him, tortures, bringing him to a state of unconsciousness, deprivation of his judgment, taking away of his human dignity. In this manner were 'confessions' acquired."

Stalin would brook no opposition. There was "the most cruel repression . . . against anyone who in any way disagreed with Stalin." He demanded "absolute submission to his opinion. Whoever opposed this concept or tried to prove his own viewpoint . . . was doomed to removal from the leading collective and suffered . . . moral and physical annihilation." Even the other members of the Kremlin leadership were suspected by Stalin and periodically purged. Khrushchev quoted Nikolai Bulganin, then Premier, as saying: "It has happened sometimes that a man goes to Stalin on his invitation as a friend and does not know where he will be sent next, home or to jail."

Stalin was blamed for Russia's staggering war casualties in the early days of Hitler's attack. "Documents which have now been published show that by April 3, 1941, Sir Winston Churchill, through his Ambassador to the U.S.S.R. [Sir Stafford] Cripps, personally warned Stalin that the Germans had begun regrouping their armed units with the intent of attacking the Soviet Union. . . . However, Stalin took no heed of these warnings" and of warnings from other quarters, so that "the necessary steps were not taken to prepare the country properly for defense and to prevent it from being caught unawares."

A hint of animosity between Khrushchev and Georgi Malenkov was revealed in the speech. With benefit of hindsight it might be seen to portend the open break between the two men less than a year and a half later, when Malenkov was voted out of the Presidium and exiled to rural Kazakhstan to manage a power plant.

At the time of Germany's attack on Russia Malenkov was Stalin's assistant and Khrushchev was head of the Party in the Ukraine. Recalled Krushchev:

"At the outbreak of the war we did not even have sufficient numbers of rifles to arm the mobilized manpower. I recall that in those days I telephoned to Comrade Malenkov from Kiev and told him: 'People have volunteered for the new army and demand arms. You must send us arms.'

"Malenkov answered me: 'We are sending all our rifles to Leningrad, and you have to arm yourselves.'"

Among Khrushchev's accusations against Stalin were the charges of defeatism and cowardice:

"It would be incorrect to forget that after the first severe disaster and defeats at the front Stalin thought that this was the end. In one of his speeches in those days he said: 'All that Lenin created we have lost forever.'

"After this Stalin for a long time actually did not direct the military operations and ceased to do anything whatever. He returned to active leadership only when some members of the Politburo visited him and told him that it was necessary to take certain steps immediately to improve the situation at the front.

"Therefore the threatening danger which hung over our fatherland in the first period of the war was largely due to the faulty methods of directing the nation and the Party by Stalin himself. However, we speak not only about the moment when the war began, which led to serious disorganization of our army and brought us severe losses. Even after the war began, the nervousness and hysteria which Stalin demonstrated, interfering with actual military operations, caused our army serious damage.

"Stalin was very far from an understanding of the real situation that was developing at the front. That was natural because during the whole patriotic war he never visited any section of the front or any liberated city except for one short ride on the Mozhaisk Highway during a stabilized situation at the front. . . .

"Stalin interfered with operations and issued orders that did not take into consideration the real situation at a given section of the front and which could not help but result in huge personnel losses."

Khrushchev devoted a considerable portion of his four-hour address to denouncing Stalin's vanity. Stalin insisted on glorifying himself, on taking credit for all accomplishments, and on demeaning the services of others. Through history books, novels, and movies, Stalin spread the legend that victory was due "to the courage, daring, and genius of Stalin and of no one else. . . ." He never acknowledged to anyone that he made any mistakes, large or small, despite the fact that he made not a few mistakes in the matter of theory and in his practical activity.

"All the more shameful was the fact that after our great victory over the enemy which cost us so much Stalin began to downgrade many of the commanders who contributed so much to the victory over the enemy, because Stalin excluded every possibility that services rendered at the front should be credited to anyone but himself."

In the postwar years, said Khrushchev, Stalin erred in conduct of Soviet relations with other Communist countries, especially with Yugoslavia. According to Khrushchev, Stalin once said, "I will shake my little finger—and there will be no more Tito. He will fall." This, of course, did not happen, and one of Khrushchev's earliest acts was to try to restore comradely relations with Tito.

Stalin had cities and enterprises named after him and statues erected in his image. He ordered thirty-three tons of valuable copper consigned to a gigantic monument to himself on the Volga-Don Canal. Khrushchev said that "Stalin, using all conceivable methods, supported the glorification of his own person. This is supported by numerous facts. One of the most characteristic examples of Stalin's self-glorification and of his lack of even elementary modesty is the edition of his *Short Biography,* which was published in 1948.

"This book is an expression of the most dissolute flattery, an example of making a man into a godhead, of transforming him into an infallible sage, 'the greatest leader,' 'sublime strategist of all times and nations.' Finally no other words could be found with which to lift Stalin up to the heavens.

"We need not give here examples of the loathsome adulation filling this book. All we need to add is that they were all approved and edited by Stalin personally and some of them were added in his own handwriting to the draft text of the book. . . . In the draft text of his book appeared the following sentence:

" 'Stalin is the Lenin of today.' "

"This sentence appeared to Stalin to be too weak, so in his own handwriting he changed it to read:

" 'Stalin is the worthy continuer of Lenin's work, or, as it is said in our Party, Stalin is the Lenin of today.' You see how well it is said, not by the nation but by Stalin himself. . . .

"And further, writes Stalin:

" 'Stalin's military mastership was displayed both in defense and offense. Comrade Stalin's genius enabled him to divine the enemy's plans and defeat them. The battles in which Comrade Stalin directed the Soviet armies are brilliant examples of operational skill.'

"In this manner was Stalin praised as a strategist. Who did this? Stalin himself, not in his role as a strategist, but in the role of an author-editor, one of the main creators of his self-adulatory biography."

Khrushchev devised the phrase, "cult of the individual," to describe Stalin's self-glorification and the national cult of Stalin-worship that Stalin had encouraged. The campaign against Stalin's reputation was waged under the banner of a campaign to eliminate the harmful cult of the individual.

The impact and far-reaching effects of this Khrushchev-inspired de-Stalinization program would be hard to overstate. The full Khrushchev indictment was read only to the 1436 delegates at the Communist congress. They could be expected to pass its contents in more easily digestible form to a populace not accustomed to such a diet. This was to be done gradually. Communist functionaries indoctrinated Party members at meetings held following the Party congress in offices, factories, and other enterprises. Five months later, the spirit of Khrushchev's text, greatly diluted and with none of the robust phrases of spiteful denunciation, was translated into a resolution of the Communist Party's Central Committee and published in the newspapers. The resolution was entitled, "On Overcoming the Cult of the Individual and Its Consequences," and contained such measured phrases of Communist idiom as this:

"The cult of the individual, as we know, resulted in certain serious mistakes in the management of various branches of Party and governmental work, both at home and in foreign affairs. Mention might be made, in particular, of Stalin's serious mistakes in directing agriculture, in organizing the country's preparedness to repel the Fascist invader, and of the gross arbitrary actions which led to the conflict with Yugoslavia after the war. These mistakes jeopardized the development of certain aspects of Soviet life and, particularly in the concluding years of Stalin's life, hampered the advance of Soviet society. . . ."

At this time, too, Lenin's long-suppressed testament, criticizing Stalin's rudeness, was published in an effort to show to the population at large, as Khrushchev had attempted to demonstrate to the select Party congress, that de-Stalinization was in the true spirit of Lenin.

But by this time, only a few months after Khrushchev's speech, the problem confronting the Kremlin was more one of holding the reins on the populace rather than of seeking justification for the program.

Certainly, no denunciation ever voiced in the non-Communist world equaled Khrushchev's, long Stalin's compatriot, in vehemence, authority, detail, and conviction.

Khrushchev's iconoclastic stroke led to a general devaluation of respect for the idols of Kremlin authority. The license to criticize Stalin was taken by some intellectuals as a right to criticize and question precepts of Communism itself. Khrushchev's words and their echoes stunned the Soviet ear. The repercussions were reflected in bold, cynical questioning by students in university classrooms, in the rewriting of Soviet textbooks, in riots in Tbilisi.

The trouble in Tbilisi, capital of Stalin's native Georgia Republic, occurred a month after Khrushchev's speech, on the third anniversary of Stalin's death.

Although it is Soviet custom to commemorate birthdays with greater public attentions than death anniversaries, editorial eulogy and front-page portraits had marked the first and second anniversaries of Stalin's death. But on March 5, 1956, there was not a single reference to him. During Stalin's three decades of leadership it was not unusual for his name to be lauded several hundred times in a single edition of *Pravda*. But on the third anniversary of his death he was mentioned only twice, and then merely coincidentally; in an agricultural report alluding to crop successes on two farms that happened to be named after Stalin. Another newspaper mentioned Stalin too, but only in a notice about a student who was defending a dissertation in the Moscow Mining Institute that happened to bear Stalin's name.

This cavalier treatment of Stalin's memory gave rise to the first outburst of violence caused by de-Stalinization. Georgians, a spirited, proud, hard-drinking mountain people felt pride in Stalin as a native son and they resented slurs against him. Under Stalin, there is evidence that Georgia enjoyed advantages in government crop collections and in other taxation. The loss of Stalin hurt many Georgian pocketbooks as well as their pride.

When March 5 passed without appropriate official observance, there was indignation, and on March 7 and 8 students, carrying portraits of Lenin and Stalin, marched through the streets of Tbilisi. On the second day the marchers were fired on as they swarmed in front of a government building, shouting protests, tearing up pictures of Khrushchev, and refusing to disperse. Repercussions continued for months; as many as 15,000 "agitators" were dispatched to Georgia to "re-educate" the people, a number of university and Party officials were dropped for the breach of student and public discipline.

Belatedly, on March 9, the Tbilisi newspaper, *Dawn of the East*, published a tribute to Stalin, a photograph of Lenin and Stalin, and an announcement that commemorative meetings would be held at factories. Subsequent articles in the Communist Party paper warned against hooliganism and added that, although it was natural for Georgians to feel a pride in a native son, they should realize that all nationalities are equal and none entitled to special favors.

De-Stalinization manifested itself in many ways. The Soviet forty-eight-hour week was reduced to forty-six. Russians were promised a seven-hour workday. (They still have no right to bargain for higher wages.)

Russians, for the first time, were given the right to change jobs. (They have no unemployment insurance, though.)

Millions were released from slave-labor camps, and effort was made to find them work and a place to live. (Other millions remain in camps.)

Four hundred thousand people of the Chechen-Ingush Autonomous Republic in the norther Caucasus Mountains were given the opportunity to return from exile in Central Asia where they were sent by Stalin for collaboration with the German army. Fifty thousand Balkars, another nationality dispersed by Stalin, were permitted to resettle in their native region. (But 400,000 Volga Germans and 300,000 Crimean Tartars remain exiled from their traditional areas.)

Russians clung like ants to delegates from England and America and India to a World Youth Festival held in Moscow in 1957 and asked questions about wages and politics and freedoms. (But a Russian girl who was seen holding hands with a young American and exchanging an innocent kiss was taken by a policeman before a "morals" board to be reprimanded.)

The Stalin prizes awarded annually for achievement in art, science, and literature were changed to Lenin prizes. Numerous Soviet equivalents of counties and provinces, factories and educational institutions bearing Stalin's name were changed. (However, Stalingrad and Stalinabad, Mount Stalin, and others have remained.) This changing of names reached ridiculous proportions when V. M. Molotov, Lazar Kaganovich and Georgi Malenkov were expelled from positions of Communist leadership for opposition to Khrushchev's policies. The Moscow Metro (subway) originally bore the name of Kaganovich who supervised its founding. Later the line had been renamed in honor of Lenin, but one station was given Kaganovich's name. When he fell into disgrace that station dropped his name and retained its original name, Hunter's Row. Something had to be done to put a stop to this musical chairs in nomenclature. A Kremlin decree ordained that henceforth names of Soviet statesmen and public figures could not be given while they were still alive "to districts, towns, communities, villages, industrial enterprises, collective farms, institutions, and other organizations."

Svetlana's Breath, a perfume named after Stalin's daughter, fell into bad odor and disappeared from cosmetic counters.

In his speech Khrushchev criticized Stalin for commissioning a national anthem which praised Stalin but contained not a word about the Communist Party. It would be necessary to compose "a new text of the anthem, which will reflect the role of the people, and the role of the Party," said Khrushchev. Adopted on May 15, 1944, to replace the "International" with its call to workers of the world to arise, the words of the Soviet national anthem were dropped. Because of the mention of Stalin in the third stanza, it was considered unsuitable for singing in the era of de-Stalinization:

Unbreakable Union of Freedom's Republics
Great Russia has welded forever to stand.
Long live the creation of will of the public
United and mighty our Soviet land.

Glory to our motherland. Glory to our Freeland.
Bulwark of nations, both friendly and strong.
Banner of Soviets. Banner of People,
Leads us from victory to victory on.

Through tempests the sun of our freedom's been shining,
Great Lenin has lit us a new way indeed,
And Stalin has reared us faithful to people
Inspired to labor and heroic deed.

Our Army has grown and matured in fighting
To all base invaders we shall put an end.
The fate of mankind in battle deciding
To glory we'll bring our dear motherland.

These words used to provide a signature at midnight to Radio Moscow's broadcasts, but with de-Stalinization only the stirring music was played—without words.

A larger-than-life-size statue of Stalin in a Napoleonesque pose, hand inserted in jacket, no longer stands at the end of the cavernous lobby of the Hotel Moscow. The day that five potted palm trees appeared in its stead, I asked the doorman about it. He winked slyly, drew his forefinger across his neck and said: "They took it out last night."

The statue of Stalin in the House of Journalists also disappeared from its accustomed place on the staircase landing. In the Tretyakov Gallery old Russian classics by Shishkin, Repin, and Kramskoi have replaced portraits of Stalin. (However, Stalin remained in lobbies of the Metropole and National Hotels and stone statues of Stalin continued to dominate Moscow's Gorki Park and Agricultural Exhibition and countless thousands of Soviet enterprises throughout the land.)

The name of the Moscow Stalin Auto Works was changed to the Likhatchov Auto Works. (But Stalin's body still lies next to the revered Lenin's in the mausoleum in Red Square.)

Ambiguity also is reflected in conversations with Russians. Shortly after the initiation of the program to revise the public's idea of Stalin, I spoke with a number of people threading their way in the queue through Red Square into the Lenin-Stalin tomb. Russians who had learned to keep a civil tongue in their heads during Stalin's time were not about to change quickly.

Yes, said a man with a tan straw hat, he had read the criticism of Stalin in the newspapers. What did he think of it? Certainly it was correct criticism, he replied, confident that he was on safe ground, at least for the moment, in agreeing with the newspapers. Other Russians farther down the line replied with carbon-copy phrases from *Pravda*. What did a man holding a child in his arms think of Stalin while he lived? A moment of hesitation and the man replied: "I didn't think about it."

On the pavement along which pilgrims to the mausoleum leave, a broad-faced Muscovite paused to chat. He had waited many months to obtain a ticket to visit the mausoleum and he said it was "good" to see the embalmed leaders. But what were his reactions to the sight of Stalin's body now that his errors and crimes had been exposed? "It reinforced the intensity of my feeling, and I felt sorry for the innocent Party comrades who suffered," was his reply. The man moved on. Others shrugged and refused to discuss the subject.

After years of experience in discipline those Russians who would talk with a stranger about Stalin were quick to agree that whatever the present leaders said was correct. Under the conditions of Stalin's oppressive rule people learned to keep their thoughts and attitudes to themselves and, when it was necessary to speak, to parrot only what appeared in Soviet newspapers. Russians are still cautious, even though they are told that things are different now, as in some ways they are.

There is less reticence in conversation in private. A friend in the Foreign Ministry tells you that tears of sympathy welled in the eyes of several old-time employees when V. M. Molotov entered a ministry elevator after de-Stalinist Khrushchev had ousted Molotov for his pro-Stalinist tendencies. A taxi driver nods his head toward black stone

Lubiyanka prison on a late night drive and says: "When Stalin lived worse things happened there than even in the Spanish Inquisition. Things are better now." An intelligent young Russian friend, born and brought up under Stalin, objected to my questions about the abundance of statues of the dictator in park, factory, and office—and about the disappearance of some. "Please don't joke about that," said the boy, indoctrinated in impressionable years to believe in Stalin as the great benefactor, "I loved that man." A Soviet journalist spoke with emotion: "You Americans think we know nothing about freedom. We know enough to realize that we lacked the freedom even to breath without fear when that evil madman lived."

There is a reticence and embarrassment among Russians in speaking to foreigners about Stalin. No one likes to admit to a foreigner that his nation has been wrong and that almost every derogatory phrase spoken about Stalin in the West now has been echoed by the Soviet leaders themselves.

The attitude of Russians was demonstrated, too, in an experience of my wife, who, with limited knowledge of Russian, set out in search of a food store in Moscow specializing in Georgian products. Not knowing the Russian words for "Georgian store," she tried to solicit directions by sign language. A small crowd gathered around an ice-cream stand as she pointed to a spot on her hand that would be Moscow and then to Georgia's relative position. No one understood. Then she recalled that Stalin had been born in Georgia. She cradled her arms as if holding a baby, and said: "Baby, Stalin." The knot of people dispersed as if stung by bees. A policeman eyed her suspiciously, wondering what kind of public agitation this foreigner was attempting.

The impact of de-Stalinization is perhaps greatest on young Russians. They were brought up in a kind of worship of Stalin. On a visit before Khrushchev's speech to a camp for Pioneers, an organization for primary-school-age Russians, I heard youngsters, age eight, singing:

> *"We were born in the land of Stalin,*
> *We were born in the land of Lenin.*
> *We were born in the land that has never been defeated,*
> *We were born in the land that will always be victorious."*

Disillusionment of youth is a serious result of de-Stalinization which may have profound consequences in the future. A girl in her last year in the Pedagogical Institute told of an incident: a history teacher, lecturing on World War II, attributed victory over the Germans to the wisdom and unerring leadership of the Communist Party.

A bold student raised his hand. "How did we ever win the war against Napoleon when there was no Communist Party?" There were cases of students raising questions of whether Stalin's successors did not in fact share some of Stalin's guilt for tortures, unfair trials, and executions since they were in positions of responsibility under Stalin.

Confusion and embarrassment were evident—and will continue to be—as the Soviet nation adjusts to the new order. A guard in the hallway of the Ministry of Communications pretended not to have noticed that a triple life-size statue of Stalin had been removed. He assured me he was on vacation and never had been aware before of a statue there. The Ukrainian Republic announced the decision of its Supreme Soviet to combine the Lenin and Stalin districts in the area of Lvov, and to no one's astonishment the resultant enlarged district retains the name of Lenin. The big Soviet Encyclopedia (which was being issued at the rate of one volume per month) skipped, for the moment, the volume containing Stalin's biography when it was due. Instead, the volume for the next letters of the alphabet was published while the editors awaited the final, approved version of Stalin. The missing volume was finally published more than a year later. With the passage of time, it deals more kindly with Stalin than had Khrushchev, for it recites the many offices held by the late dictator, referring to him as an "outstanding follower and disciple" of Lenin, and speaks of his "devotion to the working class, his selfless struggle for Socialism, for Marxism-Leninism." However, it questions certain writings of Stalin, in particular his assertion that "wars are inevitable under present conditions between capitalist countries." The Encyclopedia reiterates the Central Committee's denunciation of Stalin's self-glorification and of his errors in considering himself infallible, in using mass repressions against political enemies, in failing to heed warnings of German attack, and so on.

The Encyclopedia's section on Stalin stresses that Stalin's peculiar crime, the creation of a "cult of the individual"— a euphemism for one-man dictatorship—is "not inherent in the nature of a socialist society." This is a questionable premise.

The *Short History of the Communist Party*, which in his later years was ascribed to Stalin's authorship, had been required reading for university students. Now it was withdrawn. History courses covering the Stalin era were canceled until textbooks could be rewritten to conform with the new version of Stalin. For a period of time history examinations were called off because students had been taught the wrong answers about two decades of Soviet history.

All of this indicates what a volatile process was de-Stalinization— this attempt to moderate the extremes of Stalinism. In a way it was like setting fire to grass or dead leaves in a back yard. You want to burn the leaves (in this case the aspects of Stalin's rule which inhibit national progress), but the problem is to see that the fire doesn't get out of hand and burn down your house (in this case Kremlin authority). The fire is allowed to spread just so far in one direction and then must be doused.

It became open season for a time for criticism of Stalin, and the criticism spread to the Soviet system itself. In April 1956, just two months after the Khrushchev speech, *Pravda* drew the reins by reminding Russians that license to criticize Stalin did not mean license to criticize the Communist Party.

"Pretending to condemn the cult of the individual," said *Pravda*, "some rotten elements are trying to question the correctness of the Party's policy . . . Some rotten elements are trying to make use of criticism and self-criticism for all sorts of slanderous inventions and anti-Party assertions."

"At a certain scientific laboratory," reported *Pravda*, staff workers Avalov, Orlov, Nesterov, and Shchedrin "made use of inter-Party democracy for slanderous statements directed against the Party's policy and its Leninist foundations."

A Communist Party resolution felt it necessary to explain that it was not a lack of personal courage that deterred the men around Stalin from preventing his excesses, but rather that historical conditions were such that the people would not have understood or sympathized with efforts to restrain Stalin.

The pressure of public opinion, however feeble it may be in Russia, forced Stalin's heirs to explanations in the Party apologia:

"The question may arise: why did not these people openly oppose Stalin and remove him from the leadership? That could not be done in the conditions then prevailing. Indisputably, the facts show that Stalin was responsible for many unlawful actions, particularly during the concluding period of his life. But it should not be forgotten that the Soviet people knew Stalin as a man who fought for the socialist cause. In this struggle he at times resorted to unworthy methods and violated the Leninist principles and standards of Party life. Herein lay the tragedy of Stalin. But at the same time, all this made it difficult to combat the unlawful actions then being committed, for the successes of building socialism and the strengthening of the U.S.S.R. were, in this atmosphere of the cult of the individual, credited to Stalin.

"In these circumstances, opposition to Stalin would not have been understood by the people; it was not at all a matter of lack of personal courage. Clearly, anyone who opposed Stalin would not, in this situation, have had the support of the people."

The pace of de-Stalinization slowed down drastically when near-revolution in Poland and open revolution in Hungary demonstrated that by renouncing Stalin, whose prestige had been nurtured for a generation, the Kremlin's new leaders placed in jeopardy the very respect for authority by which they govern.

A few months after Hungary it was necessary for Khrushchev, originator of de-Stalinization, to backpedal on his condemnation. In some respects, Stalin was a model Communist worthy of emulation, said Khrushchev, correcting himself. If Stalinism meant discipline, Khrushchev, shaken by events in Hungary, could not help but covet it. Finally, the authorized version of Stalin seemed to boil down to this: Stalin did much good in his early career, but in old age he became vain and listened to bad advice, committing serious violations of "socialist justice." The excesses of Stalin must not be repeated, but Stalin must be respected, and especially the authority that he represented.

However, having lifted the lid of repression a bit, the Soviet leaders cannot clamp it down again without risking pressures of public dissatisfaction. Having breathed a bit of the sweet air of freedom, the Soviet people desire more. In taking hold of de-Stalinization, the Kremlin leaders seized a bear by the tail. They cannot very well let go of de-Stalinization completely without discrediting themselves and perhaps being devoured by public discontent.

De-Stalinization, although it has meant a more amenable attitude toward intercourse with non-Communist nations, has never meant renunciation of Communist ambitions. Khrushchev once said that if anyone thought that Communists had ceased to believe in the eventual peaceful world triumph of Communism, they were wrong; "We will bury you," he warned the West. On another occasion, Khrushchev declared that if anyone expected that demolishing Stalin's cult of the individual would mean abandonment of Communism's objectives, he could wait until the lobster learns to whistle. (When Khrushchev's remark was circulated abroad in news dispatches the phrase was translated, "until the *shrimp* learns to whistle." Actually, the Russian word used was *rak* meaning lobster; shrimp is virtually unknown in the Russian diet.) On still another occasion, the initiator of de-Stalinization declared: "We are for co-existence. But we are also for the growth of Communism. . . .

"We wish to live in peace. But if anyone thinks that our smiles mean that we abandon the teachings of Marx and Lenin or abandon our Communist road, then he is fooling himself. You might as well say that Easter always falls on Tuesday."

The term "collective leadership" rang out in speeches, declarations, and *Pravda* editorials during the heyday of de-Stalinization. It meant rule by a group rather than by an individual. It was to be a way of correcting Stalin's errors of one-man rule. But "collective leadership" lasted only as long as it took Khrushchev to eliminate the other members of the "collective" or committee.

It was a concept born of necessity. Upon Stalin's death Lavrenti Beria had attempted to use his control of the secret-police apparatus to seize Stalin's prerogatives. Without an institutionalized, traditional, constitution-based method for transferring power, the question of who succeeded Stalin became largely a question of who was strongest. Beria might have been, had not Stalin's other successors joined forces to execute him. In order to prevent any *one* of them from assuming absolute power it was necessary to *all* of them to share power. It was an alliance imposed by the knowledge that only in a committee type of leadership could each of the members protect himself from a repetition of Stalinist one-man tyranny. However, it proved to be a false assumption. Khrushchev, by gradually weeding the membership of the Party's Central Committee (which he came to manipulate as his instrument of power just as Stalin had used the secret police), was able to eliminate the other important members of the "collective leadership."

The hypocrisy and cynicism of Soviet political life was demonstrated with telling clarity in the manner in which the term "collective leadership" was foisted on the people and then, without public explanation given or demanded, it quietly waned.

Equally hypocritical was the manner in which Khrushchev permitted himself to be showered with phrases of praise. This was the sort of personal glorification that Khrushchev himself had criticized Stalin for encouraging. The phrases were not as frequent or as fulsome as Stalin's, but the similarity is there. N. A. Mukhitdinov, a member of the Kremlin's Presidium, declared in a speech: "Comrade Khrushchev, the leader of our government, Party, and people, is a faithful pupil and continuer of Lenin's great cause." This was followed—stated the official account—by applause, cheers, and shouts of "hail Khrushchev."

At the opening of a farm exhibition, agricultural leaders declared that, "We promise *you*, Nikita Sergeyevich, that targets will be overfulfilled." A small-scale version of Stalin's "cult of the individual" (or "personality cult," as it is also called) had thus been created around Khrushchev.

The nearly full circle run by the leaders of the Khrushchev era in their attitude toward Stalinism was reflected in a small news item less than two years after Khrushchev's famous speech. Members of the Communist Party, as they do in all Kremlin programs, set the course for villagers in Soviet Turkmenistan. They decided to rename their village, long called Voroshilov. Its new name, of all names, was Stalin.

CHAPTER 4

THE FOUR PER CENT BRACKET

Lenin is supposed to have remarked once with engaging candor that there could be any number of political parties in the Soviet Union but only on one condition. The Communist Party must be in power and all the other parties must be in jail.

The Communists justify their political monopoly by explaining that there is no need for an opposition party. Opposition parties are necessary only when they represent *opposing* class interests. In the Soviet Union, runs the Communist argument, there are no *opposing* classes. The only classes, the workers and peasants, have similar rather than contradictory interests. The Communist Party defends their interests. The workers and peasants would not tolerate any attempt to undermine their interests by an opposition party.

From time to time the Communist Party feels compelled to justify the existence of only one political party, without legal opposition. One such explanation, written by A. F. Gorkin, a prominent Communist who has held various positions including that of secretary of the Presidium of the Supreme Soviet.

In an article entitled "Soviet Democracy is the Highest Form of Democracy," Gorkin wrote: "Bourgeois propaganda has often pointed out that in the U.S.S.R. there is only one party and that only one candidate is voted in each election district. Thereby they seek to cast doubts on the consistently democratic nature of the Soviet electoral system.

"It is true that there is only one party in the Soviet Union. And this is not an accident but rather conditioned by history. In the struggle for the overthrow of the autocracy and the winning of power by the working class, in the struggle with the internal counter-revolution and foreign intervention, and in the construction of socialism, the Communist Party has, by its unflagging care to raise the material well-being of the working folk, won undivided prestige among the people, their love and boundless trust.

"It is not our fault that the once existing petty bourgeois parties of the Socialist-Revolutionaries and Mensheviks had sunk to the position of direct accomplices of the counter-revolution and, having lost all influence on the working people, have ingloriously departed from the historical scene. In Soviet society there is no ground for the existence of other parties. One cannot demand that after the victory of socialism, after the elimination of the exploiting classes, political corpses should be artificially resuscitated!

"Since there are no opposing antagonistic classes in the U.S.S.R. there are also no parties which would reflect the opposing interests of these classes, and there is no need to put up rival candidates in our elections. This reflects the socialist essence of our state, its moral-political unity, the inviolable unity of the Party and the people."

Gorkin might also have added the simple statement that it is in effect illegal even to suggest that another political party be formed. During the first flush days of de-Stalinization, certain professors of the Communist Party unit at Moscow University are said to have raised in theoretical discussion the suggestion that the time might now be appropriate to permit a modified form of second party. The professors are reported to have been subsequently severely reprimanded, expelled from the Party, and warned about uttering such heresy again.

The Communist Party consists of only seven million members out of a population of more than two hundred million people. Less than four per cent of the Soviet people are members of the Party. And, in fact, it is only a small portion of this four per cent that runs the country. It is the elite class, the privileged few in a country of underprivileged people. It is small wonder that *Pravda* could not restrain itself and ignore the book, *The New Class,* written by disillusioned Yugoslav Communist leader Djilas. Djilas's first-hand appraisal of the Communist Party as a new exploiting class burned deep into Communist conscience. Without mentioning the actual content of the book, *Pravda* denounced it for "insinuations and hostile attacks on the Communist Party." Djilas himself was described as a renegade belonging to the "miserable set of a demoralized, cowardly movement," a traitor to the people and the revolution. *Pravda's* real rage lay in the fact that Djilas was a traitor to the Communist class in a society which claims to be classless.

At the time of the 1917 Revolution the Party claimed to have numbered only 240,000 members; in 1938 its membership had grown to 2,300,000; and at the end of World War II, in 1945, there were about six million. The growth since then has been much slower; the leadership apparently preferring exclusivity to broad membership. A small, selected group can be more effectively controlled than a mass representative party.

It is no easy matter to join the Communist Party in Russia. It is considered an honor to belong. No one knows how many millions of Russians, if given the chance, would refuse to join because they oppose Communist principles, but it is certain that the Party could be at least several times larger than it is today if the Kremlin leadership were to decide to expand. No one can estimate, either, how many Party members pay only lip service to the Party's principles. Certainly there are many who belong because it is one of the few ways of achieving a privileged position in the Soviet Union. Money does not obtain a roomier apartment in Russia. Party membership will. Neither money nor, in fact, a responsible position as a plant manager, a scientist, or a writer in itself wields real influence in Russia. Party membership does. Prestige and influence, if not always respect, go with Party membership in Russia. One of the first adjustments a correspondent has to make in reporting from Russia is to rid himself of a feeling of self-consciousness in asking people if they are members of the Communist Party. In interviewing a person in the United States such a question is usually regarded as an insult. In Russia, of course, an affirmative answer is given with pride.

To join the Party a Russian must be nominated by three Party members (each of whom has been in the Party at least three years) in the office or factory or institution where he works. Sponsorship is not lightly given, because sponsors are held responsible for their candidates. The would-be member is interviewed and investigated by members of the Party unit to which he has applied first. To be admitted as a candidate member, he must receive a majority vote. His period as a candidate member or, in effect, as a Party apprentice, may run for months or years before he is again voted on for full membership. Usually the period of probation runs one year. A person is eligible for Party membership at the age of eighteen.

Party units of varying size in every factory, collective farm, every city district, every town and village, in schools, in offices, in military units, and aboard navy ships, form the base of the Communist Party. There are more than 400,000 units, ranging in membership from tens to hundreds.

Delegates from these units meet irregularly in Party congress. There is one delegate elected for every 5000 members. A congress, according to Party rules, should be convened at least every four years.

In the first forty years of Communism there were twenty such congresses. In the early days congresses were summoned with greater frequency than under Stalin when, for example, there was a thirteen-year gap from 1939 to 1952. A congress traditionally sets major courses in Party policy. It was at the twentieth congress, for instance, that de-Stalinization was initiated. The twenty-first congress was called in January 1959 to deal with expanding the traditional Five-Year Plans to seven years, and with other matters. The congress elects a Central Committee which in turn elects a Presidium (formerly called Politburo). Although the size of the Central Committee and the Presidium varies from period to period, as does the size of the Party itself, the Central Committee usually consists of about 130 members and the Presidium of about 15. Actually, the direction of control is from top to bottom; not from the broad base toward the apex. In effect, it is the members of the Presidium who nominate the Central Committee, and in periods of one-man rule it is a single member of the Presidium who determines the composition of the Central Committee.

Between congresses the Central Committee is summoned periodically —at least twice a year, according to Party rules—either to resolve disputes within the Presidium, during periods when that degree of democracy is in effect, or simply to give formal approval to decisions of the Presidium. At all times, Party members are kept abreast of the thinking and decisions of the leadership by Party publications and by personal conferences and communications. The Presidium is presided over by the first secretary of the Central Committee, commonly referred to abroad as chairman of the Communist Party.

As chairman of the Party, a man is able—as did Stalin and, to an extent, Khrushchev—to arrange for men of loyalty to him to be members (and candidate members, a group almost equal in size to the Central Committee and a rung lower in importance) to ensure support of his programs. Control of the Party means, in effect, potential control of every phase of Soviet life. Members of the Party hold all key positions in the government, in industry, in science, in the arts. Stalin used the secret police as an instrument to ensure his control of the Party by keeping an eye and ear on the thoughts and plans of other Party members and eliminating any he suspected.

The Party claims that the best people in the country belong to the Party. Certainly, an effort is made to bring the most talented and able people in. There are exceptions, especially among older men who were not Party members in the early days of the Revolution but who made their peace with the regime. For example, Andrei Tupolev, designer of jet planes, is not a Party member. Khrushchev and Bulganin made a great point of this when Tupolev was invited to accompany them to England. They pointed to this exception as evidence that Party membership is not an essential of success.

There is evidence since Stalin's death that decisions have been taken by a majority vote of the Presidium. Once a decision is made, no opposition is tolerated. It's obvious that a man of good faith and conviction who opposes a program in its formation is not likely to be converted by the process of a unanimous vote that goes against him. It is this phenomenon that makes for opposition parties in Western democracies. The absence of a mechanism in the Soviet system by which an opposition can patriotically continue to express its opinion makes it impossible for an opposition to survive. Immediately after Stalin's death his successors spoke a great deal about their system of "collective leadership." The Presidium at that time consisted of eleven men. Under any circumstances it is rare for eleven men to hold the same views on issues. The Kremlin eleven were no exception. Eventually, in a Central Committee vote in June 1957, against V. M. Molotov, Lazar Kaganovich, and Georgi Malenkov, Khrushchev was able to purge his opposition and demonstrate again that the nature of the Soviet system gravitates toward monolithic control. It was a tribute to the discipline and rigorous code of the Communists that Molotov alone failed to vote against his own expulsion from the Presidium and Central Committee. He had the rare temerity at least to abstain from voting.

The Communist Party has been described as a tightly disciplined civilian army, a dedicated secular priesthood. Membership entails many privileges and opens horizons of limitless opportunity. But the demands and responsibilities are tremendous too. A Party member may be called on to uproot his home and move to a Siberian farm to spur production. He may find himself at a remote army post to observe a unit's proper political indoctrination. He and other members of his unit will be held responsible for an outbreak of juvenile delinquency in their area. A drop in a factory's production will require explanations by the plant's Party members.

A Party member's personal conduct is also under close scrutiny. Ekaterina Orestova, textile factory foreman and a Party member for twenty-five years in good standing, was summoned by her Party superiors. She had accepted a gift from workers on her birthday. Some disgruntled workers had complained that they were forced to contribute. The magazine, *Party Life,* discussed the case. *Party Life* investigators had determined that Miss Orestova had not suggested that money be raised. Her best friend at the factory had initiated the collection, and some workers felt obliged to contribute because of Comrade Orestova's position. The magazine granted that allowances must be made for Comrade Orestova's excitement and confusion at the surprise presentation, and also that some workers would have been offended by her refusal to accept the gift. However, in similar cases, Party members should be guided by Orestova's error. They should refuse the gift and suggest instead that the workers hold a meeting and present a certificate of honor as a birthday present. As this case demonstrates, the Party is characterized by often oppressive, self-righteous earnestness with a total absence of any lightness of spirit or humor.

Like any political organization, the Communist Party has its petty problems too. At the twentieth congress Comrade P. G. Moskatov, presenting a committee report, complained that many members had not observed the rule that dues must be deposited in a bank within ten days of prescribed dates. Furthermore, in a period of two years, failure to pay dues was the reason for 20 per cent of expulsions from the Party. Moskatov added that from 1950 to 1954 no fewer than 30,000 documents, mostly Party-membership cards, had been lost, and some Party units did not regard this negligence with sufficient concern. Moskatov reported that 73 per cent of Party income came from dues, 26 per cent from publishing activities, and the rest from miscellaneous sources. Party income would have been greater, he said, but 42 of the Party's 102 newspapers in the Russian Republic were losing money and needed subsidies. From time to time Party publications deplore the overabundance of administrative workers. In 1956 a Party periodical announced that a 20 to 30 per cent reduction in the size of the Party apparatus—the Party's administrative and operational workers—was being carried out. Neither the number of Party functionaries before nor after the cut was given.

The composition of the 7,215,505 Party members (including 419,609 candidates) at the time of the twentieth congress was reflected in statistics issued on delegates to the congress. Among the 1436 delegates about half, or 758, had higher education. There were 193 women. Twenty per cent of the delegates were under 40 years of age. Fifty-five per cent were between 40 and 50. Twenty-five per cent were over 50. Only twenty-two of the delegates had entered the Party before the 1917 Revolution. These statistics reflect the gradually changing complexion of the Party. The core of revolutionary fanatics who plotted in cellars and fought in the streets against Czarist soldiers is fast dying. The new Communist is a man of vested interests. Stability rather than revolution benefits him. He has acquired position and property.

The term *tovarich,* meaning "comrade," originally a greeting among Communist Party members, became the national form of salutation after 1917. The word *grashdahnin,* "citizen," is used by policemen, in courts, or in a formal, impersonal way. The old practice of a patronymic—using a father's first name as the middle name of his offspring—is retained today. Thus, Dimitri Nikolayevich Ivanov indicates that Dimitri is the son of Nikolae Ivanov. (Women in professional fields often retain their maiden names.) If you knew Dimitri Nikolayevich Ivanov well you'd call him simply Dimitri. If you were not on intimate terms, but rather were his neighbor or co-worker, you'd address him Dimitri Nikolayevich. This also is the informal manner in which Russians often refer to their leaders—Khrushchev, thus, is called Nikita Sergeyevich. Name cards or calling cards are almost never used, and then only by Russians who deal frequently with foreigners who may expect a card in return for theirs.

Russians use nicknames. "Mila" is short for Ludmila. "Natasha" is the affectionate term for Natalia. Yura can be affectionately called "Yurachka."

The Communist Party starts its training of the nation's young at a tender age, starting with "Little Octobrists," in pre-school, nursery age, "Pioneers" in grade school, and the "Young Communist League" (or Komsomol) after the age of 14.

In 1938 Komsomol had 4,800,000 members. By 1949 it had grown to 8,000,000. In 1958 there were 18,000,000 members in an age group that comprised probably 25,000,000. The potentialities of the Komsomol as an instrument for indoctrination and direction of the youth is evident in these figures. It's also significant in this regard that by 1959 more than 80 per cent of the Soviet populace had been born and educated under the Communists.

Communism is a sort of religion. It has its deity, its shrine, its Vatican; Communism has its own priestcraft, its ritual, its dogma, its hereafter. The deity is Lenin. All works are performed in his name; his writings are the Communist Bible and are quoted as infallible. A random example is found in a piece published on the Revolution's fortieth anniversary on "Economic Competition Between Socialism and Capitalism":

"The socialist system is historically inevitable in all countries. V. I. Lenin wrote that 'all nations will come to socialism. This is inevitable.'" (V. I. Lenin, *Works,* Russian edition, Vol. 23, p. 58.)

The shrine of Soviet Communism is the Lenin-Stalin tomb, as macabre a memorial as can be found since the era of Egypt's mummies. Here in a high-ceilinged vault, dramatically lighted by red-tinted overhead spots, lie the embalmed bodies of Lenin and Stalin in massive caskets of glass, ribbed by carved brass. Soldiers with naked bayonets stand at rigid attention at the head and foot of each casket while silent Russians, in a pilgrimage of mixed reverence and curiosity file silently past. The red granite mausoleum, built in 1924, shaped like a stunted, flat-topped pyramid, stands in Red Square just outside the Kremlin's wall. In the wall itself, marked by lettered stone blocks, lie urns with the remains of many Communist great, including such varied names as Andrei Vishinsky, who died in New York when serving as Russia's representative at the United Nations, and John Reed, the American author of *Ten Days That Shook the World*, about the 1917 Revolution. In a strip of park, studded with proud pines, behind the Lenin-Stalin tomb and bordered by the Kremlin wall, are other resting places including "fraternal graves" of a number of persons who died in the Revolution's civil war. The most honored vault, though, is inside the tomb; two soldiers stand guard at the entrance. Their tour of duty varies with the season—the colder the weather the shorter the tour. Visitors to this Moscow Mecca from other Communist lands lay wreaths of flowers (in winter, paper flowers) at the entrance to the shrine. The line of ordinary pilgrims stretches from the Alexandrovsky Garden at the foot of the Kremlin's south wall, alongside the east wall, and into Red Square. During the few hours of the six days a week the tomb is open to visitors, the invariably long line wends its way into the sarcophagus. For Russian vacationists Moscow is the Washington and New York of the U.S.S.R., and the mausoleum is the Empire State Building and the Washington Monument. For the Communist faithful it is St. Peter's and the holy of holies. The names of Lenin and Stalin are inscribed in red letters on the black labradorite stone that borders the entrance. Covered by black, stiff, cardboardlike material, the bodies of Lenin and Stalin are concealed from the chest down. Their arms and hands lie above their black coverings. Lenin's face has an unnatural waxy appearance, and there are rumors that it is really a death mask, but authorities deny this. Stalin, a much more recent occupant, looks ashen but natural. Lenin wears a black suit with a single row of ribbons over his breast pocket. Stalin—his face pock-marked—is dressed in a brown-colored marshal's uniform with several rows of military and Party decorations. The visitor enters from Lenin's side of the mausoleum after descending the stairs into the subterranean, air-conditioned portion of the edifice. Then he climbs a half-dozen steps to a narrow, walled balcony within an arm's reach of the coffins. He takes two steps parallel to Lenin's right side and then turns to look into the glass end of the casket, square at Lenin's face. A few steps more and he is facing Stalin. The viewing balcony then turns left; the visitor walks along Stalin's left side, down the steps, and leaves the chamber by climbing another staircase to street level. The secret method of embalming that has preserved Lenin's body since 1924 and Stalin's since 1953 is said to have died since with the Soviet embalmer. Irreverent non-Communist visitors refer to the pair as the "gruesome twosome" or "the cold cuts."

The Communist Vatican is the Kremlin. The Kremlin is the original site of Moscow. Founded in 1147 as a fort on heights overlooking the confluence of two rivers (the Neglinka has long since been covered over), the Kremlin gradually grew to its present 64.2 acres and became the site of the palaces and churches of the Czars. Under the Communists the buildings within the great red-brick walls came to serve other functions. Despite the violence of revolution and civil war, neither the cathedrals nor many other Czarist treasures were destroyed by the Communists. Originally a fortification, the slightly sloping, high Kremlin wall with its crenellations and twenty towers, inscribing roughly an isosceles triangle, is a sight of majestic beauty. Few palaces of the world, including Tokyo's Imperial Palace and England's Windsor Castle, can equal the Kremlin for sheer line, imposing architecture, and color. The rich yellow of the Kremlin's building is climaxed by the green of the roofs and by the burnished gold of the cathedral towers and of the twin cupolas of the Ivan Bell Tower.

The steeplelike spires of the five main Kremlin towers are topped by glass stars of deep red. They replace the imperial eagles that were displayed in Czarist days. Although the red glass is edged with gold, the stars are not fashioned of priceless rubies as some tourists are led to believe. The stars are illuminated automatically whenever the sun is not shining and they turn like weather vanes with the wind.

Lenin and Stalin lived within the Kremlin walls. The men who followed Stalin moved out to a series of almost identical walled villas with spacious gardens on the edge of Moscow near the skyscraper of Moscow University. Lenin's apartment is preserved, and selected visitors are shown through. During Stalin's time the Kremlin's walls were sealed to casual visitors. Beginning in the summer of 1955 the Kremlin was opened to the public on purchase of tickets for 3 rubles (30 cents), and in one year alone it was visited by five million people. The Grand Kremlin Palace, built during the reign of Catherine the Great, still contains the Czar's living quarters, but now serves as the signing place for documents with foreign representatives (usually in the Marble Hall), the place for lavish state parties (in the gold-and-white, glittering St. George's Hall), and the assembly place for the Soviet parliament, the Supreme Soviet. The Assembly Hall is a combination of two Czarist halls, one of which was the throne room for receiving ambassadors.

The Soviet leaders have offices in the Presidium Building, from whose green dome the red Soviet flag flies twenty-four hours every day (the Russians haul down their flag neither at sunset nor during rain, sleet, nor snow). It is from the Kremlin that the ukases, the decrees and edicts by which Russians live, are issued by the leaders, the chief practitioners of Communist priestcraft. They claim for themselves exclusive knowledge and wisdom for interpreting the words of the deity, Lenin, for the good of the faithful. They are the arbiters of what constitutes heresy at any particular time. Under high priest Stalin it was heresy to suggest reconciliation with Yugoslavia's leader, Marshal Tito. Under high priest Khrushchev it became heresy to oppose reconciliation. Any deviation from the will of the dominant Kremlin man or faction is treated more severely and often less charitably than any church deals with heretics. The charge is framed in the priestcraft language of the Communist religion: there is an accusation of "anti-Party activity," of "dangerous bourgeois deviationism," of being "an enemy of the people." _Pravda, the daily Bible_, warns against "individuals who approach questions of domestic and foreign policy as sectarians and dogmatists." Under Stalin the punishment for heresy was forced confession, trial, and execution. After Stalin it was not always death but rather, sometimes, exile.

The rituals of Communism are many, from giving daily praise to Lenin and laying flowers at his tomb to the staging of periodic elections and the holding of parliamentary sessions of the Supreme Soviet. The ritual of adulation is as constant as daily prayers. In varying daily forms _Pravda_ writes: "The great Lenin taught the Party to safeguard the unity of its ranks as the apple of its eye and ruthlessly to fight all who tried to subvert this unit." V. M. Molotov, when he was a member of the Kremlin priesthood, wrote: "To speak about Lenin is a difficult thing. No matter what you say it seems little, it seems not to contain the desired sentiments, not to express the fullness of your feelings." There are the semiannual rituals when hundreds of thousands of Russians plod obediently through Red Square on the Revolution Anniversary and on May Day to demonstrate fealty to the high priests who stand on an upper-level balcony of the Lenin-Stalin shrine and bestow their blessings by arms lifted in salute. These occasions are graced by a ritualistic publishing of "calls," usually about one hundred in number, a kind of expanded Ten Commandments or catechism that lists in slogan form Communist attitudes of the moment. A typical "call" declares "Glory to the Soviet armed forces, brave defenders of Marxism-Leninism and of our Soviet motherland." Incantations of this sort abound in Communism. Phraseology is handed down and followed as if in a tribal ritual. (By the way, Russians of a philosophical turn of mind will tell you that their peaceful nature is indicated in their customary use of the term "Motherland," as contrasted with "warlike" Germany's traditional use of the word "Fatherland.")

Communism resembles a religion most, perhaps, in its persistent promise of a hereafter. To industrialize rapidly, the Kremlin priests found it necessary to sacrifice the welfare of a generation and more. To provide resources for machines, it was necessary to deny resources to people. The sacrifice and effort were extorted not only by the whip, but also by sacrificial effort of Party servants and by promises of a better life to come. The Russian worker and peasant had known little freedom and less comfort under the Czars, and the Revolution did not change his lot. But the Communists made promises. When the construction of Communism was completed the Soviet Union would be a land flowing with milk and honey. Each person would give according to his ability and would receive according to his needs. Communism is the promised final stage of economic development. At present, say the Kremlin high priests, the Soviet Union is in an intermediate state; only the foundations of socialism have now been completed. The faithful, or at least their children, will arrive at the Promised Land of the Communist hereafter. Temples are erected to the better, more abundant life to come. The Moscow and Leningrad subways, aptly described because of their marble and brass splendor as the "Russian Orthodox church gone underground," are completely out of context with the sparseness of Soviet life. The monumental escalators, the glittering chandeliers, the heroic mosaics of peasant, worker, and soldier, are intended to dramatize to the Russian that personal privation is contributing to a prosperity for the masses—himself, or at least his children, included. Temples to the Communist hereafter also comprise the agricultural exhibition at the edge of Moscow. Each Republic and region of the U.S.S.R. is represented by a palatial building in native architecture, where products of the area are displayed. Gilt fountains play colored-water streams in front of buildings of World's Fair dimensions. It is all contrived to impress the visiting peasant with the power, progress, and promise of his land.

The principle of separation of church and state has its counterpart in the religion of Communism. The Kremlin maintains there is a distinct division between the Communist Party and the Soviet Government. On paper there is. The organization of the Communist Party, from the Presidium at the top and down to the Party units, is separate from the government structure administering the affairs of the nation. But the line between Party and state is usually meaningless because the main jobs in government are held by members of the Party, and where this is not the case, the government official receives his guidance from the Party. The Party is omnipresent if not always omniscient. Every military commander, for example, has a party political worker of equal rank in theory, and greater influence in fact, by his side. Party members fall into two classes: those whose full-time activities are devoted to Party organization and administration, and those who hold other jobs

—as factory managers, university rectors, government officials—and whose influence and importance are enormously enhanced by Party membership.

The governmental structure is, theoretically, rooted in the people. Elections (with only one candidate for each office) are held for deputies to the Supreme Soviet—the U.S.S.R.'s two-chamber congress or parliament. The Supreme Soviet elects a Presidium. This is the Presidium of the Supreme Soviet, not of the Communist Party, but many of its members are the same. The Presidium elects a chairman, who is president of the country. There is also a Council of Ministers, consisting of the heads of various ministries. The chairman of the Council of Ministers is the Premier of the nation. He is, of course, chosen from among the members of the Communist Party's Presidium.

The Supreme Soviet, by an invariably unanimous show of hands, converts the ukases—the decrees—promulgated by the Presidium of the Supreme Soviet (which acts for the whole body between sessions) into law.

The illusion of separation of Party and state is maintained in the issuance of proclamations. These are issued in the names of *both* the Presidium of the Supreme Soviet and the Presidium of the Communist Party. The illusion was encouraged too during Khrushchev's tenure as first secretary of the Party, when he held no position in the government. Khrushchev was a member of the Supreme Soviet, but he did not hold a post in the Council of Ministers, although at that time it was Khrushchev who ran the government as well as the Party. This was sometimes a convenient device. When asked by reporters at an embassy reception when Russia might be expected to launch another earth satellite, Khrushchev replied with evasive good humor, "I don't know. This is a decision for the government to make, and I am not the government."

The Supreme Soviet convenes in the long white Assembly Hall of the Grand Kremlin Palace. The hall was formed in 1934 by breaking down the partitions between two great Czarist chambers, the Alexandrovsky and Andreyevsky Halls. A football field and more in length, the hall has a platform at one end dominated by a towering statue of V. I. Lenin. The rows of polished walnut-wood benches and desks are equipped with earphones for simultaneous translations. Speeches are translated as they are being delivered, in order to enable members of the multilingual assembly to follow the proceedings.

A deep balcony at the far end of the hall provides seats for one thousand selected spectators. Smaller balconies along one side of the hall are reserved for representatives of the various embassies. Along the opposite wall are windows of monumental dimensions, rising from the floor to the towering white ceiling where molding conceals indirect lighting.

The parliament, defined in the constitution as the "highest organ of state power in the U.S.S.R." is composed of two chambers—the Council of Nationalities and the Council of the Union. Deputies are elected to the Council of Nationalities from the various political subdivisions that compose the U.S.S.R. Twenty-five deputies are sent from each of the fifteen Union republics, eleven from each so-called autonomous republic, five from each autonomous region, and one from each national area. Representation in the Council of the Union is on the basis of population. One deputy is elected for each 300,000 people. A simple majority vote in each chamber is necessary to pass a law—but there are never votes of dissent.

The Supreme Soviet elected in 1954 consisted of 1347 deputies. Of these, 348, or more than a quarter of the deputies, were women. Intellectuals—writers, journalists, artists, ballerinas—comprised the largest group, 809 deputies. Three hundred and eighteen were workers and 220 were peasants. Most were over forty years of age, but 110 deputies were between the ages of twenty-three and thirty. With the growth of population 64 seats were added to the Supreme Soviet for the election held March 16, 1958. Thirty-one members were added to the Council of the Union to make a total of 731 seats and 33 members were added to the Council of Nationalities, bringing its total to 633.

The function of Soviet legislatures was perhaps best described by the legal journal, *Socialist State and Law,* in an article about lower-level bodies in the Republics, but it applies as well to the Supreme Soviet. The journal criticized these legislatures for having such short sessions that they were merely a parade. Speakers were designated weeks in advance and often they read lines written for them. In effect, they had become institutions for simply endorsing decrees submitted by the Presidium of the Republic. After Stalin's death the Supreme Soviet gave at least the appearance of fulfilling its constitutional role. During Stalin's rule, the constitutional provision that the Supreme Soviet meet at least twice a year was often ignored. A budget approved by the Supreme Soviet had often been already in effect for some time.

With Stalin gone, the Supreme Soviet was encouraged to assume an aura of democracy. Budgets were submitted at least a few weeks before the first of the year to which they applied. Legislative committees met months before each session to draft laws that the leaders planned to submit. There was a semblance of discussion, if not debate. A deputy named Georkadze spoke on behalf of his constituents in Tbilisi, asking for an increase of 30 million rubles in funds designated for construction in the Georgian capital. He explained that "the shortage of housing is still acutely felt, especially in view of the fact that many old buildings have fallen into disrepair because not enough money was spent on upkeep." A deputy named Komolov walked to the podium in his turn to urge that greater attention be paid to the needs of the coal-mining industry in his constituency in Uzbekistan in Central Asia. He also requested an appropriation of seven million rubles "to complete a television center in Tashkent (capital of Uzbekistan) so the people of our city can enjoy television like the people in Moscow and other places." No deputy criticized any proposed law or suggested that members of the Presidium, who occupy seats on the platform were not properly discharging their responsibilities.

Supreme Soviet sessions rarely last more than a week or ten days and manage in this brief time to pass a budget, hear a lengthy report on the status of the nation's economy, discuss a report on foreign policy, vote approval to a long list of presidium decrees, and pass a resolution or two in favor of peace and frequent contacts among the parliaments of the world.

Violators of laws, decreed by the Kremlin and confirmed by the Supreme Soviet, are tried in Soviet people's courts. Since the death of Stalin a great deal has been written in Russia about the restoration of socialist legality. This simply means that some of the most blatant secret-police abuses of elementary rights have been eliminated. However, there still is no right of political criticism, precious little freedom of speech, and small recourse for the accused. Although arrest as the result of simple denunciation by a malicious neighbor seems to have died with Stalin and his secret-police minister, Lavrenti Beria, arbitrary arrest still is possible. Although many falsely accused persons have been freed from forced-labor camps, such camps still exist. Three-man boards of the M.V.D., the Ministry of the Interior, which could sentence Soviet citizens to exile in remote sections of the Soviet Union or to forced labor on secret charges without hearing the accused, have been abolished. Soviet authorities claim that accused persons are now given the right of counsel at some stage of their preliminary investigation. Previously an accused person might be held six months by police and then for an indefinite period by a judicial investigator. Only when he was finally brought to trial would he be given the right to have a lawyer.

Articles have appeared in Soviet publications asserting that the principle must be observed that a man is presumed innocent until proven guilty. *Izvestia,* meaning "News," has attacked the principles laid down by Andrei Vishinsky, prosecutor during the Stalin purge trials of the 1930's, who maintained that a confession by the accused was sufficient evidence for conviction and that the accused is as much obliged to establish his innocence as the prosecution to establish his guilt.

One of the cruelest Soviet laws apparently has fallen into disuse since Stalin's death. The law held whole families responsible for crimes committed by one of their members; in particular, the desertion of a soldier incriminated his family. This provision was intended to inhibit soldiers, especially during the war and postwar occupation, from defecting to the West.

A Moscow court I visited is typical. Set back from the street in a courtyard shared by apartment houses, the narrow four-story building housed two courtrooms on each floor. Unlike many government buildings, there was no armed guard at the door; I was able to walk into any courtroom. Only eight people were seated on the four rows of straight-back benches divided by a center aisle in the dimly lit room I entered. Under a picture of Lenin, a people's judge, an elected official, sat, flanked by a man and a woman, so-called lay assessors, chosen in a manner analogous to jurors. The Soviet judicial system does not provide for jury trial. Verdicts are reached by a vote of the professional judge and the lay assessors; a majority vote decides the verdict. A railing separated the public benches from the judges, a court stenographer, and a witness stand. The Soviet equivalent of the attorney general or prosecuting attorney is the procurator general. The functions of the office of the procurator are not confined to presenting the state's side in a case. The procurator is supposed to safeguard the observance of law by state enterprises and to supervise adherence to law in places of detention. The prosecuting counsel and the defense counsel do less of the questioning than in an American or British court. Most cross-examination is by the people's judge. Witnesses are not sworn in, the atheistic society recognizing no deity. However, punishment is provided for giving false testimony if the lie is discovered.

On one occasion a Soviet newspaper complained about the appearance of, and decorum in Russia's courts. "Is it not time," asked the paper, "to begin giving an orderly, clean, and cultural aspect to our people's courts?

"Of course it may be said that dirty floors and dusty windows in the courtrooms, wobbly bookcases, and intolerable heat are trifles. But it is these trifles which accumulate into something bigger—namely, contempt of court."

The writer then went on to paint a word picture of a courtroom: "The court is in session. Suddenly drunken swearwords interrupt the decorous speech of the lawyers. A ragged bum with a face swollen from many days of drunken orgies ambles along the hall, rolling and pitching from side to side.

"Such is the atmosphere in which the people's judges of the Sverdlovsk District of Moscow are often compelled to work. Entrance to the courtroom is generally free. We might say too free."

Russians are very litigious. This may seem surprising in view of the frequency with which justice has been trampled upon. Yet Russians bring complaints and suits to court—disputes over housing space, wage disagreements, ownership problems. The cases heard by courts offer an insight into the stream of every day Soviet life.

Old people with insufficient means of support are entitled to financial help from their children. This is what brought Feodor Skvortzov, a man in his sixties, to a people's court in Irkutsk, Siberia. Although he was receiving a pension from the state as a retired worker, he did not have enough income to live on. There was one complication, though. Feodor didn't know the names of his children. It seems that Feodor had led a loose, philandering life; he had been married several times and hadn't bothered to keep track of his offspring after leaving each wife. But, conscientiously complying with the court's suggestion, Feodor set about finding his children. He managed to locate four of them by asking friends and acquaintances. Without summoning any of the children to court to state their attitudes in the matter, the judge blithely handed down an order for each to give the old man a small sum of money each month. As might be expected, this irked Feodor's namesakes who, having been neglected by their father in their childhood, had no intention as adults to help support him. At this point the story came to the attention of *Pravda,* which took the judge to task. The judge replied to the inquiry of a *Pravda* reporter, explaining that "a Soviet court does not take revenge." Feodor needed help, and it was not the court's place to inquire into his conduct as a parent. *Pravda* took exception to this juridical opinion and carried an article suggesting that judges stick less to the letter of the law. Youthful triflers should realize by the example of men like Feodor, declared *Pravda,* that in their weak and lonely old age their children can't be expected to lend them a hand or to sympathize with them.

A court in Yerevan, capital of Soviet Armenia, sentenced Suren Saribekyan and Leon Beginyan to fifteen and ten years' imprisonment respectively, for threatening a passenger aboard a train with a knife and stealing his luggage.

Nikolai Masliko, a factory worker, was sentenced to seven years in jail by a court in Minsk for stealing a Pobeda car.

G. Totalashvili was sentenced to death by a Tbilisi people's court for robbery and murder of a farm woman.

Anna Nikolaevna Klochneva received two years' imprisonment for swindling. She had acquired 56,000 rubles ($5600) in a period of two years by selling counterfeit theater tickets and luring victims into giving her money for providing them with nonexistent apartments.

A notorious place of imprisonment is Lubiyanka prison, situated in Moscow across a square from the *Detzki Mir* (Children's World) department store on one side and the city's only Catholic church on the other. A black stone building with an iron gate, bars at ground level, and narrow slits of windows above, Lubiyanka represents the worst days of police terror to Russians. Even so, there are jokes about it. At the time of the Hungarian Revolution, when Imre Nagy was in and out as premier, the story was told of three men in a cell in Lubiyanka. One asked the other what he was in for. "For opposing Imre Nagy," was the answer. "And you?"

"For supporting Imre Nagy," replied his cellmate.

They turned to the third occupant and asked why he was there. Came the reply: "I'm Imre Nagy."

A Russian suspected of a crime may be arrested without a warrant. There is no right of habeas corpus that requires police to produce charges against a suspect in open court or set him free. There is no provision for bail by which a Russian suspect may be released until the time for trial.

Under Soviet law a suspect may be held for many months while police authorities gather evidence for the trial.

Until 1954, capital punishment was prescribed only for "traitors of the motherland, spies, and saboteur-diversionists." At that time "premeditated murder" was added to the list. It is said that the death penalty is administered to a convicted criminal by taking him, or her, from the jail cell without advance notice (and, of course, without benefit of solace by clergy). The victim is led down a stone corridor, apparently believing that he is being taken for questioning, or perhaps to see a relative. Suddenly he is felled from behind by a shot in the head. Russians say it's less cruel this way.

Labor camps can be seen near the center of Moscow. Construction of apartment houses and other buildings is often done by persons sentenced to "corrective labor." The construction sites are surrounded by board fences with watchtowers at regular intervals.

Prisons are rarely mentioned in Soviet publications. But in 1956 *Izvestia* ran an article obviously intended to show that Soviet prison life is humane. It described a visit by reporter V. Goltsev to Butyrka prison, part of which dates back to the 1700's. The article made a point of mentioning that Butyrka no longer holds any political prisoners. Prisoners were said to work an eight-hour day (six hours on Saturday) in the prison machine shops, carpentry shops, laundry, and other shops servicing the inmates. Each prisoner had a "norm" set for his job, and if it was fulfilled and discipline maintained he was "granted a rebate of two or three days of his term for each day of work." The prisoners were paid for their work. However, many prisoners apparently malingered. "The work of the prison doctor," wrote the Soviet reporter, "is complicated and responsible. He has to be alert all the time. While seeing to it that prisoners are healthy, the prison doctor must keep a weather eye open to forestall the various machinations of criminals who often simulate an illness to escape work."

Prisoners were said to be permitted to receive three six-pound parcels a month, and fresh fruit and vegetables in unlimited quantities; visits by relatives were allowed at certain times; prisoners may spend their earnings in the canteen to the sum of 100 rubles ($10) a month. A typical day's prison fare, besides bread, included: breakfast, consisting of mashed potatoes with vegetable oil and herring; lunch—sour cabbage soup with meat and barley porridge with butter; millet porridge and vegetable oil were served for supper.

The article said that no new prisons were being built because crime was diminishing from year to year. It may be presumed that plenty of old prisons are in existence to serve Soviet needs. What may be more important, though, is the apparent conclusion by the men who have followed Stalin that it does not pay to fill prisons with innocent people because their labor is unproductive and they consume more than they contribute to the nation's economy.

Many prison sentences include denial of the right to vote for a number of years. Probably of all possible deprivations the Soviet citizen, with little voice in nominating candidates and even less voice in their election, would least miss this one.

CHAPTER 5

AGITATOR'S NOTEBOOK

Mr. Rogov, of the Soviet organization that deals with tourists, is a patient man, but an incessantly complaining British tourist was more than he could bear. The Briton complained about the toast being cold, about the poor telephone service, about his room being too hot. Finally, after a week of enduring complaints, Mr. Rogov politely inquired: "Why is it, sir, that you are always complaining?"

"Why not?" responded the British gentleman. "This is a bloody free country, isn't it?"

Mr. Rogov looked startled but offered no comment. The fact is, though, strange as it may seem, that Russia *does* have one of the most democratic constitutions in the world—on paper at least.

The people of the U.S.S.R. are guaranteed all manner of rights. But guarantee is one thing, and fulfillment quite another.

Under the Constitution adopted on December 5, 1936, the Russian is assured the right to work. He is guaranteed against unemployment. In fact, though, the right to work means an *obligation* to work and does not include the complementary right *not* to work. At times in Soviet history jail sentences have been the punishment for those habitually late to work. Only recently have workers been permitted to change jobs with two weeks' notice; previously a person was bound irrevocably to his place of work by law. There is no unemployment insurance: a person who refuses to accept a job in a Donbas coal mine or a Ural ore pit because he considers it below his ability may soon be forced by lack of money to accept it. And it's a crime to strike.

The Constitution guarantees the right to education.

At least seven years of schooling is compulsory, depending on the schoolroom availability in a particular place. Students in the Soviet equivalent of college receive monthly allowances, or stipends, as they're called, from the government. Only since de-Stalinization has tuition been eliminated. However, free education carries with it an obligation to the state. A graduate is obliged to work for as many as four years at a government-designated job. Many graduated are assigned to the Arctic, to remote areas of Siberia, and to other undesirable regions. For instance there is the case of Tamara Bogolov, a medical-school graduate with a great interest in becoming a gynecologist. She was sent to a primitive section of Sakhalin, a barren and cold island north of Japan, and told that she could only be a surgeon, as there was none there. Tamara replied that she disliked and was apprehensive of surgery, and found that she could practice gynecology if she would move to a settlement in an even less developed part of Sakhalin where there was a surgeon but no gynecologist. Of frail physique, Tamara feared for her health if she were obliged to live for three years in hardship conditions. She remained on her original assignment, and, whatever the consequences may have been for her patients, the experience took a ruinous toll of Tamara's health and spirit.

The Constitution guarantees the right to rest and leisure. Increasingly, this right *is* being observed. Until 1957 Russians worked eight hours a day, six days a week. This forty-eight hour work week has now been reduced to forty-six hours by providing a shorter working day on Saturday. A forty-two hour week is now the immediate goal, and Soviet leaders promise a six-hour workday in the indeterminate future.

Four weeks of paid vacation is usual. However, there is a shortage of resort accommodations (rest homes and sanitoria, they're called), and many workers do not have suitable places to spend their vacations.

The Constitution guarantees the freedom of street processions and demonstrations and the right to unite in public organizations. These rights may be exercised only "in conformity with the interests of the working class, and in order to strengthen the socialist system." Suffice it to say that, in reality, organizations are formed only to support policies of the Communist Party, and street processions are organized only to serve government purposes.

Such was the case when processions of Russians, bearing placards demanding "Hands Off Egypt," marched to the British, French, and Israeli embassies to protest the military action against Egypt in November 1956. The several thousand demonstrators in front of each Embassy were mostly students, dispatched from schools in organized platoons. One column blundered and showed up in front of the British Embassy, across the Moscow River from the Kremlin, with signs in French.

Youngsters, urged on by chanting compatriots and cheerleaders, climbed on the Embassy fences and walls to affix signs: "Down with War" and "Get Out of Egypt." This at the very time when Soviet tanks and troops had entered Budapest and were waging war against Hungarian revolutionaries.

One agile youth inched his way up a drainpipe to affix a placard to the bedroom windows of Lady Hayter, the dignified wife of the British Ambassador. It may have been this, as much as the other aspects of the demonstration, which occasioned the Ambassador, Sir William Hayter, to protest to the Soviet Foreign Ministry "a grave violation of diplomatic usage."

I was present at the British Embassy. Soviet militiamen stood at the Embassy gates and at the entrance to the chancellery without interfering with the demonstrators who swarmed over the garden and tennis court. During the three hours of noise and largely good-natured milling about, a member of the Embassy asked the militiaman at the door when it would end.

He glanced at his watch and, with apparent foreknowledge, replied: "In about fifteen minutes." It did.

When the demonstrators dispersed, workmen of "Burobin," the Soviet service organization for the diplomatic corps, marched to the scene as a sort of after-the-battle echelon and removed the signs and placards.

Demonstrations in the summer of 1958 were much rougher and caused considerable property damage. Crowds, organized with martial precision, converged on the target Embassy and broke windows, hurled ink bottles against the walls, and in one case flung crude fire bombs—rags soaked in gasoline—through windows. The West German and Danish Embassies were stormed in this fashion in retaliation for demonstrations at the Soviet Embassies in Bonn and Copenhagen, where the execution of Hungary's Imre Nagy was protested. The demonstration at the American Embassy in this instance consisted only of placards and jeers. However, a few weeks later, when American Marines landed in Lebanon, a mass

78   MAIN STREET, U.S.S.R.

of Russians—estimated at somewhere between 70,000 and 100,000—
snarled Moscow traffic for most of the afternoon as columns converged
on the Embassy, broke more than one hundred panes of glass, and
catapulted ink bottles to upper-story windows with slingshots. Most of the
Russians I saw and photographed seemed passive. They were there because their shop or office had closed for the afternoon so that they could
participate in this obviously non-spontaneous "spontaneous" demonstration.

A few days later, some Russians apparently were still caught up in the
spirit of the affair long after the Soviet trade union or Party organizers
intended. Two dozen beer bottles were hurled over the Embassy's back-
yard fence, damaging several cars including Ambassador Llewellyn
Thompson's Cadillac. He protested to an official of the Soviet Foreign
Ministry, who heard him with apparent embarrassment. Soviet censors
never passed accounts written by American newsmen of this unscheduled
demonstration.

Other constitutional guarantees similarly lose their democratic pretense in practice. Freedom of speech and of the press is provided in the
Constitution, but criticism of the Party is tolerated neither in speech
nor in print. Privacy of correspondence is guaranteed, but mail is opened.
Inviolability of the person and the home are Soviet freedoms that,
during Stalin's era and, to a lesser degree, now, were desecrated by
arrest without cause and (as admitted by Stalin's successors) by
imprisonment without justice.

Other articles of the Constitution are also ignored.

This supreme document of the Soviet state declares that each of the
union republics that comprise the U.S.S.R. has the "right freely to
secede." In practice, the fifteen republics have no more opportunity to
secede than "each Union Republic has the right to enter into direct
relations with foreign states and to conclude agreements and exchange
representatives with them" or to have "its own republican military
formations."

These union rights are contained in amendments to the Constitution
enacted in February 1944. These were intended to provide a basis
for the Kremlin's contention that each of the republics (then sixteen)
was entitled to its own delegate in the United Nations. The ruse helped
in achieving for the Soviet Union two extra seats in the U. N. General
Assembly—one each for Byelorussia and the Ukraine. But when the
British Government put the constitutional provision to a test in August

1947 by offering to exchange diplomatic representatives with the Ukraine, the proposal was turned down.

The Constitution provides for periodic elections by secret ballot. Representatives to the Supreme Soviet, the nation's legislature, are elected every four years. Elections for local Soviets (governing councils in towns, cities, and other administrative subdivisions) are elected for two-year terms. The right to vote is known in Soviet terminology as an "active right"; the right to be elected is described as a "passive right." Soviet citizens who reach the age of twenty-three are eligible to be elected to the Supreme Soviet. A candidate for a republican legislature must be twenty-one, and for local Soviets eighteen years old. Deputies to the Supreme Soviet are elected at large. That is, a candidate need not be a resident of a particular election district to be elected from that district.

Several months before election day in Russia red flags and signs with the word *Agitpunkt,* bordered with bare electric light bulbs appear over certain doorways.

Agitpunkt means "agitation point." The people who work out of such stations are called "agitators," a term which may raise the mental image of a bearded man in turned-up collar, stealthily making his way along the sides of buildings, a bomb hidden under his coat. But this is not the Soviet concept of the word. An agitator is a perfectly respectable citizen in the Soviet Union. As a matter of fact, by Communist standards, he is a model citizen for he carries on political education activities in the community.

A twice-monthly Communist pocket-size magazine is put out for the guidance of agitators. It bears the diverting name, *Agitators' Notebook.*

The purpose of the *agitpunkts* and the agitators is mobilizing the populace to turn out on election day. It is by this organized mobilization that 99-plus per cent of eligible voters always cast ballots in each Soviet election.

Elections in Russia are not contests. Rather they are a ritual, a preordained manifestation of public support for the Communist Party and its appointed authorities. The only question in any election is whether 99.5 per cent or 99.7 or 99.9 per cent of the ballots will be cast for the slate chosen by the Party. These foreordained results are intended to persuade the outside world, if not the election participants, of the unity of people and state.

There is only one candidate for each office. He or she is nominated by meetings of Communist Party units, trade unions, youth organizations, cultural societies, and other organizations. There may be disagreement among the various nominating groups as to who should be the candidate from a particular district. But, by means of conferences, discussions, and instructions from the local Party organization, a single candidate is finally nominated from each district. In the event that several districts nominate the same candidate (Khrushchev was nominated by more than 100 districts in the 1958 Supreme Soviet election), election boards (or, in the case of Khrushchev, Party authorities) decide which district the man shall represent as a candidate—and subsequently as a deputy. Nominations are listed thirty days before the election, and from then on there is unanimity from the beginning of the "campaign" right on through election day.

The candidates are not necessarily Party members, but each is approved and endorsed by the Party. There is, of course, no such creature as an opposition candidate.

Every Soviet citizen has the right to vote, beginning at the age of eighteen. Everyone is expected to vote. To make sure that everyone does, *agitpunkts* are set up in libraries, museums, hotels, concert halls, and apartment houses. A few tables and chairs are the only furnishings. There are no electioneering posters with earnest faces of candidates. The *agitpunkt* I visited was in the Ministry of Communications building in a ground-floor room ordinarily used for receiving telephone subscribers' complaints. The director was a slight, gray-haired, friendly woman who said her name was Larissa Balakhonov. Her staff of fifty volunteer workers was busy, she said, paying personal calls on every family in this *agitpunkt's* area.

Two schoolgirls in their late teens, members of the Komsomol, the Young Communist League, entered the room with a list of the people they had found at home and had talked with. This team of young agitators had reminded each citizen of the date of the election (election day is always Sunday, the Russian's day off) and of his duty to vote. The agitator inquired whether any member of the household would be out of town on election day and, if so, explained that the absentee could vote wherever he happened to be on election day.

The door-to-door canvass leaves no one with the excuse that he did not know about the election day, though it would have been almost impossible to be oblivious of it thanks to daily newspaper articles and radio comments.

Russians are not required to register before elections in order to vote. There are no qualifications of property ownership or length of residence in a particular place. Everyone who has reached the age of eighteen is qualified to vote, except (in the words of the Soviet Constitution) "insane persons and persons who have been convicted by a court of law and whose sentences include deprivation of electoral right."

Some people with questions dropped in at Mrs. Balakhonov's *agitpunkt*. An engineer explained that he would be leaving Moscow on a trip to Stalingrad and thus would not be present in the district where his name is inscribed. Arrangements were made to issue him a certificate to enable him to vote in Stalingrad or even aboard the train.

A housewife stopped in on her way to market to say that her son had moved to the outlying Kalininskiy District of Moscow. His name and new address were taken by Mrs. Balakhonov and sent to the *agitpunkt* in that district to be added to the lists of Kalininskiy's agitators.

Although their election is ensured, candidates are supposed to get out and shake hands with their constituents. Meetings are held in apartment houses, factories, theaters, and offices where citizens recite speeches of praise for the candidate and the candidate waxes eloquent on Lenin and the wise leadership of the Communist Party. Testimonial speeches are always delivered by a set cast of character-witnesses, as it were, including a neighbor, a factory worker, a member of the intelligentsia (a writer, scientist, theatrical worker), and, perhaps, a student. One such pre-election meeting which I attended was held in a Moscow club for cinema workers. In an apparent effort to make attendance at the meeting as attractive as possible, speeches lasted only an hour and were followed by the showing of three films. There was also a twenty-piece army brass band playing in the lobby, and before and after the meeting a number of younger voters undertook to dance on the stone floor to the band's march like tempos. Refreshments—cakes, chocolates, and flavored soda water—were on sale.

The platform was bedecked with red flags and a great portrait of Lenin. The oratory was of the florid, emotional, organ-toned type that Russians prefer. The candidate, Mrs. V. E. Fyodorova, a textile-loom operator about fifty years old, punctuated her speech to the 800 voters with the phrase *"if* I am elected," but everyone knew she would be.

On election day the polls open at 6 A.M. and close at midnight. At a polling place in the Sovietskiy district, only a short way from the Kremlin, election workers sat at tables with huge books in front of them with the names of voters in the district. As a voter entered he (or she) walked to a sign indicating the initial of his last name and presented any identification, such as a trade-union card or a factory pass; the name was then checked against the residence list. The voter received one ballot paper for each of the two chambers being elected. In the Sovietskiy district, on the white ballot paper for the Council of the Union was the name of A. N. Nesmeyanov, of the Soviet Academy of Sciences; and on the blue paper for the Council of Nationalities was the name of N. M. Shvernik, a member of the Party Presidium.

At the far end of the room, under a silver-colored bust of Lenin and bordered by pots of flowering plants, stood two sealed ballot boxes watched over by an unsmiling, bespectacled attendant. The voter folded the ballot papers and dropped one through the slot of each of the boxes.

Three green-curtained voting booths of telephone-booth size were available against one wall, where a voter might register disapproval of the candidate by crossing out his name or writing in another name. While I watched, no one availed himself of the privilege, and the several scores of voters who passed quickly through followed the much less conspicuous procedure of receiving their ballot papers and going directly to the boxes. However, three American election observers—an official delegation— who were invited (in return for a group of observers who attended a U.S. election) reported that they did see people enter the booths. Certainly, though, the action of such non-conformists would be visible to the poll officials, and presumably an agitator might at the very least pay the dissident a visit to inquire into the nature of his objections to the approved candidate.

It's made just as simple as possible for the voter. He doesn't have to mark the ballot in any way. No need to write *Da*. Just take the ballot, drop it into the box, and it will be counted as a gesture of assent for the approved candidates on the list. It's explained that there's no reason for *choice* of candidates because all elements of the populace are represented in the best possible way by the candidates nominated. There's no room for opposition candidates because the people are unanimous in following the leadership of the Communist Party. That is the rationale of the Communist.

When the Western proposal for free elections as a means of unifying

Germany was under discussion at the Geneva Conference of July 1955, Mr. Harold MacMillan, then British Foreign Secretary, is said to have countered the objections of V. M. Molotov, then Soviet Foreign Minister, by declaring: "It's too bad, Mr. Molotov, that you've never had any experience with free elections. It would do you good to run for office."

"Why?" demanded Molotov.

"Because," said MacMillan, "you would be defeated."

Theoretically, a Soviet candidate could be defeated by enough voters writing in other names in a space provided, which very few do. Even fewer cross out the names of candidates they disapprove of. A Russian has the option of not voting at all, but almost everyone does. It is easier than inviting demands for explanations from agitators and criticisms by zealous neighbors. The *agitpunkts* make it certain that no one has the excuse that he did not know how, when, or where to vote. Similiarly, no Russian is left in doubt as to what is expected of him at his place of work, whether it be a factory milling machine or a farm milking machine.

CHAPTER 6

THE SPUTNIK THAT WOULDN'T GO RED

Strategists in the Kremlin were plotting war.

"We could send ten men to the United States with atom bombs in suitcases," suggested the leader. "One could go to New York, another to Detroit . . ."

"No," interrupted his comrade, "we couldn't do that."

"Why not? We have plenty of atom bombs."

"Yes, but where are we going to get the ten *suitcases?*"

This little story demonstrates the unevenness of Russia's economy. In order to accomplish certain priority projects, other aspects of the economy have been neglected. At the time that Russia amazed the world by launching its first sputnik, on October 4, 1957, it was impossible to buy many ordinary household items in a Moscow store. A housewife could not find waxed paper or kitchen aluminum foil. Electric blankets, facial tissue, portable radios were not manufactured. Resources were not invested in air-conditioning units, window screens to keep out flies, or personal deodorants. It *is* possible to live without all of these things. Russians do.

Russia's economy has not been able to produce enough to provide both rockets *and* refrigerators. The needs and whims of the consumer have been neglected in order to fulfill the requirements of the state. The United States produces anywhere from 80 to 120 million tons of steel a year—the variation depending on what demand prevails for cars, girders, filing cabinets, and locomotives. The Soviet Union pro-

duces upwards of 50 million tons of steel a year because that is
precisely what Russia's economy is now *able* to produce. That limited,
inflexible output is rigidly channeled into priority projects.

In Russia's economy all resources are used at the discretion of a
single authority, the government. It is the government that owns the
mines, the railroads, the factories, the forests, the steel, the oil, the
stores, the restaurants. It is the government that controls the manpower.
Only in wartime is a capitalist economy able to impose controls
approximating those of the Soviet State to determine the use of
resources. Ordinarily the investment of a capitalist nation's steel and
lumber and oil, owned by privately owned enterprise, is determined, at
least in part, by the desires and demands of the population. In Russia
the assignment of resources is decreed by what Soviet authorities deem
right and proper. This has made Russia a land rich in nuclear bombs
but poor in suitcases.

At the time that the Soviet Union launched sputnik II, on November
3, 1957, workmen were putting decorations on buildings for the
November 7 celebration of the fortieth anniversary of the Revolution.
A great sign was erected on the Ministry of Communications building.
Electric lights depicted a Moscow skyscraper, a fountain, and traffic.
Then lights went on to show a rocket rising. Soon bulbs lit up to show
a globe of the world. Finally, in orbit around the earth, a series of
red bulbs, two at a time, were illuminated to illustrate the two Soviet
sputniks. Although far overhead the two sputniks were passing with
clocklike precision, it took workmen on the ground two days to get
the red bulbs to light up in proper sequence.

A similar contrast may be seen at Moscow's airport when the futur-
istic TU-104 plane with its swept-back wings and powerful jet engines
is being readied to receive passengers. Attendants trudge aboard bearing
old-fashioned teakettles of a design used by grandmother prior to the
air age.

The shortages of comfort and luxury goods is reflected in the story
of the leading Communist who died and was sent to hell. At the
entrance the demon in charge offered him the choice of two gates to
hell, one marked "Capitalists," the other "Communists."

"Which one for you?" the demon asked.

"The Communist hell, of course," the Communist replied. "There's
bound to be a fuel shortage there."

It is a never-ending source of surprise to watch floors being polished in Soviet office buildings and hotels. A workman removes one shoe and sock, places his bare foot through a strap attached to a brush, and by a jerky, jogging movement, limps along, slowly polishing the floor. It is slow, inefficient, and obviously uncomfortable for the worker. Surely a nation with Russia's advanced industry can produce ample electric floor polishers. But resources are devoted to other products. Furthermore, it is no easy matter to put a new item into production. In a society of free enterprise, an individual who recognizes a possible market for automatic floor polishers may be able to borrow several thousand dollars to fabricate a few models. These he would demonstrate to potential customers and, on the basis of their orders, obtain more money to go into business. In Russia's controlled, planned economy an idea must work its way up through a particular ministry or regional economic council for approval before a government factory is instructed to put the idea into production. This is a time-consuming process. It is against the law for an individual to engage in private enterprise. Only the state may own the means of production. There is a retarding inertia among bureaucrats in an economy of still-limited resources toward the adoption of a new product. The criterion for accepting a product becomes: can we get along *without* it? In the case of consumer goods, the answer is usually, yes. The question of whether it can make life easier and pleasanter is ignored.

After Stalin's death steps were taken to reorganize Soviet industry. Through the years, control of the government's 200,000 factories and 100,000 construction sites had become concentrated in Moscow. More than fifty ministries directed Soviet production from offices in Moscow. Such highly concentrated centralization outgrew efficiency as Soviet industry grew. It had become unwieldy. It took days or weeks for a factory manager in Alma-Ata to receive permission to undertake a simple adjustment in production. Some ministries tried to contain themselves in self-sufficient watertight compartments; one ministry, for example, built a 5000-ton-capacity iron casting plant in Leningrad even though another ministry was already operating near Leningrad with an 8000-ton surplus which was being shipped elsewhere at great cost.

Centralized control could be justified when the Soviet industrial work force numbered 13 million in the early days of Stalin's reign, but it could not cope efficiently with a work force of 50 million at the end of Stalin's lifetime. Furthermore, centralization served to deprive managers at the scene of production of any initiative.

Stalin's successors, Khrushchev in particular, undertook a gigantic decentralization of industry. Final authority was still to rest in Moscow, but day-by-day management was delegated to regional economic councils, known as *Sovnarkhozy,* which were created. Ten Moscow ministries were abolished. These were ministries whose factories and construction projects could be better managed closer to the scene by a regional economic council. These included the Automobile Industry Ministry, the Ministry of Construction of Oil Industry Enterprises, and the Heavy Machine Building Ministry.

Also, fifteen ministries, transferred previously from Moscow to Republic capitals in a preliminary effort at decentralization, were now disbanded. The functions of such republican ministries as those of the Coal Industry, Fish Industry, Oil Industry, and Construction of Coal Industry Enterprises were delegated to regional economic councils.

One hundred and five economic administrative regions were created, with an economic council to manage industry in each region. The reorganization uprooted thousands of bureaucrats who had found sinecures in Moscow ministries and were obliged now to accept jobs in remote economic councils. The dislocation freed much office space, most of which was converted into living quarters for overcrowded city dwellers. The transfer of ministry records alone was a job of staggering proportions. Almost thirty ministries and organs of ministerial status remained in Moscow, including such ministries as Defense, Agriculture, Health, Railways, Foreign Trade, and the Committee of State Security (the secret police). The balance sheet of results—the toll of the dislocation weighed against benefits of moving management closer to the production line—will take years to be written.

Whatever problems may be solved by Khrushchev's audacious, revolutionary reorganization of industry, new problems have been generated by it. Anxious for their own economic regions to do well, the heads of many a Sovnarhoz neglect or ignore shipments promised to factories outside their district in order to satisfy demands of their own factories. *Pravda* and other publications ring with indignation at this evil of "parochialism" in management.

The new freedom from Moscow's tight management has resulted in other abuses also. The personnel of the Sovnarhoz in Karaganda, in arid Kazakhstan, is charged with distributing a half million rubles ($50,000) among themselves in "incentive" and bonus payments. They had a seven-story Sovnarhoz headquarters built at a cost of 25,000,000 rubles ($2,500,000) and, to satisfy someone's whim, constructed a palatial doghouse for breeding purposes at a cost of 552,000 rubles ($55,200). Local self-indulgence of this sort would never have been possible when the reins were held in Moscow.

In personal terms, the reorganization is at best a mixed blessing for factory managers who now go to nearby regional economic councils for decisions. In the Asian heartland city of Stalinabad, a drab, provincial place, the manager of the Stalin Textile Factory explained to me that under Khrushchev's decentralization of industry it was no longer necessary for him to travel to Moscow, comparatively a capital of gaiety and glamour, to confer with Ministry officials. There was an understandable wistfulness in his eyes.

The blueprint for the use of Soviet resources and man and woman power is set down in the National Economic Plan. This is a comprehensive, coordinated plan—volumes of figures, charts and graphs—that regulates the economic activities of all persons and institutions in the Soviet Union. It prescribes, on the basis of past experience and future expectancy, how much iron ore is to be extracted from mines, how many tons of steel are to be fabricated, what quantities of this steel are to be assigned to factories in Moscow, Leningrad, Sverdlovsk, what products these factories are to turn out and in what numbers, which of these products are to be sold abroad, and what is to be purchased from foreign lands.

The basic document for the National Economic Plan has been the Five-Year Plan. Often the butt of jokes ("The Russians like their new Five-Year Plan so much it may take them ten years to complete it"), the Five-Year Plan is, in effect, a scheme for the nation's entire economy, of the sort that any capitalistic enterprise draws up for a period of time. The Plan specifies a production goal—a quota—for each industry. The Plan is drawn up by the State Planning Committee, known as the *Gosplan*. (*Gosplan* became even more important and powerful with the decentralization of industry. It inherited many of the powers and top-level personnel from defunct ministries. The factory manager in Russia does not have the independence to do such things as investing capital in plant expansion or bidding for scarce raw materials. These decisions lie with *Gosplan*. Thus, although the post-Stalin reorganization did *decentralize* day-by-day management it also served further to *concentrate* long-range control.)

In addition, there are annual plans which often revise that segment of the Five-Year Plan. Quarterly and monthly plans are prepared for important industries.

Every industry has a production target. Each worker in the industry is given a norm—the number of lampshades he is expected to produce in a week, the number of bricks he is to lay, or the number of cans of peaches to be preserved. It's readily understood how a target can be set for the number of trees to be felled by the timber industry or the number of bicycles to be manufactured. But without first consulting the fish, it may be difficult to see how Soviet fishermen can be assigned a precise number of fish to catch. Yet they are. By taking into consideration the catch of previous seasons and the availability of new equipment, a catch quota *is* set. This is done, too, for whales. Russia sends a whaling expedition to Antarctic waters each season for about seven months. The flotilla has had as its quota the blubber of 1000 whales, which it usually fulfills with the considerate co-operation of the whales.

Certain industries overfulfill their quotas; others fall below, and their officials encounter severe criticism from the Communist press. Not uncommonly quotas are overfulfilled for the sake of bonuses and at the expense of quality. Soviet officialdom realizes this. A cartoon shows a corpulent man with an oversized necktie, on which is inscribed in figures increasing in size, "100%," "200%," "300%," indicating over-fulfillment of production plans. A second section of the cartoon shows the back view of the same man; his clothing is coming apart at the seams, and superimposed is the word "Quality?"

Some Five-Year Plans (the first was in 1928) have been completed ahead of time. At other times the Plan has been revised to conform with the actual accomplishment. In 1957 it was announced that the Five-Year Plan that was to end in 1960 would be terminated instead in 1958, and a new plan, a Seven-Year Plan, would commence, lasting through 1965. The revision seems to have been caused by a number of factors: the disrupting effects of Khrushchev's decentralization of industry certainly entailed adjustment of production sights. There had been overly ambitious quotas set for some industries. In the case of other industries the truth seemed to lie in the official announcement's explanation that the discovery of new deposits of raw materials made it possible to raise economic targets. Whatever the other causes of the revision, it seemed to spell, for a period at least, the end of the historic Five-Year Plans that have become identified with the Soviet economy. Seven-Year Plans and longer were promised. The first began in 1959.

Under its all-encompassing economic plans Russia has made astounding economic progress. The comforts and freedoms of a generation and more were sacrificed to the goal of converting a backward peasant nation into the world's second industrial power in less than forty years. On the fortieth anniversary of the revolution that brought Communism to power the Soviet Union could claim that:

Steel output had increased from 4.2 million tons in 1913 to 51 million tons in 1957; the United States produced 104.5 million tons in 1956. The magnitude of growth of Russia's steel output is shown by the fact that in 1913 Britain produced two and a half times more steel than Russia, but by 1957 the Soviet Union's steel output exceeded the production of Britain, France, and Belgium combined.

In the same period coal production had risen from 29.1 million tons to 395 million tons of hard coal. The corresponding figure for U.S. coal production in 1957 was 479 million tons.

Electric power production increased from 1900 million kilowatt hours in 1913 to 210,000 million in 1957. United States electrical output amounted to 684,000 million kilowatt hours in 1956.

Soviet development, however, is uneven. Some industries and areas have been neglected. Two thirds of the Soviet Union's 78,000 collective farms still do not have electricity. Or, to use Khrushchev's own words in his fortieth anniversary speech: "All towns and nearly all industrial settlements and more than one third of all the collective farms now use electricity."

Khrushchev himself declared in his speech to the Supreme Soviet legislature on its Revolution-eve session that "we have an acute housing shortage" and "we are lagging behind, both in the quantity of the output and particularly in the quality of certain consumer goods, and that the cost and prices of these goods still are high."

In its drive toward rapid expansion of the economy, Russia also has, until recently, neglected modernization of production methods. Automation of plants has lagged seriously. An elaborate wall diagram in the Hall of Automation at the All-Union Industrial Exhibition, a permanent fair in Moscow, represents an electric power station that can be operated by one man. Natasha Kalasnikova, a round-faced girl with an easy smile, uses her guide's pointer to show dials on the control panel that would automatically regulate such a plant.

"How many such automated power stations," I asked, "are now in operation in the Soviet Union?"

"None, yet," was Natasha's frank reply. "This is a *plan* for such a project."

Like this power station at the Exhibition, automation in Russia is still, to a significant degree, in the diagram stage; but Russians are sure that, when achieved, automation will be an unmixed blessing. Problems which have accompanied automation in Western countries are disparaged as exclusively characteristic of the capitalist system. Some automation, of course, has already been introduced into Soviet production, and there are plans for automatic lines for everything from pipe-rolling mills to butter-making.

Shortly before powerful rockets sent Sputnik I orbiting around the world, emitting its historic "beep, beep," it was the occasion for a news item in Moscow's newspapers when the capital's first automatic shoeshine machine was installed. There had been—and still are—many human shoe shiners (both men and women) operating in small sidewalk booths, but this was the first Soviet automatic accomplishment in this field. A squirt of polish fell on the customer's shoe and two rough brushes rotated to apply a shine. All for 50 kopecks (5 cents)! It was considered something of a wonder by youngsters and adults who came to the Moscow cobbler's shop to see it.

In Kiev, the capital of the Soviet Ukraine Republic, crowds gather around the clock that chimes each quarter hour while supplementary dials indicate the hour in Moscow, Peking, Paris, London, and New York (incorrectly, by the way, when I saw it, because summer daylight-saving time was not taken into account).

There are now automatic dispensers for cigarettes (a 15-kopeck piece —one and a half cents—delivers a single cigarette) and for soda water. The newspaper *Soviet Russia* promises even greater wonders: "Suppose you've neglected to buy a box of matches on your way home from work. You drop in at the nearest store, put a coin into the slot of one of the many small boxes hanging on the wall. Out in an instant comes what you want—quickly and conveniently. . . . Trade-machine-building factories in Kiev, Kharkov, Kaliningrad, and Perovo will turn out automatic devices for selling sandwiches, beer, soda water, ice cream, and similar items."

Invention of such automatic equipment and of more important devices is encouraged, but the monetary rewards are small. Besides the title of "inventor" (workers who introduce minor changes in production methods and processes are called "innovators"), the return for an invention is seldom more than 6000 rubles ($600).

There is a Committee on Inventions and Discoveries under the Council of Ministers which is impowered to issue a certificate of invention to a Russian who comes up with a better mousetrap. This simply certifies that the Russian was the first to invent the particular item. He receives no money for this. However, if and when a particular ministry or regional economic council accepts the invention for use in a factory or enterprise, then the inventor receives a sum of money varying with the importance of his development. No royalties are paid during the years of the invention's use—only a flat and final sum. The explanation is that it is the duty of every citizen to use his creative talents for the good of the State, whether he's paid extra for it or not.

The automated lines at Moscow's first ball-bearing plant, originally named for Lazar Kaganovich until his expulsion from the Communist Presidium, are paragons of precision and efficiency. Entirely of Soviet manufacture, the automated lines turn out small ball-bearing units, commencing with uncut metal and advancing through stages to the final product, which automatic arms wrap and seal in individual cardboard boxes. Fewer than a score of people are employed in supervising and regulating each of these production lines. American automation experts who visited the plant pronounced it to be as up-to-date as any in the United States or Britain. But only a small percentage of the 60 million ball-bearing units produced annually by the plant, ranging in weight from five ounces to four tons, are manufactured by this automated equipment. Some operations, by contrast, particularly the transporting of products from one stage of production to another, are done laboriously by hand. As in most Russian factories, half the 12,000 workers are women, whose intensive employment reflects the nation's labor shortage.

Women do every sort of work in Russia. They sweep streets with stiff brooms made of twigs, shovel snow, operate cranes, drive buses and steam rollers, dig coal. Women are barbers, lathe operators, bricklayers, judges, and radio announcers. Of Russia's 334,000 doctors, 76 per cent are women. Seventy per cent of Russia's teachers are women. Fifty-three per cent of all specialists—persons skilled by reason of higher education in any field of endeavor—were women in 1956. One third of all the deputies elected to regional Soviets, or councils, in

1955, were women. In 1956, 45 per cent of the working force were women. In industry 45 per cent of workers were women; on state farms 46 per cent were women, in stores and other trading enterprises 58 per cent, in restaurant work 83 per cent, and in health services 85 per cent.

Women work for various reasons. Some admit that low salaries make it essential that they earn wages in order to provide an adequate family income. The official explanation, as published in a government pamphlet intended for foreigners, says:

"Our women go to work and are eager to do so, not only because their wage augments the family income, but also because their work gives them economic independence. They work because they want to devote their lives to the common interests of the people, because they want to contribute their own labor to the great construction work being carried on by the Soviet people for the sake of a better life and happiness for their children. Work has become a necessity for the Soviet citizen, for the Soviet woman." Work has indeed become a "necessity," because the Soviet Government has made it so.

The labor shortage has many causes. Great numbers of workers have been diverted to new agricultural projects in Siberia and Kazakhstan and to new industrial enterprises in Siberia. The terrible toll of World War II and the reduced birth rate during the war have diminished the labor supply. There is also extravagant inefficiency in the use of labor.

Automation in Russia will contribute to a solution of the labor shortage long before its effect is to deprive men and women of jobs. Also, automation would first contribute to giving Russians a five-day work week before it would contribute to unemployment. No one lost his job at the Kaganovich ball-bearing plant by the introduction of automated lines, the first one of which took four years to install. Workers in other sections of the factory were trained to operate the automated equipment, a series of gray painted hulls that cover processing parts. The salaries of the transferred workers were raised from the average 970 rubles ($97) per month they had been earning previously to an average 1100 rubles ($110).

An automated line in the ball-bearing plant is next door to a shop where women, instead of mechanized carts or cranes, lug pieces of work from one assembly line to another. Everywhere in the U.S.S.R. there is evidence of this uneven economic progress. At the atomic power station outside Moscow I watched two young Russians, part of the staff of 100 (of whom 20 per cent are women), seated at a control board supervising by remote control the 5000-kilowatt nuclear pile. In the wash-room on the same premises as the nuclear reactor, hot water is produced by a primitive wood-burning stove.

There is a long way to go to bring the entire economy abreast of the twentieth century. But young Communists claim to be confident that when automation comes to the Soviet Union it can bring only good and none of the dislocations experienced in Capitalist economies. An article in *Literary Gazette,* the newspaper of the union of Soviet writers, insisted that automation is a foe of workers in Capitalist societies, but a friend under socialism. It explained that a capitalist economy is inter-ested only in profits, regardless of human suffering, but that in a planned socialist economy automation will lighten the workers' labor, shorten their hours, and increase their incomes. Soviet workers, long underpaid for long hours and heavy work, hope this will be the case.

The guide Natasha, at the Industrial Fair, offers visitors the same bright prospect in her prepared text.

"People will not work just to earn a living but rather because the few hours of work each day with automation will make it a joy."

The fact is, however, that automation is not without its difficulties for Russia as well as for capitalist societies. Some workers and managers have dragged their feet and resisted the introduction of automation. Even Soviet newspapers have recorded cases of sabotage of equipment by workers in coal mines when the introduction of hydraulic mining equipment obliged them to mine more coal in order to retain the same wages.

Factory managers who have to produce prescribed quotas are some-times reluctant to introduce new machinery which (although it may increase future production) may retard output during the transition period. A factory manager risks his job if production falls short, for even a comparatively brief period. A sizable part of his income is his bonus for fulfilling or overfulfilling state quotas and can be endangered by "bugs" in newly installed automated equipment. Under these conditions a manager may try, to the extent that his authority permits, to postpone installation of automated machines.

This tendency was recognized in a speech by the then Premier Bulganin before the plenum of the Central Committee of the Communist Party in July 1955, when he accused a minister of the Machine and Instrument Building Industry of clinging to outmoded techniques "obviously because old models can be produced more simply without any bother."

Despite these difficulties the Russians do enjoy certain long-run advantages in the conversion to automation. Russia's is an expanding economy. Vast resources are still untapped. Man power released by automation can, under the Soviet system, be readily diverted to opening new mines or plowing new fields. The government claims there is full employment, and, in fact, almost all unemployed persons are those who do not wish to work or who cannot find jobs for which they consider themselves trained or suited. There are a considerable number of young people whose parents' incomes have made it possible for them to shirk work and these are a particular target of government attention. In 1957 the Russians published a law providing for deportation to remote regions and compulsory labor in slave-labor camps for beggars, vagrants, and persons living on unearned incomes. The latter category would cover idle youth. The law's preamble declared that Socialist society had eliminated unemployment and the exploitation of man by fellow men. It went on: "However, in the industrious Soviet family there still are people leading an antisocial, parasitic way of life. Such people either take up employment for the sake of pretense and actually subsist on an unearned income and enrich themselves at the expense of working people; or, though fit for work, do not do useful work, either in society or in the family, but prefer to engage in vagrancy and begging and often commit crimes."

The proposed law provided that adult able-bodied citizens who lead "an antisocial, parasitic life and persistently shun useful labor, as well as those living on unearned incomes," may receive sentences of from two to five years of compulsory labor at "a place of deportation."

The method of trial for accused persons resembled the procedure of the Salem witch trials. Verdicts were a community responsibility. A simple majority vote at a meeting of adults of neighborhoods, in the case of cities, or of the entire community, in the case of rural areas, would be enough to convict a person. In some instances a meeting of adult residents of one apartment house, attended by at least one hundred persons, could by majority vote sentence a fellow-resident to a Siberian labor camp. In effect, a handful of Communist Party members in a small community could, by taking the lead, sentence an indolent young man to forced labor.

Some gypsies, traditional nomads of sections now controlled by the U.S.S.R., have managed to evade Soviet-imposed productive labor. In 1956 a severe law was passed that decreed that gypsies coming of age, "who shirk work for public benefit and indulge in tramping," should be sentenced by people's courts to deportation from their native regions for five years to be spent at "corrective labor." The law indicated that the authorities had all but given up on converting elder gypsies into the Soviet concept of useful citizens and would now concentrate on gypsies as they reach the age of eighteen.

Most unemployment in the Soviet Union is transitory because economic pressures force people to take jobs offered, even if not jobs of their choice. There is no unemployment insurance to tide a person over a waiting period between jobs. The vicious-cycle Soviet argument is that there is no need for unemployment insurance because there is no unemployment. Thus, a worker who becomes redundant in one job because of automation may soon be obliged to accept another job, although he considers it below his experience or qualifications. There is no recourse to the trade union as in the U.S.A., France, Italy, or Britain, because trade unions serve quite a different function in Russia. In the Soviet Union the trade union's function is, in the words of a Soviet document on the subject, "to rally workers to meet and surpass production plans of the state." The state's production plans are law. The trade unions and management are committed to fulfill these goals. If plans call for the introduction of automated equipment, the trade union's legal role is to facilitate that plan. Trade unions in each factory conclude terms of work agreements with the managers. These provide how much of the enterprise's income is to be spent on social halls and toilet amenities for the workers. It is also a trade union responsibility to, in the words of the newspaper *Izvestia,* "take steps to see to it that setting-up exercises are introduced into the daily work routine of enterprises." In a state extremely conscious of its citizens' physical fitness, factory and office workers are supposed to participate in some form of exercise. As *Izvestia* explains it: "When you work in the same position for a long time productivity goes down . . . and a result is an increase in rejected pieces of work." Union officials investigate the validity of causes for firing a worker and may plead the worker's case before management. Union dues funds help in funeral arrangements of members. Membership in unions is not obligatory, but most workers do belong. In the Soviet concept, it is not a case of labor union pitted against management. Rather, unions are an arm of the state just as is management. In the case of automation, for example, a union would not seek the retention of workers in traditional jobs.

A built-in cushion against disruptive effects of eventual automation lies in the fact that control of an entire industry is in the hands of a central Moscow ministry or, for a particular region, in the hands of a regional economic council. The apparatus thus exists for the transfer of redundant workers from, say, an automated plant in Moscow to a less technologically advanced factory in Yakutsk, Siberia. The Moscow worker, replaced by a machine, does not usually have to seek a job. One (not necessarily in a place he finds desirable) is usually found for him. The released worker is free to seek other employment in Moscow where he has his home and friends. But an unsuccessful search, and economic and social pressures (including loss of accumulated pension benefits) may soon induce him to take one of the jobs offered by the ministry or economic council, with free railway fare and unimpaired pension seniority —even in Yakutsk.

Since Stalin's death, moderating features have been introduced into the Soviet economy. The working week has been reduced from forty-eight hours to forty-six. The two hours of free time are at the end of the day Saturday. Enterprises are entitled, with agreement by workers and management, to skip the lunch period and end work even earlier. Some industries have introduced a seven-hour day and a forty-two hour week, and plans are to make it universal.

A minimum-wage law, long taken for granted in capitalist countries, was introduced for the first time in Russia only in 1956. The law raised the level of wages of the lowest-paid workers, such as women street sweepers and watchmen in factories. It provided a minimum wage of 300 rubles ($30) a month in towns and 270 rubles ($27) in rural areas. The law exempted persons earning less than 370 rubles ($37) a month from income and bachelor taxes.

Of greatest significance is a post-Stalin law enabling workers to leave a job with two weeks notice. Previously it was a legal offense, punishable by a jail sentence, to quit a job without permission. Now a worker will lose his pension accumulation by leaving a job without the full consent of the management, and he may be blacklisted at other plants in order to retain him in his original job. But theoretically, and in most cases actually, the Russian is now free to leave a job. This is a far cry from the days of Stalin, when a law (since revoked) provided that a person twenty minutes late to work on three occasions could incur a five-year jail sentence.

At best, Soviet wages are low by Western standards. At the Likhatchov Auto Works, formerly the Stalin Plant, in Moscow, where 40,000 workers are employed, wages range from 750 rubles ($75) to 3000 rubles ($300) a month. Executives get more. Ivan Ivanovich Karsov, assistant director of the plant, showed me through the great shedlike buildings spread over many acres. A short, balding man with searching brown eyes, Karsov seemed to resent the question when I asked how much he earned. He had visited the United States in 1939 to purchase machinery for the plant and he said that U. S. workers get their pay in envelopes so that others may not know what they earn. "My salary is a private matter too," he said.

When I told him that some large corporations publish the salaries of their executives in public reports to stockholders, he agreed to tell: "My monthly salary amounts to 5000 rubles ($500) besides bonuses." In a good year, when the plant overfulfills its production targets, Karsov's bonus can increase his salary by 50 per cent or more. Even so, this is not an exceptional salary for the assistant director of the nation's largest vehicle factory.

There are advantages other than salary, though, for a man in Karsov's position. He has a chauffeured car assigned for the use of his family. In a country where money alone cannot purchase adequate living space, Karsov's position entitles him to a large apartment for his wife and three children. As is true of most Russians in top managerial positions, Karsov is a member of the Communist Party, the thin layer of populace that runs the country. His Party membership and managerial status lend him prestige, influence, and respect that often accompany monetary wealth in capitalist countries.

Forty-nine years old, Karsov began working at the auto plant as an apprentice in 1921, three years before it produced its first vehicle. It was then a repair shop. He learned a machinist's trade, was sent to an automobile institute, and graduated in 1935 with a rudimentary knowledge of engineering and plant management. He joined the Communist Party in 1930. Undoubtedly this helped his career greatly. Karsov's assignment to the United States to purchase machinery kept him there for two years to inspect purchases before shipment. He visited a number of American auto plants and observed the assembly-line techniques. Many of the U.S.-built machines bought by Karsov are still in use and the name "Cincinnati" stands out incongruously on pressing machines and lathes near walls decorated with posters of Lenin and "increase production" posters in the Cyrillic alphabet. There are also large machine tools made in Germany, France, and England. Now replacement parts for these are made in the Soviet Union, and almost all of the new machines, except for those from Communist Czechoslovakia and East Germany, are also manufactured in the U.S.S.R.

Karsov's son is an industrial designer, working in a government design bureau since graduating from a technical institute. One daughter is studying law at Moscow University, and a younger daughter is still in secondary school.

Karsov's responsibilities are extensive. Besides running the plant, the management is concerned with housing projects, schools, and nurseries for employees' children. There are two polyclinics on the premises where minor injuries and ailments are treated, and more complicated ills receive attention at the plant's hospital. The plant employs 124 doctors and 184 nurses. Two thousand youngsters of plant employees attend 16 kindergartens. Six thousand employees belong to 29 sections of the plant's "Torpedo" sports club. Technical schools run by the plant are attended by more than a thousand workers. The Likhatchov factory operates its own health resort on the Baltic Sea where the best workers and privileged persons like Karsov and his family are able to obtain reservations. There's also a smaller rest home for vacationing employees about fifty miles from Moscow. Tickets to other government-operated rest homes are sold to deserving workers, but by Karsov's own figures, only 8500 workers of this plant's 40,000 are able to obtain tickets for any of these vacation spots in any one year. (Almost all large vacation "sanitoria" are now operated by the Ministry of Health rather than by individual plants or ministries. This is a consequence of the demise of ministries in the reorganization of industry.)

The plant has a large recreation building, called a Palace of Culture, whose gymnasium is used for Party lectures as often as for basketball games and whose auditorium is the scene of as many classes as movies.

Each year the plant builds six hundred apartments for its workers. This is another factor to dissuade people from leaving their jobs. There's a law that an occupant of an apartment may not be evicted for going to work in another job, but pressures from neighbors can serve as well as a law to force a family out. The construction work is done by 1000 builders in the employment of the plant, but the financing of the construction is by government funds and it is the government that actually owns the apartments. The factory's role is to supervise their construction, assign their occupants, and manage them when completed. Distribution of apartments is on the basis of "a complex of factors," to borrow Karsov's phrase: a worker's seniority, the number of members in his family, and the condition of his present flat. Assignment of flats is made by the management, the Party unit, and the union.

Although the factory bears the name "auto works," very few *cars* are produced. The assembly lines—working on two shifts—concentrate on trucks and bicycles. Both are vehicles of labor in Russia. In villages and on farms the bicycle is not a vehicle of sport or recreation but rather an important means of carrying people to and from work. The plant produces 450,000 bicycles, 100,000 trucks, and 3000 buses annually. A bicycle is completed every minute, a truck every five minutes, an autobus every two hours, and a refrigerator every ten minutes. Karsov said that "several hundred Zil limousines" are manufactured each year. The Zil, standing for the initials of the plant, is made only for use of the Kremlin leaders and other government organizations. The Zil closely resembles the pre-World War II Packard in its long lines and pointed front. Asked about this, Karsov replied, rather evasively and with a trace of embarrassment, it seemed, that "with the development of auto techniques, all cars look very much alike. After all, if you build a car it looks like a car. With the exception of some midget cars, all cars look like American cars. There's nothing unusual in the appearance of the Zil as many details will be the same in *all* cars."

Although selling prices vary with the purchaser (prices for sales abroad depend on the foreign-policy considerations of the transactions), the average products of the Zil plant are: 15,000 rubles ($1500) for the several models of dump trucks; 40,000 rubles ($4000) for buses; 70,000 rubles ($7000) for the seven-passenger Zil car, and 600 rubles ($60) for a bicycle. The Zil refrigerator, white-enameled with two ice-cube trays and a small freezer compartment, sells for 2000 rubles ($200) and, as the owner of one, I can testify that it works reliably and well. The same cannot be said for many other Soviet appliances, as, for example, the telephone.

CHAPTER 7

DIAL U FOR UBISTVA

A correspondent for the British Reuters news agency was trying to make himself heard on a telephone call to London.

"Ordzhonikidze, Ordzhonikidze," he shouted, dictating a dispatch which included the name of Grigory Ordzhonikidze, onetime People's Commissar for Heavy Industry, a man from the Georgia section of the Soviet Union. A city was named for him, as well as the navy cruiser on which Bulganin and Khrushchev went to England. The correspondent tried to convey the name letter-by-letter.

"O for Oslo, R for Russia."

The line was momentarily interrupted, and the correspondent shouted to operators along the line until the circuit was finally resumed.

"D for damned," he continued.

A moment of crestfallen silence as the perspiring correspondent was chastised by the man in London.

"But," he pleaded, "I'm *not* swearing. I'm spelling."

Telephones in Russia are enough to make the most patient man curse. It is common experience for the line to go dead in mid-conversation during calls within Moscow. Faulty equipment may be the cause or, if one accepts as fact that lines are tapped, the clumsiness or whim of the monitors may be the reason.

There is no way to say for sure if the Russians listen in on foreigners' conversations. They certainly have the facilities needed for so elementary a technical job as line-tapping. American Embassy personnel operate on the assumption that their every conversation is monitored. Overly cautious members of the Embassy have been known to refuse to discuss even the most innocuous topics on the phone. I once phoned John C. Guthrie, then First Secretary, to ask what method had been used to deliver a certain diplomatic note to the Soviet Foreign Ministry. Had the Ambassador delivered it personally? Had it been sent by messenger?

"I'd rather not answer that on the telephone," replied Mr. Guthrie. "Come around to the Embassy if you want to know."

Surely Soviet authorities would have learned nothing they did not already know had he answered me. Having been the recipients of the note, the Russians obviously knew *how* it was delivered.

This is not the only instance of the cloak-and-dagger attitudes carried to an extreme by the American Embassy. The British, French, and other Embassies had a much less inhibited attitude toward the telephone.

The knowledge that someone may be listening to your conversation on the telephone, and, in fact, right in your own room can be tantalizing, upsetting, or depressing, depending on the individual.

Every coincidence assumes dire significance. A correspondent, who was convinced that his room and telephone were wired, offered this evidence: one afternoon, after his wife had been begging him to take her to the Praga Restaurant (Moscow's most expensive, if not Moscow's best), there came a telephone call from a minor Soviet official. The Russian had been trying, for reasons best known to himself, to ingratiate himself with the correspondent, and he asked the delighted wife whether she and her husband would like to join him for an excellent meal at, say, the Praga Restaurant?

This same correspondent maintained he had become convinced that telephone conversations were not entirely private after the unnerving experience of picking up his telephone a few seconds after completing a call—to hear a portion of his just-concluded conversation being played back on a recording device.

On one occasion, a Russian who visited my hotel room insisted that I turn on my radio to deafening volume so that his words would be drowned out for any recording device. He was a Russian who should know.

Imaginative visitors to Moscow have claimed that they saw midget microphones concealed in low-slung chandeliers, and there is the tale that a microphone was once discovered in the Great Seal of the United States in the American Ambassador's office. This was shortly after the seal had been returned, having just been repainted by the Russians.

It is a fact that eight microphones were discovered (during one of the periodic checks that all embassies make) in the Moscow apartment of a member of the Canadian Embassy's military staff. There were two under the parlor floor, two in the ceiling; two more were rooted out of dining-room paneling, and two were under the bed!

An Asian ambassador in Moscow was once guided by his nose to a microphone. The workman who had installed it near the base of the chandelier, in the space between the ceiling and the floor above, apparently had forgotten a piece of his lunch—an aromatic chunk of cheese that grew more aromatic with the passage of time.

An ambassador of a Middle Eastern country, in a period of strained relations with Russia, suggested that we go for a walk outdoors when I had an off-the-record interview with him. So cautious was he that he refused to ride in my car, rented from the Soviet Intourist organization, for fear of microphones.

It must be added that planting microphones in embassies is not a phenomenon unique to Russia. It's not unknown for microphones to be discovered on an embassy's premises even in supposedly "friendly" lands.

Circulation of such stories, both likely and unlikely, understandably alarmed one young lady, the fiancée of a diplomat, who was preparing to come to Moscow. She worried so much about the silent invasion of their intimacies that finally she confided her concern to a psychiatrist. "I feel inhibited," she explained. "What should I do?"

"I'd suggest," replied the practical therapist, "that when you make love, you simply do so *quietly*."

On any long-distance telephone call, even between such major cities as Stalingrad and Moscow, the chances are only about even that you'll be able to make yourself understood at all, whereas on international calls circuits are usually clearer than on many domestic conversations. Perhaps this can be attributed to superior equipment at the foreign end which compensates for the Soviet lines. An incoming international call takes priority over any local call, and without warning the operator will disconnect a local conversation to put through a foreign call.

Almost any city in the world can be called by wire or radiotelephone from Moscow. Exceptions are such cities as Madrid, for the Soviet Union has no diplomatic relations with Spain. (However, mail or telegrams may be sent to or received from Spain.) Radiotelephone service with the U.S.A. is available for only two and three-quarter hours every day, from 4:45 P.M. to 7:30 P.M., Moscow time. However, calls may be made between the United States and Moscow at any time of the day or night if the caller requests that it be relayed via London.

To make a call abroad or, for that matter, a call to any Soviet city outside of Moscow, a Russian must pay in advance. He goes to a post office, pays for the number of minutes he plans to speak, and receives a receipt. At any time within a month he may phone long distance by giving the operator his receipt number. Of course this system totally ignores the convenience of the caller or the fact that it is difficult to know beforehand how many minutes it may be necessary to speak. Similar examples of the bureaucratic penchant for making life difficult are easy to find in the U.S.S.R.

If a Russian expects to makes several long-distance calls, he may leave money on deposit at the post office and draw on it. But to phone *now* and pay *later*—this is not the practice for private calls.

A Russian may make a long-distance call from his home if he wishes, but many prefer to go to the Central Telegraph Office, where connections are usually clearer. Local conversations may be interrupted several times. It's always safest to begin by deciding who will call back when cut off. Also, Soviet telephone receivers have an earsplitting tendency to backfire violent static noises from time to time. So experienced telephone users in Moscow take the precaution of holding the receiver an inch or so from the ear. Because of this, Russians shout when talking on the telephone. However, another explanation has been offered for their screaming conversations. It seems that Russians—in a country born late into the industrial age—still feel mildly mistrustful of mechanical gadgets. That may be why they are unconscionable jaywalkers, apparently innocent to the wounding powers of the auto. That may be why they lack faith in any apparatus being able to convey their voice some miles without a very vociferous assist.

These minor inconveniences have not discouraged Russians from wanting telephones installed in their homes, for there are long application lists. It's difficult to get a telephone—the shortage lies in insufficient central telephone exchanges. A Russian told me that when he finally received a telephone set it lay idle for many months until a number became available in the nearest central office.

As new apartment houses are erected on Moscow's outskirts, telephone central offices are built there too. Occupants of these new flats get phones installed quickly, but pity residents of older sections of the city such as one correspondent's interpreter, who had the backing of the Soviet Foreign Ministry's press department and of the Soviet governmental agency which had assigned him his job. In this case, influence helped not a bit; he was unable to get a phone. The latest available statistics for the number of telephones in the U.S.S.R. are for 1943. At that time there were only 861,181. The number must have increased several fold by now. In 1957 there were more than 60,000,000 telephones in the U.S.A.; there were 31,611,280 in 1947.

In communal apartments, usually only one telephone in the common hallway serves the families occupying the various rooms. The problem that would be involved in trying to apportion the telephone bill among a half dozen families may explain why charges are a fixed amount. You may make an unlimited number of local calls. In fact, even Soviet hotels do not charge for telephone calls, quite a contrast to many American hotels which not only charge the public phone-booth rate for each call but often add a switchboard service charge besides.

In Moscow, a home telephone costs 25 rubles ($2.50). Usually bills are not sent, for subscribers are expected to pay every three months. A telephone call from the accounting office reminds delinquent subscribers, and as a last resort a bill is sent.

Public telephone booths are glass-enclosed affairs on sidewalks rather than inside buildings. No seat is provided. The single slot in public telephones takes only a 15-kopeck piece which makes this coin, slightly smaller and thinner than a nickel, desirable and it is not readily surrendered as change.

However, you need no coin to call certain emergency numbers. There's a button provided on public telephones which is pushed to enable you to dial 01, 02, or 03 free of charge. If you push the button to dial any other number a busy signal is all you get for your effort. The number 01 connects you with the fire department, 02 calls the police, and 03 summons an ambulance.

A recorded man's voice will tell you the correct time if you dial 100. The announcement is made only once. If you miss it the first time you must dial again. Weather information is obtained by dialing D-2 05 25. A lady answers and pleasantly inquires "What do you need?" You can ask for today's weather or for the forecast up to three days ahead.

Another Soviet telephone service is moving-picture information. You can ask if a particular movie is playing anywhere in town and, if so, where it's being shown on that day. Also, the schedule at any particular *kino* (movie house) may be received. Only information for the same day is given.

Ordinary Moscow telephone numbers have six digits. The American Embassy number is D-2 05 50. The National Hotel, where many tourists stay, is B-9 99 17.

You can talk for an unlimited time for 15 kopecks on a public telephone. However, if you should want someone to call you back, that's impossible, because the public phone's number is not marked on it. It's considered extremely poor form to make more than one call when others are waiting in line, and Russians often will not hesitate to rap at the glass door and tell you so.

Dials have ten numbers paired with ten letters of the Cyrillic alphabet. When the British play "Dial M for Murder" was staged in Moscow's Pushkin Theatre, it was necessary to change the title to "Telephone Call." The word murder in Russian is *Ubistva* but there's no letter U on Russian telephone dials, and a direct translation would have puzzled Russians.

Probably the busiest telephone number is 09—for information. Telephone numbers are difficult to come by in Russia, mainly because telephone directories are few and far between. The 09 information operator will give you certain numbers, but many private phones are unlisted. If you ask for the telephone of any of the embassies in Moscow the response is "We do not have the numbers of any foreign embassies." You can get the number of secret-police headquarters or of the Kremlin but not of an embassy. Russians are discouraged from any contact with embassies, particularly those of non-Communist countries. That's why policemen stationed at embassy entrances stare intently into the interior of incoming cars, and that's why Russians seeking an embassy number get no assistance from the information operator.

Public telephone booths are not furnished with directories. Most owners of telephones do not have directories either. From time to time telephone directories have been published and sold at newsstands, but the supply is quickly exhausted. There's no attempt to keep pace either with the demand or with changes in subscribers' addresses or numbers.

The difficulty in finding a telephone directory is sometimes attributed to Soviet secrecy. That may be part of the explanation. Part, too, may lie in the Soviet penchant for privacy; if someone wants you to have his telephone number he will give it to you. Most of the explanation, though, is found simply in the astigmatic outlook of Soviet bureaucracy as to what constitutes public service.

Although Russians are not as shy as they used to be under Stalin about giving out telephone numbers to foreigners, most do so only with reluctance. I became well acquainted with a Russian interpreter when I accompanied an American agricultural delegation on a five-week tour of the U.S.S.R. During the course of the trip he often suggested that we must get together in Moscow. When the trip was about over, I asked for his telephone number.

"Oh, my telephone is out of order right now," he said.

"Well, I can phone you when it's repaired," I suggested.

"No, we expect to move soon to a different apartment where we'll have a new number. Anyway, it might be better if *I* called you."

One correspondent tells of trying, during all of a three-month visit, to obtain the number of an assistant editor of *Pravda,* who found an excuse each time to refuse to give it. At the Geneva Conference, where the ephemeral "Spirit of Geneva" was born, the editor finally volunteered the number. It was of little use, however, for the correspondent has never returned to Moscow.

The Soviet public seems well served, though, when it comes to postal service. Like telephones and telegraph, post is under the Soviet Ministry of Communications. There are ordinarily four daily mail deliveries in Moscow. The first, beginning at 6:30 A.M., brings the morning newspapers, which are handled by the postal system rather than by carrier boys. Postal authorities claim that a letter, whether registered or dropped into a mail box anywhere in Moscow in the morning, will be delivered before the day is out. This may be true for mail addressed to *Russians,* but it's not always the case for letters addressed to foreigners. These may take as long as a week for delivery. Mail from abroad takes even longer. Although it takes fourteen to twenty-four hours (depending on the aircraft and route) by air from New York to Moscow and from five to ten hours from London to Moscow, I've received letters from both capitals that took two weeks or more. Seven days is average time for an airmail letter from New York. The shortest time in which I have got a letter from New York was five days; the longest, twenty-two days. Mail sent abroad from Moscow is almost as slow in reaching its destination. Obviously the delay is in Moscow. This delay and other evidence lead to the conclusion that foreigners' mail is opened, read, and probably photostated. The unusual thickness of the layer of glue which seals most envelopes gives a hint that they have been opened and resealed. I've received many envelopes bearing a Russian stamp reading, "Received in damaged condition." In each case, the "damage" had been repaired by a strip of paper, resealing the lefthand side of the envelope where it obviously had been slit.

It costs 60 kopecks (6 cents) to send a letter within the U.S.S.R. by regular mail and 10 cents by airmail. Airmail sent abroad from Russia is one ruble and 60 kopecks (16 cents) compared to 15 cents' U. S. postage required to airmail a letter from the U.S.A. to Russia.

The accepted way of addressing a letter in Russia, as in a number of other European countries, is just backwards from the practice in the U.S. The addressee's name is written last; the country and city first. A properly addressed envelope would read:

U.S.S.R.
Moscow
Ulitsa Gorkova, 10
Ivan Ivanovich SMIRNOV

If insufficient postage is affixed to a letter, the recipient must pay a fixed fine of 1 ruble (10 cents), no matter what amount of stamps is lacking. It may be the sender's fault, but the receiver pays. As a matter of fact, even if the return address is written on an unstamped envelope, the Russian postal service will not return it to the sender, but rather will collect the fine from the addressee. In this way mail is not delayed, but neither does this system encourage Russians to pay attention to putting the correct amount of stamps on a letter.

Russian postage stamps are masterpieces of imagination and detail. It is a philatelists' paradise. New stamps are issued for every occasion—there's been one for each sputnik with a likeness of that particular earth satellite, a series to mark the International Geophysical Year, and stamps to commemorate the Tchaikovsky music competition which Texan Van Cliburn won. (His picture was not on any of the stamps, of course, but for a while Russian adulation of Cliburn was so great that no one would have been surprised if it had been.)

Lenin is shown on scores of Soviet stamps. Sometimes just his bust is pictured, but more often he is delivering a speech in a historical setting or embarking on one of his periodic exiles.

Counters in stores specializing in stamps sell issues to mark Communist Congresses both in Russia and abroad, to honor Arctic and Antarctic expeditions, and even for the occasion of an international horse-racing meet. There is a series on wild life in the U.S.S.R. One block shows a figure doing setting-up exercises; each stamp depicts a different position. The whole series provides a veritable short course in physical fitness.

There are "first day issues," special postmarks, and envelopes with Soviet landscapes in color.

Mailmen in Russia are mostly women. They seem efficient, but presumably curiosity is a female characteristic in Russia as elsewhere, and one lady mailman came to grief for taking letters home to read. A court sentenced her to two years in prison when, on complaint of folks along her route, police found forty-five undelivered letters at her home. Nineteen of the envelopes had been opened, but apparently she hadn't yet got around to reading the others.

Women also deliver telegrams. They travel by Moskvitch midget cars. Early in my stay in Russia I did a broadcast describing delivery of telegrams. I pointed out that although it may take only a matter of minutes for a message to be transmitted by radio from New York or London to Moscow, delivery was only as fast or as slow as a little old lady in a Moskvitch car. It was impossible, I wrote, to make arrangements to have cables telephoned from the telegraph office. The censor passed the script. Perhaps the broadcast had nothing to do with it, but three weeks later a notice was sent to all correspondents from the Ministry of Communications, pointing out that if appropriately notified, the cable authorities would be pleased to telephone the text of cable at any hour, day or night. They do so, too. Sometimes overzealously, in fact. On one occasion, a cable addressed to me was delivered at noon to another correspondent, who phoned me right away and brought the cable over to my hotel. Later that day, I mentioned it to a clerk in the telegraph office. Fourteen hours later, at 2 A.M., my friend was awakened by a call from the telegraph informing him that a cable had been erroneously delivered to him. He said he knew, he had delivered the cable himself to the National Broadcasting Company correspondent, and did the young lady realize what time it was? Fifteen minutes later I was roused from bed by a similar call, checking whether I had really received the stray cable. It took fourteen hours for bureaucracy to catch up with its error, but once it did there certainly was a doggedness about it.

The busiest time for the Soviet Ministry of Communications telegraph operators is shortly before May Day, Revolution Day in November, and New Year's Day. It's a Soviet tradition to send friends telegrams expressing holiday good wishes. You can write telegrams in the Russian Cyrillic alphabet or in any Roman alphabet language as Soviet telegraph offices are equipped with both keyboards, and before the holidays, special stands appear in subway stations where telegrams may be written and paid for.

Usually Soviet greetings sent by telegram are of sober content, so that it may well have startled telegraph clerks when they read a telegram I sent to Louisiana Democrat, Senator William Ellender, who celebrated his sixty-seventh birthday while on a tour of Siberia. It read:

> *Russia is red*
> *You've a right to be blue.*
> *Omsk ain't Louisiana.*
> *Happy birthday to you.*

It seemed to me that anyone celebrating his birthday in Omsk in the heart of Siberia might need cheering up, even though the Russians now protest that Siberia no longer is a land of bitter cold and exile but a quickly developing new frontier with dramatic industry and a courageous program of cultivating new lands.

CHAPTER 8

TO CHEW WITHOUT SWALLOWING

One afternoon I was discussing Communist economics with a young Russian engineer, an earnest Communist. I opened a package of chewing gum and asked whether gum is manufactured in the Soviet Union.

"No," he grinned, "we Communists consider that to chew without swallowing is unproductive." Then he took a stick.

There was some truth in his joking response, because Russia is a land which has known hunger, and providing food to chew on is serious business. At the root of Soviet plenty or scarcity is agriculture. Agriculture in Russia is big in every sense. Farms are gigantic. Crop successes have been spectacular. Crop failures have been staggering. The greatest superlative in Soviet agriculture, though, is enormous inefficiency—the profligate waste of man power.

In the United States one farmer feeds about eighteen people.

In the Soviet Union one farmer feeds only five people.

Only 14 per cent of America's population lives on farms, and only about half of those actually work on the farm.

In the U.S.S.R. about 40 per cent of the labor force works on farms.

The disproportionate numbers plowing Soviet soil stems, in part, from history. When thousands of small farms were combined into huge collectives, a Soviet objective was to take advantage of the greater possibilities for efficiency in big units. However, for the most part, the bigger farm units did not mean fewer people. The families who had cultivated their small farms remained to work on the collectivized fields, although with the expansion of acreage and introduction of machinery fewer hands should have been necessary.

There are two types of farms in the Soviet Union—state farms and collective farms. A state farm is on land owned by the government and operated as a factory would be, with wages paid to workers. A collective farm is on land which the government permits a large number of farmers to use jointly under prescribed conditions, presumably forever.

An individual farmer on a Soviet state farm does not share in the profits, which go entirely to the government. A worker on a collective farm receives only small return because profit is spread among a great many families. Therefore, on both types of Soviet farms the motivation to reduce personnel and increase efficiency is vastly diluted. The profit instinct that motivates an individual farmer in the United States to operate as efficiently as possible and with as little help as possible is surely diminished by collective management.

Another reason for inefficiency is Soviet failure to take full advantage of machinery. A harvesting combine in the United States or Canada will move over rolling plains cutting and threshing wheat with one or two workers involved in the operation. In Russia the same operation requires nine or ten persons.

Granted that Soviet combine machines are generally less automatic than American, there still seems little real need for two men instead of one at the controls of the tractor hauling the combine, or for two women helping the thresher.

One of the Americans on the 1955 tour of Soviet farm areas, Herbert Pike, had, with his wife, operated a 700-acre farm near Whiting, Iowa, for ten years. Their only help was one hired man and part-time hands at harvest. Pike's favorite gambit in conversation with Russian farm workers was to describe his farm, then ask the Russians to guess how many people it took to run it. The answers ran from 40 to 100. The reaction to Pike's response drew incredulous expressions from more restrained Russians, and a frank "I don't believe you" from others.

It's not unusual to find that mechanization on a particular Soviet farm will have increased by 50 per cent during the past decade. The manager will proudly list the trucks, tractors, and combines used now as compared to ten years ago. However, the number of workers on the farm usually will not have decreased in proportion to the mechanization but, in fact, may have grown. The acquisition of machinery has not meant a significant reduction in man power.

A farm that claims to be 95 per cent mechanized may have 500 horses in its barns. A highly mechanized American farm often has horses only for riding, if it has horses at all, for work horses consume feed and require tending. However, in the case of Russia's horses there may be military considerations. There is reason to believe that Soviet farms are required to keep great numbers of horses to supplement Russia's still limited motorized transport in case of war. Many of the roads in the Soviet Union are unpaved and better adapted to horses than to trucks.

It's a mistake to assume that Russia's farms employ wasteful numbers of hands because there's an overabundance of labor. This is not the case. There's a labor shortage, largely because of inefficient use of man power. Factory managers complain about not having enough workers for the job. That's why women are employed in every sort of work. There just aren't enough men.

The success of a manager of an individual collective farm or state farm depends on fulfilling government quotas of grain. The relief afforded the payroll by eliminating a hundred workers is less of a consideration than the consequent possible diminishment of crop gathered. Labor is cheap when compared to the penalties of failure to meet a grain target. This mitigates against efficient use of labor or land.

An American farmer would soon go broke on fields that yield from 16 to 30 bushels of corn per acre as do Soviet farms I've seen. In Iowa 60 bushels of corn from an acre of land is average.

An adequate harvest has been the paramount consideration in Russia; not the number of hands it takes to provide that harvest. To guarantee sufficient wheat, women are assigned to trudge after giant combines and pick up single stalks of grain.

To assure sufficient pork one woman is assigned to tend 10 sows on a typical Russian farm. An American farmer will take care of 50 sows himself in addition to his other work. However, where an average of eight piglets live out of every litter on American farms, white-coated Russian pig tenders manage, by devoted care, to save 12 piglets in an average litter.

Even with this prodigal expenditure of human energy, the Soviet Union, with its larger population and greater area, has not yet been able to overtake the United States in agricultural output.

In 1956 there were 55,002,000 pigs in the U.S.A.; 52,155,000 in the U.S.S.R. Cows in the United States numbered 48,674,000; in the Soviet Union there were 29,237,000 cows.

With all its limitless land, the Soviet Union has never grown as much total grain as the United States (although the U.S.S.R. has at times surpassed the U.S.A. in wheat and rye).

In expanding agricultural output, the Russians have encountered greatest difficulty in increasing the livestock population. The extensive slaughter of cattle by disgruntled farmers in the 1930s depleted Russia's herd. Furthermore, with limited quantities of grain reaped, Russia had to use its grain to feed people *today* rather than to feed cattle which might be used to feed people *tomorrow*.

In 1916 in Czarist Russia there were 28,820,000 cows. It took almost forty years of phenomenal treadmill effort for agriculture, under Communism, to re-attain that figure. It was only in 1955 that Soviet statisticians for the first time reported more cows (29,237,000) than before the Revolution.

One of the earliest projects of the men who succeeded Stalin was to try, once and for all, to raise Soviet agricultural output significantly and rapidly.

The objectives were several. The Kremlin leadership wanted, of course, to provide ample grain for the people. Furthermore, it sought to raise sufficient feed for cattle to break the bottleneck of meat supply. Finally, the availability of surplus grain would strengthen Soviet foreign policy in providing wheat to sell or donate to foreign governments.

The gigantic "virgin-lands program" was launched in 1954. The public announcement was a decree by the Central Committee of the Communist Party on March 2 declaring its purpose: "To satisfy the growing needs of our country's population for consumer goods and to provide . . . raw materials in the coming two to three years in abundance on the basis of the mighty growth of socialist industry."

In other words, an attempt was to be made to bring agriculture abreast of industry, for it has lagged behind since the Revolution. In 1955 Communist Party First Secretary Khrushchev spoke of it in a speech before the Supreme Soviet, the parliament of the U.S.S.R.:

"In 1955 the Soviet Union's gross production exceeded the level of production of 1937 twenty-seven times . . . the generation of electric power 86 times and the output of the machine-building industry more than 160 times.

"The agriculture of our country is growing and developing."

In context this modest tribute to agriculture was abject admission of failure.

Soviet agricultural gross output, it is estimated, has been increasing at the annual rate of about one per cent, while the population has been outdistancing the food supply by growing at the rate of one and one-half per cent. The virgin-lands program was undertaken to correct this deficiency.

The virgin lands were not entirely virgin. Some acreage had been plowed and planted in the 1930s. But the crops had been so meager that the land was soon deserted.

However, plows had never broken most of the vast areas of virgin Siberia and Kazakhstan, northernmost of the Central Asian republics, where marginal rainfall and a short growing season had conspired to render its steppes unprofitable for farming.

The man behind the decision to work the virgin lands on a huge scale was also behind many other post-Stalin innovations, including de-Stalinization and de-centralization of industry—Nikita Khrushchev. Whatever his other characteristics, he could never be said to lack daring.

It was a gamble on a truly national scale. It meant staking on the roulette of Russian rain hundreds of thousands of men and women who might otherwise be employed in pursuits of guaranteed production. It meant diverting quantities of Russia's limited resources from other products to the manufacture of tractors and farm implements for cultivation that might yield giant harvest *or* might only grow stubble.

So far the answer to the gamble is not known.

The first year's harvest was good. The second year's poor. The third years's crop was excellent; the fourth, indifferent. The fifth season brought a bumper crop. The future may bring abundance, or it could produce the largest dust bowl known to man.

All the instruments of social pressure at the state's disposal were mobilized to recruit young people. Leaders of the Komsomol, the Young Communist League, suggested to unmarried members and to young childless couples that they could best demonstrate their allegiance to Komsomol principles by volunteering. Meetings were devoted to soliciting members to sign up and go. Similarly, in factories it was the trade union "activists" or "agitators" or "propagandists" who hounded eligible workers to leave for the virgin lands. Factory foremen and plant managers added their words of encouragement. In every enterprise the

Communist Party group, the elite core behind any Soviet program, keeps the heat of propaganda burning: it was the duty of youth to volunteer. It was a heroic opportunity. It was a patriotic obligation.

One should live in such an atmosphere to appreciate its effectiveness. Anyone who has served in the armed forces in wartime may have sensed a few of the ingredients. Social pressures, which are totally alien in a civilian society, cause men to volunteer for dangerous or distasteful missions. There is the desire to win approval of the members of the squad. There is the need to observe the standards set by the platoon leader. It takes a confirmed cynic to resist these pressures.

I met a nineteen-year-old factory apprentice at the bar of the Sovietskaya Hotel in Moscow on the eve of his departure for Siberia. Several buddies were commiserating with him and he had been drinking liberally.

"I'm not sure *why* I agreed to go. I guess I just couldn't say no after so many people told me I should go. The Komsomol members made me feel that I would be a coward if I refused. They didn't say so, but I know that's what they were thinking."

Of course, some young Russians, fired with a love of adventure and a pioneering spirit, needed no urging to become a part of the dramatic project.

Besides social pressures, material benefits were offered to attract volunteers. The inducements offered to Anatole Doroshev, who works at the Egorgivsky State Farm in Siberia, were typical. Anatole, 26 years old, worked as an electrician in a tractor plant at Lipetsk, some 250 miles southeast of Moscow, where he earned 1000 rubles (about $100) a month. Then the shop's union organization enlisted Anatole for the virgin lands. He received three month's salary in a lump sum as a state subsidy, and he and his recent bride received free train tickets from Lipetsk to Rubtsovsk, site of the farm.

Although Anatole would have been exempt from army service in his job at the tractor factory (only youngsters who are not employed and not in school are usually inducted), several of his friends volunteered in order to evade the Soviet draft.

The wage scale in the virgin lands is higher for most jobs than elsewhere, and is known as the "Siberian super-wage." However, after learning how to drive a tractor, Anatole earned the same salary as at the Lipetsk factory. His living quarters consisted of one room as they did at Lipetsk. The toilet facilities had been indoors at Lipetsk, but here only a primitive community outhouse was available.

However, there was one notable advantage. Like other families on the Egorgivsky State Farm, Anatole and his wife received a small plot of land, about one third of an acre, which they could cultivate for their personal use. A certain portion of their crop would go for taxes, but beyond that, what they did not eat they could sell. Anatole grew potatoes, onions, watermelons, and cucumbers in his personal plot, and this contributed considerably to his income. (Later the tax was abolished.)

Anatole, a blond, soft-spoken lad, said he enjoyed the outdoor work as a tractor driver more than the factory job. He liked the idea of being associated with a dramatic new project and was obviously fired with a spirit of patriotism.

Since their move to Siberia, Anatole's wife has given birth to a daughter whom they have named "Nadezhda," meaning Hope, to express their outlook toward their virgin lands adventure.

The birth rate on virgin-land farms has been high because of the youth of the settlers, the frequent unavailability of contraceptive supplies in farm stores, and the possibility of roomier housing. Crowded conditions have played a part in depressing the birth rate in cities. Anatole and other rural dwellers have been offered liberal mortgages by the government to construct their own homes.

This phenomenon of an active birth rate inspired one correspondent to write that "there are few virgins in the virgin lands"—a phrase which the censors saw fit to delete.

The Egorgivsky State Farm, named for the region, was founded right at the outset of the virgin-lands program, on May 1, 1954. It began with a crew of 298 people, who constructed a few buildings and set their tractors to plowing the land. This was soil that had been planted once before, in the 1930s, but poor crops had forced abandonment. Now, under the Khrushchev program, another attempt was to be made.

The Egorgivsky farm is huge by U. S. standards, but considered just average size in the virgin lands. Its 75,000 acres would comprise about 300 average-size Iowa farms. Founded on flat steppe, fields for cultivation were laid out in mammoth rectangles of two-and-a-half miles by a mile and a quarter. These vast dimensions lend themselves to mechanized farming. Combines in staggered ranks of three and four roll across oceans of wheat; but dust can be seen rising in billows from the roads whenever trucks pass.

By its second year, the Egorgivsky farm had grown to 950 people.

Three-story apartment houses of wooden construction were going up. There is a community building with a hall, graced by a portrait of Khrushchev, for meetings and movies. Outside is displayed a "wall newspaper" which chronicles the achievements of the farm's populace, especially those who exceed their quotas.

A crude elementary school was built on the farm's premises for the first four grades. Older children travel seventeen miles to a higher school, where they live in dormitories, returning home only after school on Saturday.

Many of the state-employed farmers have built their own homes with the loans offered. These are two- and three-room wood or adobe brick structures, sometimes with a one-room attic under a slanted roof.

The community area of the Egorgivsky farm and other virgin-land farms bears a resemblance to the American frontier of the mid-1800s complete with dirt road, crude board houses, men in boots and caps, the patient horse drinking at the village watering trough.

A half million people were transported to western Siberia and Kazakhstan to plow up 75 million acres of land, an area about one fifth the total farm land in the United States and more than double all the land under cultivation in the British Isles. The Soviet pioneers suffered privations of frontier dimensions in their Gargantuan undertaking.

Many slept in trailers and railroad boxcars. Others actually lived in caves dug out of hillsides. Allowing for the inclination of those who experienced the early days of the virgin lands to glorify their roles, their accounts in Soviet newspapers indicate what they endured.

"It was very cold in the trailers, and the water froze. Spring seemed to have forgotten about us and was very long in coming," wrote Raisa Shevchenko. "Then the thaw set in, making the roads impassable. We could not transport bread from town. Our only neighbors were geologists who had a baking stove in which they baked six loaves of bread. But there were four hundred of us. Our girls set about baking pancakes. They were small and there were not enough to go around.

"In summertime, in the blazing heat, the state farm was left without drinking water. Hardly a cup of muddy water mixed with clay could be drawn up out of the dried-up wells. The tractor drivers' cabs blistered with the heat; they sweltered inside as if in a furnace, without a gulp of water; but the youths did not grouse or whimper."

Another pioneer, Nikolai Sukochev, wrote: "Some of the families, and mine, too, are seeing in the New Year (1956) in trailers, which are warm, of course, while another fifteen families are still living in dug-outs, just above the river. But we didn't come here expecting everything on a silver platter."

There were a lot of people who couldn't take the privations of the virgin lands. Just how many quit to go back to the city is not known, because this statistic has not been made public, but the attention devoted by Soviet newspapers to "deserters," as they were called, indicates it was a problem of some magnitude especially in the early days.

The same social pressures that motivated the man or woman to volunteer in the first place were brought to bear against deserters. They found it difficult to get back their previous job or a new one. Legal action was possible, too, for, having presented the volunteer with three months' wages as a bonus, the state could require that it be repaid or that the recipient face a court on charges of embezzling state funds.

In an interview Sergei Shevchenko, chairman of the executive committee of the Supreme Soviet of the Altai section of Siberia, indicated to me that if a virgin-lands volunteer stuck it out for a year, no attempt was made to recover the bonus payment. Action was taken, though, against short-term deserters.

Such action may account for the repentance of Pyotr Lyutikov. His case was described in the newspaper *Komsomolskaya Pravda*.

"Pyotr Lyutikov, who slunk away from our state farm at a grim moment, has come back. You see, he didn't like the steppe, the climate was not for him, and so he deserted. Now, when we've built so much and lived through so much, he has come back and moves around the state farm with his eyes downcast in shame. There were lads and lasses much younger and weaker than he, but they were not daunted by the difficulties. Many an angry word was hurled at Lyutikov's head at the meeting they had in the first team (part of the farm organization), and he got it good and proper. Nevertheless, they decided to take him back, and now Lyutikov is working in good style."

Volunteering for the virgin lands and staying there was presented as a patriotic duty above all. It therefore caused considerable shock to the Communist leadership when a play called *We Three Came to the Virgin Lands* opened in a Moscow theater. For it credited motives rather divorced from patriotism for the movement to the new farmland in its story of why three young people volunteered to make the trip.

One of the characters, effete Mark Rakitkin, signed up because he feared himself in jeopardy of arrest for gambling; he had been expelled from the Komsomol youth organization for his association with convicted hooligans.

Ira Kulkova's reasons were similarly unrelated to devotion to the motherland. She was an orphan, without any real friends, lonely in a workers' dormitory in which she lived. Depressed, bored, she was attracted by the promise of good money, travel, and a life that might be more eventful.

Perhaps least worthy was the motivation of Alyosha Letavin. Plain and simple, he was stood up by a girl on a date. Indignant, he decided to get even with her and with the world in general by packing off to Siberia.

When *Pravda* finally reviewed the ideologically erring play it stated "not one of them went off to the virgin lands at the command of a patriot's mind and heart."

This was unforgivable. *Pravda* flew off in several directions against the playwright, the theater, and the critics who had taken the wrong cue and given the play a favorable review.

Did not the playwright know, demanded *Pravda,* that Soviet youth "were drawn to these unpopulated steppelands not by selfish interests or desire for adventure, nor by the wish to rid themselves of their past, but by the lofty romance of labor heroism and selfless devotion to the socialist homeland?"

As for the management of the Central Children's Theatre. It "erred greatly by listing this play on its repertoire."

How about the television authorities who had carried the play live on TV? They, scolded *Pravda,* "took an exceedingly irresponsible attitude by hastening to popularize through television such an obviously unsuccessful work."

Critics, whose only fault lay in jumping to the conclusion that the play must have had Party blessing, got it as severely as anyone from *Pravda* for failing to "expose the play's ideological and artistic failings."

The playwright, N. Pogodin, apologized and promised to rewrite the play.

The erring critics published retractions.

The TV officials admitted undue hastiness.

The Children's Theatre withdrew the play from its stage.

Pravda had righted a wrong.

CHAPTER 9

VALENTINA'S PIGLET

The story is told of a group of venerable old men, all over ninety, who were brought to the Kremlin from Stalin's native Georgia region to honor Stalin on his seventieth birthday.

The nonagenarians carried signs displaying a slogan often expressed by school children during Stalin's lifetime: "We thank you, Comrade Stalin, for a happy childhood."

Stalin is supposed to have done some swift mathematics—subtracting his own seventy years from the visitors' ninety—and then commented:

"But I wasn't even born during your childhood."

"That's why," replied the old men in unison, "it was happy."

Surely one of the most unhappy, brutal chapters in Stalin's career opened in 1928 when he undertook to merge privately owned Russian farms into the peculiar Soviet institution known as collective farms.

It was a colossal project. Only an iron-willed Stalin, oblivious to human cost, could have carried it through.

The peasant constituted the largest part of the Russian populace. Like farmers everywhere, he was devoted to his soil. He would not give it up without struggle.

Events had forced the Communists to wait more than ten years after the Revolution of 1917 before attempting to do away with private farming. Other problems came first. It was necessary to consolidate power. There was the civil war, the war with Poland, the great famine of 1922–23, and, not least of all, differences among the Soviet leaders themselves as to timing.

In 1928 Stalin and his colleagues began with mailed fist to convert Russia from an agrarian economy to an industrial power. The first Five-Year Plan was announced. It was inspiringly ambitious, but it was also a blueprint for human misery. The people were to be worked at forced draft. Human comforts were ignored to make Russia a first-class industrial power.

Russia began its first Five-Year Plan with only a certain quantity of coal, iron ore, railway track, timber, leather; with only a certain number of men and women. All of these resources were to be concentrated on one objective. The objective was to industrialize Russia faster than any nation has before or since. (It remains to be seen whether Communist China can do it faster.)

Once this forced mobilization of *industrial* workers was set in motion under the initial Five-Year Plan, the *peasant* could no longer be permitted to remain an individualist, to engage in free enterprise. A first step in eliminating the private farmer actually had been taken only days after the Revolution. A decree on November 9, 1917, had abolished private ownership of land. All land in the U.S.S.R. became the property of the state. Farmers did not legally own the land they tilled, but the crops it yielded were theirs, and they considered the land theirs too.

The Soviet Government set the price it would pay farmers for grain to be converted into bread at state bakeries to be sold at state prices at state stores to workers in state factories. The independent ideas of the Russian farmer frustrated this plan. The farmer who considered the government's price too low refused to sell. He preferred to hoard his grain or to sell it privately or to feed it to his cattle or to let it rot. In 1926 about 85 per cent of the Soviet grain crop was grown by peasants of middle class or below. Yet of this 85 per cent, only about 11 per cent was made available to the government.

This was a situation which the Soviet state could not tolerate, especially as the population of cities was increasing with the growth of government industry. The campaign to eliminate the private farmer began with heavy taxation to force him to sell to the state. There were frequent confiscations of grain from wealthy peasants who refused to sell their grain to the state at its arbitrarily fixed prices.

A principal target of the Kremlin was the *kulak*. The kulak was the more prosperous farmer. When taxation failed to bring the kulak to heel, the decision was made in Stalin's own words to pass "from the policy of restricting the exploiting proclivities of the kulaks to the policy of *eliminating* the kulaks as a class." Obviously the kulaks and the less prosperous peasantry could not simply be exterminated, because who would then cultivate the fields? But something must be done to ensure that the farmers, like the workers in the factories, toiled for the state according to the state's plans for the development of the country and not for the farmer's individual profit.

In more recent times the emphasis has been on the creation of *sovkhozes* or state farms which may be loosely described as "agricultural factories"; the employees of the state farm are basically employees of the state just as is a worker in a state ball-bearing factory. The sovkhoz farmer gets paid an hourly wage just like the worker on an assembly line.

But it would have been dangerous to attempt overnight to convert the individual Russian farmer, with his inbred instinct for private enterprise, to a day laborer on the government fields of a sovkhoz.

A less drastic intermediate step was necessary. This was the *kolkhoz,* or collective farm. A collective farm is an amalgamation of a number of adjoining peasant holdings. The peasants would be organized into a collective farm organization under a chairman selected by the Communist Party. In this way the crops to be planted could be dictated by the Communist leadership, and, most important, the proper channeling of the crops could be controlled by the state. By farming larger units of land, presumably greater efficiency might be attained, and thus larger crops. The peasant members of the collective, or amalgamated, farm would share in its profits. This presumably would provide an initiative.

It had been decided by the Communist Party as early as two years after the 1917 Revolution that farming in the U.S.S.R. would take the form of sovkhozes and kolkhozes. But at the time the mass program to eliminate private farmers was undertaken eleven years later, less than 7 per cent of all farm acreage in the Soviet Union had been organized into state farms and collective farms.

Now, the decision made, events moved quickly. Twenty-five thousand tough, trusted factory workers were dispatched from cities to the countryside to cajole, convince, and coerce farmers into pooling their land and their livestock into collective farms.

By March 1, 1930, the strong-arm methods of the state had driven

55 per cent of the private peasants onto collective farms. Peasants were beaten up. There were executions. Provinicial authorities were authorized to confiscate property and to send reluctant kulaks into exile in Siberia and other places remote from their homes.

Peasants joined collective farms out of desperation. But desperation does not produce crops. Fields were neglected. Cattle were slaughtered by the thousand by their owners rather than surrender them to the joint ownership of the collective farm. Other peasants left the countryside to seek work in the city or to attempt to escape from Russia.

In the spring of 1930 bitterness and resentment had reached such proportions that the planting of seed was disrupted. A poor harvest resulted. By 1932 there was widespread famine.

During this period Stalin had to retreat temporarily. This was first revealed publicly in typical fashion in an article in *Pravda* entitled "Dizziness from Success," published on March 2, 1930. It blamed the dislocations in agriculture not on the Kremlin's policy but on the over-zealousness of police units, factory-worker squads, and youth groups which had been sent to the countryside to carry it out. With feigned innocence the article denounced the "unseemly threats against the peasants" which had the result of "strengthening of our enemies and the discrediting of the idea of the collective farm movement."

Indeed the collective farm movement had been discredited. In an attempt to allay rebellious peasants, permission was granted in some cases for them to withdraw from collective farms. Many did. In a two-month period in 1930 the number of collective farms dropped from 110,200 to 82,300. Even more dramatically, the number of households which belonged to collective farms plummeted from about 14,300,000 to 5,800,000.

But Stalin had not forsaken the aim of eliminating the private farmer. Only his tactic had temporarily changed. Now, by taxation, it was made almost impossible for the de-collectivized peasant to make ends meet. Every advantage in seed, machinery, and tax benefits was given to collective farms. The poorer peasant especially was forced to rejoin the collective. Finding it impossible to make a living under the crush of taxation, unable to obtain credit, and, in some cases, with only a portion of his cattle and buildings returned by the collective, the small farmer was squeezed from his regained independence back into the collective.

In October of 1930, 25 per cent of Russian agriculture had been collectivized. A year later it was 60 per cent. By 1936, almost 90 per cent of the peasant population had been amalgamated into collective farms.

The cost of collectivization was heavy. It has been estimated that five million kulak families were deported to Siberia and other god-forsaken regions. Perhaps half of the nation's livestock perished at the hands of enraged peasants. For a time the death penalty was imposed on persons found guilty of stealing grain. Sections of political police were stationed in the larger centers of farming to guard the crops.

Although there is no present evidence of enthusiasm for collective farming among Russians born to the soil, open resistance ceased long ago. Today in Russia a few privately owned farms still survive. They comprise about one per cent of Soviet agricultural areas. They are tiny, isolated plots which have survived only by their remoteness from other farms with which they could be readily amalgamated. There are 78,000 collective farms in the U.S.S.R., which makes this the pre-dominant form of agriculture. As new farm areas are opened, in the virgin lands, for example, they are organized as state farms. Certainly, Communist planners prefer the state farm to the collective. There is no question on a state farm of the farmers sharing in the crop. There is none of the constitutional theory, as on a collective, of the farmers enjoying tenancy of the land free of charge in perpetuity. At the present time the Soviet Union admits to having two classes—workers and peasants. (It may be argued that there are other classes, too; for example, a class of intellectuals. But Soviet theoreticians explain that members of the intelligentsia are drawn from the workers' and peasants' classes and do not comprise a class in themselves. It may be argued that a new *bourgeoisie,* a middle class, has grown up in Russia, a class possessing some property and having an interest in perpetuating this class. Soviet theoreticians angrily deny this. In any event, contrary to the frequently ex-pressed view abroad, the Russians themselves do not say that the Soviet Union is now a classless society.) The aim *is* a classless society. This will come—so runs the Soviet explanation—when collective farms are elimi-nated and all land is included in State farms. Then members of the present peasant class will be wage-earning workers for the State just as we are lathe operators in a factory. Eventually, it is hoped that all farms will be state farms; collective farms will be eliminated. But with the costly struggle for collectivization only so recently won, the Soviet leadership is moving slowly. Now there are only about 5000 state farms in the

U.S.S.R., some 600 of them created only since the inauguration of the virgin-lands program.

The Soviet Union's richest land lies in the so-called "black soil belt" that stretches through the Ukraine and eastward into the Kuban region which borders the Black Sea. Forty miles from Odessa, the Black Sea port in the southwest part of the Ukraine, lies the Budënny collective farm. Its fertile, black soil is known in Russian as *chernozem,* a name which has found its way into English to describe that desirable type of earth. The farm is named after Marshal Semën Mikhailovich Budënny, Russia's flowing-mustached Czarist-army sergeant who joined the Communist Party in 1919 and organized the Red cavalry; severely defeated at Kiev, capital of the Ukraine, by the Germans, Budënny spent most of World War II in the rear, training troops, but he retains an honored place.

The chairman of the Budënny farm is Makar Posmitny, a barrel-chested man with a booming voice. Some kolkhoz chairmen are women. I met Mrs. Felka Mitosova, chairman of the *Strana Sovetov*—meaning soviet land—farm near Rubtsovsk. A woman of iron grip, hair pulled back in a bun, husky voice, and bronzed face, she directs a farm of 7000 acres where 360 families live. A member of the Communist Party since 1928, Mrs. Mitosova, aged fifty, has a son, two grandchildren, and her father was still living at the age of ninety. Her husband is completely in her shadow; a smallish, quiet man, he tends horses on the farm.

Like all collective farms, the Budënny farm is vast, covering 8500 acres. Even that is below average size. Nearly 15,000 acres is average for a Soviet collective farm. By contrast, the average acreage of U.S. farms in 1950 was 215 acres. There are 1172 people living on the Budënny farm, not all of whom actually work on its collectivized fields; some commute to factories and other enterprises near Odessa. Like much of the Ukraine, the Budënny community was razed by the Nazis. Of the 117 Budënny men who went to war, 92 did not return. The four sons of farm chairman Posmitny were wounded in battle.

Like chairmen of other collective farms, Posmitny was elected by a meeting of the collective farmers. However, the choice is not really theirs. A kolkhoz has a Communist Party group as do all Soviet organizations. The Party indicates who is to be elected, and he is. During one period, in an attempt to evoke greater production by tighter supervision, chairmen were sent to farms from cities. Each was a proven Party man of steely determination but often ignorant in agriculture. The result was that wily collective farmers were able to malinger more than before, and harvests suffered. Most of the outsiders were withdrawn, and chairmen now are largely chosen from among Communist Party members on the farm itself. These are men with considerable agricultural experience who can command some respect from fellow farmers.

Each year a collective farm pledges itself to deliver a certain quantity of grain, milk, meat, and other produce to the government at prices arbitrarily fixed by the government. The size of the pledge is, in fact, dictated by Soviet agricultural authorities on the basis of the capacity of the particular farm. Produce beyond that quota is the farm's profit and may be used in several ways. It can be sold on the so-called "free market," a vestige of free enterprise in Russia where prices are fixed by the traditional capitalistic laws of supply and demand. Finally, it may be divided up among the farm workers as part of their share of the farm's income. The farm's profit is invested in improvements, in a fund against poor years, and for pensions for farm members. Each farm, rather than the government, provides for its members in their old age. This, of course, differs from the status of workers in factories, offices, and other segments of the Soviet society who draw pensions from the Government when they are old enough to retire.

Traditionally there had been two sets of prices which the government paid to collective farms for their produce. There was a low price for "compulsory deliveries" to the state. There was a higher price for so-called "state purchases" of grain and meat over and above the minimum quota set for the particular farm. Khrushchev broke that tradition too. Farmers had resented selling produce at the derisory price set for "compulsory deliveries." Whenever possible the best barley and corn and pork were saved for payment to farm members or for sale in the "free market" rather than for delivery to the state. As part of the pattern of providing incentives to stimulate greater effort and more output, Nikita Khrushchev inaugurated a system of one set of prices for produce purchased by the state. The price varies from region to region and according to the size of the crop, but the hope is that it will result in bigger harvests through increased incentives.

Crops and money are divided among farmers under a system of "workday units." The workday unit is a peculiar creation of the Soviet economy. A farm worker in the United States or Britain gets paid a certain sum per hour. In some cases he may share in the crop. A farmer on a Soviet collective farm earns a certain number of workday units for a shift depending on the importance of the job, the skill required, and the difficulty of the task.

Men and women are divided into brigades. There are brigades for cultivating fields, brigades for milking cows, pig-tending brigades. Each brigade has its scale of workday units. A tractor driver must plow a certain number of acres to earn a workday unit. On an eight-hour shift a good tractor driver may make from four to seven workday units. A milkmaid must fill a certain number of pails to earn a workday unit. A thresher operator must feed a certain number of bushels of wheat into a machine to earn a workday unit.

The labor required to earn a workday unit, or a "WDU" as it is usually abbreviated, will vary from farm to farm for each job. What a WDU means in terms of payment varies too, from farm to farm. A model Ukrainian farm named after Khrushchev is cited in the Soviet Encyclopedia as paying 17.30 rubles ($1.73), 2.6 pounds of wheat, and 2.6 pounds of potatoes and vegetables per workday unit in 1955. A year later the same farm's crop and income was such that it was able to pay only 12 rubles ($1.20) but 6.4 pounds of wheat per workday unit.

On the Budënny farm, also a very prosperous collective, in a good year a workday unit paid 12.40 rubles ($1.24), six pounds of wheat, and four pounds of forage for livestock. It's not unusual for a collective farmer on the Budënny farm to earn 8000 rubles ($800) a month. This approximates the wages of a Moscow factory worker. And, besides, the farmer gets a portion of the crop of the collectivized fields as well as enjoying the right to cultivate a small personal plot. When several members of a family on a well-to-do farm work, they enjoy high income by Soviet standards.

Arriving at a scale of workday units for any particular farm seems part mathematics and part guesswork. The amount of work that a farmer may be expected to accomplish in a day in comparatively easy field work is taken as worth one WDU in pay. All other work is estimated above or below that. As might be expected, there is frequently bickering on a farm over the scale of workday units. A worker in the hot sun argues that a farm comrade in a cool barn should be entitled to fewer workday units for a day's labor. There is frequent revision of the pay scale.

This complicated system of paying workers in the *same* sort of job *different* sums for a day's labor necessitates an army of bookkeepers. A disproportionate number of people on a collective farm is kept busy tallying workday units for the labors of other people.

Most of the rolling, fertile fields of the Budënny farm belonged to a German landowner named Josef Heuss. At the time of the Revolution the land was divided among the peasants who lived on Heuss's property. Then, when collectivization began, the peasants were called upon to give up their fields to the collective. These, with adjoining smaller farms, comprise the Budënny collective. The farmers are permitted to retain ownership of their homes but not of the land under it. Only the government may own land in Russia, but the peasant is given tenancy forever under the Constitution. A strange sidelight of the history of the Budënny farm is that a son of original owner Heuss lives on his father's former property and earns workday units as a combine operator.

Although considered a "millionaire" farm because its crops earn more than a million rubles ($100,000) a year, the Budënny kolkhoz has many hovels for homes. One I visited was made of mud-and-straw bricks a foot thick, whitewashed and painted blue. A crude wooden door opened into a small kitchen with dirt floor. I had to stoop to get through the doorway into the four-by-five-foot kitchen where a clay, wood-burning, low fireplace provided both cooking facilities and heat. In the next room, eight-feet square with dirt floor and a single window, stood two narrow beds, carefully made up with white lace counterpanes and a smaller coverlet draped over two overstuffed pillows on each. A peasant woman and her child, barefooted, were eating Ukrainian borsch at a small table. On the wall was a photograph of the man of the hut in army uniform; now he worked as a horse tender. Near his picture hung a framed certificate of an animal husbandry school he had attended on the farm. The border included a profile of Lenin and Stalin. That was the only Soviet symbol, and in a corner hung a crude icon of the Virgin Mary. On a bureau three large picture frames leaned against the wall, with an assortment of faded family snapshots. The only bright color in the room came from a red flowering plant on the single window sill.

It was the family's hope to move soon into a new wood house. Most of the Budënny farm families enjoy better quarters than did this stable hand, his wife, and child. But by Western standards, the material possessions of a collective farmer are few, although he does have more than enough to eat and in far greater variety than the Russian city dweller. For example, on a collective farm near Odessa named after Karl Liebknecht, the left-wing German Socialist martyr, there are only three privately owned cars among the 3800 people living on the farm's territory. Many of the Libknecht farmers have income enough to afford a car, but the cars are not available. Two hundred of the farmers on this prosperous collective own bicycles.

The Liebknecht farmers collectively own two small passenger cars and sixteen trucks. These are community property and, besides being used for work, sometimes take a group of collective farmers to town for shopping or a movie. It's not unusual on a Sunday in Moscow or in other cities to see open trucks with four rows of benches holding farmers bundled in blue padded jackets, women with warm shawls over their heads, on an outing to town.

Like other collectives, the Liebknecht farm has a large community hall for meetings, movies, and dances. There is a seven-year school on its 4000 acres, a nursery for youngsters whose mothers work in the fields, and an impressive collective of barns, pens, and sties. There is a wine cellar for storing a white, fresh vintage called Pearl of the Steppes. Electric milking machines are used in cow barns, but many of the agricultural methods are a half century behind the times. In highly developed Western farm operations wheat is cut and threshed in one operation with a hydraulically controlled combine run by one operator. On the Liebknecht farm it is a long-drawn-out process; the wheat is cut, then gathered and carted to a stationary thresher where the wheat is separated from the straw, the grain from the chaff. Several dozen people are occupied in this unduly complicated task.

Although the Liebknecht farm is considered highly mechanized by Soviet standards, it has 192 horses. They are used for less than 10 per cent of the farm work. This is not unique. The Budënny farm, equally mechanized, has 250 horses.

An American farmer touring one of these Ukrainian farms is struck by its size, excellent soil, wasteful use of man power, and old-fashioned, inefficient methods for many operations. Such were the reactions of Asa Clark, a Washington state wheat farmer. At dinner, a collective-farm chairman, a burly fellow with a gold star medal of the Hero of Socialist Labor on his lapel, began a toast by saying: "We are pleased and honored to have the chance to show you our work and our humble achievements. . . ."

"And they *are* humble," murmured Clark, unable to resist the temptation.

It was Soviet government policy for decades to keep the principal mechanical means of farming out of the hands of the collective farms and under the exclusive control of the state. Although *state* farms always had their own tractors, combines, and other machinery, collective farms did not, except for some trucks and a garden tractor or two. The history of peasants' resistance to collectivization and to government collection of quota-designated crops had resulted in the Soviet institution known as the Machine Tractor Station, or MTS. This was a garage, parking area, and repair shop where great numbers of farm machines were concentrated, maintained, and assigned to collective farms in the area. The purpose was simply to keep the collective farmers dependent on the government. As mechanization of farming increased, so did the dependence. The government charged the collective farms in money and in produce for the use of the machinery. The charges varied with government policy from punitive to solicitous. The tractor operators and other workers at an MTS were employees of the government. They received hourly wages, bonuses, and had the privilege of cultivating personal plots of land near their homes at the Machine Tractor Station. By keeping the possession of cultivating and harvesting machinery in its hands, the government was able to exercise a powerful influence on the conduct of collective farms and to help assure that the farms actually deliver the quotas imposed by the government. Party propaganda claimed that the MTS was intended for efficiency, to spare collective farmers the expense of buying farm machinery, and to make the maximum use of machinery. However, this explanation becomes transparent when it is realized that some Machine Tractor Stations serviced only one collective farm in cases where the collective farm was exceptionally large or isolated. Obviously it would be more efficient for the farm to have control of its own machinery, but this would have deprived the government of one of its most effective controls over the historically troublesome peasant. However, there is reason to believe that the need for efficiency has taken precedence over the need for control, in the case of the MTS at least. To fulfill Khrushchev's promises to raise Russia's meat, milk, and butter production above America's, Soviet farms will need to operate more efficiently. Man power and machinery must be used with greater productivity. Apparently aware of this, Khrushchev declared in early 1958 that plans should be made gradually to eliminate the Machine Tractor Stations and to sell the equipment to collective farms. The MTS would continue to exist only as a repair shop and a supply depot for spare parts.

This revised institution is known as the Repair Tractor Station, or RTS. It also serves as the Soviet counterpart of a sales showroom for display of new agricultural machinery offered for sale to collective farms.

After Khrushchev had spoken events moved swiftly. The appropriate Party and government bodies formally voted the necessary decisions. By early 1959 some 70 per cent of the nation's more than 8000 Machine and Tractor Stations had been liquidated, and the rest would be before long. A major upheaval in the structure of Soviet agriculture had been accomplished. For the sake of efficiency the sacred agricultural precepts of the past were swept aside. With the customary "flexibility" that enables Communism's propagandists to switch points of view without any noticeable self-consciousness, the Russian people were told that the abolishment of the MTS was in accordance with the teachings of Lenin, just as they had been told that the creation of the MTS conformed with his doctrines. If an ordinary Russian had been foolish enough to advocate openly abolition of MTS's and farm ownership of machinery he would have been branded a dangerous heretic before Khrushchev's tradition-shattering decision. Afterwards it was heresy to question the orthodoxy of the move.

As in other cases where the Soviet Party and state apparatus seek to get something done in a hurry, economy was no consideration. The price of MTS agricultural equipment was set at a price within reach of the budgets of most collective farms. Since the government was selling the machinery to farms to use in the state's behalf, price was of less concern anyway than in a private transaction. It was a case, in effect, of the State transferring funds from one of its pockets to another.

An example was the Stalin Collective Farm near Stalinabad, north of the border of Afghanistan, where the chairman, Sultan Zamanov, a brown-skinned Tadzhik with a coarse mustache, told me that his farm had been able to purchase all the machinery of the MTS that serviced the farm (and that farm alone) for 1,500,000 rubles ($150,000). The previous year the farm had paid twice that amount for the use of the MTS's machinery, tractor drivers, and advice. The MTS machinery, including 100 tractors, obviously was worth several times the amount charged the Stalin Farm.

The jobs of MTS managers and other administrative personnel were swept away. Drivers of tractors, mechanics, experts in animal husbandry moved from the MTS to the collective farms which they had served. As a matter of fact, some of them had been living on the farms anyway as members of farm families. But now they are no longer on the government's payroll but rather on the farms'.

The Khrushchev hope was that by placing the machinery in the hands of the collective farms it would eliminate the factor of inefficiency that was necessarily present when an artificially created gulf existed between the farms and the machines the farms used. The hope is that the farmer's initiative will be increased by the knowledge that the farm community to which he belongs owns the machinery that it uses. At the very least, abolition of the MTS eliminates a mountain of bookkeeping and paper work both on farms and in the defunct MTS.

Although it is a clear step toward good sense and efficiency, it is also a major step away from the conventional Communist concept of state ownership of the means and machinery of production. It is a step backward from making the farmer a government-employed worker in the fields. In the sense that he is a member of the collective farm community, the farmer is now a part owner of machinery. It enhances the independence-from-state-control of the collective farm. But for the moment, at least, the Kremlin is willing to take a temporary step backwards for the sake of the more immediate goal of greater output.

It is an instructive experience to fly over Soviet collective farms and observe that, in a striking number of cases, the vast expanses of community fields are incompletely harvested, bundles of wheat lie ungathered in fields and rain-soaked by roadsides. By contrast, the small squares of garden and orchard behind each house of the village or several villages that compose the collective farm are tended with manicured care. These are personal plots, or household plots, which each family on a state and collective farm is entitled to cultivate for its own use. Although the Soviet farmer may remain aloof about the collectivized fields and care little about how crops there fare, he has a personal deep interest in the remaining vestige of private-land trusteeship, if not ownership, in Russia.

The care which is lavished on the household plots is indicated by the considerable crops they yield to the nation's economy. Through the years Communist authorities gradually cut down on the size of household plots and took a portion of the plots' harvests in taxes. The aim seemed to be eventual elimination of this hang-over of another era. However, in 1958 taxes on household plots were eliminated. In their drive to obtain more food for a growing population and for export, the Kremlin leaders after Stalin apparently decided that produce was more important than principle.

The collection of taxes, in money and in produce, was not without its seriocomic aspects. A farm girl named Valentina wrote a letter to the editors of *Komsomolskaya Pravda*, the Communist youth newspaper ("Youth Truth," roughly translated), complaining about the actions of the local tax collectors. It seems that before dawn three village officials arrived at the farm homestead where Valentina lived with her mother. The officials trussed up a pig which Valentina had received as a piglet for her fine work as a collective-farm pig tender. Summoned by the pig's nocturnal squeals, Valentina and her mother rushed outdoors just as the officials were driving off in a truck with the animal. They explained that they were taking the pig because the family had failed to pay the state enough meat in taxes. Valentina's mother produced receipts at the state office the next day, but it did no good. The officials said that even though they might be in error the pig could be applied to next year's taxes. Valentina's letter was indignant. She wanted her pig back.

On a representative collective farm such as *Strana Sovetov,* with its woman chairman, household plots run from half an acre to an acre and a half in size. Farmers also are permitted to own one cow, two calves, a half dozen sheep, and two hogs, as well as chickens, geese, and other fowl. The number and type of livestock that may be privately owned vary from time to time and from region to region. For example, in mountainous areas of the central Asian section of the Soviet Union where feeding conditions are poor for other animals, collective farmers are permitted to own small herds of mountain goats. Also in parts of that Asian frontier area ownership of camels and donkeys is allowed. The farmers on this collective average an income of 5000 rubles ($500) a year from their crops and 3500 rubles ($350) from privately raised livestock.

The effectiveness of the private enterprise impulse in Russia was well demonstrated by the results of a law issued in August 1953 which was intended to correct a shortage of milk and meat in cities. The law permitted persons living in suburbs of cities, as well as those living on farms, to own limited numbers of livestock. In the period of two years, cows owned by workers and office employees living in and near towns increased by 300,000, pigs by 600,000, and sheep by 1,300,000. The milk and meat shortage in most cities was partially solved, but another problem was created—a bread shortage. The livestock owners bought bread and other grain products at government shops at low, fixed government prices, fed these to the livestock, and sold the milk, meat, and eggs at the free market at the high prices caused by great demand. This practice was so profitable that the new suburban livestock dealers were force feeding their animals and fowl, milking their cows three and four times a day, and reaping profits. Some workers left their jobs at desks and factory benches to devote full time to plying their trade between back yard and market. In July of 1956 the drain on grain products in state stores and the depletion of the labor force in some areas was so considerable that the Kremlin found it necessary to issue this decree:

"The Council of Ministers thinks it necessary to reconsider the laws encouraging the development of cattle breeding under private ownership by town dwellers. Primitive cattle breeding in towns, with considerable waste of bread and other foodstuffs, attracts working power from productive labor in society, resulting in huge labor expenses per unit of production, corrupting the unstable part of the population, and resulting in elements of disorganization in our Socialist production." The decree provided that persons who feed cattle with bread, flour, groats, potatoes, and other foodstuffs bought in state stores will be fined 500 rubles ($50) for the first offense and 1000 rubles ($100) for a repetition. To encourage suburban dwellers to sell their livestock to state and collective farms, taxes were imposed on ownership. The tax was 500 rubles ($50) a year for a cow, 150 rubles ($15) for a pig, and 40 rubles ($4.00) for a goat or sheep. More important, the suburban farmer was obliged to sell to the government, at low prices set by the government, quantities of meat for each head of livestock owned. For example, 45 pounds of meat per year must be delivered for each pig owned. Although meat and other produce taxes could be paid in the money equivalent, this heavy, new punitive tax, required many owners to slaughter animals in order to pay the government its due. Besides reflecting the potent instinct for private ownership that persists in Russia, the episode also demonstrated how the Kremlin uses its taxing powers to encourage or discourage any activity.

The free market, or "collective-farm market" as the authorities prefer to call it, is a colorful, bustling place—a noisy combination of an oriental bazaar and a pushcart market. The market in Kharkov is typical. It occupies a vast open area, part of a bombed-out portion of the city, only three blocks from a main trolley line. In one section, women crouch over straw baskets they have woven and are offering for sale. The first price is only a bargaining figure. The customer is expected to make a counter offer. In season, bunches of flowers and plants are displayed in colorful disarray. Farther into the market there are rows upon rows of blue-painted stands where women, shawls tied over their heads, sell beets, carrots, cabbage, tomatoes, onions, apples, and a Russian favorite, mushrooms, strung in great chains. There are barrels of sour pickles, *schi* (a sour soup), and *kvass,* a ciderlike beverage made of fermented bread. A customer is offered a taste of sour cream being sold in an open vat. Then the spoon is dipped back into the vat for the next customer. Meat is displayed in long, roofed sheds. The types of meat are difficult to recognize, apparently hacked without any particular concern for cuts. An axe rather than a saw is used so that meat often contains splinters of bone. Sometimes the head of an animal is hung conveniently to help a customer identify what she is buying. The animal's eyes stare down accusingly at the shoppers. Chickens are sold with heads, feet, and most of the plumage attached. There is supposed to be government inspection of products, but hosts of flies in the summer defy attempts at sanitation. A customer is handed a piece of meat in her bare hands; she is expected to bring her own wrapping and containers to the market.

On Sundays only there is a "bird market" doing business in Moscow. Here are sold canaries, parakeets, pigeons, tropical fish, and hedgehogs, which are often kept as pets. Pigeon-raising is a popular pastime on Moscow roofs. In an open lot near the "bird market" dog owners gather to await prospective customers.

Goods are sold either by individual farmers from the produce of their personal plots or by representatives of collective farms for the entire farm. The collective-farm produce is surplus after deliveries have been made to the government at fixed prices, and after a portion has been set aside for payment in kind to members of the farm. Prices are almost always higher than in state stores, but goods which are not ordinarily available elsewhere can be found in this "free enterprise" market. The quality of fruit and berries and vegetables is often superior too, indicating that the collective farms often deliver their quotas to the government in inferior goods and save the better portion of the crop for the free market, where the profit is greater.

There are thirty collective-farm markets of varying sizes in dispersed sections of Moscow. The central Moscow market serves 50,000 shoppers a day. The daily average receipts of a trader at the market are officially reported to be from 1500 to 2000 rubles ($150 to $200) a day. In 1955 the sale of foodstuffs in all Soviet free markets amounted to more than 15 per cent of all retail food sales in the country. There are more than 8000 such markets in the U.S.S.R. Twenty per cent of the income of collective farms came from these markets.

The importance of this free-enterprise segment of the Soviet economy is indicated by these figures: in 1955 collective farmers privately owned 42 per cent of the nation's cow herd, 29 per cent of the nation's pigs, and 55 per cent of the goats. Their small plots of land accounted for 33 per cent of the total area under cultivation in potatoes, vegetables, and melons.

The reason for tolerating this anachronism of free enterprise in a controlled economy is simple. The socialized segment of the economy has not been able to supply the needs of the people. In agriculture, as in housing, whenever a lag occurs, the Kremlin is forced reluctantly to revert to methods of capitalism to solve its problems.

CHAPTER 10

A COVER ON THE BORSCH

A cartoon in *Krokodil*, the Soviet satirical weekly, shows a passerby bursting into a room that is dark with black smoke. A man and wife are lounging unconcernedly.

"Something is burning in the kitchen," shouts the intruder.

"Don't worry about it," responds the complacent couple, "it's only that our neighbor has forgotten her cakes in the stove."

The situation is peculiarly Soviet where a number of families occupy the rooms of a single apartment and share a common kitchen and bath. Under these crowded, communal conditions it's not unusual for animosity to grow of the sort when one family is delighted to see a neighbor's cake burn even if it fills *their* room with smoke.

Even new apartments in Russia often consist of three-room units—one family to each room. There's a common entrance hallway for coat racks. From this hallway opens a door to each family's room and other doors to the communal kitchen and bath. Older apartments have six, eight, and even a dozen families sharing common premises.

Crowded housing is easily Russia's number-one domestic problem. Nikita Khrushchev recognized this in a speech on the fortieth anniversary of Russia's Revolution: "We have an acute housing shortage. The reasons for that are understandable. First, Soviet power inherited an incredible housing shortage from the old order. Second, in Soviet years the population in towns and workers' settlements has increased more than three and a half times. Third, in the prewar years we were compelled to economize on everything, including the construction of dwellings, so as to be able to put every kopeck into heavy industry. Four, tremendous damage was caused to dwellings during the war which left nearly 25 million people without a roof over their heads."

With a few alterations the Khrushchev analysis is correct. The third reason should be first on the list, because it was neglect of housing construction in the Soviet race for industrialization that brought the problem to its present proportions. Industrialization compounded the crowding by causing the transfer of millions into urban areas.

The Kremlin contempt for housing persisted long after the war, except that greater lip service has in recent years been paid to the problem. Slowness of construction and, often, poor quality of workmanship were other factors ignored in the Khrushchev speech.

In 1956, Maxim Saburov, then Russia's chief economic planner as chairman of *Gosplan,* the state planning commission, said that it would take twenty years for Russia's standard of housing to catch up with the United States'. Somewhat more vaguely, Khrushchev promised in 1957 that twelve years would bring adequate housing for all.

The climb toward adequate housing is a steep one. A city ordinance ruled that people will no longer live in basements. A walk down many Moscow side streets shows that they still do. Windows opening below sidewalk level reveal, through parted curtains, darkly lit, dank rooms. Often the window shaft, a cement-lined hole in the sidewalk to permit light to enter, is not even covered with grating and presents a hazard to the incautious pedestrian.

It is not at all uncommon for four persons to live in a single room. When Moscow was in the throes of an Asian-flu epidemic, doctors published recommendations on how to treat and to prevent spread of the disease. Isolation was suggested. In Soviet terms, isolation meant hanging a sheet to separate the flu victim's bed from that of the other members of the family.

Foreigners are seldom invited to the homes of Russians. Long indoctrination in suspicion of Westerners is one reason; even though a Russian may not believe the indoctrination, he realizes that it is best not to court official suspicion by defying it. Another potent reason is that many Russians are ashamed to show their crowded quarters. The home of a factory foreman in Rubtsovsk, in Siberia, which I visited, was lavish by Soviet standards. On the third floor of a five-story building without an elevator, it consisted of a living room, a bedroom, and private kitchen and bathroom. The toilet had no flush mechanism but consisted of a removable basin. The bedroom contained two beds for the mother, father, and youngest child. An elder daughter slept on a bed in the living room which, in the Russian custom, held a jungle of rubber plants and other space-consuming greenery. The beds were the customary Russian iron bedsteads with a thin mattress and two great, overstuffed pillows at the head, covered by bridal lace. This counterpane of lace, an umbrella-sized orange or yellow lampshade, and spreading plants are almost inevitable features of Soviet apartments.

A friend's apartment in Moscow was in an older building. It took many months of association before he invited me to dinner. It was his suggestion that we meet two blocks from his home just after dark. Nervously, he led me by a devious route, apparently to throw any followers off the scent, and then, with a quick glance up and down the empty street, he motioned me into a dark hallway. The elevator was not working; it never did work, he said. The four flights led past doors padded like quilted jackets against winter's drafts. The staircase was unlit, unpainted, and unheated. It reminded me of the stair well of a bombed building in Vienna after the war. Our entrance into his rooms was even more ceremoniously secretive. He had warned me not to speak until he gave the word, but he took the added precaution of holding a finger to his lips as he slipped a key into the lock of the apartment's common entrance. We hurried by an open door of a room occupied by another family; there was a closed door across the hall, and the entrance to his quarters lay straight ahead. The first small room was a bedroom, in which his son already was asleep. There was another big bed in the room. We entered the next room, no more than fifteen feet square, with a round table and chairs in the center. In solid array around the walls stood a china closet, a radio and phonograph, a bookcase, and a couch. The single window was trimmed with the customary lace curtain, seemingly made of the same material as the traditional bed covers. My friend's wife was in the communal kitchen preparing what turned out to be an excellent meal.

This Russian certainly was more cautious than most. Other Russians have invited foreigners to their homes with little more ceremony than is involved in an invitation by a family in Kansas City. However, it's not at all uncommon for a member of the U. S. Embassy staff to serve a two-year tour in Moscow without ever having the opportunity to visit a Russian's home.

Another apartment I visited was assigned to Leonid Scherbakov, hop, step, and jump event contender on the Soviet Olympic team. With his wife, he lived in one room of a three-room, three-family unit with one kitchen and bath. Because of his privileged position, Scherbakov enjoyed better quarters than most newlyweds who more often than not must live with parents.

The housing shortage has its effects on Soviet health, the birth rate, and morals. Overcrowding is partly responsible for Russia's high incidence of tuberculosis. Overcrowding contributes to the fact that Russian children are rarely heard crying; there's almost always someone just across the room to rock the crib or fondle the child. Even in extremely cold weather park benches are usually full, and in the evenings sidewalks abound with strollers, for even in the winter it's more appealing than a crowded room. Every seat at post-office writing tables is occupied until closing time. There are few dogs and cats kept as pets in cities for the simple reason that there's so little room for humans.

Since several families live in separate rooms of a single apartment, signs above the doorbells at the entrance indicate how many long and short rings are intended for the Fedeyev, Masevitch, or Dubronov family.

Congested housing contributes to alcoholism; it's a way to forget the discomfort. The enforced close quarters contributed to the denunciation by neighbors that led so many innocent Russians to jail as "foreign agents" or "economic saboteurs" during Stalin's time; not uncommonly neighbors accused a person falsely in the hope of obtaining his vacated space. Now, in order to break the habit, cases are reported in newspapers of persons going to jail for making false accusations.

Regulations assure each person in Moscow of nine square yards of floor space—that's an area measuring three yards by three yards—but this guarantee is not always fulfilled. Five square yards is more often the case in the capital. (Rent is seldom more than five per cent of the salary of the head of the family, but electricity and other utility charges often double the figure.)

To contribute to the inconvenience of living in crowded rooms, Soviet-manufactured paint (even in the Kremlin) comes off on your clothes if you rub against a wall.

Although an extra person might seem like an imposition, the grandmother (*babushka*) is a pillar of Soviet society; she does the time-consuming shopping, acts as cook (with the man and wife of the family away at work), she baby-sits, and her monthly pension contributes to the family income.

Heating might not seem a problem under crowded conditions, but Russians are great respecters of the Russian winter. Windows are almost always double panes, and edges are taped with strips of paper to keep out winds. Coal (there is also oil and natural-gas heat) is piled up in courtyards, but usually central heating does not go on until October 15, no matter how early the winter. In summer, electric fans are widely used in homes and in enterprises, but the only air conditioning I've experienced has been in the Bolshoi Theatre, the Kremlin, and the Lenin-Stalin mausoleum.

To facilitate cleanliness under crowded conditions there are public bathhouses in most neighborhoods. Overcrowding discourages large families. The government tries to encourage a high birth rate; there are great unsettled areas for an expanding population to fill. A mother of five children is entitled to a pension on that basis alone. A news item reflects the solicitude of the government toward large families:

"Anastasia Sergacheva, a worker at the Magnitogorsk metallurgical plant, has just had triplets. She already has three-year-old twins. The plant administration is taking great care of the Sergachev family. They have been given a larger and more comfortable apartment and a big grant of money. The trade-union committee of the shop where the mother works has bought three cots and complete layettes."

The newspaper *Red Star* devoted unusually frank attention to the effect of housing on the birth rate by publishing letters on the subject from military personnel. A second lieutenant in favor of large families wrote: "It would be hypocrisy not to take into account a lack of adequate living conditions or the fact that soldiers are constantly on the move. These things are of importance, indeed. But not of paramount importance. My wife and I have been kicked around not less than my colleagues. We have had to live under all sorts of conditions in crowded rooms and apartments without all modern conveniences. At times it was difficult. But never on any such occasion did it enter our heads that life without children would make us more free, or that children bind us hand and foot."

The other side of the argument was presented by another lieutenant who denied that the reasons against having children were that they prevented the couple from attending dances and movies. "There are more weighty reasons," he wrote, "I mean the lack of adequate living conditions, first of all, the housing shortage. My wife and I have one child. We three lived for over a year in one room of 24 square feet. Well, I must say, you wouldn't want two or three children under such conditions."

Bizarre situations are created by the desperate housing shortage. Crowded conditions may easily cause tensions and animosities among neighbors. Another cartoon in *Krokodil* shows a busybody neighbor, in the first panel, peeking through the keyhole of the people next door. In the second panel she is caught in the act by the neighbor, who suddenly opens his door. The third panel shows the busybody now indignant because the neighbor has transplanted his doorknob and keyhole to the top of the door, well above her head. In real life, a Russian told me of a six-room apartment shared by six families in which disputes about sharing of electric bills had reached such acrimony that each family had its own electric-light bulb installed in the common toilet. The switch for each bathroom bulb was operated from each family's room. Each communal apartment shares a single electric meter and, in harmonious situations, the neighbors apportion the charges. Under less harmonious circumstances it is possible to buy individual electric motors which are installed in a family's room; this family contributes to the communal bill only the charges that appear on its meter.

Gas charges are less easily broken down. Bitterness among the families of a four-room apartment was so intense that each family kept its burner on the communal stove going at all times even when not in use to make sure that it got the maximum "use" out of its portion of the bill. Even this instance of communal enmity pales by comparsion with the case, described by a Russian friend, where intense suspicion caused housewives to tie down their pot covers for fear that a neighbor might contaminate the boiling borsch.

One method of coping with the shortage has been to convert office buildings into apartments. That was cited by Party publications as one of the benefits of Khrushchev's decentralization of industry; by eliminating ministries and transferring others out of Moscow, office space became available for living quarters. The availability of a comparatively few apartments became news. A typical newspaper item appeared under the headline, "Office Space Freed for Flats." The article read:

"Minsk—Steps are being taken here to reduce the floor space under the republican offices of the Byelorussian Department Stores, Gastronom Groceries, State Trade Inspectorate, and other trade institutions. The vacated premises are being refurnished as housing. Minsk trade workers will get as many as 50 flats.

"A number of steps are being taken to cut office space and remake it for flats at the Grodno, Brest, and Gomel regional consumer cooperatives. In six months alone some 200 apartments will be remade from floor space currently occupied by offices."

There is increasingly extensive construction of massive apartment buildings in most Soviet cities. The first sight of Moscow that greets a visitor driving in from the airport is of a vast community consisting of scores of ten-story apartment houses, some completed, others still under construction. The scale of the project is impressive, but it will take construction of huge dimension just to replace war destruction, to keep pace with the normal growth of population, to permit families living together to obtain separate quarters, and to compensate for old buildings that have become uninhabitable through age.

The discontent over housing has motivated the government to encourage private building and ownership of homes. This encouragement takes the form of liberal mortgages. Although private enterprise is discouraged under the general precepts of Communism, it has been considered expedient to bring instincts of private ownership into play to contribute to a solution of the housing problem. The trend of private building is particularly evident in rural areas. The government offers to lend prospective home owners from 10,000 to 20,000 rubles ($1000 to $2000) depending on the region of the country. Even by Soviet standards this mortgage does not build much of a dwelling. Mostly such private homes are about 20 by 35 feet, a good-sized living room in many homes in other countries, but usually subdivided into two or three rooms in the Soviet version.

Some of the houses are fashioned of adobe bricks, composed of mud and straw. These primitive bricks are left to dry and harden in the sun so they will not shrink later, exposing cracks to winter winds. The bricks are laid upon a wooden framework, and then the mud and straw surface is whitewashed with lime and water. Often the roofs are thatched with straw. It is common to see a man and wife working on their privately owned home. Sometimes several women neighbors help on a reciprocal basis.

Steel, which has more critical uses in the Soviet Union, is seldom if ever used on private homes, nor, for that matter, is it used in quantity in construction of large four- and five-story city apartments. In multistory buildings the walls are thick at the base to compensate for the lack of structural steel support; they gradually taper upward. That's one reason why new buildings quickly look old in Russia; the lack of steel in construction causes sagging, cracks in the plaster, and doors that won't close properly. The solid buildings are often prerevolutionary, like the Bolshoi Theatre, its last reconstruction having been in 1856. One visitor noted with considerable truth that in Russia it is the old buildings that look new and the new that look old.

A brand-new six-story apartment house on Yaroslavskaya Chausee in Moscow was made available to members of several foreign embassies. A bachelor member of the Norwegian Embassy was assigned a small flat on the top floor. Cracks began to appear in the walls, and more annoying, was the appearance of large blotches on the ceiling after the winter's first snowfall. He summoned the *dvornik,* the caretaker, and pointed to the water dripping on his new rugs and furniture.

"Of course it's leaking," shrugged the caretaker. "The snow is melting on the roof."

To a Russian, accustomed to the inadequacies of Soviet construction, nothing could be more natural.

The private-home-building program got under way on October 17, 1954, when the Ministry of Agriculture's newspaper *Solskoye Khozyaistva,* meaning "Agriculture," published a notice of certain "privileges" to families which moved from cities to farm areas "where there is need of more workers." The "privileges" of private home ownership and easy payment mortgages were originally intended as an inducement for city dwellers to move to the virgin lands in Siberia and Kazakhstan. Also, it was impossible for the government to cope with the housing demands of the almost half a million people recruited for the virgin lands without soliciting their help in building their own dwellings. Subsequently the privilege of mortgages to build homes was extended to other regions.

The lenient terms of the loan would dishearten any Western banker. Repayment may be made over a ten-year period. The first three years are free of interest. For the remaining seven years interest is only 2 per cent.

As an added inducement to set up private housekeeping in rural areas, the government offered loans of from 1500 to 3000 rubles ($150 to $300) to families to purchase livestock. One cow was the limit per family, and several pigs, chickens, geese, rabbits, and such.

Not infrequently several families will pool their resources to build a common dwelling. Such was true in the case of Victor and Yuri. Victor was a translator for a government foreign-language publishing house; he had accumulated considerable funds from piecework payments. Yuri was an engineer whose connection with a government construction ministry gave him access to materials needed for building a somewhat more complex home than along adobe lines. In Russia the ability to obtain scarce goods is far more important than money. A man who undertakes to construct his own home is entitled to purchase the required materials. But having permission on paper to make a purchase is one thing and finding a seller quite another. When a would-be home builder presents his papers at a supply bureau he is often informed that there's a waiting list for construction supplies. Employees at the bureau have priority. Newspapers have exposed cases of bribery to obtain materials and of embezzlement on the part of those entrusted with the distribution of such materials.

Victor applied to the town Soviet in the suburban village, forty minutes by train from Moscow, for permission to build an all-year *dacha*, a villa or country house. The permission was granted and a plot of land was made available on which to build. With this permission went papers authorizing him to buy the necessary materials. Victor turned these papers and his funds over to Yuri, who used his ministry connections to purchase lumber, cement, plumbing fixtures, and all the other ingredients that go into a house.

On weekends the two men work on the house, and they have hired several part-time workmen. Such employment of workmen for a private project is not precisely a violation of the law forbidding an individual's hiring of others to work for his profit. Rather it was justified on the same principle as contracting the services of a cobbler to mend a pair of shoes. By this rationalization, a carpenter is hired to perform the specific job of, say, roofing the building.

In fact, though, Victor is a financier who provided the funds for the project, and the others are working for him, although in a somewhat less than classic capitalistic fashion.

No papers were exchanged between Victor and Yuri. It is entirely an unsigned gentlemen's agreement, born of a marriage of Soviet inconveniences. When the seven-room house is completed, they will have it approved for occupancy by the appropriate town authorities. They then will receive separate ownership papers; by their own arrangement, Victor's document will say that he owns four rooms, and Yuri's will confirm his ownership of three rooms. Each will move his family and possessions from their present one-room quarters and will gradually purchase additional furniture; first of all, each says he wants to buy a television set.

CHAPTER 11

BOY LOVES GIRL LOVES TRACTOR

Television in Russia sometimes provides instructive insight into the Soviet way of life.

Such an insight was provided by the showing of a film entitled *This Is How It Began*—the story of young people who had been recruited to cultivate new farms in Siberia. In one scene a young couple in love is daydreaming in a wheat field, planning their future together. The picture fades. Superimposed on them is an image of their dream house—one room of an apartment. But this dream room is larger than most. There are twin beds, a dining table, several chairs, and a sideboard. Overhead hangs the usual umbrella-sized tassled lampshade that is sold in government stores and graces almost every home.

The girl shakes her head. She has other ideas about their fantasy home. As she talks, the picture fades again. A new superimposed image begins to appear.

Would the new dream home be a large apartment? A private bungalow? Would it include a two-car garage? A swimming pool? After all, dreams are free. No. When the image came into focus again there was the same room, but the umbrella-shaped lampshade had been replaced by a neat, modernistic chandelier.

Of such things are dreams made in Russia.

For a long time another Russian dream was to be able to *buy* a TV set. There were not enough manufactured. It wasn't that the price was so high (although my set with a screen that measured 14 inches in its diagonal cost 2600 rubles—about $260). It's possible for even a low-income Russian household to own a TV set, because often everyone in the family works. By chipping in they could afford to buy a six-inch set.

The midget screens, incidentally, led to a joke told circumspectly by Russians:

"Have you heard? The government is recalling all six-inch TV sets."

"Why?"

"Because Khrushchev has gotten so fat he can't fit on a six-inch screen."

Sets manufactured by various Soviet factories bear such names as *Rubin* ("Ruby"), *Znamya* ("Banner") and *Avangard* ("Vanguard"). The *Rubin,* with a 12- by 14-inch screen, sells for 2600 rubles ($260) and is the most expensive set.

Repairmen are in demand. It's usually necessary to wait a week or more for one. They are employed by the Government and earn a ruble wage equivalent to about $70 a month.

The impact of TV on Russian family habits is indicated in a book of 1000 proverbs published by a state publishing house. It includes a TV-age proverb: "TV in. You out." So, as in the early days of television in the United States, the owner of a set has to expect uninvited neighbors to drop in in such numbers as to evict him.

Although the Russians began TV transmissions on a regular, although infrequent, schedule before World War II, TV has lagged far behind the United States in number of sets, number of channels, and hours on the air. Even the most unbiased critic would probably agree, too, that Russia has lagged in quality of programs. Even the censor, who must approve correspondents' scripts, tacitly acknowledged some criticism of Soviet TV.

An article had been published in the Communist youth newspaper, *Komsomalskaya Pravda,* which discussed prospects for flights to the moon. It might soon be possible, wrote the scientist author, to transmit TV signals to the moon and bounce them back to the earth. This would make it possible for half the world to see Moscow TV. "A questionable privilege," was my comment in a broadcast script. The censor passed it.

In 1955 there were about one million sets in the Soviet Union. A year later it had grown by a half million. By 1957 there were over two million sets, more than half of them in Moscow. By 1959 the number of sets exceeded two and a half million. This was about one twentieth of the number of sets in use in the United States. In fact, the number of sets in households in the state of Michigan alone equaled the number in the whole of the U.S.S.R. New York had twice as many as the Soviet Union.

However, it would be a more valid comparison to note that there were more sets installed in Soviet homes than in most European countries. In an economy of shortages, significant resources were invested in the development of television, and this is evidence of the importance attributed to the medium by the Soviet leadership. In fact, Russia ranks fourth—after the United States, Canada, and the British Isles—in the number of sets in use.

There is, of course, no individual or private ownership of television stations in Russia. The government, originally through the Ministry of Culture, and more recently through a special committee created under the Council of Ministers, operates TV stations. Major cities—Moscow, Leningrad, Omsk, Sverdlovsk, Vladivostok, and a score of others—have stations. The number of stations grew from about 20 in 1956 to 35 in 1959, and there are plans for 60 by 1960. There are experimental transmissions in color, but no regular color programs. There is no "rating" system, so important in the economics of American television, that measures the popularity of programs in terms of how many sets are tuned in. There is no regular network, although it is planned eventually to link the various stations by cable.

On several special occasions a number of provincial capitals were able to look in on events in Moscow by means of airplanes sent aloft with television relay transmitters aboard. The military parade in Red Square on the fortieth anniversary of the Revolution was transmitted in this manner to Leningrad, Kharkov, and Kiev. Something went wrong on the Leningrad relay aircraft, and although the audience in Leningrad could hear the music and roar of tanks, their screens were blank. However, by a freak of transmission, television sets in Warsaw and Prague were able to pick up the picture of Red Square.

The main Moscow station provides films of entertainment and propaganda, but the local stations originate most of their other programs.

Moscow television goes on the air weekdays at about 7 P.M. The word "about" is used advisedly, because there's a certain whimsical contempt for precision in schedules. A program may begin five minutes early or end fifteen minutes late. There are no paid commercials to compel adherence to a schedule nor rival networks to attract the viewer (although the government's Moscow station has a supplementary second channel which transmits programs for one and a half or two hours every night).

TV goes off at 11 P.M.—or rather at *about* 11. When the 48-hour Russian work week was abbreviated in 1956 by two hours on Saturday, Moscow's station began transmitting an hour earlier, at 6 P.M., on Saturday only. Apparently, the reduction in Saturday's working hours eliminated the objection to "daytime" TV the rest of the week— the danger of distracting men and women from their jobs. Sunday is the only day off, and Russians are able to watch several hours of afternoon programs, if they wish, commencing at 2 P.M.

Soviet television programs generally fall into three categories:

1) Movies. These are mostly Soviet or from one of the other Communist countries. When it suits the Soviet point of view, a movie from a non-Communist country will be shown. Such was a film entitled *Wetbacks*, produced in Mexico, which related the tragedy of Mexicans who swim the Rio Grande and enter the United States illegally in search of work. It showed the Mexicans mistreated and exploited by American capitalists. The film track was dubbed into Russian except for certain gum-chewing, side-of-mouth phrases like "Okay, Jack," and "Let's go, boy," which were in English.

2) "Live" transmissions from theaters, stadiums, and the scenes of other public events. The pick-ups from theaters, although involving no special production for TV and using only three cameras, are often the best Soviet TV has to offer. The quality of the program depends on the production being televised. A Bolshoi Theatre production of the "Sleeping Beauty" ballet cannot be spoiled even by unimaginative camera work.

Few plays are produced in TV studios themselves, largely because of lack of space. Moscow's facilities, until completion of a new building, consisted of a single studio which would not have been large enough for the waiting room of a vice-president's office at a New York network. The new space consists of two medium-size studios with modern Soviet-manufactured cameras, lights and control-room equipment.

Amateur talent is used where available, like a dramatic group at the Likhatchov auto plant which presented scenes from Mark Twain's *Tom Sawyer* from their clubhouse stage. It was a good adaptation, even though the rich boy, in the scene where Tom gets into a scrap with him, was a little overdressed for the part—just as western TV hams it up a bit when depicting a Russian spy. *Tom Sawyer* was followed by an earnest-looking factory chorus singing songs of the Bolshevik Revolution.

The stadium transmissions are mostly sports events or rallies to honor a state visitor. Soccer sells out Dynamo Stadium which seats 80,000 or Lenin Stadium's 100,000 places, so that the U.S.S.R. sports committee does not worry about TV cutting into its receipts.

Other televised public events include the May Day parade through Red Square with shots of the Soviet leaders waving from the top of the Lenin-Stalin mausoleum, a concert of American violinist Isaac Stern from the Tchaikovsky Hall, or a ball in the St. George's Hall of the Grand Kremlin Palace in honor of young farmers from Siberia's virgin lands.

3) Features of a fairly regular nature. This category includes newsreels, five to ten minutes in length, which consist mostly of scenes from factories, farms, and construction sites where workers have excelled. About once a week newsreel film from foreign countries, including the U.S.A., is shown. The American footage is usually pretty innocuous. It is provided by an American news-film company in exchange for Soviet film and consists of scenes of a New Hampshire ski race, a New York furniture show, or perhaps a race in California among youngsters in soapbox "cars."

Regularly, editors of various Soviet publications are invited to present the Soviet point of view on world issues. TV has no commentators of its own. Leading workers from factories, often without neckties, appear before the TV camera to tell how they were able to exceed their production goals.

There are regular dance lessons, presented in a solemn, businesslike manner. There are programs of household hints: a lady will demonstrate how to set a table for a party, or how to cook *blinichi* (meat pancakes), and there was a rather catastrophic demonstration for amateur flower-box gardeners. The somewhat unco-ordinated lady expert became hopelessly entangled in branches of various species of flora she had brought with her as visual aids.

About once every three months a program is presented on "How to Handle Your TV Set," in which viewers are shown the proper technique for tuning and focusing. Somewhat more frequently, television indulges in the "self-criticism" that is a peculiarity of the Communist society. Letters from listeners are read by an announcer. Complaints are answered. Yes, it was a mistake not to have announced beforehand that a movie with war scenes had best not be watched by children under sixteen. Yes, an effort would be made to present movies of more recent origin. And so on.

The evening schedule regularly begins with a half hour of programs for children. This may be an animated cartoon, (which Russians do very well) or a puppet show (which they do even better). Regularly, an actress from the Moscow Art Theatre dressed in peasant costume with embroidered blouse, wide pleated skirt, and ruffled tiara hat will tell fairy and folk stories.

The give-away-type television program, so popular in capitalistic countries, enjoyed a great but extremely brief popularity in Moscow. Called "Evenings of Funny Questions," the program gave boxes of candy and neckties as prizes to contestants who could imitate the poses of Pushkin's and Gorki's statues or recite childhood nursery rhymes from memory. One Saturday night in September when the first chill of Russia's winter was in the air, the master of ceremonies announced that since it was time for Muscovites to begin digging out winter clothes, the first three people to get to the studio clad in winter garments would win prizes. Others who cared to come out to the Moscow University Club, where the program was originating that night, would find a hospitable welcome awaiting them. The lure of free prizes was stronger than expected. Within minutes, Russians of various ages, all dressed in boots, thick coats, and fur hats, began rushing onto the small stage of the club, within full view of the TV audience. They came in droves, tripped over camera cables, blocked the camera lenses, and argued about who was first. Absolute confusion reigned. Television screens went blank as distraught TV personnel cut the program off the air. A flustered announcer came on to utter a meaningless phrase: "The sponsors of this evening will take time in order to make out the situation." It was a half hour before impatient TV viewers saw anything on their screen. Then another announcer appeared to say that the evening's transmission was canceled because of "organizational difficulties." There was no more television that evening, and there have been no more give-away programs since.

Much of Moscow's schedule consists of movies. Someone has described the theme of Soviet movies as "Boy Loves Girl Loves Tractor," and this aptly applies to an unfortunate percentage of films on TV. A young man on a collective farm who shirks his job falls under the charm of a robust and devoted Communist worker in a field brigade.

She will permit her hand to be won only after the erring youth has changed his way of living and become a quota-exceeding tractor driver.

A film which Danny Kaye did on his travels for the United Nations International Childrens' Emergency Fund was shown on Moscow TV— but a month and a half later than in twenty-five other member countries of UNICEF, and in far shorter form. The ninety-minute film of Kaye's travels to hospitals, camps, and other institutions to entertain underprivileged children was cut to precisely eleven minutes. It was preceded by G. A. Mitriev, chairman of the Soviet Red Cross and Red Crescent societies, speaking about UNICEF and the role of the Soviet Union in relief work among children.

Mitriev spoke for eight minutes, and then the film was run to show children being helped by Soviet contributions. Danny Kaye's role in the film was only incidental in the Russian editing. The Russian narrator's voice in the background did mention him three times as a famous American comedian "Dahnee Kane" who was shown mugging and singing with undernourished and sick children in Italy, Africa, and Greece.

Presumably the film was cut down because it gave too much prominence to an American, or because eleven minutes is all Moscow TV authorities thought it was worth. However, an hour or two each night, for a complete month, was devoted to coverage of a world-championship chess match. There may be less exciting subjects for TV, but they are difficult to conceive. There were interminable closeups of chess players' scowling faces and exhaustive interviews on chess strategy, those with foreign players protracted by translation. To many Russians chess is absorbing; to non-chess players the transmissions of the tournament from Tchaikovsky Hall were incredibly boring.

The programs actually transmitted by Moscow's station often bear little resemblance to those listed in a sixteen-page pulp publication, published weekly by a government printing house and costing 40 kopecks (4 cents).

A viewer never really knows what he's going to see on TV until it appears on his screen. Programs are canceled and changed with flippant casualness, but the absence of sponsors relieves TV officials of the worry of loss of revenue.

On the fiftieth birthday of Soviet composer Dimitri Shostakovich (who had been in and out of trouble periodically during Stalin's time for writing music that was said not to be understandable to the masses), a program to honor him was scheduled from the Great Hall of Moscow's Conservatory of Music. Either his Stalin-era experiences or his personal nature has made Shostakovich unusually shy. The composer of eleven symphonies (his first written at the age of twenty) telephoned the director of Moscow TV and asked that the transmission be canceled.

"Too many people would see it on television," explained Shostakovich, "and it's really just a private affair."

The television director acceded, although the "private" birthday celebration was attended by two thousand members of Russia's music world and was carried on radio. Moscow's TV audience was told that the program would not be carried because of "reasons beyond our control."

As is usually the case, an old movie was televised instead.

In this case it turned out to be a *good* old movie—*Romeo and Juliet* as danced by the Bolshoi Theatre's prima ballerina Galina Ulanova and Yuri Zhdanov. This film, shown abroad, has received acclaim in many countries.

Since the government operates the movie studios, as well as the theaters and the Bolshoi Ballet, there are fewer problems involved in transmissions of movies and from theaters than in the United States and other countries.

A movie may be shown on TV twelve days after it opens in movie houses. In the United States and other countries it's customary for movie producers to insist on a lapse of many months or years before dissipating a movie's box-office appeal on television. Of course, the limited number of TV-set owners in Russia makes it less likely than in the U.S. that a television showing of a film will substantially reduce its theater audience. However, as in America, Russian theater managers complain about the ruinous effects of television on their ticket sales. Theater managers in Russia are employed by the government to supervise government-owned theaters and are responsible for showing a profit. The best programs on Soviet television are the live transmissions from theaters, especially ballet performances from the stage of the Bolshoi: all four hours for a ballet like "Swan Lake." Whenever the show is about to change at Moscow's single-ring circus, the outgoing troupe is televised for the full performance of three hours. The biggest name in Soviet circus is a clown called Karand'ash (Pencil), whose penchant for political humor seems to be the reason for his periodic disappearances from the sawdust ring. When the circus troupe, including Karand'ash, was televised the biggest laugh of the evening came as the clown, whose mustache and garb resemble Charlie Chaplin's, trudged across the ring, laden down with a window frame, a sink, a radiator, and a toilet seat.

"Where are you going with all that stuff?" asks the master of ceremonies.

"To my new, fully completed apartment," is the reply, which to a Russian is a hilarious gibe at government housing authorities, who often consider apartments fit for habitation even when lacking elemental facilities.

Television has produced other telling political criticism, unrehearsed and unexpected. It is a practice of Moscow television to invite some foreign ambassadors to deliver short talks on dates of special importance to their nation. An ambassador invited to appear cannot very well be asked to submit his remarks for censorship. It's taken for granted, though, that a diplomat will not abuse the invitation by words offensive to the nation to which he is accredited. However, diplomats are often skillful speakers, and Russian audiences are not without perception. The Norwegian ambassador dwelt on the nature of democracy in Norway where all segments of political opinion, he said, are represented in parliament. The Ambassador of India referred to the "events" in Hungary as a great "tragedy," a description never used by Soviet organs. Britain's Ambassador expressed pleasure that Charles Dickens's works are made available to Soviet citizens but added that it is an error to judge Britain today in terms of Dickens's day. Moscow television audiences heard France's visiting Premier Guy Mollet tell them and their leaders that "people living in cloistered solitude cannot get rid of fear." It was a subtle way of telling the Soviet leaders, in the presence of their people, that those people should enjoy the same free contact with the outside world as their leaders. U. S. Ambassador Llewellyn Thompson accepted an invitation—the first extended to an American envoy—to speak on the Fourth of July, 1958. A moderate, soft-spoken diplomat by nature, Thompson abstained from intemperate remarks but *did* advocate freedom of travel and an end to censorship of information.

Such pinpricks on Soviet television are rare. And when Moscow's cone-shaped transmitter is not beaming straight culture and entertainment it is usually sending outright political indoctrination.

An example was a film giving the Soviet version of the Hungarian revolution. The revolt began on October 23, 1956. It was not until just a few days before the New Year that the events in Hungary were mentioned at all. Then the carefully edited and narrated ten-minute film was shown two and three times a night for a week. It represented the revolution as a Western, principally American, imperialist plot that resulted in "white" terror and lynchings of honest Communists. Order was restored because the mass of the populace, loyal to the Communist leaders, repelled the "counterrevolutionaries." Soviet tanks *were* shown, but only a brief glimpse, and the narration explained that they had been invited by the Hungarians to assist in the defeat of the Fascists, organized by American and other imperialists who sought to overthrow "people's power" in Hungary.

The Russian is subjected to a form of the longest "commercials" in the world. These are known as "product-popularization" programs, but by any other name they *are* commercials—protracted and dull. When a state factory manufactures a product that needs "pushing," Ministry of Trade authorities arrange to put a "product-popularization" commercial on TV. One of the most yawn-provoking consisted of a full five minutes of instruction on the use of a sewing machine named for the city Tula. Another recommends a canned baby food. The most imaginative advertises the government's "cash and valuable goods" lottery; this is an animated cartoon that shows a lucky Ivan playing a winning number accordion or riding a motor scooter. It's intended to send the TV viewer to the nearest lottery counter to buy a fistful of chances, but instead it may drive him to the complicated set of dials to turn it off. Occasionally there are other government announcements. Before New Year's Eve viewers were informed that the Praga Restaurant, one of the most expensive, was accepting reservations for New Year's Eve parties. Every three months there is a reminder that the quarterly tax of 30 rubles ($3.00) on the use of a TV set is due. This tax, which is paid at the post office, is the only direct source of income from television; the government's budget provides additional revenue. It's not easy to forget TV-tax time, what with the on-the-air reminders and the fact that notices are sent out. Inspectors are employed full time and may knock at the door at any time to demand a tax receipt. The TV tax evader must pay a 100-ruble ($10) fine on the spot.

The government gets full return for its investment. The authorities are completely aware of the impact of television in the indoctrination of a populace. That's why resources are being invested in the manufacture of TV sets, studios, and transmitters while there's still a crying need for more housing, better clothing, and indoor plumbing.

When the Kremlin undertakes a propaganda policy of any sort, the full facilities of television are made available. This was demonstrated in the Sixth World Youth Festival, held in Moscow from July 28 through August 11, 1957. Groups of students and young workers were invited from places as disparate as Canada and the Congo, from Britain and Bali. There were concerts of national songs and dances by each delegation. There were displays of handicraft. There were meetings of hobbyists —stamp collectors, coin collectors and such—and discussion groups on furtherance of student exchanges and what youth could do for peace.

For the Russians it was an opportunity to dissuade the young visitors of preconceptions of Russia as the land of Stalinist oppression. It was a chance to convince the youth of other lands, by talking only about peace and by omitting any reference to the size of the Soviet army or its role in Hungary, that Russia wants only peace and that other nations, allies of the United States, cause tension and war. Although any American with a passport could travel to Russia without restriction at that time, the U. S. State Department opposed the attendance by any Americans at the festival. (About 160 came anyway.) An argument could have been—and was—made that 2000 young Americans, full of enthusiasm for Democracy, might have made a greater impact on the Russians than the Communist youth would have made on them. However, the obvious propaganda intentions of the Soviet Union in sponsoring the event made the United States Government wary of participation by Americans.

In any event, Soviet television was fully mobilized to present events during the festival, and for two months prior to its opening TV carried a series of programs called "Festival Phrase Book" on how to pronounce elementary words in a variety of tongues, in anticipation of the foreign visitors. There were presentations of the Soviet youth groups that would perform at the festival, speeches by festival officials, interviews with Soviet and foreign participants. If by the time the festival actually got under way the populace of Moscow was *not* fully festival-minded, it was not the fault of television.

Visits by heads of foreign states get the full TV treatment and sometimes result in memorable pictures:

There was the stadium rally for President Sukarno of Indonesia. The sun beat down on Khrushchev's head and caused him to pause in mid-speech. "Excuse me, Comrades," he said a bit shyly, "but I think I'd better put on my hat."

There was the look of obvious disapproval on Khrushchev's face when Marshal Voroshilov spoke at a Kremlin mass meeting on his return from an Asian trip and told of his astonishment at discovering that ally Mongolia was such a poor, barren land. The expression of dissent disappeared when Voroshilov developed his thesis, explaining what great progress had been made in civilizing Mongolia under Communism.

There was the momentary lapse of the TV cameraman who kept his camera focused on leaders Bulganin and Mikoyan exchanging remarks of some apparent hilarity, when Khrushchev was in the middle of a serious oration on the merits of Yugoslav co-operation with the U.S.S.R.

Television transmission of such arrivals and departures and "friendship meetings," as they're called, usually takes place in the afternoon, outside of regular TV time, without any prior announcement in the printed schedules.

Depending on how you care to look at it, television in Russia is far ahead or far behind the United States in at least one respect—there are no regular television critics in the Soviet Union.

Intermittently, the newspaper *Soviet Culture* has run articles of criticism and evaluation under the signature of "Teleobserver." Teleobserver is a number of people. In each city reviewed—Leningrad, Kiev, Tallin, Omsk, Tomsk, Minsk—a correspondent for *Soviet Culture,* who may possess no interest in TV and not even a TV set, is assigned to evaluate television in his precinct.

I telephoned a gentleman at *Soviet Culture* to ask about the Teleobserver column; he explained that their news correspondent in each city consults with local officials and viewers before writing his criticism. In Russia it always pays for a Soviet writer to know what the official attitude is on any subject from Stalinism to television before writing about it.

A reason why there is so little published about television is that Soviet newspapers are so small. In Moscow only the *Evening Moscow* publishes TV schedules a day in advance. None of the other newspapers does this.

What television criticism may lack in volume in Russia, it makes up for in influence. A criticism in *Pravda* may be sufficient to stimulate drastic changes in the personnel of the yellow stucco building that houses Moscow television. It was probably not mere coincidence that a letter appeared in the columns of *Pravda* criticizing dull and repetitive shows, and shortly after the director of Moscow's station was replaced—the third director in two years.

Letters from readers are a favorite technique for presenting the views of Soviet authorities. It gives the opinion an air of popular spontaneity. You will never read a letter-to-the-editor that contradicts the editorial, and thus Party, view.

The letter that preceded the change in management of Moscow TV was signed by a Comrade Nikolai Chibisov, an engineer, and was entitled "When Will *Barmalei* End?" *Barmalei* is a children's cartoon which, according to Chibisov, had been presented on television no fewer than eighteen times in three years.

"The work of the Moscow TV studio leaves much to be desired," he wrote. "There are more than twenty theaters in Moscow whose repertoires number not less than 200 plays. This gives television ample opportunities for selecting programs of interest.

"Yet, our TV viewers have forgotten when they last saw transmissions from the Operetta Theatre or the Stanislavsky Theatre or from many other Moscow theaters.

"Movies are often canceled all of a sudden. Who is to blame for this? The TV studio or the movie officials?

"When memorable occasions are observed the press carries articles on the subject and the radio arranges special broadcasts before and during the holiday.

"Yet, on Builders' Day an old movie, *Dance Teacher* was shown on TV.

"Another movie *Goalkeeper* was run eleven times in three years. It seems that this movie is kept for emergencies.

"The movie-distribution department now has 150 feature movies and more than 100 animated cartoons available.

"However, only 10 or 15 animated cartoons are run regularly on TV and they are repeated every two or three months. The animated cartoon *Barmalei* was shown 18 times in three years so that people are asking if the end is yet in sight.

"I would also like to say a few words on telecasts before and during holidays. A shorter working day precedes work holidays. One gets home in a real holiday mood and wants to rest up completely and to enjoy a good television program.

"But holiday TV shows are dull as a rule.

"Let them improve their work at the TV studio!"

The fund of figures and facts available to Chibisov lent weight to the impression that this was no ordinary letter, but rather one inspired by authorities.

Not all the television comment is critical. Teleobserver, reviewing television in the Estonian capital of Tallin, had words of praise for TV reporter Heino Mikkin who exhibited a competitive spirit rarely seen in Soviet reporters. Rather than wait in Tallin for the train which bore victorious Estonian athletes back from the Olympics, reporter Mikkin went out to a way station on the railroad line. He interviewed the athletes about their exploits and their long train trip from Vladivostok across Siberia, and when the train pulled into Tallin, he escorted a group of medal winners from train to studio for the first interview of their homecoming, thus scoring a scoop on the local newspapers.

Teleobserver had some words of stern criticism, too, for Tallin television, and especially for a group of visiting Russian artists who had not bothered to memorize their pieces. "People were surprised," wrote the critic, "to see that singers and musicians had not taken the trouble to learn the songs by heart, but rather kept their eyes fixed on their music."

The only stars or "personalities" developed in Moscow television are its announcers. Unlike American and British TV, which has its own performers under contract, Soviet television borrows its talent from other Soviet media. The popularity of an Ulanova may be enhanced by an appearance on television, but she is already an acknowledged star from the ballet stage. The announcers—more women than men— are the only Russians seen regularly on TV screens.

Valentina Michaelovna Leontyeva, one of the announcers, is often recognized by people in the subway who ask her for her autograph. She receives mail requests for photographs which she provides only for school children, never for male admirers, lest her husband object.

This prudery is characteristic of Soviet television. Low-necked blouses are never worn by the girl announcers and almost never by guest performers. The only "cheesecake" is on the regular Sunday program on physical culture. Demonstrations are given to the accompaniment of piano music while an off-camera narrator counts *ras, dva, tree, chitiri*. The demonstrators are a young man and a shapely girl in shorts and tight-fitting blouse. The Soviet cameraman indicates that he is only human by focusing frequently on tight close-ups of the most attractive portions of the young lady's anatomy.

There was a bit of unexpected cheesecake when a group of British models demonstrated made-in-England clothes in Moscow. The girls were putting on fashion shows in Gorki Park's exhibition hall, and on the last evening of their three-week stand they were seen on television. Despite the anxious word of caution by a Soviet official that it was considered improper in Russia to show one's undergarments, one model, demonstrating a dress with full skirt, lifted it to permit a view of her ruffled crinoline petticoat and her shapely legs. Russians had something to talk about for days.

Women have technical jobs in Soviet TV as well as performing and announcing. On a visit to Moscow's cramped studio you see husky women pushing heavy Kleig lights and operating the control panel. For a time a woman, Valentina Sharoyava, was director of the station. Large in build and hearty in nature, Mrs. Sharoyava, a Party member, wife of a teacher in a music institute, earned 2500 rubles per month (about $250) and delighted in talking about her work and herself.

How are tickets obtained to visit the Moscow studio?

"People write in or telephone," explained Mrs. Sharoyava, "and, because our space is so limited, we have a waiting list three months ahead."

Are requests taken in order?

Mrs. Sharoyava smiled, showing several gold teeth: "All of us are human, and so, not always just. No applications from individuals are given consideration now. Letters come in from Party committees, from union committees and from factory groups. We give them first consideration."

Why is there so little concern about keeping to a schedule?

"This is largely explained by national characteristics. When there was a delegation from the German Democratic Republic visiting us, they told us that they are absolutely rigid in the time of their programs. When time is up an artist is switched off. It sometimes happens that our programs run overtime. The Germans are too punctual. We are Russians and are more flexible."

Does it present any problems for a woman to be director of a TV station?

"Well, of course, in our country women do every kind of job. But sometimes being a woman has its disadvantages in this job. There are many football [soccer] fans in our country, and when, for some reason, we are unable to carry an important match in Dynamo Stadium there are complaints. Once a man insisted on speaking to the director:

" 'Well, girl,' he said, 'I'm waiting. I'd like to talk to the director.'

"I told him that I was the director.

" 'Look here, girl,' he said, 'don't joke with me. I want to talk to the director.'

" '*Tovarich*'—I tried to persuade him—'take my word for it. I *am* the director.'

" 'Everything's clear to me now,' he exclaimed. 'If a *woman* is director of an institution of this kind I can understand why there's no football.'

"With that he hung up. This was especially unjust because I happen to be a football fan myself," chuckled Mrs. Sharoyava.

Until 1953 scripts were lettered on cards which were held up out of view of the camera for guest speakers to read. This seemed stilted, however, and cards are no longer used. Television in Russia has not yet developed automatic prompting devices like America's telecue or tele-prompter; kinescope, which permits on-the-air filming of programs, is only being experimented with.

During the interval between programs the screen is filled with the picture of an ordinary stage curtain. An announcer appears briefly to tell about the next program, and that it will be on in five or ten minutes, as the case may be. Then the curtain is shown, without sound, until it's time for the next program.

For about a half hour before the day's programming begins, a test pattern is shown. A test pattern is a scientifically arranged pattern of lines, circles, and numbers in various shades of black which permits studio cameras to adjust and focus properly. The test pattern is transmitted in Russia as a service to viewers to permit them to tune their sets.

The test pattern is also shown for a number of hours during the day when there are no TV programs. This is to enable government television repairmen to have something to tune to when fixing sets. Sets are sold with a six-month guarantee on the picture tube. Mine lasted a year and a month and then blew out right during a speech by Soviet President Voroshilov.

There are technical failures, too, *in* the studio. At Moscow TV they recall the evening that the red light on the TV camera, indicating to a performer that the camera is "on," blew out. It was just when Nina Kondratova, an announcer, was to recite the program schedule for that evening. Nina was making up, powdering her nose (like the other Moscow announcers, she wears very little make-up). Nina went right on doing so while a floor manager tried to call her attention to the camera. With the composure of an experienced professional, Nina confidently replied to the manager (as well as to the "live" camera, microphone, and astonished audience): "Don't worry, Igor, the light's still off."

A number of listeners complained about Nina's on-camera conduct, but it was written off as a mistake.

There was another event in the life of Nina Kondratova which indicates that Moscow television has a heart. She was injured in an auto accident and lost an eye. After months in the hospital Nina lacked the confidence to face the television camera with her new glass eye. Finally, at the urging of friends, she did. The false eye is apparent on the TV screen, but no one seems to mind. Nina has a pleasant personality, and Russian audiences don't expect glamour girls.

The Russians claim to have been the first to develop both television and radio. Radio Day is celebrated annually on May 7 in commemoration of the day in 1895 that Alexander Popov, a Russian scientist, gave a public demonstration of—so the Russians say—the first radio set in the world. Soviet accounts take note of Western claims that Guglielmo Marconi was the father of the radio and they dismiss these claims. One Soviet version reads this way:

"Besides the work of Popov and his collaborators, Marconi's achievements are also widely known. In June 1896 in Britain, Marconi took out a patent for his method of transmitting electric signals without conductors. Marconi's system later proved to be based on the same principle as Popov's. Although he was not the first to invent radio communications, Marconi, nevertheless, played a very considerable role in developing it. In 1899 he established radio communication between England and France and in 1901 sent radio messages across the Atlantic."

The Soviet Union's broadcasting activities are centralized in an unimposing brown stucco four-story building on a small street, a five-minute ride from the Kremlin. Although its furnishings are drab, its equipment is excellent. Russia operates some of the most powerful transmitters in the world, both for sending out broadcasts and for jamming broadcasts from other lands. Radio Moscow has a domestic and a foreign service. The domestic service consists of three "programs"—

or three separate places on the dial where completely different programs emanating from the Moscow studios can be heard. The words, *Gavarit Moskva* (Moscow speaking), can be heard at the beginning of every hour on radios everywhere in Russia. Certain hours of the broadcasting day are designated for local programs put on by the staffs of the Soviet radio system in major cities. But mostly the transmitters of the stations (all government-owned-and-operated, of course) in provincial cities and towns are used for relaying the voice of Moscow.

The first "program" begins broadcasting at 6 A.M. and signs off at 1 A.M. This is the main channel and carries a wide variety of news, commentary, music, and propaganda. The second "program" commences at 8:45 A.M. and also runs until 1 A.M. The third "program" operates only in the evening hours, from 7 P.M. until midnight, when the national anthem is played. The second and third "programs" consist mostly of literary and musical content but also carry fifteen-minute news programs and readings of the editorials from major Soviet newspapers.

Since the early days of Soviet control the Communists have recognized the power of radio in indoctrinating the populace. Radio is not considered primarily an entertainment medium; it is a means of getting the words of the leadership to the people. Great resources have been invested in carrying radio to every part of the country. Almost all automobiles are furnished with radios; like a heater in Russia's cold, it is not considered an extra accessory but rather a necessity. Most car radios are short-wave models, rather than customary sets of short-range reception capability, to enable reception over the long distances between transmitters in Russia's vastness. Short-wave radios can also receive broadcasts from abroad, and it came as a surprise while driving in the Black Sea port city of Odessa to see the chauffeur turn on the radio with a wink at me just as the B.B.C. was beginning a news broadcast. The Russian chauffeur couldn't understand English, but he knew where on the dial to find the B.B.C. To limit the extent that Russians can listen to foreign broadcasts, Soviet short-wave sets are built to include only several of the so-called bands or wave lengths on which overseas stations broadcast. However, to enable Russians in remote areas to hear Moscow, the Soviet authorities have had to provide sets with at least some capability of tuning in to broadcasts from the capitalistic world.

In 1958 there were an estimated 25 million radio loudspeakers and 10 million radio sets in the U.S.S.R. This number did not completely cover the country, though. An article in the newspaper *Soviet Russia* complained that in a certain Kirovsk district only two out of fourteen collective farms had radio facilities and, moreover, in the Dolmatovsky district, where Alexander Popov himself had lived and studied, only half of the farms had radios.

The loudspeaker is small in size, about five inches in diameter, and plugs into wall outlets to receive only the first "program" of Radio Moscow. The loudspeaker has a volume control but no dial for choosing stations. The first "program" is fed by a network of telephone wires to loudspeakers in homes, hotel rooms, hotel lobbies, parks, city squares, factories, railroad waiting rooms, even to beaches in the Soviet south. Radio loudspeakers are installed aboard river boats and even in trains. The Soviet citizen can never get far from the voice of the Kremlin. On trains and in some hotel rooms the only way to silence the voice is to find the plug (not always easy) and disconnect the speaker.

On a visit to a collective farm in the Ukraine I heard loudspeakers in barns, in pigpens, and in some fields beaming a broadcast criticizing America's foreign policy concerning the refusal to seat Communist China in the United Nations. I asked a dozen men and women, busy at their jobs, what they were listening to. Most shrugged and replied with various versions of, "Who's listening?" This acquired ability to ignore the insistent radio may explain in part why Russians feel friendly toward Americans despite the anti-American propaganda beamed at them for years. When I asked a commentator on Radio Moscow about this, he explained: "Of course we feel friendly toward the American *people*. Neither our radio nor our newspapers have any complaint against the American people. It is only the American ruling circles whom we attack for seeking war."

Radio sets, in appearance very much like sets of other countries, sell for prices ranging from 250 rubles ($25) to 1700 rubles ($170). Loudspeakers are much less expensive, costing 60 rubles ($6.00). Small transistor sets are not yet manufactured, although newspaper articles promise sets the size of a matchbox.

The Russian who tunes in his radio first thing in the morning hears the national anthem, fifteen minutes of news (read by a man and woman alternating on items), and a program of setting-up exercises to music. News is broadcast frequently throughout the day, but without any attempt to make the content of one newscast different from another. The items—the exceeding of quotas by a Sverdlovsk factory, the visit to Moscow of a Syrian trade delegation, the names of outstanding workers on a collective farm who received prizes—are read in the preaching, patronizing tone that characterizes Soviet broadcasting. There are no radio soap operas, but frequently there are readings of books or dramatizations of a classic or new play. Long periods of time are devoted several times a day to readings of the editorials from Soviet newspapers. Every Sunday during the campaign of recruiting people for the virgin lands Moscow's radio carried a program entitled, "Letters to Relatives and Friends from the Virgin Lands." A sort of quiz program is sometimes presented in which a number of musical compositions are played and listeners are invited to name the tunes by mail. There are no prizes, just the pride of hearing your name read as a winner.

There are all types of dull lectures; a typical program title is, "Lectures of the Scientists and Advanced Workers at the All-Union Agricultural Exhibition." There are talks on increasing industrial output, on agricultural developments, on Communist ideology.

Concerts and operas are often carried. There are readings of fables and stories for children, transmissions of soccer matches, and reports from Radio Moscow's reporters stationed abroad in London, the United Nations, Peiping, and elsewhere; seldom is the correspondent's voice heard, rather his dispatch is usually read by an announcer.

Radio Moscow broadcasts about 900 hours a week in many foreign languages including English, Arabic, French, and Chinese. The object is to spread the Soviet viewpoint on international issues, to win friends and perhaps converts to the Communist cause.

A great many Soviet transmitters are devoted to the task of interfering with or jamming broadcasts from non-Communist countries that are beamed to Russia with the intention of telling Russians the truth or, in some cases, subverting them. When you turn the dial of a short-wave set in Moscow your ears are assaulted by a succession of insistent noises on every wave-length band. These noises are intended to drown out the broadcasts in Russian, Ukrainian, and other languages of the U.S.S.R. transmitted by the Voice of America, Radio Free Europe, and the British Broadcasting Corporation. However, by freaks of atmospherics, these voices from the West sometimes do get through. English-language broadcasts of the Voice of America and the B.B.C. are not ordinarily jammed.

Apparently there is a limit to the number of transmitters and personnel that the Russians can devote to the task of blocking the reception of foreign broadcasts. Furthermore, by not jamming English language broadcasts, Soviet authorities can argue against accusations that Russians do not enjoy the basic freedom of listening to what they wish. Although very few people in the U.S.S.R. understand English, the broadcasts seem to be effective. There is a "grapevine" or "jungle tom-tom" of spreading news; especially since Stalin's death, with Russians less fearful of denunciation by neighbors, is news spread by word of mouth. The potential effectiveness of foreign broadcasts is demonstrated by the considerable resources Kremlin authorities invest in silencing them. Another demonstration came at the time of the Hungarian Revolution. At first the Soviet radio ignored the Western version of the uprising. Then hours of radio time and columns of newspaper space were devoted to offering rebuttals to the accounts broadcast from abroad. The Voice of America, Radio Free Europe, and other foreign transmitters were mentioned by name and denounced. Surely the Soviet authorities knew that by replying to the foreign broadcasts they were in fact calling attention to them. Those Russians who had not heard the foreign version were made aware of it through the rebuttal. However, apparently the Kremlin considered that the foreign propaganda stations had spread their word so effectively that it was imperative to try to counteract it by Soviet radio and newspapers.

CHAPTER 12

NO NEWS IN IZVESTIA

"Have you heard? *Pravda* is running a contest for the best political joke. The first prize is twenty years."

So runs a wry little story that reflects the fact that jokes that poke fun at the Communist system or leaders never appear in Soviet newspapers. There are a great many newspapers published in the U.S.S.R., but their contents are restricted and much of a sameness. Often events that produce headlines almost everywhere else in the world are not even mentioned in Russia. What's more, events *within* Russia of great public interest are frequently ignored.

For example, November 17, 1956, was a day of much news in Russia. It was a day when the Russians exploded a nuclear bomb, proposed a disarmament conference, and when Western ambassadors walked out of a Kremlin party in protest to a Khrushchev speech. It was also the day when Galina Ulanova pulled a tendon in her leg.

Soviet newspapers carried columns on the disarmament proposal, one paragraph on the nuclear test explosion, and nothing on the walkout. Also, not a word was published about Ulanova.

Galina Ulanova, although then forty-eight years old, was still prima ballerina in a country where ballet is sometimes as much an obsession as an art form. She still convincingly danced the role of teen-age Juliet in the magnificent Russian ballet version of the Shakespeare classic. Ulanova, acknowledged as the world's leading ballerina, is an idol to Soviet citizens of all ages. Her activities should be of greater news interest to Russians than those of Margot Fonteyn to Britishers or those of Greta Garbo, Marilyn Monroe, and Margaret Truman combined to Americans. Yet the events of that November Saturday night were never reported in any Soviet newspaper.

Ulanova was dancing the title role in "Giselle." The Bolshoi Theatre was sold out, as it usually is even for lesser performances. It was well after 8:30 P.M. when I finished writing my account of the Kremlin walkout, and I hurried to the Bolshoi, arriving as the intermission was drawing to a close. I sank into my seat and for the first time in a hectic day prepared to relax. The curtain went up on the second act, the eerie graveyard scene where jilted maidens who have died before their marriage rise from their resting places. The maidens dance for some minutes, and then Giselle rises from her grave through a trap door. Ulanova did so, performing several pirouettes and then dropped prostrate on her face.

The fall was so graceful that for a hushed moment no one seemed to realize what had happened. Then a gasp from the audience. The curtain was drawn. A Russian woman seated next to me began to weep quietly. The audience was hushed as the house lights went on. In about ten minutes the director of the Bolshoi appeared before the curtains to explain that it was nothing serious, Ulanova had simply pulled a tendon. The audience applauded briefly in relief. Raissa Strutchkova danced Ulanova's role for the remainder of the performance.

The few minutes of that second act were all the ballet I saw that night. I went back to the Central Telegraph Office to send a story about the dramatic accident at the Bolshoi.

Some months later I had the opportunity to ask a member of the staff of the *Soviet Culture* newspaper why this news story had been ignored. Why had no explanation been given for Ulanova's prolonged absence afterwards from the Bolshoi stage?

He replied that this was considered a personal affair of Ulanova's, that its publication might be an intrusion into her private life. Besides, he added, "hardly anyone outside of Moscow heard about the accident anyway." The implication seemed to be that if no one had heard of it, why mention it?

The private lives of important Russians are never referred to by Soviet newspapers. Human-interest features of the kind that frequently appear in American, British, or French newspapers about the family lives of leaders, their wives, their children, their hobbies—these are unknown in the Soviet Union.

It was learned for certain that Khrushchev had a college-age son only when he took the boy to England with him. It became known that a Khrushchev grandson (the child of a son killed in the war) was attending military school only when Khrushchev told this to a guest, Mrs. Eleanor Roosevelt. Confirmation of rumors that Mrs. Bulganin taught English in a Moscow school became known only when she discussed it with an American visitor.

To judge from Soviet newspapers, Russia is a land virtually without catastrophes. There's almost never a line about an automobile accident of any sort. Fires are never mentioned. As far as Soviet newspapers are concerned, Russia seems to be a land immune to floods, hurricanes, tornadoes, gas-main explosions, suicides, train crashes, and airplane disasters. Plane crashes are acknowledged only when they would be known to the outside world anyway. In the summer of 1955 an Aeroflot plane carrying a delegation of Norwegian women crashed, killing all aboard. It was evident to Soviet authorities that sooner or later the Norwegian Government would get around to asking what had become of its peace delegation, so the disaster was published. Such was the case, too, when a Polish airliner crashed into a field near Moscow's airport in the spring of 1957 with Americans and other foreigners aboard. The same year, when an Aeroflot plane hit a smokestack and plummeted into the bay near Copenhagen, it was also announced in a brief paragraph.

A Kamchatka volcano eruption in March 1956 rated only a few sentences, although scientists elsewhere compared its magnitude with that of the historic Vesuvius eruption in 79 A.D.

On June 27, 1957, a severe earthquake rocked the city of Chita, with a population of more than 100,000, in the mountainous region north of Mongolia. The entire coverage devoted to the event was a dispatch, reading: "At 9:11 local time an earthquake took place. The epicenter was north of the Lake Baykal area. It had a force of nine on a scale of 12. In Chita the force reached five. Cracks appeared in some houses in Chita as a result of the tremor."

Reports published in Soviet newspapers of authorized demonstrations at the American, West German, and Danish Embassies omitted any reference to damage inflicted by the crowds. Although unruliness was encouraged at the demonstrations, it was apparently considered unwise to imply generalized endorsement for brick-hurling.

Murders are usually ignored by newspapers, but there was an exception in the case of a murder that occurred twenty-eight years prior to the publication. A paragraph-long account was published of the arrest of a man who had committed a double murder in Moscow in 1929, with a motive of robbery. He wandered from Siberia, Estonia, and back to Moscow where the long arm of Soviet law caught up with him. The newspaper's account said simply that his sentence was severe and left it at that.

An insight into the philosophy that motivates Soviet authorities to repress news was given by a remark of the then Defense Minister Marshal Zhukov at a diplomatic party. He was asked why Soviet authorities did not announce each nuclear-test explosion as it occurred, as was done by the United States and Great Britain. Zhukov explained that such announcements would perform no public service, but would only alarm the populace and increase international tensions.

The explanation for ignoring fires, floods, and such seems to lie, in part, in Soviet official reluctance to reflect instability of any sort. Disasters, especially those which result from negligence, might contribute to public lack of confidence in authority. This is to be avoided. Furthermore, Soviet newspapers consider their mission to be more indoctrination than information. The front pages of *Pravda,* the U.S.S.R.'s leading paper, and of other newspapers that follow *Pravda's* lead, often are taken up with speeches by the Communist leaders, progress reports on the successes of the Soviet state, and decisions of the Party and government. A full page will be devoted to an article explaining the need for closer ties between Party officials and the masses. An editorial, occupying half of the front page, will exhort the populace to greater productive effort, and the rest of the page will be covered with detailed reports of the fulfillment of production targets in factories and farms down to the remotest district. These are intended as examples to be emulated.

Although Soviet newspapers omit news of disasters in the U.S.S.R., the same standards are not applied to disasters in other countries. These are considered of legitimate public interest. The Soviet press *does* mention a flood in Yugoslavia. A paragraph a day was carried on each of President Eisenhower's illnesses. Major plane crashes in other countries are sometimes described. Suicides in the United States are often of morbid interest to Soviet editors, who portray them as a barometer of America's economic decline. An auto accident involving an American in Athens, Greece, was headlined in *Pravda* as "New Crime by American Militarists." A U. S. Army officer had run down a deputy in the Greek Parliament. "This," said *Pravda* "is another horrible example of American imperialists lording it over foreign territories." But when auto accidents, major or minor, occur in Russia they are ignored.

Most Soviet newspapers consist of four pages. *Pravda* alternates four pages on one day with six pages on the next, and the intention is to have six pages daily. There are few pictures, mostly of the leaders at an official function, or of outstanding workers, or of a new power plant or factory. Occasionally, there are photos of a more original nature. Five days after it was launched, the first Soviet earth satellite was pictured on a display stand with its four antennae extended. During the Southern school-integration crisis in the U.S.A. photos were reprinted from American publications of Arkansas National Guard troops barring Negro school children from entering the high school and other pictures of a Negro being kicked in the face by extremists. A montage of front pages of foreign newspaper headlines about the sputnik was carried.

There are no banner headlines, no extra editions, no comic strips, no crossword puzzles (although some Soviet magazines do publish them under the adopted title *krossverd*). The emphasis on political indoctrination, the avoidance of the sensational, and the drabness of make-up, all combine to yield dull newspapers. Even *Pravda* felt forced to admit this in declaring that Soviet newspapers are "colorless, lifeless, boring, and also hard to read." This confession was made in May 1957, on the forty-fifth anniversary of *Pravda's* first appearance.

There are more than 7500 newspapers in the Soviet Union, and they appear in sixty languages, with a total circulation of 57,500,000. More than 3000 magazines and periodicals are published. At a time when the number of newspapers and periodicals in the United States is being constricted by increased costs of production there is a steady growth of publications in the Soviet Union to keep pace with a growing population, settlement of previously unpopulated regions, and greater availability of resources for printing presses and paper. The Russian Republic, largest of the Soviet Republics, has 4600 newspapers of all sorts, with a total circulation of 35 million.

As the organ of the Communist Party's leadership, *Pravda* is the paper that sets the tone for other Soviet newspapers. Most Government Ministries have their own newspapers. *Medical Worker* is published by the Ministry of Health. The Ministry of Culture publishes *Soviet Culture*. The Ministry of Defense has several newspapers: *Red Star* is the army paper; *Soviet Fleet* concentrates on navy matters, and for news and indoctrination of special air interest, Air Force men read *Soviet Aviation*. The Central Council of Trade Unions publishes *Trud,* meaning labor, and the Union of Soviet Writers publishes *Literary Gazette.*

There are a variety of magazines. *Screen* is a weekly movie magazine. *Questions of History* interprets history from the Marxist point of view. *Party Life* is a Communist Party journal.

There are provincial and regional newspapers. These often are published jointly by the Communist Party's Central Committee and the government's Council of Ministers of the Republic. There's *Dawn of the East* in the Georgian Republic's capital. There's the *Baku Worker* in Azerbaidzhan. There's *Pravda of the Ukraine,* published in Kiev.

Pravda, the Party paper, and *Izvestia,* the government paper, are the biggest national newspapers with circulation throughout the country. *Pravda* means "truth" and *Izvestia* means "news," which has led to the comment among Soviet cynics that there is no truth in *Pravda* and no news in *Izvestia.* Matrices of these newspapers are flown by jet planes each day to the far reaches of the U.S.S.R. to be printed.

Most newspapers have full-size sheets, but *Soviet Sports* is tabloid size, as is *Moscow News,* an English-language paper, intended for the consumption of tourists and the diplomatic colony and for sale abroad. But tabloid size does not add zest or sensationalism to the content or make-up. There is no competition among newspapers to be first with the news. It is not at all unusual for several days to elapse after a news event before it is mentioned in Soviet newspapers, if at all. It's interesting to compare a copy of *Pravda,* for example, with the airmail Paris edition of the New York *Herald Tribune* or with *The Times* of London, which reach Moscow usually several days late. Their contents of world news would make one believe that the editors drew from events on different planets. With much of the little available space in Soviet newspapers devoted to editorials and articles of exhortation and indoctrination, a certain amount of world news must be omitted. Other items are omitted as detrimental to, or as not contributing to, Soviet interests.

The lag in publishing news stems from several causes. It just isn't in the Soviet tradition to rush into print. The "stop the presses" tradition of competitive news is alien. Furthermore, the contents of Soviet newspapers are planned a day in advance. Therefore, it requires breaking up a planned page, which *is* sometimes done, in order to publish a late development. Also, editors require time to decide what interpretation to place on an event that will conform with Communist policy.

Even with this lack of flexibility there's little predictability to the time that *Pravda* or *Izvestia* or *Trud,* all morning newspapers, will make their appearance on any particular day. The trucks may start loading at midnight—or at 6 A.M.

Home delivery of newspapers is by mail. Papers are usually distributed quickly in the morning mail. They also are available at newsstands run by a government agency. There are very few "paper boys" in the Soviet Union. However, it's recognized that a greater number of papers can be sold if paper boys are out hawking them, and the practice is being encouraged. It was reported in the Soviet press in 1958 that there were only fifty paper boys in Moscow, a city of almost five million inhabitants —4,847,000 according to the latest *Moscow Handbook,* a guide book sold at newsstands.

A type of Soviet newspaper that requires no delivery is the wall newspaper. Many Soviet enterprises—factories, offices, collective farms, educational institutes—post items of interest to their personnel on bulletin-board newspapers. The photographs of the most productive workers are put up for all to see as an intended incentive. "Innovators," those who develop new techniques for speeding up production, are invited to describe their methods. Often letters of criticism are published. A bricklaying team led by a Comrade N. Ermoshin wrote a letter to be published in the wall newspaper of Moscow subway workers. It read: "Work in our section is going too slowly. Much time is wasted on auxiliary operations. The crane stands idle due to the inefficiency of Antonov, the head of the section. Bricks are supplied by hand. This has told badly in our earnings. Yaremchuk, the chief of the building administration, has ignored our request to improve the organization of the work. It seems that the central administration of Metrostroi [the organization dealing with the continuing expansion of the subway] and its chief are not interested in this section of the work." The power of the "wall press" was demonstrated by changes being made to the satisfaction of the bricklayers.

There are no circulation wars among Soviet newspapers. Prices range from 20 kopecks (2 cents) to 40 kopecks (4 cents). Some papers such as *Pravda* vary their price with the number of pages: 20 kopecks for four pages; 30 kopecks for six. Annual subscriptions to newspapers are accepted only twice a year—at the end of November and May.

The emphasis is on getting as many people as possible to read newspapers (and thus to be familiar with Communist policies and ideologies) rather than on selling one newspaper or another. In line with this objective, newspapers such as *Pravda, Izvestia, Soviet Culture,* and others are posted on many buildings in long display frames behind glass to protect them from inclement weather. Passers-by pause to read the day's papers without charge.

Although Soviet newspapers do not compete for readers, they occasionally do engage in private feuds. Such was the case when the publication *Physical Culture and Sports* ran a piece reporting that Vladimir Kutz, Russia's great long-distance runner, had rushed out to the airport, about twenty miles from Moscow, to meet an arrival who he thought would be his friend and competitor Gordon Perry, the British track star. It turned out that the man who stepped from the plane was Fred Perry, the tennis player. The reason for Kutz's wasted trip, reported *Physical Culture and Sports,* was that Russia's main sports publication, *Soviet Sports,* had printed Gordon's instead of Fred's name. In its next edition *Soviet Sports* defended its reputation, indignantly denying that it had published anything about the arrival of either Fred *or* Gordon Perry, and calling the editors of *Physical Culture and Sports* a bunch of fabricators.

On another occasion *Pravda* took the editors of *Soviet Estonia* to task for not following through on their exposés. It was not enough, declared the big brother of Soviet publications, for *Soviet Estonia* simply to point to errors; the newspaper must stick to a complaint until the situation is remedied. For example, reporters of the Estonian newspaper had discovered that rough handling of bricks hauled by trucks from railroad sidings to a construction site resulted in damage to 25 per cent of the bricks. During the following month the newspaper published another report on the subject and ran an appeal to the head of the construction project to correct the situation. But this did not satisfy *Pravda.* A month had passed, complained *Pravda,* without another word having been published in *Soviet Estonia* on the subject. "Is this the proper attitude, to take a stand and then back down?"

asked *Pravda*. "Of course not, a newspaper must see to it that its criticism is effective."

That was not the sum total of *Pravda's* grievance. It seems that sometime earlier the newspaper's canny reporters had discovered that timetables were not posted at two bus stops. How long should it take to rectify such a simple omission, asked *Pravda* rhetorically. A day or two, estimated *Pravda*. But, it took *Soviet Estonia* two weeks before it published a response from competent authorities, stating that in the near future there would be timetables at all bus stops. *Pravda* took umbrage neither at the construction authorities for breaking bricks nor at the bus officials for neglecting to post timetables, but it berated the Estonian newspaper for lack of persistency in correcting these errors.

The editors of *Soviet Estonia* dutifully reprinted the *Pravda* complaint in full, without comment and without any subsequent conspicuous alteration in its editorial practices on exposés.

A rather more serious deviation was detected in a publication of the Defense Ministry by the editors of a newspaper of the same ministry. The *Military Herald,* a journal with a circulation limited to military men, published an article in April 1956, stating that Stalin had ignored warnings of the military intelligence of impending German attack and had thus left Russia unprepared. This was a mild denunciation, indeed, of Stalin compared to that uttered by Khrushchev four months earlier at the Communist Party congress. But now Kremlin authorities were drawing the reins on criticism of Stalin, lest license to denounce certain features of the Stalin era be taken as license for criticism of Communist authority itself.

What's more, in this case criticism of Stalin might be taken as criticism of the military and, worst of all, by a *military* publication. At that time Marshal Georgi Zhukov, already Defense Minister, had been named to full membership in the governing Communist Party Presidium. There is reason to believe that Zhukov jealously guarded the military against the slander of any association in Stalin's excesses and abuses.

An article in *Red Star* corrected the *Military Herald's* concept of what constituted permissible criticism of Stalin insofar as his military errors were concerned.

"Absolutely wrong and harmful views contained in a leading article in the *Military Herald's* fourth issue of 1956 could not but cause surprise and sorrow. This article asserts that our army had to wage the hard running battles of the retreat allegedly because the troops were not in a state of military readiness. . . .

"Whether the authors of the aforementioned article in the *Military Herald* wanted it or not, they played down the importance of our victory in the last war and the decisive part of the Soviet people and its armed forces in winning this victory.

"These incorrect views of the *Military Herald* are presented under the pretext of the struggle against the cult of the individual. It is indisputable that the struggle against the cult of the individual and its negative aftermaths are of great theoretical and practical importance, but there cannot be any putting up with such a state of affairs when, under the pretext of exposing this cult, the role of our party and its central committee, the role of our people and the Soviet Government both in strengthening defense capacity and in the organization and carrying out of the rout of Fascist Germany are minimized."

Red Star continued to set the record straight:

"The Communist Party, its Central Committee, the Soviet Government, long before the war started bore in mind that Fascist Germany would attack the U.S.S.R. sooner or later. They bore this in mind, taking practical steps to rebuff aggression.

"The Party, the government, tirelessly pushed the development of heavy industry as the main material basis of the defense capacity of our country. Thanks to this, our army and navy were equipped on the eve of the war with excellent types of military techniques and armaments in terms of those times."

This episode illustrates how cumbersome is the task of attuning all publications, even when, as in this case, controlled by the same organ of the state, to a precise prescribed theme.

Usually, there is uniformity among Soviet newspapers on the presentation of news. Such was the case in the Hungarian Revolution of 1956. The uprising began on October 23, 1956. For two days, while newspapers around the world recorded the words of Radio Budapest and of reporters on the scene, the event was totally ignored in Russia. On the twenty-fifth all Soviet newspapers carried the same brief dispatch circulated by Tass (Telegraphic Agency of Soviet Union, the official Soviet Government news agency) under the headline (also distributed by Tass), "Failure of Anti-Popular Venture in Budapest." It said that an attempt to provoke "a counterrevolutionary revolt" had been prepared for a long time with "forces of foreign reaction systematically egging on anti-popular elements to rise against lawful rule."

The dispatch continued: "Hostile elements pounced on yesterday's (October 23) student demonstration in the capital as a pretext for sending into the streets shock groups of rebels, standing in readiness, and to sow confusion among the people in an attempt to provoke mass disorders. A number of state and public institutions and enterprises were attacked. Unbridled Fascist thugs began to loot shops, break windows in houses and offices, and tried to spoil equipment of industrial establishments. Gangs of rebels who had managed to seize arms provoked bloodshed in a number of places."

The Tass report added that martial law had been declared and that Soviet military units had assisted troops of the Hungarian People's Republic to restore law and order. Probably Soviet authorities would have preferred to blanket the events in silence, but the fact that broadcasts of Radio Budapest could be heard in Moscow made it imperative for Soviet news publications to acknowledge that something was going on.

For three subsequent days after acknowledging trouble, Soviet newspapers hopefully ran variations of the same headline, "Counterrevolutionary Attempt Crushed." But events did not conform with the Soviet headlines. Soviet troops (briefly withdrawn) returned in force to the streets of Budapest. Russians learned of developments from English language broadcasts from abroad. Soviet authorities acknowledged that the Hungarian uprising could no longer be regarded as a minor mutiny, quickly crushed. Overnight, Soviet meager mention was transformed into a torrent of attention. The events were presented as a counterrevolution, inspired by the United States and its "imperialist" allies against the popular will of Hungarian workers and peasants who had appealed to their Soviet "brothers" to deliver them from "Western oppression." Day after day, Soviet newspapers played on and elaborated this theme in columns and columns of newsprint.

By November 20 Soviet newspapers were publishing their accounts by Tass and their special reporters under the headline "Life in Hungary Is Rapidly Becoming Normal." This headline replaced one which had been running for several days: "Life in Hungary Is Slowly Becoming Normal." The accounts, however, mentioned "resistance and even direct terroristic acts of counterrevolutionary elements." To Soviet readers, who have learned to read between the lines, this seemed somewhat unlike normal life, slow or rapid.

Soviet newspapers almost always are humorless except for occasional attempts at satire. Such was the case in the treatment of a report from New York that two citizens had been denied fishing licenses because of their Communist affiliations. This motivated *Soviet Russia* to propose "Rules and Statutes for Orderly and Well-Behaved, Piscatorial Pursuits." The satirical statutes included these:

"1. Fish must not be removed from ponds without labor. Accordingly, every town dweller must testify under oath that neither he, his friends, nor chance pedestrians met, have any affiliation with the Communist Party or any sympathies for Communism. The inhabitants must necessarily submit all fingers used in the handling of fishing tackle for the purpose of their fingerprinting." (This was at a time when American regulations requiring fingerprinting of foreign visitors irked Soviet authorities. The Kremlin maintained that fingerprinting was an insult, suitable only for criminals.)

"2. Honest fishermen are forbidden to see brother-anglers from afar. Farsighted vision and human intercourse undermine the pillars of American democracy.

"3. Any fish charged and found to have been hooked by a Communist or any person disapproving of American policy shall be summoned to appear before the Un-American Activities Committee.

"4. Fishes shall be forbidden to seek for deeper pools to swim, that town dwellers may not be encouraged to seek better places for human habitation. There are no objections to fishes spawning pearls before swine, the powers-that-be."

Vicious comment is not limited to attacks, satirical and direct, on capitalists. When in power the Soviet hierarchy is exempt from all but praise, but once deposed, the Berias, Molotovs, Kaganoviches, Zhukovs are heaped with venom. Lesser personages are vulnerable at any time. An old woman who tends a newsstand near the Bolshoi Theatre told me that readers prefer *feuilletons* to politics. A *feuilleton,* a word adopted by the Russians from the French, is an article of criticism or an exposé. "I always fold my papers," confided the woman, "to show a *feuilleton* on top. People will buy that paper first. It's because we Russians like gossip."

The director of the Kiev zoo, Joseph Vasilievich Kravchenko, was exposed in a *feuilleton* published by *Truth of the Ukraine* for failing to provide proper winter quarters for the elephants. Several caught cold. The director purchased great quantities of first-class vodka to nurse the animals back to health, but, according to *Truth of the Ukraine,* during the Revolution Day holiday in November much of the vodka failed to reach the ailing elephants. The director and the zoo's veterinarian intercepted it for human festivities.

Not infrequently these *feuilletons* reveal aspects of Soviet life which ordinarily are concealed. *Trud* ran such an article on beggars (who, visiting foreigners are told, no longer exist in the Soviet Union). *Trud* gave the case history of one vagrant with nine court convictions for theft by the time he was thirty years old. Upon his release from jail the ninth time, he decided that it was easier to beg than to steal. He married a woman named Valya (who had been in jail eight times and apparently shared his outlook). He put a bandage across his eyes, she took a pair of crutches, and together they embarked on a career as beggars. They averaged 350 rubles ($35) a day, which is better than a factory worker's week's wage. Recently, said *Trud,* the couple took a month off to vacation at a Black Sea resort.

Warming up to its subject, *Trud* told of another Russian beggar whose technique was to enter a subway train and shout:

" 'I'm not a wounded soldier nor a cripple, but just a guy off my nut. I don't like to talk much and I'm not responsible for myself.' Then, casting a savage eye at the passengers and brandishing a cane over their heads, he would yell: 'Come on brothers, shake out your pockets.' "

This brand of begging by intimidation paid off well too, said *Trud.*

Quite another technique was employed by a beggar operating on Moscow suburban trains. As *Trud* told it, he would limp through the train whining:" 'Brothers and sisters. Old folks. Don't leave a veteran of three wars without help. Help your country's defender with your well-earned kopeck.'

"He then slowly rolled his eyes at the ceiling, jerked his head twice, and limping on both legs, slowly moved through the coach.

'Help me brothers. Help me sisters,' he nodded to either side like a puppet on strings.

"Taking pity, the passengers gave alms, some a 10-kopeck bit, some a 20-kopeck coin, and the kinder-hearted, a whole ruble.

"After traversing the entire train, this (self-styled) 'veteran of three wars' disembarked at Perove station."

"Here," continued the *Trud* account, "we witnessed a miraculous transformation. He easily straightened out his legs and made haste for the station's refreshment bar.

" 'A quarter bottle of vodka and a chaser,' he shouted at the bartender.

"He gulped down the vodka straight from the bottle and finished it off with a glass of beer."

Trud's feuilleton entitled "Without Shame, Without Conscience," expressed indignation that additional laws were needed effectively to prevent panhandling. (Such a law was subsequently decreed.)

In another *feuilleton,* the weekly satirical magazine *Krokodil* took to task the managers of "The Road to Communism" collective farm in the Far Eastern region of the Soviet Union for an unorthodox and expensive wolf hunt. Instead of ridding the farm of the wolves by organizing hunting groups, it was decided to rent an airplane from the state's Aeroflot line and to pursue the animals from the sky. After seventy-one hours of aerial hunting and the firing of 600 bullets, the hunters had a bill of 95,124 rubles ($9512) and three dead deer, who hadn't been bothering anyone, to show for it.

Krokodil's chief contribution to Soviet journalism is the cartoon which lampoons features of Soviet life although the main target is capitalists and imperialists. The common fault of Soviet enterprises of having a disproportionately large managerial staff is reflected in a cartoon showing the manager of a state store declaring: "We are not overstaffed. There are only two chiefs and one worker." The weekly magazine *Ogenyok* (meaning "Little Flame") also carries cartoons among its short stories and articles. One cartoon is aimed against dogmatism on the part of directors of certain institutions. A museum director is shouting at his assistant as they stand before a statue of Venus de Milo, "This is shameful. Why are there no arms?"

The assistant replies timidly: "Comrade director, this is a Venus."

"Indeed," fires back the director, "I won't have people injuring even a Venus. Have the arms restored immediately."

Another *Krokodil* cartoon comments on the failure of police to stamp out hooliganism (a word that has found its way into Russian). The cartoon shows a street filled with young toughs. Fist fights are going on. Several hooligans are throwing bricks through store windows. Others are snatching pocketbooks from struggling women. A policeman, his back turned to the violence, is giving an order to a meek, frightened street cleaner, "When the fighting is over, see to it that you have the street cleaned up of debris right away."

One of the few Moscow newspapers that carries advertising is *Evening Moscow,* published by the *Mossoviet* (the Moscow City Council). This is Moscow's liveliest newspaper, largely so because page four of its four pages is devoted to ads. Russians line up at newsstands to buy copies.

In general there's a great deal less advertising in the Soviet Union than in capitalistic countries. There's less reason for it. In a country with rival manufacturers of the same type of product, advertising is necessary to induce customers to buy one product instead of a competitor's. There is no question in Russia of what manufacturer's tooth paste or champagne to buy. There's only one manufacturer, the government. This eliminates competition in the capitalistic sense; it also eliminates competitive advertising among manufacturers to attract the buyer.

Advertising is supposed to serve quite another function in the Soviet Union. It is supposed to inform. On occasion, the Soviet style of advertising has been criticized in Russian newspapers for failing in its function; it is not enough for a sign to say, as do some, "Drink Tomato Juice." A proper Soviet advertising sign should serve the Soviet citizen explaining why it will benefit him to drink juice, what uses juice can be put to, and so on.

There is no advertising on either radio or television. Besides the one page in *Evening Moscow* there are increasing numbers of neon signs on buildings. One depicts a moving taxi and reads: "Use Taxis. The most convenient type of transport." Nearby, an electric sign over the Metropole Hotel urges Russians to use air transport for speed. There are neon signs instructing people to dial 01 in case of fire, to drink "Narzan" mineral water, and to take vitamin pills. A running electric sign of the sort that fringes the New York *Times* building in Times Square graces *Izvestia's* modern building just off Gorki Street. However, it's not the latest news that plays across *Izvestia's* sign; rather various products are repetitiously advertised.

Advertising is serious, sober, entirely devoid of "sex appeal." Attractive blondes in low-cut dresses—so widely employed in selling everything from aspirin to automobiles in the U.S.A.—are never used in Soviet ads.

It is not at all unusual to find that a product displayed in a store-window advertisement is not available inside the store.

Roof-top green neon signs urge citizens to: "Buy 3% Lottery Loan Bonds." On the same subject of advising people what to do with their money, red neon suggests: "Save money in savings banks." Other neon tubing reads: "State insurance. Insurance of property. Insurance of life."

Brand names are omitted because there are no brands. Moscow signs simply read:

"Buy canned goods."

"Buy cakes, sweet and plentiful."

"Subscribe to newspapers and magazines."

"Best gift to buy—at the jeweler's."

One of the most colorful neon signs in Moscow advertises no product, but rather a precautionary word to Muscovites: "Take fire-precaution measures to save your home from fire. Carelessness leads to fire." A bold red and green neon sign in Dzerzhinskiy Square across from the Children's World department store and secret-police headquarters reads: "Dial 01 in case of fire."

Another ad on the same subject urges Russians: "To avoid fire, switch off electric gadgets and gas equipment when leaving your home."

Pravda carries a brief listing of theater performances for that day, but only *Evening Moscow* carries a schedule of television programs; radio and television keep their audiences informed on the air of what's coming, and there is a weekly publication that consists of program listings.

Evening Moscow is also the only newspaper that carries divorce notices. Before a divorce becomes final in the Soviet Union, it is necessary for a notice to be published. About twenty-five such notices are printed daily, and it's said that some people wait a year or more before they are able to complete the legal requirements for divorce because of the bottleneck of lack of divorce notice space in the four-page newspaper. When published the notice reads like this:

"Grishin Nikolai Vasilievich, living on Solyanca 10, apartment 3, brings divorce suit against Grishina Margarita Josefovna, living in the same place. Case to be considered by the people's court, 1st division, Proletariat district, city of Moscow."

Movies also are advertised in *Evening Moscow* in conservative ads. "Today and every day. See on the screen in the capital a new feature movie, *One Night,* based on a play by B. Gorbatov. Produced by Lenfilm" (the Leningrad film studio).

Another ad reads: "The All-Union Research Institute of Horse Breeding invites a junior scientific worker for its economics department. A candidate's degree in economics or agricultural sciences is required."

"A new monthly magazine," announces an advertisement, "is put out, called *Questions of Literature,* published by the Union of Soviet Writers and the U.S.S.R. Academy of Science's Gorki Institute of World Literature. The magazine will print research works on the theory of literature, its history, basic problems of modern literature, and its teaching in both secondary and higher schools. Scientific controversies will be held on the pages of the magazine and reviews published. The subscription for twelve months is 72 rubles ($7.20)."

Occasionally, a more unusual ad appears. Once the Moscow film studio asked people to sell or rent the studio Caucassian style daggers and belts for a movie under production.

A Moscow store advertised, "We will buy clothing at your home." For a fee of 10 rubles ($1.00) the store would send a purchasing agent to the home to set a price on second-hand clothing, fur items, and shoes. "Save time. Use our service," urged the ad.

Typical of ads in the Tbilisi newspaper, *Dawn of the East,* is this Ministry of Communications announcement prior to a Revolution Day celebration:

PUBLIC NOTICE.
CITIZENS!
In all post offices in town congratulatory telegrams on the fortieth anniversary of the great October Revolution are being received ahead of time with the time of delivery marked.
These are received at favorable rates with 50 per cent discount. Don't forget to congratulate your relatives and friends on the holiday. Sending these cables ahead of time saves you time and money.

Ads offering to exchange apartments are displayed on glass-enclosed notice boards on Moscow buildings, where for a small charge a Russian may offer his apartment or his services as, say, an English teacher or typewriting instructor. Provincial papers carry a limited number of personal ads such as this one in *Dawn of the East*:

TRADE APARTMENTS.

Would exchange two rooms, 49 square meters, conveniences provided, for equal space in Kalinin district. Inquire daily from 2 to 5 P.M., address: Tzeretelli Street, 18, second entrance, Dolidze's apartment.

A Soviet newspaper office is a far cry from those of Western dailies. There is no large city room or news room, astir with the activity of meeting a deadline. There are no reporters seated at desks, no horseshoe-shaped copy desk where headlines are written and dispatches edited.

Pravda reporters and editors work in separate, private offices in a quiet atmosphere like a library's. "This arrangement makes more thoughtful work possible than in a noisy room with many people," explained Danyil Kraminov, American affairs editor, when he received me. It had taken two weeks to arrange the appointment. An elevator took me to Kraminov's fourth-floor office in the gloomily gray *Pravda* building, three miles from the center of Moscow. Kraminov sat behind a small, glass-topped desk in front of a map of the world and described *Pravda's* operations. There are eighty people on the editorial staff. This is a small number by comparison with a metropolitan daily in Paris, London, Tokyo, or New York. But then, *Pravda's* size does not warrant a larger staff. The twenty editors who comprise the editorial board are members of the Communist Party. Only one in five of the other staff members are, though.

The staff is divided into fifteen departments, including Party life, economics, cultural, agriculture, literature, and arts, and foreign affairs, which itself is divided according to regions of the world. There is also a department devoted entirely to *feuilletons*. "We must be very cautious with *feuilletons*," said Kraminov, "because most of those we write about consider themselves unjustly accused. We spend time gathering the facts so that we can prove them wrong if they argue afterwards. Sometimes a *feuilleton* writer will spend several weeks on one."

Besides the editorial staff at work in Moscow, *Pravda* correspondents are assigned to each republic capital, and there are twenty correspondents stationed abroad in New York, Washington, Berlin, Bonn, Vienna, Peiping, New Delhi, Paris, Rome, and elsewhere.

Kraminov himself sent free-lance pieces to newspapers while a student, then went to work for *Izvestia* and transferred to Tass before going to *Pravda*. As a Tass correspondent, Kraminov had worked in Stockholm and London. About twelve members of the staff are graduates of the Institute of International Affairs. Others have completed courses in institutes of journalism. Several members of the editorial staff began by writing letters from collective farms and factories. The paper receives an average of a thousand letters per day. Most *feuilletons* originate from a complaint or tip in a reader's letter.

The working day at *Pravda* begins at three in the afternoon. *Pravda* publishes seven days a week; most Soviet newspapers take Monday off. The day begins with a brief editorial conference, lasting usually less than a half hour, at which the contents for the next morning's paper are reviewed and the contents for the day after that planned. The editorial conference decides the layout of news, but Kraminov denied that other newspapers follow *Pravda's* lead on what to print where. "It's not difficult," shrugged Kraminov. "All of our newspapers have the same tradition. Foreign items are regularly published on pages three and four. Domestic news on pages one and two." However, the similarity of make-up of Soviet newspapers leads a regular reader to believe that some liaison more dependable than tradition or coincidence causes *Izvestia* and other papers to follow *Pravda's* standards. *Pravda's* statements and editorials may be taken as Communist policy. No pretense is made on this score. *Pravda* is the publication of the Party. Its top editors are members of the Party's Central Committee. They are in close daily contact with the Party's leaders. There is no mere chance involved when *Pravda* takes a stand on an issue. Rather, it is an expression of Communist doctrine. However, Kraminov disclaimed that guidance is necessary whenever *Pravda* prints an editorial of importance. "We would be very bad journalists," he said, "if we couldn't interpret correctly, for example, the foreign policy of our government when an international issue arises."

Kraminov considers himself a political worker. There is no attempt at objectivity. That is not considered necessary or desirable. The paper's job and the role of the journalist are not to present news in an objective way but rather in a way that furthers the interests of the Party and the Soviet state. This is also the Kremlin's objective—but one much more difficult to fulfill—in the case of news sent out of the Soviet Union. Foreign correspondents are permitted into the U.S.S.R. because it is the price of reciprocation that the Kremlin must pay for its reporters to be stationed abroad. Soviet authorities try to control the news sent out of Russia by imposing censorship on the words written by foreign correspondents stationed in the Soviet Union. To use a favorite phrase of *Pravda's* the censors do not always "fully fulfill the glorious state task" assigned to them.

LEFT: Women workers painting fence near museum church in Leningrad.

BELOW: Moscow classroom. Teacher. Boys and girls at double desks, in uniform.

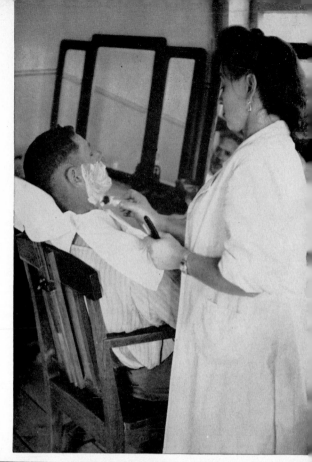

RIGHT: Woman barber gives customer shave in a Ukraine town shop.

BELOW: Moscow subway train.

RIGHT: Children at play in Soviet Park of Culture and Rest.

BELOW: Open-air "free market" in Kharkov.

RIGHT: Two Russian girls with typical long braids at Moscow Agricultural Exhibition.

BELOW: Collective-farm-village street.

CHAPTER 13

THE SOVIET LEADERS WERE EQUALLY LIT UP

It was the Soviet Revolution Day holiday. The magnificent St. George's Hall of the Kremlin's Grand Palace was the scene of a party for the top thousand Russian officials. Long buffet tables were covered with cold delicacies and wines, champagnes, vodka, and liquors. Everyone drank freely. Around midnight, dancing began in the adjoining domed Hall of St. Vladimir. Anastas Mikoyan, his mustached mouth laughing, led buxom, usually businesslike, blond Ekaterina Furtseva in a vigorous Armenian dance. Mikoyan tried several times to draw Nikita Khrushchev onto the dance floor, but Khrushchev resisted. Finally, Khrushchev took Mikoyan firmly by the arm, talked earnestly into his ear, and Mikoyan desisted. There are those who believed that Khrushchev had reminded Mikoyan of the time that Stalin had intimidated stocky Khrushchev into performing a Ukrainian *gopack* dance against his will—a recollection which Khrushchev had submitted as testimony of Stalin's cruelty in his famous denunciation of Stalin.

This little sidelight encounter between Khrushchev and Mikoyan did not detract from the boisterous gaiety. I tried to take pictures. Plainclothes security police quickly placed themselves between me and the dance floor each time I raised my camera. The Presidium leaders may have been in their cups, but their bodyguards were very sober and determined to prevent this minor orgy from being recorded on film. At midnight a galaxy of fireworks burst over the Kremlin.

In describing the occasion in my broadcast the next day I wondered how I could convey the atmosphere of inebriation that had prevailed. The Soviet censors, who must place their stamp of approval on every news story before it leaves Russia, certainly would not pass any intimation that the Soviet leaders were drunk.

Finally, I began my broadcast script:

"Fireworks lit up the sky over the Kremlin, and inside the Soviet leaders were equally lit up."

The censors passed it.

The idiom apparently escaped the censor, perhaps himself a bit sleepy from his holiday libations; or else he interpreted "lit up" to mean that the Soviet leaders were radiant in celebration.

Censorship in Russia is in some ways capricious, in some ways predictable.

You can be sure in advance that any criticism of the Soviet leaders will be deleted. Any attempt at humor or sarcasm is, in this respect, discouraged.

For example, on one occasion a number of royal visits were taking place in Western Europe, and Khrushchev was lecturing to a Soviet agricultural conference about the growing of cabbages and other crops, I began a broadcast script this way: "In these days when Kings and Queens of England, Holland and Iran are off on pomp-and-circumstance visits to foreign lands, the unkingly proletarian leader of Communism, Nikita Khrushchev has been absent, too, from the Kremlin palaces to talk to his people about cabbages."

The censor crossed out the word "unkingly," although Comrade Khrushchev, as a good Communist, would probably have been the first to deny any monarchial traits. For good measure the censor also deleted the word "palaces," perhaps more to deny that Khrushchev frequented the palaces in the Kremlin grounds than to deny that such palaces exist.

During a period when diplomatic notes were being dispatched from the Kremlin at the rate of one a day, I speculated, "You can't help wondering how many people the Kremlin has on the job of writing letters to leaders of other countries." Out went the phrase. Apparently any speculation that anyone but Premier Khrushchev himself was engaged in the composition of these notes was considered derogatory to Khrushchev.

Words that may be passed for a period of time later become forbidden. For instance, after Khrushchev's denunciation of Stalin in February

1956, almost any word describing Stalin would be approved. A correspondent could speak of Stalin's "cruelty," "oppression," "sins," "crimes," or "excesses." Then came the Hungarian Revolution, caused in part by the easing of controls consequent on de-Stalinization. Khrushchev revised his evaluation. He described Stalin as a "model" Communist in some respects and said that he and his colleagues were all "Stalinists" when it came to the class struggle. The censor fell into step. Reference to Stalin's "errors" would be passed, but anything more drastic fell victim to the censor's pencil.

At a time when the Kremlin was in the process of formulating policy toward Premier Charles DeGaulle and his new French constitution the censors were extremely sensitive about any speculation on the possible resultant Soviet attitude. In fact, when a correspondent submitted a cable simply quoting, without a word of comment, the section on DeGaulle from the official Soviet Encyclopedia, the dispatch was not returned by the censor. The correspondent was told that it would not be passed. The Encyclopedia was sharply critical of DeGaulle but at that time it was not sure that Soviet policy would be too. (Later it was.)

At a time when Nikolai Bulganin had been deprived of his position as Premier and was about to lose his seat on the Party Presidium, the censor would not place his stamp of approval on any reference to Bulganin. Even when I mentioned in a script the simple fact that it was Bulganin's birthday the censors stopped it.

In writing about present Soviet leaders there's little gamble involved. Anything complimentary gets passed. Anything smacking at all of disdain, disrespect, or disparagement gets killed.

However, on other aspects of the Soviet scene there's a greater element of chance. A censor on duty in the morning may delete a phrase that a censor in the evening will approve, or vice versa There's the human element involved, even among censors. One is stricter than another, or braver in sticking out his neck, or more careless

At different times, on the same day and in different stories, I've had the phrase "Soviet satellite nations" approved by one censor and deleted by another. One censor has passed the reference to Stalin as an "iron-fisted dictator"; another has crossed out "iron-fisted" but left in "dictator." In still another script, both words were eliminated.

The censors have been known to edit what the leaders say—presumably on instructions from above. Once Khrushchev lost his temper with a visiting lady member of France's parliament who expressed astonishment that women perform hard physical labor in Russia. According to accounts by the parliamentary group, the Communist chairman pointed out that, at least in Russia, the women were engaged in honest toil whereas in France women were reduced to prostitution. You could not, he continued, walk down the street in Paris without being accosted by a prostitute.

This portion of Khrushchev's conversation, as well as some of his off-the-cuff remarks to correspondents at receptions were deleted by the censors.

The element of capriciousness does not simplify a correspondent's job. It does add a bit of levity, though, to the enraging and rather degrading procedure of submitting material to a censor. The story is told of one newspaperman who submitted an account of Soviet housing conditions which spoke of every "nook and cranny" being utilized for living space. The censor left "nook" but deleted "cranny."

During Stalin's latter years censorship was extremely severe. It was impossible during one period for correspondents to do more than transmit what was contained in Soviet government statements and in Soviet newspapers. Even a parenthetical mention of the weather, in describing a May Day parade, was stricken from a dispatch. Apparently weather was considered information of military importance to an enemy planning a sneak attack.

Censorship eased up considerably after Stalin's death. It became feasible to describe crowded Soviet housing conditions, to mention student restlessness, to refer to mistakes in Soviet policy toward Tito.

It would be self-delusion to believe that the knowledge that material must be submitted to a censor does not tend to create inhibitions in writing. When the clock is ticking away the minutes before broadcast time, the tendency is to avoid a phrase that may delay the broadcast script on the censor's desk. You tone down a phrase. You omit an adjective.

It works the other way too. The resentment that censorship generates may tend to color a correspondent's attitude even toward Soviet statements or events which are not deserving of criticism.

Like other correspondents, a working rule which I soon made for myself was that I would try not to write *for* the censor. Recognizing the inhibitions and aggressions engendered by censorship, I would try to write things as I saw them and let the onus of making alterations fall on the censor. If a news story was so altered by the censor as to change its intent or attitude, then I would simply scrap that story. I did this more times than I care to remember. But often I was more surprised by what got through than by what was killed by the censor.

These are the mechanics of censorship:

A correspondent hands his copy to a girl clerk seated at a counter in a second-floor suite of rooms provided for foreign newsmen in the Central Telegraph Office, a gray stone, six-story building on a corner of Moscow's main thoroughfare, Gorki Street.

She assigns it a number and takes it into a back room. Some minutes or hours later, a light flashes on her desk as a signal that the censor has completed his work.

Correspondents are required to write at the bottom of dispatches intended for cabling: "Corrections at my risk." This euphemism serves as permission from the correspondent to the censor to make deletions.

These deletions are usually accomplished with a black pencil, less often in ink, and occasionally are obliterated with typewriter X's. An especially offensive script may be given the scissors treatment; the page being returned in truncated form, inevitably with the writer's most precious phrases remaining in the censor's basket.

Sometimes a story is delayed for a day or longer. This may be due to the censor's checking with an official concerned with the subject of the story. Sometimes a story is killed. In such cases the clerk informs the correspondent. Since you never see the censor you cannot argue with him. Occasionally correspondents, crowded by a deadline, have found it useful to hand the clerk a note for the censor, either berating him or pleading with him, according to the nature of the correspondent. Depending on the nature of the censor this has been useful or fruitless in producing a decision on the copy.

There are various ways a correspondent may transmit a story. In the case of "feature" material it may be sent by airmail. Most often it is either sent by radio (or cable) or it is telephoned. Since one copy of the three sheets which a correspondent submits to the censor is sent to the telegraph operators, cables are transmitted exactly as they come off the censor's desk. However, instead of cabling, if a correspondent telephones his story to London or Frankfurt or New York he may try to dictate a word or paragraph that has been deleted by the censor. Sometimes the correspondent will get away with it. Sometimes not. An alert censor monitoring the conversation will pull the plug or switch and leave the correspondent with a dead line. Such is also the case for my broadcasts.

When I try to broadcast censored lines I succeed sometimes, but more often I lose my Moscow-London-New York broadcast for that day.

Soviet authorities usually shun use of the word censorship. When asked by correspondents about it, Leonid Ilyichev, at that time chief of the Foreign Ministry's press department, responded that there is no censorship, but that facilities exist to assist a correspondent in avoiding mistakes in his dispatches. This, of course, is not precisely the case. Ordinarily, the censors have no interest in eliminating errors. A correspondent may write, for example, that there are 12 or 100 Soviet republics (rather than the 15 which there are) and the censor will not lift a black pencil to save him the possible embarrassment of the mistake getting into print or on the air.

There was the instance when Soviet authorities were roundly criticized for their extravagance and bad taste in architecture. Included in the newspaper editorial criticism was the name, among many others, of Alexander Vlasov, described as the "former" chief architect of Moscow. An American correspondent took this to mean that Vlasov had been fired from his job, as were some of the other architects mentioned in the piece. He wrote in his dispatch that Vlasov had been denounced and fired.

It was true that Vlasov was the *former* chief architect of Moscow. But he had left that job a number of months previously to take a higher post in the Soviet Academy of Architects.

At the time of the editorial criticism of architects, Vlasov was completing a tour of the United States with a delegation of Soviet construction experts. His presence abroad gave the story prominence there. When Vlasov's ship arrived in France he was astonished to find himself the object of unsought solicitude by scores of anti-Communist Russian *émigrés*. He required police escort to protect him from Russian expatriates who were convinced that he would want to seek haven in France rather than face the wrath of Kremlin authorities for his architectural errors.

Apparently the demonstrations were a source of embarrassment and anxiety to Vlasov. When he returned to Moscow he must have expressed his chagrin. Soviet newspapers ran articles bitterly berating the perpetrators of this "provocation." It was an "anti-Soviet plot, an insult, a defamation."

The correspondent who made the mistake was called before Ilyichev and sharply warned that any repetition of such inaccurate reporting would have serious consequences. (The correspondent later was given seven days to leave Russia.) However, there was no suggestion—which would have been consistent with the Soviet claim that censorship was a corrective service—that a duty lay with the censor in the first place to have caught the erroneous dispatch that Vlasov had been fired.

Only very rarely does the censor's pencil modify a dispatch. During the Hungarian affair a censor inserted the word "counter" before my description of the uprising as a "revolution." In Soviet semantics it was a "counterrevolution," which is an uprising by reactionaries against the true "revolutionaries," namely, the Communists. Another instance of editing by the censors is said to have occurred years ago when a correspondent reported that he and others had stood "within a stone's throw" of Stalin. The censor inserted the words, "but no one threw a stone."

Semantics work two ways. The censors never objected to the description of the Soviet leaders as "proletariat dictators." In the Communist lexicon the Soviet state is a "dictatorship of the proletariat," the working class. This phrase has one ring to the ears of a Communist; quite another to an American or Briton.

Occasionally, bitter to admit, the censors are actually helpful.

When Anna Pankratova, a leading Soviet historian, died, I wrote a broadcast in which I compared her in importance with other leading Communist Party women such as Ekaterina Furtseva, candidate member of the Party's Presidium, and Maria Dimitraeva Kovrigina, Health Minister. The script concluded, "At the most recent Communist Party congress, historian *Kovrigina* stood up and acknowledged that she'd used the wrong approach on Stalin. Her textbook *History of the Soviet Union* was rewritten. History is flexible in the Soviet Union."

The last sentence was too flip for the censor's taste. It was deleted.

But, with rare helpfulness, the censor caught my error in writing "historian Kovrigina" rather than "historian Pankratova." He underlined Kovrigina's name and placed a question mark above it.

From time to time censorship has had certain loopholes. Prior to 1945 censorship applied only to material cabled from the Soviet Union. A correspondent could telephone his stories to the outside world free of censorship. He might be subject to a warning or expulsion if something particularly objectionable appeared abroad, but there was no censorship of the actual telephone call. This loophole was sealed.

In 1955 it became possible to send television news film from Moscow.

What's more, it was not necessary to develop the film or submit it to censorship. This was an inconsistency. Prints of still photographs were supposed to be submitted to the censor for approval prior to sending abroad by radio or by mail, but a roll of movie film for newsreels or television could be sent through the Soviet post or by air freight without being inspected. Eventually the authorities sealed this loophole too. In any event, there always was at least a degree of *pre*-censorship in the authorities' controlling to an extent *what* could be photographed.

Also, radio recording tapes could be sent out without a censor hearing what had been recorded. Presumably a correspondent was supposed to have submitted in advance the script to be recorded, and there was always the knowledge that anything particularly offensive on the tape might come to the attention of Soviet Embassy officials abroad when it was played on the air.

Where loopholes did not exist correspondents often tried to make them.

Such was the case when the censors refused, for a time, to pass references to the execution of five security-police officials and the imprisonment of three others in the city of Tbilisi (also known as Tiflis). This seemed particularly illogical, because a broadcast of the Tbilisi radio had been monitored in London, announcing the trial and sentences. Correspondents in Moscow were receiving cables from their home offices (incoming cables are not censored) informing them of the Tbilisi broadcast and asking for confirmation and any details. Even when the Tbilisi newspaper arrived in Moscow with a court item recording the event the censors continued to cut out any mention of it in outgoing dispatches.

Finally, when one correspondent was telephoning another story of an innocuous nature to his London office, he remarked:

"Say, about what you've been asking me. It's true that there's a basketball team down in that city named after that terrible social disease (syphilis, as in Tiflis) that's been put out of action for good. Three other guys on the team have been benched for ten years."

Actually, the Russians hurt themselves by censorship.

The knowledge that material from Russia is censored convinces people abroad that much is untold, that dark secrets are withheld from publication even outside Russia. In effect, everything that is known by foreigners in Russia about Russia is also known outside. The only feasible way to impose effective censorship is to seal the frontiers of a country. However, the presence in the Soviet Union of diplomats, the flow of tourists, including visiting journalists and Russian-speaking professors, in and out of Russia makes it impossible to keep any secrets that are known to foreigners in Russia from getting out of Russia. Even accredited correspondents resident in Moscow are permitted to enter and re-enter the Soviet Union whenever they wish. It's not unknown for a correspondent on such a trip to write about student restlessness or about detrimental effects of Khrushchev's de-Stalinization speech or about strains in Soviet-Chinese relations (any of which the censors would alter), and to have the story released by a bureau of his organization in another city without attribution to him.

During Stalin's time a correspondent going abroad received only an exit visa and had to apply all over again for a visa to come back. This inhibited any inclination to break censorship by such devices.

Censorship in a country where travelers enter and leave can at best (from the Soviet viewpoint) only serve to delay a story. At worst (again from the Soviet viewpoint) it encourages exaggerations and distortions being published abroad. The fact that a story is cut by the censors naturally stimulates imaginations. Surprisingly, the censors permit correspondents to send their editors a cable informing them that a story has been distorted or shortened by censorship. Soviet experts and not-so-experts take the limited information as cue for elaboration and speculation.

Such was true in the case of the "mystery patient":

The story broke in Bonn, capital of West Germany. Professor Hans Schulton, a specialist in blood diseases at the Cologne University, was asked by a diplomat at the Soviet Embassy in Bonn to fly to Moscow to treat a patient described as a member of the Soviet government. Dr. Schulton was met at Moscow's airport by representatives of the Ministry of Health and was told in reply to his inquiry that the patient's name was "a secret." Even when Dr. Schulton examined the patient he did not learn his identity.

The censors passed accounts of Dr. Schulton's arrival, his comment that the patient was critically ill, and even that he did not think it was one of the top Presidium members whom he likely would have recognized from photographs. But, the press department of the Soviet Foreign Ministry, to which such inquiries from correspondents must be directed refused to identify the "mystery man."

This led to wild speculation abroad. The most fantastic story was published in a New York tabloid which reported an argument in the Kremlin which ended with Lazar Kaganovich, first deputy premier, being shot. Apparently, as Kaganovich lay bleeding to death, the assassins among his Kremlin colleagues thought better of it and decided to save his life, enlisting the aid of a West German specialist. The story was completely false.

The doctor remained several days and departed, unable to contribute to the patient's recovery. A few weeks later the "mystery" patient died, and obituaries in the Soviet newspapers announced the death of V. A. Malyshev, Minister of Machine Building.

Diplomats had learned earlier, to their satisfaction, by the doctor's description of the patient and by cocktail-party conversation with Russians, that the "mystery" man was Malyshev. At least one correspondent had passed on the information to his office before his telephone line was cut. (He was later summoned to the Foreign Ministry and warned that future violations would have serious consequences.)

Censorship in this episode seemed to serve no useful Soviet purpose. It only delayed identifying the man. It only prompted erroneous speculation in the outside world.

In an interview with Turner Catledge, managing editor of the New York *Times,* Khrushchev was asked about censorship. The transcript of the exchange, as recorded by Khrushchev's interpreter, Oleg Troyanovsky, son of the Soviet Union's first ambassador to the United States, is instructive.

Catledge: "As a representative of a big American paper, I stand for a free exchange of information. In this connection I would like to ask you whether you do not think that the censorship which exists in the Soviet Union is unjustified and creates more problems than it solves. The dispatches of foreign correspondents in the U.S.A. and the other Western states are not subject to censorship."

Khrushchev: "The control of press reports or, as you put it, censorship, is practiced in the Soviet Union only with regard to slanderous dispatches. The Soviet people cannot remain indifferent to slanderers who distort reality in their dispatches and write all sorts of concoctions.

"Neither can we remain impartial to those who call for the disruption of the normal life of society or for murders. If the statements of these people are restricted, it does not mean a restriction of the freedom of the press. And so, when some correspondent or another wants to send abroad misleading dispatches that do not correspond to the real state of affairs, our authorities take measures to prevent such incorrect, slanderous dispatches from appearing. I believe this is right.

"I would say that, as a matter of fact, this is not censorship but only a more rational employment of the material means of society, so that funds are not wasted on telegraph communications, paper and so on. We wish to use all for the benefit of society and not to its detriment. Thus, when the proper authorities hold up erroneous or false dispatches, do not publish them, this is for the good of society. This is our understanding of the question."

Khrushchev's concern about wasting the money of American news organizations on cable and broadcast-circuit tolls, and especially his concern about conserving paper were the source of wry comment among correspondents for some time.

However, it soon became evident that Khrushchev's words had lent the censors new confidence. Whatever doubts they may have had about the quality of the support they enjoyed on high, Khrushchev's words dismissed those doubts. Judging from the line upon line of deletions that subsequently came through the censor's door at the telegraph office, the censors bent to their task with new energy and self-assurance.

In the autumn of 1958 Soviet authorities expelled Roy Essoyan of the Associated Press for what was described as a "gross violation of censorship." Essoyan had written that Nikita Khrushchev had suffered his most serious political setback up to that time on his trip to Peking in July 1958. The reporter speculated that Khrushchev might lose political stature in Russia as a consequence of his concessions to the Chinese Communist leaders. Soviet censors did not pass the story. Essoyan, after being cut off several times, finally was able to telephone the story to London during a momentary lapse of vigilance on the part of the censors. His dispatch was widely published in the United States, in some cases with an editor's note indicating that it had been *passed* by the censors. This gave the impression that Essoyan's dispatch bore official Soviet endorsement. Instead of issuing a denial of Essoyan's story, the Russians threw him out. By stating the bona fide reason—violation of censorship—instead of contrived reasons (such as violation of currency regulations cited in some previous expulsions), the Russians were attracting undesired attention to their censorship, but it was a price they were willing to pay to make it clear that Essoyan's story did *not* bear the mark of official approval.

Shortly after Essoyan's expulsion, the Russians ordered Paul Niven, Columbia Broadcasting Corporation correspondent, to shut down the

C.B.S. bureau and leave, himself. This was retaliation for a CBS television drama entitled *The Plot to Kill Stalin* which depicted Khrushchev in the role of an accomplice to Stalin's death.

Both expulsions indicated Khrushchev's personal sensitivity. The action against CBS introduced a new and unique factor in Soviet censorship. In effect, the Russians were trying to exercise a form of censorship over whatever a newspaper printed or a television network carried in the United States of a displeasing nature to the Kremlin by threatening to shut down that organization's Moscow bureau.

Correspondents are supposed to initiate all requests with the Press Department of the Foreign Ministry, or, more recently, with an organization known as the State Committee for Cultural Relations with Foreign Countries. Correspondents are not often permitted to forget this. Such was the case when a correspondent obtained an appointment with the acting rector of Moscow University simply by telephoning his office. The university official denied that students had been expelled for expressing politically objectionable views under the giddy influence of de-Stalinization. He denied the rumor then current that several students had been expelled for posting transcripts of English-language broadcasts of the British Broadcasting Corporation. The acting rector gave answers which should not have been objectionable to the Foreign Ministry.

Yet, soon after his interview was deposited at the telegraph office, the correspondent was telephoned by the Foreign Ministry with courteous but firm instructions that all requests for interviews or any other information were to be channeled through the Foreign Ministry.

A West German correspondent, in a similar case, was asked by his newspaper to track down reports that two hundred Russians had suffered ill effects from nuclear fallout from Soviet H-bomb test explosions. By dint of two hours of telephoning, the energetic correspondent managed to reach the very man at the Soviet Academy of Science concerned with problems of fallout in Soviet test explosions. He patiently explained to the German that the report was not true, and replied to other questions on the subject.

It took several days for the press department to get around to chastising the German. "You should have telephoned the State Committee for Cultural Relations," instructed the Foreign Ministry voice. The German thought he had a perfect answer: "The existence of the State Committee was not announced until two days *after* I had the interview."

"In which case," responded the Foreign Ministry, "you should have called *us*."

Unlike the acting rector of Moscow University and the fallout scientist at the Academy, most Soviet functionaries are aware of the rules for dealing with foreign newsmen, and automatically refer any callers to the Press Department.

A radio reporter wanted to tape record some samples of Russian jazz.

He learned that the workers' club at a Moscow rubber factory was noted for its jazz music. The director of the club informed the correspondent that he must get permission from the Press Department. The correspondent turned to other matters, but within an hour his phone rang. It was the Press Department.

"We understand that you would like to record music at a workers' club. Don't you know you are to call the Foreign Ministry on such requests?"

"I know," replied the correspondent. "But you haven't given me *time* to call you."

In this case, a familiar excuse was given for refusing the request. The club was under *rehmont* (repair).

The authorities are also alert to any violations of the rule that permission must be obtained to travel more than twenty-five miles from the center of Moscow. An Italian correspondent was considering a trip to the historic town of Vladimir, whose history dates back to 1147. He inquired at the Soviet travel bureau about the cost of transportation, hotel, and food. It would take a day to get the price, he was told. Within an hour he was telephoned by the Press Department. Did the correspondent not know that he could not travel to Vladimir without applying for permission?

Patiently, the Italian explained that yes, he knew, but was there any objection to his inquiring as to the cost *before* he decided to go? If he did want to make the trip, he would then apply for permission.

"Oh," said the Russian at the other end of the phone.

It was a rare case where Soviet bureaucracy had moved too fast in dealing either with Russian citizens or with the influx of foreigners who have visited Russia since Stalin's death.

CHAPTER 14

INCLUDED: A MEETING AND A SENDING OFF

A group of fifty American businessmen, visiting the Soviet Union as tourists, were eating breakfast together in Moscow.

With them were several Russian interpreter-guides.

A late riser joined his fellow-American tourists.

"Good morning, gentlemen. Is everything under control?"

A particularly eager guide sat bolt upright.

"*Nothing* is under control here," she exclaimed, "this is a *free* country."

Shortly after Stalin's death an occasional non-Communist visitor was granted a visa to Russia. By the summer of 1955 it had developed into a trickle of several hundred American tourists. The following summer there were two thousand Americans, and in 1957 some 2500. Nineteen fifty-eight saw about 8500 Americans visiting Moscow. Besides the customary trademarks of camera and sunglasses, the American tourist to Russia bears an Intourist coupon book.

Intourist (in the words on the blue plaque at its office entrance on Moscow's Gorki Street) is the "Organization for the Travel of Foreigners in the Soviet Union." It is charged with the care and feeding of foreign tourists and assigns interpreter-guides who, of course, are under instructions to put the best face on all things Soviet.

Under the Soviet system of tourism a visitor must purchase in advance a coupon book with as many pages as days he intends to stay in Russia. He pays the tourist agent representing Intourist in New York or London or Paris from $15 to $30 a day depending on the class of accommodations. Each page contains coupons entitling the tourist to a night's lodging, three meals, tea, the use of a chauffeured car, the services of an interpreter, and—in the words of the coupon book— "a meeting and a sending off" at airport or railroad station by the interpreter.

An Intourist booklet offers a variety of tours lasting from five to twenty-three days. Although many cities are closed to foreigners, the Intourist itineraries include Moscow, Leningrad, Kiev, Minsk, Odessa, Kharkov, Stalingrad, Tbilisi, Yalta, Sochi, and Sukhumi.

In 1957 it became possible for foreigners to tour Russia along prescribed routes in their own cars. The tourists were asked to reserve a seat for an Intourist guide who met the car at the border.

In almost every city open to tourists there is an Intourist Hotel. (In the few instances where this is not the case, the foreigner stays at the available hotel which is usually well below standard, especially in toilet facilities.) In Moscow, although it is a metropolis of five millions, there are fewer than twenty main hotels (and only sixty hotels in all—some of them with dormitory-type rooms for Russians). Tourists are usually put up at the gloomy Savoy, the Metropole with its bare, endless corridors, or the National, a baroque relic of Czarist days.

On entering the National, the visitor is confronted by a bigger-than-life-size portrait of Stalin hung behind the "Administrator's" desk. Other paintings of the late dictator still hang in the National's corridors long after Khrushchev's famous speech denouncing Stalin and exposing his crimes. However, literature by Stalin quickly disappeared from the bookstall near the entrance.

The National is one hotel where there's not a Bible to be found, but its windows do command a magnificent view of St. Basil's Cathedral, its nine brightly painted onion-shaped cupolas crowned with golden double crosses of the Orthodox Church.

Like other of Moscow's older hotels, the National is furnished in Victorian style. Heavy red or green plush drapes grace french windows. Gold-painted figures of Grecian women entwine around lamps. Glass cabinets serve only to display porcelain figures. It was into such a high-ceilinged room in 1890 *décor* that cartoonist Saul Steinberg entered late one evening on his arrival in Russia. He stopped short at the door in disbelief. For a moment he thought someone had contrived a grotesquely elaborate practical joke in decorating the antique room precisely in the style of one of his line drawings.

On arrival, a tourist surrenders his passport to the lady clerk seated below the somber gaze of Stalin and behind a gigantic umbrella-shaped lampshade trimmed with kinky fringe. The passport is sent to police authorities for purposes of registration, as is done in many European countries, and usually is not seen again by its owner for at least forty-eight hours—a deprivation which contributes to a newcomer's anxiety.

The tourist's name is entered in the hotel guest book in Cyrillic alphabet so that checking a registration depends in part on pronouncing the name the way the hotel clerk chose to inscribe it. This is not always easy. There's no *h* sound in Russian that corresponds to English. The *h* may be transliterated as the deep guttural *kh* sound of Russian. Or, as is most often the case, it may be rendered as a *g*. Thus, it took some mental gear shifting for a university professor named Calvin Hoover to realize that it was he who was being addressed as *Gospodin* (Mister) Goover. Similarly, Shakespeare's melancholy Dane is known as "Gamlet."

Written in Cyrillic approximation in the National's book are the names of Senator Estes Kefauver, Congressman Patrick Hillings. Senator William Ellender, author Truman Capote, columnist Leonard Lyons, showman Billy Rose, and Eleanor Roosevelt. In fact, in one busy day at the National, you might have encountered on its red-carpeted staircases such varied personalities as Supreme Court Justice William O. Douglas, Mexican artist Diego Rivera, since deceased, French existentialist Jean-Paul Sartre, a trim U.S. airline stewardess, or members of a Canadian ice-hockey team.

The remoteness of Russia, the expense of getting there, the lack of vacation resort comforts, at first brought special kinds of tourists to Moscow. There were wealthy people, often retired, who had traveled everywhere else. There were people with professional, rather than recreational, reasons for coming to Russia—writers, legislators, professors, individuals of Russian origin, often in search of lost relatives. Increasingly, though, ordinary tourists are making the trip into the Soviet Union with curiosity as their main motive.

Whatever the other interests and impressions of visitors, they seem to share several reactions in common. Inevitably there is great curiosity as to whether hotel rooms are wired with listening devices. Almost without exception a visiting tourist who would call on me would glance furtively around the room and inquire in a low voice: "Is the room wired?" One visitor, a Boston lawyer traveling with wife and two children, informed me with self-assurance that the listening devices in their rooms were quite in evidence. "Look," he said, "you've got them here too. Those wires along the walls." He seemed somewhat disappointed when we traced the wires and found that they seemed to be just the telephone connections.

Another universal reaction of tourists is to delight in besting their Intourist guides in political discussion. Tourists would recount with glee that Mischa or Ilyena or Natasha was struck dumb when confronted with a brilliantly phrased question concerning lack of political freedoms in Russia.

The guides, whose primary job is simply to show tourists the sights, naturally often resented these exercises in political proselytizing. They resented more, though, being taken for Soviet secret-police agents whose mission was to spy on visitors. A guide named Nina told me that on trips with tourists she would often try to stay in her hotel room and encourage her charges to go out alone to try and dissuade them from the suspicion that her assignment was to follow and spy.

The fact that tourists are not usually "tailed" comes as a surprise to many.

On the second day of his visit, an American tourist was thoughtfully spreading caviar on a slice of black bread when suddenly he looked up at his wife and declared: "You know, I have the funniest feeling that we're *not* being followed." There was a trace of sadness in his voice.

Because tourists to Russia usually have a curiosity about the Soviet Union, not only as a foreign country but as a system of government, they ask to see things that would not interest them in Paris or Rome or London. A visit to a Russian worker's apartment is considered a great coup. A collective farm, a ball-bearing factory, an ice-cream plant, a ballet school are on the list of tourist attractions along with an interminable number of museums—including such unique ones as the Museum of Labor Protection, V. I. Lenin's Mourning Train Museum, and the Museum of the Underground Print Shop.

Intourist tries to satisfy most requests.

Senator Richard B. Russell asked for permission to drive to the Borodino battlefield where the Czar's troops in September 1812 had made a valiant defense against Napoleon's army advancing on Moscow. It was difficult for the Russians to comprehend that the Georgia Democrat's hobby was touring historic battlegrounds, and they were suspicious. The request was refused. Then Senator Russell learned that, unknown to him, a military attaché at the American Embassy, in an effort to help the distinguished visitor, had put in a request to accompany him. Senator Russell realized that the reason for the Russians' suspicion may have been the attaché's application. Perhaps, reasoned Russell, they read into it a plot to spy on the ancient approaches to Moscow for some atomic-age purpose. The Senator asked the American colonel to withdraw his application. He did, and in a matter of hours the Senator had permission to travel.

Alabama's Senator John J. Sparkman and Mrs. Sparkman wanted to visit a school. That was easily arranged. It was more difficult to accommodate William Benton, former assistant Secretary of State, who, incidentally, was the inaugurator of Russian-language broadcasts of the Voice of America which are so distasteful to Soviet officialdom. Benton asked permission for his thirteen-year-old son John to attend classes at a Moscow school during their two weeks' stay. Once this had been arranged, John's classmates quizzed him about American jazz and "hot-rod" cars. When invited to John's room at the National for cocoa all accepted, but none showed up.

This is a common experience of tourists. Occasionally a Russian whose acquaintance is made during a theater intermission or in sidewalk conversation will come to tea or dinner. Sometimes a tourist will be invited by a Russian to his home. These are rare cases, though. Russians learned during Stalin's era to be wary of foreigners. Denunciation by a neighbor or a fellow factory worker as an associate of Westerners might be enough to lead to prison. Russians have told me that they actually went a block out of their way rather than walk past the American or British Embassy during the deepest days of the Cold War. Even now, after Stalin's death, with the policy of hospitality to tourists, Russians are not encouraged to develop personal relations with foreigners. There are government agencies for that.

With the threat of Stalin-era punishment removed, some Russians have mustered the courage to try tentative contacts with tourists. Some foreigners who have sought out relatives in Russia have met with warm, emotional welcomes. Other Russians have refused to see their relatives.

American tourists are asked by clerks in their hotel service bureau what they'd like to see. Many settle for a walk through the Kremlin grounds and museum, an afternoon at Moscow's horse-race track, a look at a Russian fashion show, or a tour of the skyscraper university.

Some have had more unorthodox requests. One said he'd like to see a slave-labor camp. The Russian clerk maintained a poker face and agreed to inquire if that would be possible. It wasn't.

A vacationing American, Gari Ketchem, co-pilot for a U.S. airline, decided that he'd like to fly the Soviet TU-104 passenger jet. Authorities of the government's Aeroflot line considered the request with understandable reluctance when they learned that Mr. Ketchem had never piloted a jet, American or otherwise, but they did give him a ride in the plane.

An American cookbook writer decided it would make a good story if she could prepare an American-type meal for Kremlin leader Bulganin. The Russians received this unusual request with certainly no less aplomb than might be expected from the White House staff if a visiting Russian should ask to fix dinner for the President. So she settled for baking a cake for students at a Moscow cooking school.

Considerably more successful was a seventy-year-old former president of the National Education Association, Miss Charl Ormond Williams, who announced that she would like to meet the wife of the then Premier Bulganin. This was received with incredulity by the timid Russian girl in the hotel service bureau. Miss Williams had heard that Mrs. Bulganin taught English in a Moscow school and she thought they might share subjects of mutual interest to talk about. The Russian girl proposed that Miss Williams go instead to see a hospital. She did this and expressed an interest in watching the birth of a Russian baby. The next morning at five she was awakened by a call from the hospital telling her to come right away; the time was now.

Undismayed by lack of Intourist support, Miss Williams addressed a letter to "Mrs. Bulganin, Kremlin, Moscow," appealing to their mutual interest in education. A few days later she received an invitation to tea. Miss Williams reported that Mrs. Bulganin lived in a most unproletarian apartment, used gold-bordered chinaware, and spoke English haltingly but correctly. Asked what Mrs. Bulganin had to say, Miss Williams thought a few seconds and replied: "My goodness, I do believe that *I* did all the talking."

A rather unusual American tourist was Homer A. Tomlinson, age 65, who modestly identifies himself in literature he distributes as "King of the World." Mr. Tomlinson startled his Intourist interpreter by setting up a portable aluminum "throne" covered with gold-colored cloth in Red Square. Dressed in a soiled, embroidered Chinese Mandarin robe and holding an inflatable globe of the world, Tomlinson spoke about peace and brotherhood to Russians who gathered around him. Red Square, which saw executions during the reign of Ivan the Terrible and nowadays witnesses twice-a-year military parades, has been the scene for few more bizarre spectacles than Tomlinson preaching in English to bewildered Russians. Tomlinson later decided that he must hurry to Leningrad to greet Adlai Stevenson on his arrival in Russia. The following encounter took place in the Astoriya Hotel lobby:

Tomlinson: "Governor Stevenson, you remember me."

Stevenson (who didn't): "Why, yes, what are you doing here?"

Tomlinson (a trifle annoyed): "You know. I'm King of the Universe."

Stevenson: "Oh yes, it had slipped my mind for a moment."

Another noteworthy exchange took place between an American visitor and Soviet Minister of Culture Nikolai Mikhailov. It was during the filming of an interview with Mikhailov for use on American television— an exchange arrangement in which American students interviewed five Soviet public figures and Russians interviewed five leaders in various American fields of endeavor. During a pause in the filming one of the American students tried out his rather fluent Russian on Mr. Mikhailov. The Culture Minister hospitably suggested that the American come to Moscow for a longer period to polish up his conversational ability. The boy agreed with enthusiasm, saying he'd like to do just that when he finished his studies. He would like, he pointed out, to work in his field for a while in Moscow.

"A fine idea," agreed Mikhailov. "Where do you go to school now?"

"Yale Divinity School," replied the young man.

That abruptly ended the conversation between the aspiring preacher and the government official of the atheistic Soviet state.

From time to time Soviet leaders receive distinguished tourists. In 1955 Senator Ellender had an audience with deputy Premier Anastas Mikoyan, whose name Ellender had difficulty remembering at a news conference he summoned immediately after the meeting. The following year the Louisiana Democrat was received by Nikita Khrushchev, chairman of the Communist Party. Ellender emerged from the Kremlin office obviously shaken to have discovered that Khrushchev was—as the Senator put it—a confirmed, sincere Communist. On his third trip to Russia, Ellender had an interview with Mikoyan again. This time he remembered the name.

A group of eighteen American women in radio and television work, on a tour of Europe, were received in the spring of 1957 by the head of the Soviet Government, Premier Bulganin. After engaging in chitchat about the rewards of being a grandfather, Bulganin revealed what was his motive for taking the time to see them. It is, in fact, much of the motive behind the opening up of Russia to tourists by the men burdened by Stalin's heritage of world-wide ill will.

"We know we are sometimes depicted as frightful devils," said Bulganin. "Bad things are written about us—that we are bloodthirsty. But they are not true. We wish to be friends. If we know each other better it will create confidence, and world peace will benefit."

Americans of lesser note are sometimes tendered hospitality by minor-rank Russians. Officials of the restaurant section of the Ministry of Trade took an owner of one of New York's most expensive restaurants to lunch at the Grand Hotel. The American was courteously invited to make any comments on food and service at the Grand's restaurant, a cheerless hall with grotesque urns on window sills and marble statues reminiscent of the late 1800s. The American was profuse in his suggestions—the silverware was too large, the tables badly arranged, the waiters poorly trained. The Soviet hosts listened patiently but showed a tinge of annoyance when, at the serving of beef stroganoff, the American tasted it and cried: "We wouldn't serve this to pigs in my restaurant."

Another member of the same restaurant firm came to Moscow to see about purchasing Soviet caviar. He was given a dinner at the Praga Restaurant, and a number of correspondents were invited. The guest of honor quickly downed several glasses of vodka and proceeded to append obscene remarks to each toast offered to peace, friendship, and international commerce. The girl interpreters understood enough of the idiom to blush. By the time the main course was served the American was singing loudly and balancing champagne glasses on his head—none too successfully, for one spilled all over him. When a quartet with Georgian string instruments began playing in the private dining room the drunken guest of honor seized his stocky host, an official of the Ministry of Trade, and danced him around the floor, finally landing in a potted palm. As he was unable to stand up, the Russians supported him into a car, where he became ill, and to his hotel, where they put him to bed. When he awoke in the morning he began shouting that his wallet had been stolen. It was right where the Russians had left it when they folded up his clothes. Not a word ever appeared about this episode in Soviet newspapers.

Such incidents are the exception. If anything, the influx of tourists has served to enhance rather than diminish the warmth and admiration that Russians show toward American, British, French, and other foreigners. In provincial cities, and less often in Moscow, where foreigners are seen more frequently, it is not uncommon for crowds to congregate around a tourist to ask questions about wages and prices and politics in his country. It is a common experience for a tourist to be escorted to the head of a queue, whether at the cloakroom at the Bolshoi or at the Lenin-Stalin mausoleum in Red Square. It may seem incongruous that after years of still-persisting invective against the West by Soviet radio, newspapers, official statements, and speeches that Russians should display such genuine friendliness. Part of the explanation lies in curiosity grown from years of isolation. It is the same hungry curiosity that causes knots of Russians to swarm around the most ordinary car of foreign manufacture. It may be, too, that the drum beat of anti-Western propaganda has dulled on Soviet ears.

An Intourist guide, when asked if she thought Americans were better liked, now that Russians had the opportunity to see them, replied: "Well, at least those Americans we meet obviously don't want war, although we've always heard they did."

Despite Intourist (an invented word from *Inostrani,* meaning "foreign," or "other country," and *tourist,* which is a word common to Russian and English) red tape and inertia, the patient tourist has the opportunity to learn much about Russia in a short visit. The visitor may be surprised to find that all theater programs list the time the performance begins *and* ends. Magazines are never predated as in the United States; in fact, some magazines carry no date at all—just the number in the annual series. Cigarettes, all manufactured by the Government, come in various brands, including one named *Droog,* meaning "friend," and the latest brand called *Laika* after the second sputnik's canine passenger; the blue-and-white package bears a portrait of *Laika* with the sputnik space kennel overhead. The tourist finds that Russian women wear wedding rings on the fourth finger of the right hand and that very few men wear gold wedding bands. He finds that Russians measure in kilometers, meters, kilograms and centigrades. Tips are accepted happily by waiters, chambermaids, barbers, and other personnel in Intourist hotels with only an occasional exception, but tips are never solicited.

One tourist described the dress of Muscovites as looking as if "they were all going to a 'hard times' party." This unstylish dress and the provincial appearance of many of the capital's back streets caused another visitor to call Moscow "a big cow town." Struck by the tasteless attempts at style and the Oriental shabbiness of many neighborhoods, Moscow may seem like the place where "East meets Midwest." However, Muscovites love their old city and retain such proverbs as "Moscow is mother to all cities."

The visitor discovers that when a Russian jabs his thumb to the sky with his other fingers rolled up he is indicating that something is very good. When a Russian flicks his forefinger from his thumb against the underside of his chin he is indicating that someone is drunk.

At the airport or railroad station the tourist finds that he must fill out a form declaring that he is bearing no opium, elks' horns, or firearms, but usually the baggage inspection is cursory. There are exceptions, though, and a rare foreigner is stripped of clothing. Mostly the inspectors are looking for anti-Soviet printed or recorded material. The visitor learns that mothers' milk is sold in bottles, that there is no "formula" food for infants, no diaper service; there is also no facial tissue or sanitary napkins.

The streets are watered every night, but it is perfectly permissible to spit on the sidewalks.

The tourist may be surprised on occasion to hear a recently made Russian acquaintance (often in a show of bravado) recite a "shocking" local joke: "Do you know the difference between capitalism and communism? In capitalism man exploits man. In communism it's vice versa." Or: "Lubiyanka prison is the tallest building in the world. From its cellars you can see Siberia."

Tourists in Moscow learn that it's customary in Russia to use elevators only for going up, and to walk down. Tourists are surprised to find that not only is hotel laundry service fast but even socks are pressed. In at least one case, a visitor was taken aback to discover who had once occupied his bed. V. I. Lenin lived for a short period at the time of the Revolution in the National Hotel before moving across the street to the Kremlin. The hotel now bears a plaque with the Soviet equivalent of the inscription of "Lenin Slept Here." Lenin's room, 107, consisting of a small bedroom alcove and a parlor of stiffly stuffed sofa and chairs covered with green plush, has been occupied by Western tourists. A double door, now sealed, led to a series of other rooms including a parlor with a fresco ceiling and a balcony from which Lenin addressed crowds. It was a curious coincidence that this room should be assigned to Senator George W. Malone, as conservative a Nevada Republican

RIGHT: Woman worker at Kharkov tractor factory with picture of Lenin in background.

BELOW: Beach at Yevpatoriya on Crimea's Black Sea.

LEFT: Rarely seen Soviet oil wells. Shot through moving car window near Black Sea's east coast.

BELOW: Russian women standing in line at store to buy food in snowstorm.

ABOVE: Ground-to-ground rockets parade through Red Square on November 7, 1957.

LEFT: Women plaster house made of adobe mud and straw bricks.

LEFT: Advertisement of 3 per cent government bonds on side of building. Above it is an ad for Soviet champagne. Stands in foreground are of outdoor "snack bar."

BELOW: Ballet scene from opera *Faust* in the branch theatre of Moscow's Bolshoi.

as ever fought Communism. However well Malone may have slept, some say Lenin tossed in his tomb.

A dramatic episode of the post-Stalin years occurred on the cold night of February 11, 1956, in room 101, an ornate but run-down lounge. Two British correspondents were telephoned by the Soviet news agency, Tass, and asked to come there. A pair of well-dressed men awaited them. One spoke up in well-schooled British accents. "My name is Guy Burgess. This is Donald Maclean." In this manner did the long-missing British diplomats, whose disappearance from Whitehall had caused an international furor, confirm that they had indeed defected to Communism.

A New York *Times* editorial on the incident conveys a good deal of the flavor of the National:

"Moscow's National Hotel, across the street from the Kremlin, is a natural locale for a tale of mystery or intrigue. A faded relic of a past era, its heavy furniture and primitive bathroom facilities remind the visiting foreigners it houses that much of the old Russia persists in the new. On any typical day its expensive first-floor restaurant serves the same heavy and greasy food impartially to Chinese Communist officials and British businessmen, to Bulgarian engineers and American correspondents. In few other places do citizens of the free world and the Communist world rub shoulders so often and so intimately. E. Phillips Oppenheim would have applauded the choice of the National's shabby lounge, with its fine view of the Kremlin, as the place for ending such mystery as remained in the case of Guy Burgess and Donald Maclean."

Other rooms in the National also have unusual histories. Several rooms served as the first Embassy of the United States of America when President Roosevelt extended diplomatic recognition on November 16, 1933. Ambassador William Bullitt stayed there when he came to Russia in December to present his credentials at the Kremlin. Bullitt soon returned to Washington to gather a staff for the new Embassy, leaving behind at the National young George Kennan who later was to become Ambassador himself.

On one momentous occasion during World War II the furnishings of the National—heavily carved wooden chairs, massive oaken tables with curved claw legs, tasseled pillows—were transported lock, stock, and vodka barrel to Yalta. The retreating Germans had thoroughly looted the Crimea, but nevertheless Stalin chose it as the site for his meeting with Roosevelt and Churchill. The manager of the National

Hotel, Gogo Beridze, a burly man with bullet-shaped shaven head from Stalin's native Georgia Republic, was charged by Stalin to furnish quarters in bare Livadia Palace, a former summer mansion of the Czar on a cliff overlooking the Black Sea. Beridze emptied the National to provide furniture for Stalin, Roosevelt, and Churchill to eat, sleep, and negotiate on.

After Stalin's death Gogo Beridze was demoted to manager of an obscure Moscow restaurant, the Uzbekistan, which features a spicy Central Asian soup and *shashlik,* lamb on a spit.

Not only has the United States had an Embassy in the National Hotel; West Germany's first Embassy was in rooms 113 and 115, the hotel's proletarian equivalent to the royal suite. Ambassador Wilhelm Haas and Mrs. Haas lived in two rooms for several months until an Embassy building was provided by Soviet authorities.

Another distinguished occupant of that suite was Mrs. Eleanor Roosevelt. It is a quirk of the National's history that the furnishings of the two rooms with their gilt-edged tables were in President Roosevelt's quarters at Yalta. Eleanor Roosevelt's secretary, Maureen Corr, and her physician, Dr. David Gurevitch, had rooms down the hall, and it was at Mrs. Roosevelt's request that they set forth to Moscow's department stores to try to buy a bathing suit for Mrs. Roosevelt prior to flying down to the Black Sea resort of Sochi. They could find nothing in Mrs. Roosevelt's size until an eager salesgirl at the GUM store on Red Square said she thought she had just the thing. She returned from a storeroom with a scrap of cloth in each hand. It was a black Russian bikini. Miss Corr and Dr. Gurevitch politely explained that it would not quite fit Mrs. Roosevelt nor her taste. When Mrs. Roosevelt boarded a plane of the Soviet airline the next morning for her flight to Russia's seashore it was without a bathing suit in her luggage.

CHAPTER 15

FIRST FLIGHT BY MOZHAISKY

Not the Wright brothers, say the Russians, but rather a man named Mozhaisky made the first flight in history.

On December 17, 1903, at Kitty Hawk, North Carolina, the Wright brothers accomplished what is usually thought to be the first controlled and sustained flight in a power-driven airplane. But, long before, Alexander Fyderovich Mozhaisky had flown over the plains of the village of Krasnoye Selo (Red Village), near Leningrad.

At least, that's the Soviet Government's claim.

Captain Mozhaisky is supposed to have built his plane in 1882 when Wilbur Wright would have been eleven years old. For the next three years he is said to have carried out successful flights of his crude aircraft.

Soviet authorities become indignant when anyone questions this.

In 1956 two Russian historians wrote an article in the Soviet magazine, *Questions of History,* which implied their doubts of the Soviet claim.

This angered the editors of *Red Star,* the Defense Ministry's newspaper, who wrote that it was bad enough when "dirty and untenable insinuations by bourgeois hacks" denied the "undisputable priority of our country in the construction and testing of the world's first airplane."

Red Star continued:

"We, Soviet people, are accustomed to malicious attacks and preposterous slander upon the Soviet state, which, for forty years, have been spread by our ill-wishers from the bourgeois camp. There is a popular saying that lies and slander have short legs. Indeed, each time the reactionary bourgeois press tries to discredit the great gains of the Soviet people, the truth of our radiant life puts it in a most ridiculous position. We do not doubt that the bourgeois hacks, who are seeking to take away from us our national due, the priority in the construction of the first airplane, will be put to shame as they have always been."

However, it is quite a bit more serious matter when Soviet historians raise doubts. This "evokes in the Soviet people a sense of disappointment and legitimate perplexity."

The historians with the temerity to cast doubts on Mozhaisky's first flight were Y. F. Burche and I. Y. Mosolov. They argued that there is a lack of any convincing historical evidence, that there's reason to believe that Captain Mozhaisky was actually abroad when he was supposed to have been building his machine, and that on the day in July 1882, when he was supposed to have gone aloft for the first time, meteorological records show that a storm was raging.

In fact, it was not until 1945 that the first claims of Mozhaisky's flight were advanced. Even Soviet advocates of the claim admit that, although they now have gathered a hundred documents of various sorts to substantiate their thesis, there are no diaries or any other works by Mozhaisky himself which describe his experiments in flight.

However, if any Soviet citizen doubts Mozhaisky's pre-eminence in aviation, he need only bear in mind that the Soviet Encyclopedia has canonized Mozhaisky. Furthermore, as *Red Star* reminded its readers, a special decision of March 11, 1955, of the U. S. S. R. Council of Ministers, proclaimed that the memory of Mozhaisky was to be perpetuated by a bronze bust to be set up in the village of Krasnoye Selo where, said the Council, "the world's first airplane was built and its air tests begun."

And when the Council of Ministers decides, the judicious Soviet citizen does not challenge.

Other Soviet firsts in aviation are less vulnerable to challenge.

The first polar flight, for example, from Moscow to the United States was completed by three Russian flyers on June 20, 1937. The flight of 5700 miles over the North Pole from Moscow to Portland, Oregon, took 63 hours and 16 minutes in a Russian ANT-25 plane designed by Oleg Antonov. It was capable of a top speed of only about 110 miles an hour.

The three pilots were Georgi Baidukov, Valery Chkalov, and Alexander Belyakov. On the twentieth anniversary of the flight, Baidukov wrote his recollections in a piece which, true to the Soviet technique, included political commentary and moral-drawing:

"This flight by three Soviet pilots was recognized by the whole world as a tremendous achievement in aviation and a step forward in the conquest of the Arctic.

"I shall never forget the embarrassment of the American pressmen when they looked over our engine AM-34 and saw that it bore the trade-mark of a Moscow aircraft plant.

"They expected the engine to be either American- or British-made. The American press and radio put out all sorts of cock-and-bull stories about us, and, therefore, great was the surprise of ordinary Americans to see us cheerful and full of pep after our long flight.

"Recalling the hospitality of American people, I bitterly regret the present coolness in the American-Soviet relations. I can only regret that the Cold War has brought about this situation. I am confident that the American and Soviet people wish to be friends. The Soviet Government is taking measures to ease international tensions, but there are certain quarters in the West that sabotage these proposals."

The immense size of the Soviet Union naturally lends itself to travel by air. Every city of any size in the U.S.S.R. is serviced by airplanes in a complex network that links Vilnyus and Vladivostok, Kiev and Karaganda. The Soviet Union's domestic air service covers more miles than that of any other nation. There is only one airline in the U.S.S.R. —Aeroflot, meaning air fleet, operated, of course, by the Soviet Government. It flies mostly IL-12's and IL-14's, slightly different models of the same two-engine plane with tricycle landing gear that may be compared to a cross between the American Convair and the Douglas DC-3. As in all Soviet planes, the identification letters stand for the name of the designer; in this case, IL represents Ilyushin.

Rapidly, though, the Russians are acquiring a fleet of ultra-modern jet and turboprop aircraft. Until completion of new hangars at Moscow's Vnukova airport it's not unusual to see the enormous new jet giants with their tails jutting through holes cut in old hangar doors. It's not unusual, either, to see two dozen or more sleek, silver-colored Soviet jet and turbojet passenger craft lined up in arrow-neat rows on an airport apron.

The new arsenal of Soviet aircraft, quickly replacing the old IL-12s and 14s, includes the IL-18 (Moskva), the Ukraina, the TU-110, the TU-114 (Rossiya), and the increasingly familiar TU-104. The Moskva is intended to carry from 75 to 100 passengers and great cargoes of mail and freight at a cruising speed of 400 miles an hour. It is powered by four turboprop engines. It looks something like the British Britannica plane. The Ukraina, a squat, low-slung plane that looks almost like an amphibian, has its wing high on the fuselage with four great turboprop engines. The Ukraina seats 84 passengers in the first-class version or 126 tourist class. It travels at a speed just under 400 miles an hour. The TU-114 (which, like other planes, comes in various development models indicated by the letters A, B, C, D, and so on after the number) is designed for carrying a small number of passengers and mainly freight over very long distances. It has four turboprop engines of big capacity, designed, as are many Soviet aircraft engines, by N. D. Kuznetsov, a holder of the award of Hero of Socialist Labor. On proving flights a TU-114 has flown a route over all fifteen Soviet Republic capitals, landing only four times and completing a distance equal to that around the world at the equator in about forty-eight hours.

The TU-110, a four-jet version of the TU-104, but longer and wider with angularly swept-back wings, whose fuselage may, by stretching the imagination, be compared with that of the Douglas DC-8 jets, has a maximum speed of 625 miles an hour with a range of about 2100 miles. Carrying between 78 and 100 passengers, depending on the cabin configuration, the TU-110 is a plane Aeroflot hopes to use extensively on international routes.

The work horse of the Soviet jet age is the TU-104 which, after the disasters of the pioneering British Comet jet, became the first jet-powered passenger craft to fly regular commercial schedules. The TU-104 has also flown across the Atlantic—on special flights with members of the Soviet United Nations delegation. However, its comparatively short fuel range disqualifies it for safe transatlantic flying. As a matter of fact, on a trip to London with members of the Bolshoi ballet troupe, a TU-104 was diverted from London's International Airport because of bad weather. The increment of flying time involved in changing course to a field outside London brought the plane to a landing with only about ten minutes-worth of fuel left. A British Air Force attaché from the Moscow Embassy who was on board feared that if the plane had been unable to come directly in for a landing, because another craft was ahead of it, the TU-104 would have run dry of fuel. Seating 50 to 70 passengers, the TU-104 has a range of under 2000 miles and a cruising speed of 500 miles an hour, but it can attain speeds up to 625 miles per hour. It is a civilian version, as are all

Soviet civil jets and turboprops, of a military plane; in this case it is the civil version of a Soviet bomber. (The head of Aeroflot is a marshal in the Soviet Air Force.)

The tremendous speed of the TU-104 was demonstrated to me when I flew to Tashkent, capital of Soviet Uzbekistan in central Asia, a distance of about 2000 miles from Moscow, in just four hours. On the return trip the jet was canceled because of poor weather conditions, and it was necessary to take an IL-14. The return flight required thirteen hours, with several stops. I've also been a passenger on the TU-104 on flights to or from Copenhagen, Brussels, and Tbilisi—each was smooth and swift, although the vibration of take-off and the incredibly fast landing speed can be unnerving.

The streamlined TU-104 with its swept-back wings flies regularly to other cities too—Paris, Amsterdam, Prague, Peiping, and, within the U.S.S.R., to principal cities including Kharbarovsk in the Far East and Irgutsk in Siberia. Western aviation experts consider the fuel consumption of the powerful TU-104's engines too great to make it a commercially economic plane by privately owned airline standards. To conserve fuel the TU-104 is towed by an anachronistic-looking truck from the loading apron at Moscow's Vnukova Airport to the end of the runway, and only then are the jet engines turned on.

The plane was designed—as are all aircraft bearing the letters TU— by Andrei Tupolev.

Tupolev is a friendly man in his sixties who often attends embassy receptions with his wife, one of the best-dressed women of Moscow society. Tupolev has a ready gold-toothed smile, and when his pudgy fingers are not folded over his paunch he will likely be examining some object through horn-rimmed glasses with a technician's curiosity. At a party at the Swedish Embassy he was studiously inspecting porcelain ash trays. At the Norwegian Embassy when I approached him he was looking with curiosity at a tray of little cakes. I took one, and his face brightened.

"See, you too have taken one with chocolate frosting," he said with the pride of a man having a theory confirmed.

The cakes were arranged in rows of different colored icings. At that point, early in the party, only the row of chocolate frosted cakes had been sampled by the guests. This phenomenon excited Tupolev's curiosity.

Tupolev, a rare creature among Soviet dignitaries in that he is not a member of the Communist Party, seemed to enjoy himself immensely in England when he accompanied the Soviet leaders on their trip.

The London trip marked the first appearance of the TU-104 on non-Communist territory. One of the jets shuttled back and forth, prior to the arrival of "B and K," as they were called by Britain's headline writers, with supplies and advance men. When newspapers speculated that the Russians had only one of these craft in operation, as if in retort, three landed a few days later.

At one of the London events in honor of "B and K" I chatted with Tupolev about his plane. He was modest, but obviously pleased with its performance. The plane was working fine, he said. When I asked about the possibility of my returning to Moscow aboard a TU-104, his evaluation of the plane diminished. "It's not quite ready for passengers yet," he smiled.

The flight from Moscow to Copenhagen in aircraft powered by two piston engines used to take more than six hours with a one-hour stop for refueling and a meal at the Latvian city of Riga. The Soviet jet reduced the flying time to two hours and ten minutes and eliminated the Riga landing. The seats are roomier and more comfortable than on most Western airlines. The passenger cabin has fewer mid-Victorian-era ornaments, curtains, and lamps than Russia's older planes, the interiors of which resemble railroad parlor cars of the gaslight age. The jet's cabin is divided into three sections. The rear compartment consists of fifty-four seats, two abreast on the left-hand side and three abreast on the right. Next there is a roomy galley, and then a forward compartment with sixteen seats in pairs.

I was permitted to visit the cockpit on a flight out of Russia and found it to be an exceptionally large place with a complicated array of instruments. The cockpit is built on three levels. In the front, seated in a plexiglass nose, the navigator follows the course of the plane with charts and maps and other navigational tools. Presumably this would be the bombardier's place in military versions of the plane. On a level above and behind the navigator sit the pilot and co-pilot, and behind them on a third level, the radio operator and engineer.

Riding in the front of the plane, a passenger experiences little noise or vibration; in the rear, though, behind the jets, it is noisier than an engine-driven plane and there is considerable vibration. On take-off the plane roars down the runway, accelerating at a rate that forces the passenger back into his seat. The jet requires a long runway to become airborne and then climbs at a steep angle that soon leaves the ground far below. It customarily flies at altitudes of seven miles. The landing is the most dramatic part of the jet flight. The approach for landing is made from a score of miles distant from the airport, and the jet streaks in low over the countryside at great speed. A giant parachute can be released as soon as the plane lands in order to assist the brakes to stop it.

Hot meals are served aboard the jet, unlike other Soviet planes where the hostess offers only cold sandwiches, fruit, and tea, if food is served at all. As in old-fashioned Soviet planes there are clock faces at the front of the passenger cabin showing the time, temperature, and altitude. Unlike Western aircraft there is no sign that lights up, warning passengers to fasten their seat belts and not to smoke during landing and take-off.

Most Soviet planes I've traveled on have been furnished with seat belts, but these were almost always tied behind the seat, and no one has ever suggested that they be fastened. Sometimes seats have only half a belt; apparently the other half had torn away and there seemed no reason to replace it. When I've asked Russian stewardesses why they don't require use of seat belts, the reply is that "our pilots are so good that it is not necessary."

However, more and more the barnstorming quality of flying on Russian planes is disappearing. Aboard jet flights the hostess does check each passenger to make sure the seat belt is fastened. Hard candy is passed out at take-off, along with cotton for the ears and a cellophane envelope for fountain pens to prevent leaking at high altitudes under conditions of incomplete pressurization. On the TU-104 each place is equipped with an oxygen mask held in a pocket in the back of each seat. A rubber tubing extends from the mask to an outlet in the cabin wall, lending a kind of dentist's-office-chair *décor* to the seating arrangement.

Russians often behave on planes as if they were riding a Moscow bus. They mill about in the aisle before take-off, visiting with friends, shouting to each other the length of the plane, pulling packages off the racks and boosting them back up, pulling jackets off and putting them on again. Sometimes they seem like undisciplined children going home on the school bus. It's not at all uncommon for the plane (except for the jets) to take off and land with passengers standing up and smoking.

Stewardesses on Russian planes are selected for qualities other than pulchritude. Plain, with hair tied severely back, they usually wear a uniform of blue jacket and skirt, white blouse, and an earnest expression. In most cases they spend the greater portion of the flight in the crew compartment and come out only when summoned or to pass out Soviet magazines or tea.

The tea served on flights is usually a flavorful Russian brew, drunk from a glass with a metal holder bearing an embossed replica of the Kremlin's Spasky Tower. The tea tasted somehow different on one flight; moreover there was a tea bag dangling in the glass. Tea bags are not manufactured in the U.S.S.R. There was a label at the end of the string—"Lipton's." Almost no nonessential items are imported, and of all the commodities the Russians *might* import to make for more pleasant living, tea bags seem the last thing that's needed!

On some flights the stewardess passes out a blue and white printed sheet headed by the word "Information" in Russian and English. In small squares appropriately illustrated, the paper lists the names of the pilot, the cabin attendant, the plane type and its number, the altitude, the temperature, the speed, and the expected arrival time.

In the folder holding one's Aeroflot ticket is also contained a schedule of the flight as well as a picture post card of a Russian plane and a form for any complaints or expressions of approval.

My first flight in a Russian plane was from Helsinki to Moscow. At the airport in Helsinki, with permission of the airport police, I took photographs of the Soviet plane, a red flag with hammer, sickle, and star painted on its tail. Members of the crew in blue uniforms and bell-bottomed, baggy trousers stood in the shade under the wing and, while they did not object to pictures being taken of their plane, they turned their backs whenever the camera pointed toward them.

Aboard, a Russian-speaking American passenger asked the hostess, Galena Petrova, what time we would get to Leningrad, an intermediary stop. With precision rather than with rudeness, she replied: "We are not aloft yet. When we are in the air I shall be able to tell you."

A few minutes later a somewhat less finicky Finnish representative of the Helsinki airport came aboard and announced: "The flying time to Leningrad is one hour and twenty minutes. From Leningrad to Moscow, three and a half hours. You will fly at 6000 feet. You should have a smooth flight."

Before we took off Mrs. Petrova made an announcement: "Please put your cameras in your suitcase or hand them to me." On subsequent flights, Russian stewardesses did not take this precaution, although photography from planes over the Soviet Union is prohibited. Like almost everything else in Russia, this rule, too, seems to have exceptions. One

American lady tourist told me of her experience aboard a flight from Helsinki when the co-pilot came back to tell her they had just crossed into Russia and to suggest that she take her first photograph of the U.S.S.R.

However, the announcement on my first flight apparently chilled the American who was seated across the aisle from me. When I began typing on my portable machine during the flight, he leaned over to me and asked rather anxiously: "Do you suppose that's forbidden?"

"Why should it be?"

"Well, they told us not to take pictures, and they might suspect you of taking notes," responded the cautious traveler.

During the flight, when I went into the lavatory at the rear of the plane, I discovered that the amenities included only a single cloth towel and one small bar of soap but a complete shoeshine kit.

Russian pilots of other than jet planes seem to prefer to fly low, which permits them visual contact with the ground but sometimes makes for turbulence in flight. They take off with only a perfunctory warm-up and bank almost within touching distance of the ground. Despite these unnerving practices, I've never had a suspenseful flight in an Aeroflot plane which, regrettably, is more than I can say for foreign lines on which I've flown in and out of Russia.

The Russians almost never announce any airline accidents. They say this is because they almost never have any accidents. It seems unlikely that any airline could fly as many miles as Aeroflot without more mishaps than are reported. As for any minor accidents or illnesses in flight, a woman attendant in a white smock and first-aid case in hand usually awaits each plane at the airport and inquires solicitously whether anyone requires treatment.

Even some major Soviet airports have dirt rather than concrete runways. Landing at Kuibyshev, wartime capital city, shortly after a rainstorm, I was somewhat surprised to notice the Aeroflot plane descending to an unpaved runway speckled with pools of rainwater.

However, paved runways, too, can be of dubious standards. Such is the case at the Baltic coast city of Riga. I was on a two-engine plane bound for Copenhagen. The aircraft poised at the end of the cement runway, warming up for take-off after an hour spent for lunch and customs inspection at the Riga airport. Suddenly the plane lurched sharply to the right side, and the right propeller dug noisily into the ground. The pilot cut the engines. The plane rested at an angle with its right wing tip almost touching the ground. On the opposite side of the plane the door, opened hurriedly so that we could get out, was tilted toward the sky; it was impossible to use the ladder normally used for entering or descending.

The plane's right landing gear had broken through some of the hexagonal-shaped pieces of concrete which make up the runway. During the war the airport was bombed by the Germans. In repairing it, the Russians apparently had failed to pack sufficient dirt and rocks into bomb craters before laying down the concrete again. Our plane had the misfortune to put its full weight over one of the covered-over bomb craters which had been washed out. It seemed lucky that this had not happened during actual landing or take-off, although the pilot told us later that the plane in motion probably would not have imposed so much weight on the crust of concrete as when standing still.

It took fifteen minutes before a Russian truck drove out from the airport terminal building and the passengers were helped to the ground.

The plane's landing gear and right engine were badly damaged. It had to be abandoned until spare parts and a new engine were flown in. The Russians, acknowledging liability, paid in full for the damage. For some weeks, until the runway was inspected and repaired, planes landed and took off on the bumpy grass.

The inordinate amount of time that it took for the Russians to get to our plane in that minor emergency made me wonder about the efficacy of Soviet rescue operations. Some months later I was to have my doubts confirmed.

Also, I came to doubt the wisdom of traveling on foreign airlines within the Soviet Union.

Early in 1956 part of the de-Stalinization effort was to enlarge contacts of all sorts, including commerce with the non-Communist world. The Russians concluded an agreement with Finnair, the Finnish airline, granting it permission to fly between Helsinki and Moscow several times a week. Soon after that, an agreement was concluded with Scandinavian Airlines System for scheduled flights from Stockholm and Copenhagen. For years Soviet Aeroflot planes had been flying the Helsinki route so that the permission granted to Finnair was simply delayed reciprocation. In the case of the S.A.S. agreement Aeroflot planes were to fly the route on alternate days. Subsequently the Russians entered into agreements with other foreign carriers including Air France, Royal Dutch KLM, British European Airways and Belgium's Sabena.

It's been my experience that Scandinavian Airlines System maintains the best schedules on the Moscow route and provides the most personalized, comfortable service. The Russians insisted that comparable equipment be used, so as not to give the foreign line a competitive advantage. Since the Russians were flying their twenty-one-passenger IL-14's on these runs to the north, Finnair and S.A.S. were obliged to fly two-engine planes, although they might have preferred to use larger, faster, and more economical craft. Later, when the Russians put their jets into service, they agreed to the foreign lines using larger craft too.

In June 1957 I was returning to Moscow from Helsinki with two other correspondents, Roy Essoyan of the Associated Press and Howard Norton of the Baltimore Sun. We had been covering the state visit of Khrushchev and Bulganin in Finland. About fifteen minutes before our scheduled landing time in Moscow our plane encountered evil black thunderclouds. The pilot stayed above the billowing darkness for a while, but soon began the descent. The plane bounced and bucked. Only occasional streaks of lightning made it possible to see beyond the wing tips' red and green lights.

It was a half hour past our landing time. The plane groped its way through the storm. The stewardess asked us to fasten our seat belts. We already had done so some time earlier. Norton and I, each feeling ill, exchanged helpless glances. Essoyan kept his attention fastened on the comics page of the Paris edition of the New York *Herald Tribune* long enough to memorize each strip thoroughly.

A member of the flight crew came back into the passengers' cabin. We asked him what was happening. We were waiting our turn to land, he said. The Moscow tower wouldn't let us in yet. No, the plane was not able to use G.C.A. (ground controlled approach). This system enables planes flying blind in bad weather to find their way into airports. Operators on the ground, following the plane's approach to the field on their radar screens, communicate by two-way radio with the pilot, guiding him to the unseen runway. Obviously it's necessary for the pilot and the men at the radar sets to talk the same language in order for this "talk-down" system to work. The language of most control towers all over the world is English. At Soviet airports the language used is Russian.

The Moscow airport *was* equipped with G.C.A., and the Moscow control tower could see our plane on a radar screen. However, instructions in Russian, from the control tower to the pilot in the plane's cockpit, had to be translated by an interpreter, a necessary member of the crew on all such foreign carrier flights into Russia. Anyone who has ever had to use an interpreter is aware of the confusion and delays that can occur in communicating even the most elementary intelligence. Should last-second instructions from the control tower to the pilot to take the plane aloft again—because it was not lined up with the runway, for example—become confused in translation, a crash could result.

Nor was it reassuring to learn that foreign airlines had permission to land at only four fields in Russia. Originally, the foreign lines were permitted to put down at only *two* airfields, but the obvious jeopardy involved in lack of alternate fields caused the Russians to grant two more. Soviet planes in trouble may put in at any number of military and secondary airports. Presumably, a foreign craft in difficulty would not be shot at if it sought an emergency landing at a military fighter base. But it would first have to *find* such a base. Pilots of foreign planes were not furnished with location data on any but the four fields open to them.

We were told that the storm clouds formed a ceiling three hundred feet over Moscow's Vnukova airport. When we finally emerged from the clouds, ground lights looked even closer than that and so very welcome! We were over the runway, too high to attempt a landing. The pilot, gunning the engines to high power to counteract the effects of any downdrafts of the storm, continued along the axis of the runway, then swung to the left to come around and make a new approach for a landing. Every few seconds we would lose sight of the runway's lights in a low-hanging bulge of cloud. It was a thankful group of passengers who got off that airplane. We soon learned how thankful we should be.

The control tower's reason for keeping us aloft in the storm had been that it had lost contact with another plane, a Polish airliner, that was due in a half hour before us. The Polish plane had radioed that it was at six thousand feet, could see the airport, and was heading in to land. This surprised the control-tower personnel because the ceiling at the airport was only three hundred feet. That was the last radio contact with the plane. The tower operators thought that perhaps the Polish pilot was actually seeing another airfield and had confused it with Moscow's Vnukova. Phone calls were put in to other airfields, military and civil, in the Moscow area to ask if a Polish airplane had landed.

At midnight, just after we had put down, and about an hour after the control tower had lost track of the Polish plane, a bruised, bare-footed, mud-caked Polish stewardess walked into the airport terminal. The Polish plane had crashed, but she had survived.

Thrown clear of the wreckage, she retained consciousness and saw moving lights on a distant road. Her shoes lost in the impact, she struggled through thick woods to the road and stood in the oncoming glare of a car's headlights. By gestures, the resourceful girl managed to convey to the Russian, who understood no Polish, that a plane had crashed. He drove her to the airport. She was able to lead a rescue party back to the wreckage. Only then did she succumb to hysteria.

When the courageous girl stumbled into the airport building, we were in a room filling out papers for the customs and waiting for our passports to be stamped. Harold Milks of the Associated Press had driven out to the airport to meet Roy and me. Norton's wife was there to meet him with their car. As Milks, Essoyan, and I were walking out of the terminal building we got our first inkling of what had occurred. A Russian friend working at the airport told me in a low voice, "There's been a catastrophe. A Polish plane has had an accident." She knew no details and no one else at the airport would talk. We were able to learn only that a rescue party had just left the airport.

We drove along the road that leads twenty miles into Moscow, and about five miles from the airport we saw three vehicles drawn up beside the road, their headlights focused on the edge of the woods several hundred feet from the roadside. There was an old army ambulance and two small airport buses. We could see two men just heading into the woods, followed by a Russian woman in a white frock, a nurse, bearing a stretcher. Milks, who luckily carried a flashlight, Essoyan, and I climbed down the embankment off the road, caught up with the nurse and made our way through the woods. We could soon hear men whistling signals in the distance. A quarter of a mile farther and we broke out of the woods into a newly plowed field. At the far end of the field, against the black sky, we could see the dim silhouette of a plane's tail. In the darkness a dozen men stood about aimlessly. It came as a start to notice that several of them carried rifles and apparently they were soldiers, which meant we might be on a Russian military reservation.

Milks had the only light on that weird scene. Neither did the Russian rescue party have an axe to break into the wreckage if necessary.

There was not a single piece of fire-fighting equipment. Not even a hand fire extinguisher.

The light's beam picked out the fuselage broken in two, the tail section comparatively unshattered, the front section crushed. The wings were nowhere to be seen. We learned later that they had broken off on impact and rolled away from the main wreckage. A twisted propeller lay far to the right of the fuselage. An engine was partially buried in the mud. There were bits and pieces of seats, luggage, clothing, strewn on the field.

Then the flashlight picked out a body. A woman lying face down, her body disjointed like some sort of rag doll. A moan in the inky distance froze the aimless rescuers. The Russian woman in white shouted, *Tikho, tikho,* meaning "quiet," and we hurried toward the moans. A woman lay on her back in a furrow of the field. She cried softly in English: "Help me, help me. It's cold. It's so cold. My leg hurts."

The Russian nurse bent over her, bandaged her bleeding head, and began to administer an injection. Nearby, another of the Russians began calling for the flashlight. The nurse insisted that it be kept on the woman until the injection was completed. Then we focused it on the other Russian, as the nurse and two others gently lifted the woman's broken body onto the stretcher. The Russian who had been calling for the light was standing over the almost naked body of a corpulent man. In the bizarre way that disasters operate, his clothing had somehow been stripped from him by the impact. The Russian who was being referred to as "doctor" by the other Russians said the man was dead.

From the woods we could see a light approaching. I signaled with Milks's light and soon two policemen came up. The doctor ordered that the woman be carried out to the ambulance. We lit the way back through the woods. I walked beside the stretcher, brushing aside branches and trying to comfort the woman, who was crying, "What happened? Where's my baby? Where's my child Michelle?"

"You're all right now," I assured her. "There are Americans with you."

"What happened?" she insisted.

I told her she'd been in an accident.

She again asked for her daughter.

I asked her name. It sounded like "Margo Tamper." She said she was from Michigan.

When she had been driven off in the ambulance to the airport hospital, we continued on to Moscow, where we telephoned the chargé d'affaires of the U. S. Embassy to inform him that Americans had been involved in a plane crack-up.

We tried to telephone the story to our offices in London, but the censors cut us off after only a partial report. It was seventeen hours before the Soviet censors passed the complete story.

When we were talking to the American chargé, unknown to him or us, a telephone call had been received by the Embassy's duty officer from a Moscow hospital. An American man, Richard Cheverton, was calling to say that he had been in an airplane accident. The duty officer later sent the Embassy's doctor to the hospital.

Later the pieces began to fit together.

When the plane smashed into the field the burst fuselage scattered its occupants into the mud field. For those who landed face-down, the mud may have been the cause of death. They smothered. For the fortunate, the mud was a cushion that saved their lives. That was true for the Polish stewardess. It was true for the woman we saw at the wreckage, Mrs. Margaret Tremper. This was the case, too, for Cheverton and Michelle Tremper, the twelve-year-old child for whom Mrs. Tremper had been asking.

When we spoke to Cheverton later that morning in the hospital he told us that he had found himself up to his knees in mud after the plane had grazed the treetops and smacked the ground in a violent downdraft.

Cheverton heard someone near him calling "I'm caught, I'm caught." It was Michelle. She was partially buried in mud. He helped her to her feet. She was in near-hysterics. Cheverton began looking for other survivors but then noticed a smoking engine. Fearing an explosion or fire, he took Michelle's hand and headed toward the lights on the road.

Three cars passed the disheveled couple. A bus stopped a hundred feet down the road from them, and several of the occupants cautiously approached them. Taught by their newspapers to be vigilant of foreign parachute spies, the Russians seemed suspicious. Then Cheverton drew a picture of an airplane on a piece of paper and made gestures to indicate a crash. Cheverton's and Michelle's faces were bruised and their head wounds were bleeding. The Russians took them aboard the bus and continued into town. On the way, they picked up three police-men who escorted the foreigners to a Moscow hospital on the road. There Cheverton was able to make it understood that he wanted to speak to the American Embassy. A call was placed for him.

The three Americans were members of a tourist group from Grand Rapids, Michigan. Two others died. So did seven other passengers of other nationalities.

The Soviet press took note of the occurrence, but just barely.

With evident reluctance, the Soviet news agency Tass covered the entire episode in a paragraph:

"A passenger plane belonging to the Polish airline, L.O.T. crashed four to five kilometers from Vnukova airport on June 14. The plane hit the ground for undetermined reasons when attempting to land. Four members of the crew and five passengers were killed. The cause of the catastrophe is being investigated."

As for the four survivors: the Polish stewardess was flown back to Warsaw the day after the accident. Cheverton and Michelle suffered only slight concussion, painful bruises, and minor wounds. They left by plane, too, several weeks later. Mrs. Tremper had severe concussion, major leg fractures, and bruises from head to foot. It was several months before she could be moved, and she was carried on a stretcher aboard U. S. Ambassador Llewellyn Thompson's plane to be flown out of Russia. (Whenever the U. S. ambassador goes "out"— to use the word always employed by Americans in Moscow to describe their journeys abroad—a United States Air Force plane is sent from West Germany. It must put down in Berlin coming and going to pick up and let off a Russian radio operator and navigator for the flight over Soviet territory.) Despite their harrowing experiences, the air crash survivors preferred taking their chances on flying again rather than endure the rigors of other modes of Soviet transportation.

CHAPTER 16

WE CAME BY TROIKA

An American correspondent brought a new Chevrolet to Moscow at a time when Soviet assembly lines were overdue in producing the first long-promised Volga cars. The automobile attracted considerable attention. The correspondent, making his way through a crowd of curious Russians peering at the car, heard his Russian chauffeur confide to some of them: "It's the new Volga."

The Russian's wishful fabrication reflected the yearning among numerous Russians to see the Volga and other Soviet cars in mass production. Many Russians would like to own private cars, but very few do. When a visiting editor of an American magazine was explaining to a Moscow University student in a restaurant that his publication does not contain propaganda, the Russian solemnly responded: "It doesn't need propaganda. The best propaganda your country has is that every worker can own a car." Whatever the merits of the student's comment, Russians probably did feel envy, rather than the pity a Soviet writer intended when he reported from the United States that many workers in California are obliged to go into debt to buy cars. They must drive to work because their factories are so far from their homes. Many Russians would like the opportunity to go into debt if there were cars to buy.

As in so many aspects of the Soviet economy, first things have had to come first. Private cars are given low priority in the allotment of resources. When the Volga car finally did appear (looking like an abbreviated 1950 Dodge) the first batches were assigned to municipal taxi fleets.

A small number of cars are made available for private purchase. There are 26,000 privately owned cars in Moscow, according to official statistics. That's about one car to every two hundred people. And the proportion in Moscow is higher than elsewhere in the country. Soviet production of autos is about 7 per cent of that in the United States. In Moscow there is only one auto showroom, no ads for autos. There are no used-car lots; there's no need for them because anyone who wants to sell a car can find a plethora of customers, and cars are driven until worn out. At one time, a Russian who wanted to buy a car went to an open lot on the outskirts of Moscow where registration tables were set up on Sundays. The experience of a Soviet journalist friend was typical. Upon payment of a registration fee of about one ruble (10 cents), he was told to come back in six months, thus indicating that he was still interested in buying a car. When he came back, his name was checked on the list, where it had moved up a few notches, but, he was told, it would take at least another two years before he could expect to get one. He was asked to come back in twelve months in order to keep his name on the active list. However, as in the case of many scarce goods in Russia, persons in important positions or with sufficient influence are able to bypass the waiting line. Once the car becomes available, payment is in cash; there's no installment plan.

Early registrants one Sunday morning found a table already set up and a man busily recording names and collecting registration fees. Just before the usual opening time, the man suddenly folded up his table and hurried away, moments before the regular registrars arrived. Several hundred hopeful applicants for cars had trustfully paid fees to the Soviet confidence man in this particularly simple Sunday swindle.

The great demand for cars leads to a black market. A car may be sold by its owner but not for a profit. This is true in the case of the sale of any personal goods. To make a profit by private sale is speculating, and speculation is punishable by imprisonment. Such was the fate of A. D. Sotnikov in Shadrinsk, east of the Urals. It's surprising that Sotnikov was able to operate with impunity for more than a year in the little Siberian town of 10,000. When finally apprehended, he admitted to a people's court that he had purchased a Moskvitch car at a speculative price (that is, at a profit to its owner) and then in a week sold it at a profit to himself. He bought and sold two other cars, making 50 per cent profit on each transaction. Actually, it was not cars but cucumbers that proved Sotnikov's downfall. When he purchased a fourth car he decided to keep it awhile. Sotnikov found he could buy cucumbers at a low price in Shadrinsk and, by transporting them a bit more than a hundred miles, sell them at a sizable profit in the city of Sverdlovsk. For indulging in such profitable private enterprise, Sotnikov was sentenced by People's Judge K. Molokov to seven years in jail. Also, his latest Moskvitch car was confiscated by the state.

A tiny three-wheel, two-seat car with special controls is manufactured for war veteran amputees in addition to a kind of motorized tricycle wheelchair. No foreign sports cars nor even more conservative models are imported for sale, and nothing attracts a crowd of Russians so quickly as a brightly painted foreign automobile. The only non-Russian cars on Soviet streets are those driven by diplomats, other foreign residents, and visiting tourists. The Moskvitch looks like an old baby Austin and seats four. Next in size is the Pobeda; it is exported and is used as a taxi in Finland. The Pobeda looks like a Ford of the 1930's and provides most of Russia's taxis; it accommodates five persons, but then the back seat is crowded. It is against the law in Russia to seat three in front. The Volga, slightly larger than the Pobeda, made its first appearance in 1957, and it is a tribute to Soviet assembly lines that, once production began, Volgas began appearing in great numbers on Moscow streets—many of them as taxis. The Volga's hint at modest streamlining—slightly coned mudguards and reluctantly swept-back body lines—gives it the most up-to-date appearance of Soviet cars. Production of Pobedas is being discontinued as assembly lines are converted to the Volga.

The larger-size cars are the Zim and the Zil, taking their names from the initials of the factories producing them. Both are blatant copies of American cars. The Zim, with utilitarian lines, curved radiator grille, and rounded protruding truck in the rear, unmistakably used a prewar Buick as its model. The Zim is the more comfortable, seating five and with space for two additional passengers on jump seats that fold out of the rear of the front seats. The Kremlin and Soviet Ministries use the Zil limousine, a long, high car, obviously copied from Packard with sharply pointed front grille. The unusual length of the Zil gives a back-seat passenger the sensation of being on the end of a tandem when on curves.

The Zil is equipped with jump seats for two passengers, and the driver is separated from the passengers by an unproletarian window that may be raised or lowered automatically by a switch near the rear-seat armrests. Old-fashioned loops-of-plush hand straps for passengers to cling to are provided at either side window. These windows also are controlled by automatic switches, but the automatic gear shift, power steering, and power brakes are modern conveniences of the future in Russia.

Many Zils and some smaller cars have curtains, usually ruffled white, concealing the back seats. It's a sinister sight, reminiscent of an Al Capone-era gangster movie, when an elongated, black Zil speeds down the street, curtains drawn and passengers hidden. (A car called the Chaika, meaning "sea gull," is intended eventually to replace the Zim.)

Soviet cars are monochrome, black, tan, gray, occasionally a bright blue or green. Two-tone models are rarely seen. Except for the grille, headlights, and bumpers there is no chrome work to speak of. Russian cars have electric cigarette lighters on the dashboard, along with a windup clock that almost invariably tells the correct time. There are ash trays, seat covers are always used to protect upholstery, and almost always there's an extravagant rug of floral tapestry.

Windshield-wiper blades are never seen on Soviet cars. When a sudden shower descends, cars stop abruptly, drivers dig their rubber-edged wiper blades from favorite hiding places—under the rug, behind the seat, from the glove compartment. They scurry out into the storm to affix the blade to the wiper's arm. Windshield wipers (called "janitors") are in short supply, and to leave one exposed is to invite theft.

The shortage of spare parts torments Russian motorists. Factory managers are more interested in producing complete vehicles, in order to fulfill state quotas and win bonuses, than in turning out time-consuming spare parts. A typical case of poor planning was described in *Izvestia,* prompted by a letter from a reader, V. Zhuravlyov:

"I've got a K-125 motorcycle. It used to be quite a good one. Now some parts are worn out, so my motorcycle stands idle. It's impossible for me to do without it. I'm head of a tractor brigade and have to travel frequently. I've asked about spare parts in Kharkov and other towns in the Ukraine, I've been writing to Moscow, but all to no avail."

As *Izvestia* pointed out, this man is far from being alone. In eight months, 111,000 orders had been received by Moscow spare-parts agencies, but only two thirds of the orders were filled and these with considerable delay. To make matters worse, one of the motorcycle plants manufacturing the K-125 had begun production on a new model, the K-55. In doing so, it ceased production on spare parts for the old K-125, thus adding to the thousands of K-125 operators who were unable to use their now obsolete machines.

Izvestia editorialized: "'Where can I get spare parts for K-125s?' many people ask. There's no answer to their question. The conclusion seems crystal-clear: the output of spare parts should be increased. Millions owning motorcycles in this country must be assured that when some part of their machine is worn out the motorcycle won't just become a heap of metal junk because a spare part is not easily available. We also hope that *Gosplan* (State Economic Planning Committee) will bear in mind the spare-part needs of private owners while planning industrial output quotas." Such pious hopes often go unrealized in Russia.

There are very few convertibles in Russia. The reason lies partly in the climate, which does not lend itself to top-down driving many weeks of the year. Unlike the United States where a convertible is more expensive than a standard hard-top model, it's just the opposite in Russia. The explanation is that more steel is used in the hard-top model, and steel costs more than style in the U.S.S.R.

Each year does not bring a new model; the same body appears year after year with improvements in engine and engineering. In 1956 a new edition of the Zil was contemplated. A factory model was put on display at the Moscow Industrial Exposition, a permanent exhibit. It was no longer copied after the Packard. Rather, the Zil looked just like a Cadillac. After several months on display, the model was taken away, for the new Zil was to be redesigned. Apparently someone in authority, sensitive to sarcastic comment of foreign visitors, decided that originality must prevail. Later photographs of the forthcoming Zil were published—still looking like a Cadillac.

Most Russian cars have radios and all have heaters; that is a must in Russia. In the severe winter, windows quickly steam up and frost over. Visibility is as effectively cut off as if by curtains. The driver's gloved hand and the feeble efforts of a defroster keep a pancake-size hole free of frost to see the road ahead. Tire chains are scorned; precious steel has more important uses. Tires are manufactured with deep tread which helps somewhat, but skidding is frequent and regarded with nonchalance by Soviet chauffeurs, who simply pull out of a skid by greater speed.

This may be disconcerting to a foreign passenger, but no more so than the practice of Soviet drivers of accelerating for a short distance, then disengaging the gears and coasting until the car is creeping before re-engaging and picking up speed. Some drivers even shut off the ignition during the coast. It's a maddening practice, especially when you're in a hurry. Soviet drivers will not be dissuaded from the conviction that it saves considerable gas.

Buying gasoline is a complicated affair in Russia. First, the driver must stand in line at a government agency to purchase coupons. These he signs and presents to the gas-station attendant who, in return, gives him the amount of gasoline specified on the coupon. Different stations sell different qualities of gas, so that a coupon entitles one to receive gas only at certain stations. There are special stations for high-octane gasoline for big Zil cars, still other stations for smaller cars and for trucks. The price for each type varies, but an average is one ruble 50 kopecks (15 cents) per gallon. There are separate stations for government-owned vehicles (which comprise the bulk of Soviet traffic) and for private cars (where cash rather than coupons are used).

Filling stations are utilitarian—unadorned and Spartan in appearance. There are no public rest rooms, no soft drink dispensers, no neon signs advertising the brand of gas; the only signs read "Gas" and "No smoking." Stations are situated in obscure sections rather than on prominent corners. On highways there are 150 miles and more between stations. Three or four pumps, often cranked by hand and with a glass tube through which the gasoline gurgles into the hose, stand in a row. Attendants are usually women. Often customers take the hose themselves; the attendant simply watches and collects the coupons. The patron may fill his tires with air if he wishes, but like windshield cleaning, it's self-service. Repair work is done at auto workshops, separate establishments not necessarily close to a gas station. There are no large garages for parking private cars, no parking lots other than those operated by state enterprises for their state-owned cars, for there are not enough private cars to make parking a problem. The Kremlin's fleet of cars was kept in the long, yellow stucco stable outside the Kremlin walls in Manege Square until, for the fortieth anniversary of the Revolution, the stable was converted into a picture gallery. Now there's a less prominent Kremlin garage. Taxis and trucks of various government transportation organizations are often parked in fenced-in lots. Parking is permitted on most side streets, and the "No parking" sign is a rarity in Russia. Privately owned cars are often parked overnight in courtyards of apartment houses or in metal, crate-like garages which barely contain the vehicle. The key for one car will usually fit other cars of the same type. However, there's not a great deal of auto theft in Russia; with so few privately owned cars the sudden possessor of a car would be a marked man.

Soviet license plates bear four numbers with letter prefixes. They are issued for the life of the vehicle, so there's no need to renew them annually. Moscow plates are black with white numerals; trucks in Moscow and all vehicles in other areas have orange plates with black numbers. To obtain a driver's license in Moscow, an applicant must pass an oral quiz and a test of ability at the wheel. There's also a medical examination to ascertain that the applicant is physically fit to drive, and he or she (there are few women drivers in Russia although some *are* chauffeurs) may be required to demonstrate a mechanical knowledge. A license is issued only for a particular size car; there are first-, second-, and third-class drivers, depending on the size vehicle they are authorized to operate.

With the license (a small cardboard folder with photograph) the driver receives a card with lines for three entries. In case of a traffic offense a policeman is authorized to collect a fine and describe the offense in one of the three spaces of the card. When the third entry is made the driver loses his license and must report to traffic headquarters within six days to plead his case. If the violation is a flagrant one, the policeman may confiscate the license without the formality of waiting for three offenses. There are no "tickets" handed out nor parking summonses attached to windshields. In most cases the policeman on the spot acts as judge.

The rarity of private cars usually makes it impractical for Russians to learn to drive under instruction from friends. Such friends are few. Also, it is against the law. Driving instruction is given in official schools where students pay tuition. There is a lengthy book of traffic regulations to study. Moscow traffic signals usually have the red light on the bottom, next an amber light, and on top one or two green lights; when one green light is on it means "go," two green lights permit a left turn. A right turn is usually permitted even on a red light, which presents a hazard for pedestrians. Even when a green light permits a pedestrian to cross, he may be struck down by a car whipping around the corner. The Russian pedestrian shows no inhibition from this or other dangers in crossing the thirteen-lane-wide thoroughfares in Moscow and other Soviet cities. They plunge ahead into the street in droves in the face of red lights. Cars plow relentlessly forward, and the crossing humanity somehow divides to open a path at precisely the last moment before being annihilated. One Russian told me: "Oh, it's much better than it used to be. Now at least people mostly cross at the crosswalks. You should have seen it when people would wander into the street anywhere." Another Russian with a philosophical turn of mind explained it this way: "After all, the streets belong to the people. And besides, man created the automobile. Why should he be intimidated by it now?" Police are authorized to fine pedestrians 10 rubles ($1.00) for crossing against a light, but (although I've seen people struck down by cars) I've never seen a fine imposed. Often a blue and red police car with a cluster of loudspeakers on the roof will park at a busy intersection, and a paternal voice will try to reason with pedestrians and coax them to wait for the light. "The lady in the green hat," said the voice on one occasion. "Get back on the sidewalk. The minute you save now will be of no importance if you are killed."

A lane marked in the center of broad avenues provides an island of safety for the pedestrian who finds himself in a swirl of traffic. It is also kept free of traffic for ambulances, fire engines, police cars, the cars of leaders, and an occasional procession of schoolchildren bound for the Lenin-Stalin tomb with flags and a wreath. Only emergency vehicles are permitted to sound horns—a train-hoot noise rather than a siren. Hornblowing was made illegal in 1956 in Moscow and in a number of other cities. This reduced the din but increased the risk in crossing the street. (Of course, in an emergency, drivers may and do blow their horns.)

Traffic policemen, known in official parlance as "workers of the Division for the Regulation of Traffic Movement," direct traffic with precise and graceful movements of their bodies and gyrations of their white batons. At busy intersections policemen work in pairs; one in the center of the crossroads, directing traffic, the other in a glass-enclosed booth on a corner, changing the traffic lights at his colleague's cue. The policeman's face or back means "stop"; traffic moves from the directions toward which the policeman's sides are turned. The upraised arm or baton of the policeman corresponds to the yellow light, warning that the traffic signal is about to change.

It is a complex matter to make a left turn in Russia. Sometimes it's necessary to drive a half mile out of the way to get from one building to another just two blocks away. Left turns are generally forbidden because a car must cut in front of the stream of oncoming traffic. Instead, a driver must proceed beyond the intersection where he wants to turn left and continue straight ahead until he comes to a place marked with a looping arrow. Here a U-turn is permitted. Then the driver retraces his route to the intersection. Since he is now approaching it from the opposite direction he makes a right turn toward his destination without interfering with traffic. It's even more complex for the driver than it may be for the reader.

There are certain other traffic rules peculiar to the Soviet system. The enormous energy devoted to keeping streets swept and clean gives rise to this rule: "Manual cleaning and watering of streets, roads, and squares must be conducted in a direction opposite to the movement of traffic."

In a country where most vehicles are owned by government enterprises, it's a violation of law to leave a state car "elsewhere than in parking lots or, particularly, to park a car for the night somewhere near the driver's home." This is intended to discourage private use of public automobiles.

Processions are so frequent in Russia that special traffic provisions are required. Factory workers are periodically marched to airport or railroad station to provide "spontaneous" demonstrations of greeting or farewell for foreign dignitaries. Groups are often paraded to the Red Square mausoleum. School children march to museums and movies. Section V of *Traffic Regulations for the City of Moscow* is entitled "Movement of Columns and Organized Processions." Columns are not allowed to march in time when crossing a bridge for fear of setting up vibrations that would cause the suspension to sway. Red flags must be carried at the head and tail of the column in daytime and red lanterns after dark or in a fog.

A regulation reminiscent of the army's "trip tickets" requires drivers of all but privately owned cars to carry "a trip sheet of approved form and an itinerary sheet." The regulations provide that a policeman may commandeer a vehicle "unconditionally and free of charge" in order to "pursue a person running away" from the law, to transport a person in need of medical attention to a hospital, or "to hasten to a place where an accident or a breakdown has occurred." A policeman using a vehicle in this manner "is required to make a note to that effect in the trip sheet and to write his name, position, number of his work certificate, and number of his office telephone."

The Moscow speed limit used to be 60 kilometers per hour (37.5 miles an hour), but cars often drove faster on wide main streets, and the speed limit has been abolished. It is now the driver's responsibility to regulate his speed according to road conditions, and the policeman's responsibility to fine him if he jeopardizes life and limb. Another regulation frequently ignored concerns the transport of people in trucks. There is a lengthy list of rules that requires trucks carrying passengers in the rear to be equipped with benches fastened with cables of prescribed strength. More often, though, Russians will simply loll precariously atop a load of laundry, vegetables, or furniture. Another safety provision requires that if a car backfires within forty-five feet of a gasoline station, "the driver must immediately stop the motor and move the car, by pushing it, to a safe zone."

There are regulations for horse-drawn vehicles (while in motion keep hands on the reins) and for bicycles (a license number must be fastened front and rear).

A driver who violates traffic regulations may be fined from 10 to 25 rubles ($1.00 to $2.50) right on the spot by a policeman. The driver gets a receipt and may go on his way. I've been in cars a number of times when stopped by a policeman. The Russian chauffeurs behaved in ways not unfamiliar in similar circumstances in other lands. "I'm sorry, officer," pleaded one, "I had my eye on those pedestrians so I didn't notice the light had changed." A taxi driver who made a U-turn where none was permitted explained that he was so confused by the instructions of the foreigners in his cab that he scarcely knew where he was going. The driver of an Intourist car tried to cajole the policeman: "After all, we're both workers," he said. "Be a good fellow now." All three got away with it.

A driver of a vehicle owned by a government enterprise may lose his license for up to six months if he uses the car for his "own business purposes." Drivers often take the risk. For example, I was waiting for a cab one day when a tan Pobeda drew up to the curve and the driver beckoned to me. For 10 rubles, he said, he would take me where I was going. He was the chauffeur for a minor official in the Ministry of Trade, his boss was at a protracted lunch, and this was a not uncommon way to engage in a bit of private enterprise for self-profit.

Taxis are recognizable by a checkered band around the waist of the car just below the window line and by a light that burns green inside the windshield when the taxi is not engaged. Taxi stands are marked by signs with a large T. Most taxis are Pobedas, but there are also Volgas, Zims, a few Zils, and some Moskvitches.

A meter just below the dashboard is hand-wound but does not register any fare until the taxi has traveled a quarter mile. It's considered proper form in Russia's classless society for a single passenger to sit up front with the driver. Taxi drivers get a salary, about 400 rubles ($40) per month and a percentage of their fares. They also accept— and expect—tips. However, I've never heard a taxi driver make an ugly remark as New York, London, or Paris cab drivers will do if a tip is not forthcoming or if its size does not please them. Taxi drivers receive bonuses for proper care of their vehicles, for conservation of gas and tires. That's why some Soviet drivers will shut off their engines while waiting for a traffic light to turn green. That's also why there have been swindles. A taxi fleet in Riga consistently had shown the best maintenance record. Its drivers received handsome annual bonuses. They used the least gas and their tire conservation was particularly admirable. However, on a routine check up, an inspector from Moscow discovered that lack of wear and tear on the taxis had been achieved by the simple expedient of turning the mileage ahead by means of a matchstick inserted in a hole under the speedometers.

Swindles are also not unknown on Soviet railroads. *Pravda* once disclosed that big government bonuses were being paid to freight employees who were fulfilling their quotas fraudulently, for workers in rail transport are paid according to the volume of freight shipped. Freight is measured in numbers of great crates which make possible mechanized loading and unloading. The crates are supposed to be filled to capacity with goods when shipped. However, freight workers were cutting corners by shipping half-filled crates. The *Pravda* article noted with heavy sarcasm that this might account for the unusual weather in various sections of the Soviet Union. The Ukraine was experiencing unseasonably chill Siberian weather, and Siberia was enjoying Crimean warmth. Perhaps it was caused by the air being shipped from area to area in the empty portions of crates.

The oldest railroad in Russia runs in a perfectly straight line. The Czar who ordered the rails to be laid from Leningrad (at that time St. Petersburg) to Moscow had his own concept of what a railroad should be. He would hear no arguments from engineers and surveyors that costs would be cut by detouring certain rivers, marshes, hills, and forests. The tracks were laid from 1843 to 1851, a distance of 400 miles by air or rail. Although the track is somewhat bumpy, the trip by train between Russia's two largest cities is free of any swaying around curves. It's now called the "October Line," in honor of the Revolution month. (The letters OK on trains stand for "October" in Russian.)

The story is told that, when the railroad had been completed, the merchants along the line whose commerce would benefit from it sent a delegation to call on Czar Nicholas I to express formal gratitude. The Czar received them and is said to have asked with obvious pride: "And how did you enjoy your trip here by my new railroad?" The conservative merchants seemed confused by the question, and their spokesman replied: "But, Excellency, we came by *troika* (three-horse carriage)."

Train travel in Russia is slow but not overly uncomfortable. The "Red Arrow," considered a crack Soviet train, leaves Moscow at midnight and arrives in Leningrad nine and a half hours later—an average speed of about forty miles an hour. Other trains are slower. A trip from Moscow to Kharkov, about the same distance as Moscow to Leningrad, took me more than fifteen hours, and the train was on schedule.

According to the number of stops and speed of a train it is listed in the printed schedule as "local," "speedy," or "express." There are several classes of sleeper trains besides the ordinary coaches. A "hard sleeper" contains compartments for four persons with narrow slabs of thinly mattressed wood providing the bunks. Besides the compartment-space fare of 130.85 rubles ($13.09) from Moscow to Kharkov, a passenger must pay an additional 10 rubles ($1.00) for a thin mattress, a sheet, a blanket, and a towel. A "soft sleeper" provides the covering for the berths. The price is 174.40 rubles ($17.44) for the Kharkov run. On some trains a "soft"-class sleeper has four to a compartment, in others, two. So-called "international" sleeping cars—either cars provided for foreigners or cars attached to trains that cross Russia's borders —contain compartments for one and two persons. Usually there is a washroom shared by two compartments. The Russians see nothing improper in assigning strangers to the same compartment, men and women at that.

Sleepers are attended by a white-coated attendant who stokes a coal samovar at one end of the car and serves frequent glasses of tea to passengers. Few trains have dining cars, and those that do seldom offer choice of menu, as is commonly the case on European trains. Each meal is served in several sittings to accommodate all who want to eat. Between sittings, and on trains that have no dining car, open sandwiches of cheese, caviar, and salami are purchased at station-platform stands. Russian travelers come equipped with great boxes and bags of bread, sausages, pickles, jars of yogurt, and other heady provisions. There's an informality to Soviet train travel; it's perfectly acceptable to don pajamas for the duration of a trip. At protracted stops, passengers sometimes get off the train and do group calisthenics to stretch cramped muscles.

Soviet trains are wired to carry the programs of Moscow's radio. Passengers in coaches are a captive audience. In private compartments the plug may be pulled out if you can find it. (Sometimes there is a dial to regulate the volume, but often it does not enable you to turn the set off altogether.)

Surprisingly, in a land which supposedly caters to the masses, the international tradition of private railroad coaches for the use of officials persists. Many a district manager has fixed up a coach with private kitchen and bar to contribute to his personal comfort on business trips along the line. On occasion Soviet newspapers criticize this practice. *Soviet Russia* singled out one Ivan Petrovich Kechik, the chief of a Caucasus rail district, pointing out that his special coach is used only four or five days a month and is idle the rest of the time, even though there is a shortage of rolling stock.

Railroad personnel have been criticized for other sorts of self-indulgence. *Gudok,* the official railroad newspaper whose name means "train whistle," carried an account of behavior "reflecting on the honor of all railroad men." It seems that a train was delayed for thirty minutes at the Kursk station because the chief conductor, who must give the engineer the signal to start, was nowhere to be found. Finally, the engineer descended from his locomotive cab in search of the chief conductor. He found him locked up in a compartment of car number 36. It seems that the chief conductor, named Bunin, had taken over the train at Kursk. He immediately saw that something was amiss. The cars were untidy. In many cases the conductors of individual cars were wearing improper uniforms and they reeled drunkenly. Chief conductor Bunin sought out the train brigade head, next in command, and tried to expostulate with him. As *Gudok* reported it, the brigade head replied: "Who are you anyway to give orders around here?" When Bunin identified himself as the chief conductor, the brigade head exclaimed thickly, "Well, to me you're nobody at all." At about this time an irate passenger sought out Bunin to complain that the conductor in his particular car was drunk, rude, and had tried to extort money from them. The guilty car conductor was a man named Kunov. The harassed chief conductor Bunin managed to cajole Kunov into the conductor's compartment of car 36 for a confrontation with the complaining passenger. Kunov turned the tables by locking both Bunin and the passenger in the compartment and going on his tipsy way. *Gudok's* purpose in publishing the incident was to complain that no action had been taken against the reveling trainmen, even though the misconduct had occurred a week earlier, but the article showed that the Keystone Cop era has not passed in Russian railroading.

Long-distance bus travel is less frequent in the Soviet Union than in many Western countries. The vast distances between cities, the lack of accommodations along the way, and the poor quality of many roads and most buses are the reasons. However, bus schedules often compare favorably with train times. It takes thirty hours by either bus or train from Moscow to Simferopol, a distance of some 800 air miles. There are five buses a day from Moscow to Kharkov, and the schedule lists the trip as taking sixteen hours, an hour less than by train. The price of a ticket is 88 rubles ($8.80); a train ticket with a "hard" sleeper costs 104.40 rubles ($10.44).

Water transportation is highly developed in Russia. Many principal cities in the European part of Russia are linked by rivers and by an extensive system of canals. Although Moscow is four hundred miles from the nearest great body of salt water, ships from five seas are able to bring people and goods to Moscow's port, called Khimki, by canal and the Moscow River. Moscow is accessible to the Black Sea, White Sea, Sea of Azov, Caspian and Aral seas.

The Soviet Union boasts the longest river- and canal-shipping system in the world, a claim that would be difficult to challenge. A canal connects the White Sea and the Baltic. The Moscow-Volga Canal connects the capital with the mighty Volga. A more recent link in this river system is the Volga-Don Canal, joining the great Volga and Don rivers. The sixty-three-mile-long canal was built in only two and a half years with extensive use of German prisoners of war. A red ribbon across the canal's entrance was cut on July 27, 1952. A river ship named the *Joseph Stalin* was the first to enter and begin regular passenger and freight service between Rostov and Stalingrad.

The Russians like to do things on a grand, almost Gargantuan scale, and the Volga-Don Canal is testimony to this characteristic, as well as to Soviet engineering skill. The canal was one of Stalin's pet grandiose projects. He died less than a year after its completion, and it bears Lenin's name. Other similar Stalin projects were quietly canceled by his successors for being uneconomic. These included plans for the tallest skyscraper in the world, to be called the Palace of Soviets and to house government offices and assembly halls. A gigantic statue of Lenin was to crown its tower. The foundation was excavated, and great cement pilings were sunk in a vast cleared area near the Kremlin. Interrupted by World War II, the construction site soon became an untapped rain reservoir. Postwar shortages of steel delayed resumption of work, and the excavation was surrounded by a board fence. Among cynics there is the saying that "an anti-Communist is someone who can't tell the Palace of Soviets from a hole in the ground."

The Volga-Don Canal may well be as uneconomical as the abandoned Palace of Soviets, judging from the amount of traffic it seems to carry. However, the canal's greatest value may lie in the hydroelectric power it has indirectly created. Big, new industrial projects have been built along the canal's route, and they receive their power from the waters of artificial lakes that resulted from joining the Don and the Volga. These lakes are contained by thirteen hydroelectric dams and dikes. The largest lake is called the Tsimlyanskoye Sea, covering former villages and farm lands of 1400 square miles in area, somewhat smaller than the Great Salt Lake in Utah with its area of 2000 square miles. Thirteen thousand people were moved from their homes before the man-made inundation took place. The valleys of the submerged terrain make for depths of seventy-five feet in some parts of the Tsimlyanskoye Sea. By comparison with the Volga-Don Canal's sixty-three miles of length and fifteen locks, the Panama Canal is fifty miles long and has five locks.

My trip through the Volga-Don began at Rostov; the side-wheel ship *Aleksei Tolstoi,* filled mostly with vacationing Russians, cast off at six on a summer's evening. That night, the next day, and the following night were required for the trip of just over a hundred miles up the broad, quiet Don River to the entrance of the canal, through its locks, and into the Volga River at Stalingrad.

It was Saturday when we left Rostov, an industrial city of more than half a million, and many people were swimming off the sandy strips of beach on the river's east bank and from the steeper embankments on the west bank closer to Rostov. Flocks of small sailboats, some owned either by individuals or factory and office clubs, skimmed briskly with the good breeze around the bow of our ship, its whistle often tooting in warning. Farther from the city, small family groups could be seen picnicking in grassy indentations in the bank. The river's channel often brought the side-wheeler close to villages, their houses roofed with primitive thatch. Single cows, often tended by a vigilant old woman with the care the lone animal of the family's private "herd" deserved, grazed near the water's edge. Primitive ferry boats, really flat rafts, bridged the river at intervals. These ferries were drawn from bank to bank by cables wound around a drum; the cable lay on the river's bottom to allow ships like the *Aleksei Tolstoi* to pass. Occasionally, there was a tug pulling a series of barges loaded with grain or coal toward Rostov. A navy patrol boat with sailors aboard sped past.

Looking much like a Mississippi side-wheeler of the Mark Twain era and carrying 350 passengers, the *Aleksei Tolstoi* was named after Aleksei Nikolaevich Tolstoi, the Russian novelist and man of letters who died in 1945. Groups of university-age boys and girls with knapsacks traveled deck-class, sleeping out in the open. Most cabins are closet-size compartments with bunks for two or four persons, mixed indiscriminately as to sex in the same ingenuous fashion as on trains. The public toilets are poorly tended and made all the more intolerable by steam pipes which pass through them. As is usual in Soviet public rest rooms, toilet paper is rarely supplied and then only sheets of old newspaper cut in squares. The hot water is scalding in rest-room sinks and nonexistent in the compartments. As on trains, a loudspeaker system throughout the ship carries the words and music of Moscow's radio from morning until midnight. The loudspeakers are contained in the lampstands, so that if you pull out the plug you leave yourself without reading light. The lack of conveniences and consideration for passengers' comfort and privacy provide typical Soviet contrast to the tremendous investment in the monumental canal through which the ship passes. It is the same sort of inconsistency as on Moscow's or Leningrad's subway—a setting of wasteful grandeur for people dressed in hand-me-downs.

A crew of thirty-six work on the *Aleksei Tolstoi,* including a doctor. The captain, Vassily Sharonov, age fifty-two, started as a deck hand on an ocean-going Soviet ship and worked his way up to his present post and salary of 1200 rubles ($120) a month. In addition, he usually receives an annual bonus amounting to about 40 per cent of his salary for maintaining schedules, keeping the ship in proper condition, and for continuous service on the job. The ship's chief mechanic gets 1150 rubles ($115) a month. The ship's doctor, a physician for forty years, earns 1200 rubles ($120) per month—more than most doctors, because of his long hours—and treats sunburn and stomach-aches in an office smaller than the passenger compartments.

An easy informality prevailed on the river vessel. At each of the score of stops passengers got on and off, some disembarked for a few minutes to buy fruit and bread from peasant stands. All river stations look alike; an anchored barge with a mid-Victorian-era superstructure that resembles a stunted showboat deprived of bow, stern, and side wheel. Passengers gathered at the ship's rail and struck up conversations. An American was the target for many questions. Most seemed prompted by editorials in *Pravda*. Why did the United States drop the atom bomb on Japan? Do the American people want war? What are you, as a correspondent, doing to fight for the cause of peace? What do you like about the Soviet Union? Why are Negroes mistreated in the United States? Who can afford to go to school in the United States? Are Americans worried about unemployment? Replies were listened to politely, without argument, but also without any sign of belief.

While it was still light on the first evening, the *Aleksi Tolstoi's* great side wheels brought it to the entrance of the canal at a bend of the Don. It is marked by a white stone monument shaped like a towering lighthouse, with four black metal ship prows jutting out in the four directions of the compass. For a half mile the canal consists of a ditch, scarcely wider than the ship itself, paved with white stones. Flat meadowland stretches on either side. The gates of the first lock yawned open to receive the ship. On either portal of the gate rises a tower with heroic statues of hard-riding Cossacks. As the giant metal gates swung shut behind the *Aleksei Tolstoi* there was a rush of water through holes opened in forward gates. It took fifteen minutes for sufficient water to enter the lock and raise the vessel about thirty feet. The ship was hooked to the sides of the lock to prevent the rush of water from driving it back against the rear gate. Raised to the water-level of the second lock, the ship passed into it, and once the entrance gates to the second lock shut, it was possible to open the gates leading to the first lock, lowering its water again to the level of the Don to receive the next ship. Each lock is more imposing than the preceding one, with statues and mammoth arches adorning each. The first eight locks raise a vessel 132 feet, and then the descent begins through 270 feet to the level of the Volga River.

The only Soviet transportation projects more grandiose than the Volga-Don Canal are Leningrad's and Moscow's subways. A guidebook published by the government's Foreign Language Publishing House explains the subway origin in the customary terms of class struggle:

"The question of building an underground railway in Moscow was first raised before the Revolution. The city *Duma* (council) discussed it repeatedly. But house owners, operators of public conveyances, and owners of real estate stubbornly opposed the venture. It went against their interests. After the Revolution these obstacles were eliminated. When the progress made by socialist building provided sufficient resources for an undertaking of such magnitude, the Central Committee of the Communist Party of the Soviet Union and the Soviet Government adopted the decision to build the Metro."

Construction on the Metro (it adopted the name of the Paris subway) was begun in 1932 with the help of engineers from the U.S.A. and the resources that went into it are staggering. It is a showpiece for foreign visitors. Each station is designed on heroic lines with gold chandeliers hung from the vaulted ceilings and walls of mosaic designs depicting the triumphs of the Soviet army or the art and culture of the U.S.S.R. Each station has its own motif. The Serpukhovskaya Station, for example, has marble bas-reliefs depicting the friendship of the various Soviet Republics. A great panel of colored glass shows a parade in Red Square. The Paveletskaya Station is adorned with eighty snow-white marble pillars, and its polished granite floor is fashioned to resemble a gigantic carpet. Novokuznetskaya Station is ornamented with stucco bas-reliefs of battle scenes and with medallions bearing portraits of celebrated Russian generals. The first branch of the subway was completed on May 15, 1935.

Above ground, the entrances to many of the Metro stations resemble temples with Grecian columns. Passengers buy tickets for 50 kopecks (5 cents) a ride, and books of ten tickets are sold for convenience but at no reduction. Women act as ticket takers, and the attendants who signal the trains' departures from the spotlessly clean platforms are women too.

Moscow's transportation system also consists of electric trolley-buses, gasoline-powered buses, streetcars, mostly in sections away from the city's center, and, during the summer, swift, two-deck tram-boats ply up and down the Moscow River. But the Metro is the fastest and cleanest means of getting around. At rush hours trains consisting of six or eight cars run every minute and a half on the two track lines. Cars are simple, with long, lightly padded benches facing each other. There are no advertising panels. Men seldom give their seats to women, but it is customary in Russia for parents to stand so that their children can sit. The first section of benches is reserved for elderly and crippled persons and women with children.

In a sense the Metro is intended to excite the imagination of the Russian people. It is a symbol of the richer life that each Soviet citizen may expect when Communism reaches fruition. Under Capitalism, runs the Soviet logic, only a few may enjoy splendid apartments, but under Communism, everyone can enjoy the sumptuous subway. From the leadership's point of view, an enormous project like the Metro or the Volga-Don Canal or Moscow's Lenin Stadium, seating 100,000, is better able to inspire the people with a sense of the power of Communism than a one per cent rise in the standard of living.

Yet, in the millions of dollars and the gigantic quantities of resources that have gone into the Metro its planners forgot one important convenience for the people. There are gold chandeliers, marble statuary, heroic mosaics. But in none of the underground stations is there a single public toilet.

Such a minor privation can be easily ignored by a people which has become inured to cavalier treatment by the government of its rights, dignity, comforts, property, and money.

CHAPTER 17

A PIG CANNOT SEE THE SKY

Russians are fond of proverbs, and many Russian proverbs concern money. "A kopeck saves a ruble," recommends one proverb, but a contradictory one warns, "Extra money, extra trouble." There are proverbs that offer solace to the poor ("Poverty is no shame," and "Sleep is better without money"), and those that reflect envy of the rich ("It's always a holiday for a rich man".)

These proverbs were born in an era when money meant more to Russians than it does today. Now, under Communism, there's less that money can buy. Money will not purchase a larger apartment or a car. These are acquired only by a long wait or by influence. Whereas money is often a measure of influence in capitalistic countries, membership in the Communist Party rather than wealth is the main source of prestige and influence in Russia.

Although Soviet salaries are low, many families do have substantial incomes just because every member of the family works. Take the example of the Sergeyev family. The mother is a doctor earning 850 rubles ($85); the father is a fabric designer in a textile organization and earns 1300 rubles ($130) per month; a son works as a translator and makes 2200 rubles ($220) a month. A younger daughter is a student in an institute where her monthly stipend from the government contributes nothing to the family income but covers a few of her personal expenses for food, movies, and an occasional dress. With a total family income of 4350 rubles ($435) each month, the family's rent for their two rooms is about 40 rubles ($4.00) per month.

By pooling their income the Sergeyev family could afford to purchase a "Temp II" television set at 2200 rubles ($220), a suit for the father once a year at 1270 rubles ($127), and to eat out in restaurants occasionally.

Experience has made the Sergeyevs and other Soviet citizens wary of savings. After World War II a currency reform that confiscated most savings disillusioned Russians. Then in 1957 the government reneged on repayment of bond obligations. A Russian is inclined to prefer to convert his money into goods. This tendency is nurtured by recurrent rumors of a new currency reform. The authorities do their best to discourage such rumors. For example, in its characteristic style, *Pravda* ran a moralizing article to try to spike rumors that were causing a mild run on shops. Entitled "Short-tailed Magpies," it reported a conversation between two women:

" 'Have you heard?'

" 'What?'

" 'About a reform?'

" 'What reform?'

" 'Don't shout!'

" 'Don't you whisper! What reform?'

" 'As though you don't know. A reform to cut off all the zeros.' "

Then the gossip passed on the rumor that money would be devalued by "knocking off a zero." Fifty rubles would become 5; 100 would become 10.

The person who spoke for *Pravda* in the dialogue asked her informer, " 'Olga Semyonovna, how old are you?'

" 'Fifty. Why?'

" 'Which means that without a zero you'll be just five years old. Just the age to make sand pies in a kindergarten.' "

Having shamed Olga Semyonovna by this biting sarcasm, the voice of *Pravda* then sought to trace the source of such rumors by asking, " 'Who spoke to you about the cutoff of zeros?'

" 'Well, Marya Antonova from the fifth apartment spoke of it.'

" 'But you yourself know that she is the main gossip and chatterbox in our yard. She lies like a trooper.'

" 'She didn't invent it. Aunt Dusya told her.'

" 'All the worse. Aunt Dusya is a speculator. She was arrested more than once for her shady deals, and you believe *her*.'

" 'I don't. But everyone is speaking of it. I just pass on what I hear.'

" 'You are spreading nonsense. You ought to be ashamed of yourself, Olga Semyonovna. I considered you an intelligent woman, but you are a gossip.'

" 'And Kuzma Silych, in your opinion, is also a gossip? He is a book-keeper and yesterday he said that all zeros are to be knifed.'

" 'There are gossips who wear pants too. I would put a dress and a bonnet on your Kuzma and parade him this way in the bookkeeping department.' "

This does not silence *Pravda's* imaginary antagonist, Olga, who replies:

" 'Never mind. I am not the only one. Everyone is chattering.'

" 'Everyone? That isn't so. Our people are not like sheep, the entire flock following the ram. But there still are some who fall for the bait of the speculator. They run and buy everything whether they need it or not. Then the speculator buys the things they do not need from them for a song. Just like the pickpockets arrange a crush in a streetcar to ply their trade, so do speculators drive the suckers to the shops, to fleece them afterwards.'

" 'So everybody is a sucker?'

" 'Not everybody. Some are 100 per cent suckers. Others are gullible people, still others are of little intelligence. But for the speculator they are all equal. He fleeces them all.' "

At this point in the *Pravda* moralistic drama, Olga sees the light, admits gullibility, and asks why the militia, or police, do not apprehend the rumor mongers. *Pravda's* protagonist has the answer, a word of criticism for the militia, and a moral for all its readers:

" 'The militia goes after them, although in a halfhearted way. But it is not only up to the militia. It deals with scoundrels, but there is no need to catch the gossips and fools. They ought to be educated and ridiculed. You, Olga Semyonovna, ought to tell your Maria Antonova: "My dear, stop spreading nonsense all over the yard," and the gossip would have died a natural death.' "

The rumors of a change in the ruble's value reached a crescendo early in 1957 when the government announced what amounted to a devaluation in the ruble's conversion rate for tourists. The Soviet announcement described it as a ruble "premium" to be paid tourists for foreign currency rather than a devaluation. Previously an American dollar would buy 4 rubles. This made Moscow prices prohibitive. A breakfast of stewed fruit, toast, butter, jam, and tea at 10 rubles would amount to $2.50. A simple clay peasant art doll, five inches high, priced at 28 rubles meant $7.00 to the tourist. However, tourists buy Soviet coupon books before coming to Russia at the rate of $30 per day to cover a first-class room, three meals, tea, chauffeured car, and guide. Thus the unrealistic exchange rate was less important in terms of prohibitive prices the tourist might pay for a few souvenirs than in terms of the impression the visitor carried away. He saw a poorly stitched man's suit in a store window priced at 1800 rubles. If the tourist were to purchase rubles at the government-set four-to-one rate he would have to pay $450 for this suit.

The tourist left Russia convinced that almost every essential item, food as well as clothes, was well out of reach of the Soviet worker. The tourist, with a much higher wage than the average Russian worker, could himself not afford to pay $450 for a suit.

The four-to-one rate of exchange had been arbitrarily chosen by Soviet authorities without any regard for reality. None of the factors that come into play in determining exchange rates between other currencies—purchasing power, demand for a particular currency, trade balances between nations—played any role in setting a price on the ruble in relation to the dollar.

Thus it was inaccurate (and unfair to the Soviet government, although it seemed the last to realize it) to evaluate Soviet prices on a four-to-one scale. Russian prices have meaning only when considered in terms of how many hours a Russian has to work to purchase an item. A well-paid factory worker, earning 1200 rubles a month, would have to work a month and a half to buy the 1800-ruble suit of clothes, if he spent money for nothing else.

The same worker would labor more than a year to afford a small Russian-made car, if it were available. His wages for a week would buy a pair of shoes. A day's wages would pay for the best seat at the Bolshoi Theatre. He could also pay for the family's monthly rent with only one day's wage, and his average monthly medical needs cost him nothing at all.

At the time of the four-rubles-to-one-dollar rate, rubles could be purchased at money brokers in New York or London at prices ranging from 10 to 20 rubles to the dollar. Realizing the unreality of their rate,

Soviet authorities forbade tourists and other travelers to bring rubles into Russia and, for that matter, to carry rubles out.

Even Russia's allies had little respect for the ruble as currency. Once, on a flight to Vienna, I bought a cup of coffee and a piece of cake at the Budapest airport during a brief stop. The waitress said, "You may pay in any money—pounds, dollars, francs, kroner."

"How about rubles?" I asked.

"Any money except Russian money, I mean," she smiled.

A number of important visitors such as U. S. Congressmen and British Members of Parliament who at that time had interviews with various Soviet leaders, mentioned the inequity of the Soviet exchange rate. The reply was invariably the same: "Our ruble is pegged at exactly what it is worth and it will not be changed."

The fact was that, at four to one, the ruble was *not* pegged at its worth, and it *was* changed. To stimulate tourist travel and especially to give the tourist a favorable impression, the decision was made to grant tourists and other foreigners in Russia a "premium" of 6 rubles on every dollar exchanged in the U.S.S.R. Proportional "premiums" were given on the pound sterling and other moneys. In effect, this raised the four-to-one exchange rate to ten to one. The 10-ruble breakfast now cost the tourist $1.00, the clay doll $2.50, and the price of the suit in the window would be translated into $180—still overpriced but not quite so exorbitant.

Assurances by *Pravda* and other publications at the time of the rate increase that this did not portend a devaluation of the ruble in the Soviet domestic economy failed to convince some Soviet citizens. One such citizen was a Comrade Piscunov, described by the *Soviet Latvia* newspaper. It seems that Mr. Piscunov was a man of some means. He owned a car and a house. He had bought his wife four fur coats. He was able to send his eldest daughter to the Black Sea summer resort of Sochi for the entire summer. Mr. Piscunov, whatever his other shortcomings as described by the Latvian newspaper, certainly was no piker. Recently he bought his son a new television set and he presented his son's mother-in-law with a combination radio-phonograph. Mr. Piscunov's sources of income were not discussed beyond a reference to his "ill-begotten money." In any event, Piscunov told his neighbors that he had seen a truck unloading bundles of a new type of Soviet currency at the Riga bank which would soon be exchanged at a disadvantageous rate for old rubles.

Some of Piscunov's neighbors withdrew their savings from the bank and bought up all the gold rings they could find, considering rings more secure than rubles. Piscunov himself hastened to a government insurance office and took out a 25,000 ruble ($2500) life-insurance policy on himself, his wife, his son, and daughter, and, of course, on that mother-in-law of his son. The Latvian assumed somehow that in case of a monetary inflation the ultimate payment on a life-insurance policy would be raised in proportion.

With broad sarcasm *Soviet Latvia* asked why Comrade Piscunov was suddenly concerned for their lives. What was the danger? Was it that the blowing of auto horns, now outlawed in Riga and other Soviet cities, had increased the threat to life and limb? No, replied the paper, it was that, fearing a deflation in the value of the ruble, Piscunov wanted his money invested in something that would remain stable in value.

Soviet Latvia dismissed Piscunov and his ilk with these words:

"The Piscunovs and their like are groaning and rattling their money. Honest working people have nothing to worry about and they don't bother worrying. Their honestly earned rubles are quite safe in Soviet savings banks. The Soviet ruble stands firm and unshakable. Its purchasing capacity goes up with every passing day. Our factories and plants are turning out more and more goods, and our ruble becomes stronger and more stable."

Intermittently Soviet authorities feel compelled to offer assurances of this sort to skeptical Soviet citizens to bolster their faith in their money.

Soviet money is based on the decimal system. One hundred kopecks equal a ruble. Kopecks are coins of one, two, three, five, ten, fifteen, and twenty-kopeck denominations, ranging in dimension from the dime-size 10-kopeck piece to the somewhat smaller-than-a-quarter three- and twenty-kopeck pieces. Most are silver in color except for the one-, two-, and three-kopeck coins which are copper shade. Their design is simple: a number on one side indicates the value and, below it, the date; on the other side, a hammer and sickle with the Cyrillic letters "CCCP" (U.S.S.R.) underneath.

A one-ruble paper note (10 cents) is about the size of a dollar bill, and ruble notes get bigger in size as their value increases until the top-value note, 100 rubles ($10), which is two and a half times larger than a dollar bill. Ruble notes come in values of one, three, five, ten, twenty-five, fifty, and one hundred rubles. The 100-ruble note is gray with black, green, and blue lettering and designs. The front is graced

with an oval portrait of Lenin at one end of the bill. The opposite end
is blank until held up to the light. Then a watermark appears, which—
no surprise—is another portrait of Lenin. In the center portion is a
hammer and a sickle, imposed on a green globe, with the inscription: "Banknotes are secured by gold, precious metals, and other assets
of the State Bank." The words, "one hundred rubles," are printed at
the bottom of the bill in fifteen languages of the Soviet Union's Republics.

On the opposite side is an engraving of the Kremlin with the Moscow
River in the foreground. In small letters is the warning: "Forgery of
U.S.S.R. banknotes is subject to prosecution under the law."

If forgery is widely attempted in Russia it certainly is never publicized.
Nor are attempts at bank robbery, although a visit to a Soviet bank gives
the impression that it would be a bank robber's delight. The central
Soviet State Bank and its department banks, such as the State Bank
for Foreign Trade, are more in the Western tradition than are small
neighborhood banks. A guard stands inside the entrance to the central
banks. High-ceilinged rooms open off a drafty hallway. Tellers sit
behind generous openings in glass windows, and there are no bars. It
may well shake a foreign depositor's confidence to notice that the tellers
perform their calculations on an abacus, by sliding wooden beads along
rods in a rectangular frame. The type of abacus best known now is
the frame used for scoring in billiards. An apparatus, not dissimilar to
the abacus still used in Russia, was known in antiquity to Egyptians,
Greeks, Romans, and Chinese who performed computations by moving pebbles or other movable counters. Adding machines and even
cash registers are not often seen in Russia. Cash registers, when used
by store cashiers, often bear the raised lettering, "National Cash
Register Co., Dayton, Ohio."

The branch bank on Moscow's Gertsena Street is typical of the small
state banks situated in every district of all Soviet cities. A sign over
the entrance to the small room—wedged between a grocery store and
a shop selling musical instruments—identifies it as a bank. There is
no depositor-luring display in the window, advertising the security of
the institution or its high rate of interest. A simple brown curtain is
hung on a rod to conceal all but the tops of the heads of the clerks
inside. The only furnishings in the poorly lit room are two tables
provided for the convenience of customers. A portrait of Lenin is
dutifully displayed behind the counter, where the clerks work at two
windows. There are no bars in front of them, no automatic devices for

exchanging money between clerk and customer. No guards are on duty either inside or outside the bank.

Surprisingly, savings by children are discouraged. There has been talk in the columns of government newspapers of passing a law flatly forbidding savings accounts in the name of a minor. The explanation is that savings accounts make children greedy, egoistic, and overly fond of accumulation. In a land where private ownership of means of production is against the law, where loan or investment of money at a profit is forbidden, the concept of a child depositing money in a savings account is officially despised. The newspaper *Komsomolskaya Pravda* ran an article entitled "Unwholesome Passion of Little Depositors." It explained that banks are intentionally called "Labor Savings Banks" because they are intended as a service to those who work, to save money earned through work. If a child is saving, stated the article, to purchase a musical instrument or a bicycle, the parents can just as well save the money for him. In the words of *Komsomolskaya Pravda:* "Becoming a depositor from his school days does not contribute to a child's being thrifty, but rather to his being an acquisitive, stingy egoist." Few concepts demonstrate a greater gap between Soviet philosophy and that of the West where a child is taught early that thrift is desirable.

Open from 10 A.M. to 8 P.M every day including Sunday, the main activity of the bank seems to be the payment of electricity, gas, telephone, and other public-utility bills. Operated by the Ministry of Finance, the repository of funds for all enterprises in the Soviet Union, the banks act as central collection agencies. People customarily pay bills either in cash or by writing letters authorizing the withdrawal of certain amounts of money from their savings accounts.

Checking accounts are only very rarely used, although only a minimum deposit of 5 rubles (50 cents) must be maintained, and there is no charge for checks—which are a quarter the size of American checks —that are drawn.

There are two kinds of savings accounts. The minimum deposit for either type is 5 rubles. The first type pays 2 per cent interest annually, and deposits and withdrawals may be made at any time. The second type pays 3-per-cent dividends, but withdrawals may not be made in small sums; a withdrawal, when made, must be of the entire amount, and the account closed.

The same slip is used for deposits and withdrawals; one side is printed in black for deposits, the other in red for withdrawals.

Insurance offices are even less imposing than banks. One of the capital's twenty-five district offices is in a run-down, two-story building with a faded yellow stucco front. Like so many of Moscow's buildings, poor construction and the passing of time have caused beams to sag and lend it a crooked appearance. I entered through a wooden door, walked down three steps, along an unlit, dirty, plastered corridor, and into a small room where two women worked at desks. Two other desks were piled high with folders. On one wall of the narrow, crowded room hung a portrait of Lenin. One of the women went upstairs to call the manager, who—although responsible for several million dollars' worth of insurance each year—wore a frayed-at-the-collar shirt of subdued rainbow stripes, a necktie creased into formlessness, and an unpressed blue suit. The manager left whatever he had been working at and devoted an hour to patiently answering questions about insurance in Russia. There is only one seller of insurance in Russia—the Government. In the United States there are more than 1300 companies selling life insurance alone.

Russians may insure their lives, they may insure their property and possessions against fire, but there is no insurance sold against theft. The manager explained that it would only serve to encourage robbery if policies covered losses by theft. A woman clerk, working in her coat and shawl as protection against the winter air filtering through the side-walk-level window, chimed in the opinion that insurance against theft would, in a way, legalize theft. Since all insurance in Russia is sold by the government's Ministry of Finance, theft insurance might be taken as some sort of state concession to theft. The manager and his clerks were surprised to learn that theft policies are common in other countries.

Whether or not recognized by insurance, theft, of course, exists in Russia. There are no statistics published to indicate its prevalence. A Russian can only report a theft to the police and hope that his property will be found. Crowded living conditions make for frequent charges of petty theft: a pair of boots disappears from a common hallway; a room occupied by a family in a communal apartment is entered and small articles stolen.

Foreign visitors to Russia have found that they need no insurance to receive compensation for their loss. During the 1957 World Youth Festival an American girl reported her wristwatch stolen. After a cursory investigation, the police handed her 350 rubles ($35)—the value she had placed on the watch. An object of the Youth Festival was propaganda; to give Americans and the young people from many other countries of the world the very best impression of Russia. But even without the festival atmosphere, a British woman journalist reported that pickpockets lifted money from her pocketbook while she was walking through a Moscow market. Police authorities insisted that she accept from them the amount of her reported loss.

Only under one set of circumstances may a Russian put in a claim for stolen property. If the theft has occurred while his house is on fire or being swept by hurricane or flood, he can put in a claim for the stolen items along with those destroyed by the elements.

Crowded Soviet living conditions do serve to prevent fires. With so many families living under one roof, someone is bound to be at home at almost any time to smell smoke before an electrical short circuit or a pot of boiled-over borsch causes flames.

In the case of fire, the district insurance office sends an investigator to appraise the damage. An American, whose trunks had become soaked en route to Moscow, was instructed by his insurance company in the United States to hire a Russian appraiser to submit a report. Arrangements were made for an investigator from a state office to survey the damages. If the investigator's attitude on that occasion was typical, Russians obviously must argue for every kopeck they receive. A woman's evening jacket had been ruined by the immersion of half the jacket. The Russian appraiser examined the garment, and announced "50 per cent damage." The wife protested that the jacket was useless.

"But only half of it was spoiled by water," insisted the Russian.

When he came to a crate of water-soaked facial tissues, he ruled that no damages could be claimed because the tissues had dried. The Americans explained that the thin sheets had become stuck together in drying and could no longer be used. Unfamiliar with the product because it is not manufactured in Russia, the Russian was not convinced. He began going through each of several dozen boxes, sheet by sheet. When he realized that each box contained a thousand tissues, he conceded the damage.

Unlike policies sold by privately owned Western companies, Soviet government insurance policies contain no clause disclaiming the company's responsibility in case of civil uprising, riot, or revolution. The inclusion of such a clause might be taken by policyholders as official admission that civil disobedience is possible in Russia—an admission that Soviet authorities would never make.

There is a novel clause that provides that a Russian who happens to be at home during a fire and does not help the firemen loses his right to claim compensation.

A Russian car owner may insure himself against damages to his automobile and to other property resulting from an accident. Insurance will pay for a dented fender, but there's no personal liability insurance for injuries inflicted on people involved in the accident.

"There's no need for such insurance in the Soviet Union," explained the manager, "because medical care and hospital care are free no matter for what reason they are required. If a person is struck by a car, his broken leg is set by a doctor whose services are free, and he is treated in a government hospital without cost."

The driver of the car is criminally responsible, although he has no financial responsibility for treatment of injuries. He can be tried and put in jail for carelessness or negligence in running down a pedestrian.

Foreign insurance companies are understandably reluctant to write insurance on automobiles operated by diplomats and foreign correspondents in Russia because, in the past, Soviet authorities have not been willing to admit insurance-company investigators. There was the case of a Russian chauffeur, driving the car of an American news agency. He crashed into a truck, killing a Russian woman riding in the car with him. The driver was sentenced to five years' imprisonment. A Soviet court awarded the victim's mother 80,000 rubles ($8000) compensation. The insurance company paid without opportunity for investigation in order not to jeopardize the news agency's right to maintain an office in Moscow.

Fire insurance is widely held by Russians. There are three rates; the lowest, 4 rubles (40 cents) annually, covers 4000 rubles' ($40) worth of furniture and other possessions for residents of stone apartment buildings. The rate is twice as high to insure possessions in apartments only partially constructed of stone, and four times as high for wooden buildings.

Life insurance is less a "must" in Russia than in many other countries. Since it is considered normal practice for a woman to work until retirement age, and since there are state pensions and other forms of social security, there's less need for the head of a family to provide income for members of his family in case of death. Small payments buy a policy that pays only in case of death from natural causes; there's a higher premium rate if the policy is to pay in case of death from accidental as well as from natural causes. The rate depends on how dangerous a person's job is. A Russian may name anyone as his beneficiary, a relative or not, and, contrary to widespread belief, money and property may be inherited in Russia. Russians make out wills and have them certified at a state notary's office. The terms of the will are honored.

One aspect of insurance is similar to that in the United States and other capitalist lands, namely, the insurance agent. Soviet agents, employed by the government's Ministry of Finance, are paid a commission, and most of their income depends on how much insurance they sell. Soviet insurance men sell door-to-door and have a reputation for persistency.

In investing in insurance, a Russian need not take into consideration how much cash he may need at the end of the year for payment of income taxes. Taxes are deducted from wages—which are customarily paid every two weeks in Soviet enterprises. There are no income-tax forms to fill out; deductions are computed in advance from the withholding tax. Persons earning less than 370 rubles ($37) a month are exempt from taxes. Bachelors have traditionally paid an added tax; this is because the state believes a bachelor has fewer expenses and also because the state tries to encourage marriage in order to maintain a steady increase in the population. Bachelors pay from ages twenty to fifty; single women from twenty to forty-five. The tax structure is varied by government decision from time to time. Basically, it is a graduated tax, ranging from about 8 per cent of earnings up to 1000 rubles ($100) per month to 13 per cent above 1000 rubles. There are variations in the tax rules for various categories of income; a writer, for example, whose income from royalties on a book reached 70,000 rubles ($7000) annually would lose about 80 per cent of it in income tax. The withholding tax is reduced for each child dependent on the wage earner.

The main form of taxation, however, is the "turnover" tax, an amount added to the actual production price of a product. Although a price tag is not divided into cost and tax for a customer to see, it's estimated that, with income and "turnover" taxes, the Russian pays about 60 per cent of his wages back to the government. There are no sales taxes or state taxes—the central Soviet Government has the exclusive right to tax.

Whatever money a Russian is able to save after this taxation cannot be invested in anything but government bonds, insurance, or savings. He may not invest in a private business. This is unlawful under the Soviet system; only the state, in the name of the people, may own the means of production. It is against the law to employ anyone for private profit. A person with a special craft or talent, such as a basket weaver or a playwright, may work outside of a collective, although in the case of the basket weaver his baskets would probably be marketed through a group organization, and in the case of the playwright he would belong to the writers' union, a government-sponsored group intended to direct his creative activity into channels acceptable to the authorities.

There is no stock market to invest in, because Communism does not tolerate private investment in industry. U.S. stock exchanges are a favorite and frequent target of Soviet commentators and editorial writers. When stock prices slump it is interpreted as a symptom of the Capitalist depression that Communist economists predict. When the market rises it is explained as an indication of the vast profits munitions monopolists anticipate from an increased tempo in the arms race. It may be questioned how seriously the economists themselves take their flexible interpretation. At a cocktail party at the Ethiopian Embassy I struck up a conversation with a Russian who identified himself as a professor at an Economics Institute. He said his job was studying the American economy. What stocks would he recommend? "Oh, I suppose General Motors, Douglas Aircraft, and Du Pont," he replied with a chuckle, "After all, *Pravda* says they make the biggest war profits."

It would have been a good tip; the stocks rose in subsequent weeks.

Although Russians cannot invest—or gamble—in stocks, they are encouraged to take a chance in Government lotteries. At intervals lotteries are conducted by the Republic governments. A Russian Republic lottery offered tickets at 5 rubles (50 cents) each. The prizes were worth 400 million rubles ($40,000,000) and the Government realized 600 million rubles ($60,000,000) profit. Chances are sold at tables set up on sidewalks; sometimes a Moskvitch car is displayed on the pavement as bait. An advertisement in a Riga newspaper of a lottery conducted by the Latvian administration urged:

"Hurry to buy tickets for the cash and valuable prizes lottery!

"In this lottery 250,000 winning numbers will be drawn in the sum of 8,000,000 rubles.

"Among the valuable prizes are cars—Pobedas and Volgas—motorscooters, motorcycles, television sets, radio sets, combination radio-tape recorder sets, refrigerators, cameras, washing machines, sewing machines, bicycles, and other valuables. A ticket costs 5 rubles. It can be bought everywhere: at places of work, at savings banks, at stores, and news-stands."

Russians are encouraged to invest their money in government bonds but they may be excused for skepticism as to the soundness of the investment, because the Kremlin has defaulted on payments of many bonds. Nikita Khrushchev had a ready explanation for the government's action.

"Just as a pig cannot see the sky," said Nikita Khrushchev in his earthy idiom, "so a capitalist cannot understand our psychology, the psychology of our Soviet man."

Khrushchev spoke with insight. It *was* difficult for people of capitalist countries, and probably of socialist countries too, to understand how a nation could be expected to swallow hard, square its shoulders, and accede to its government's confiscation of a sizable sum of its money.

This speech in April of 1957 was one of the most remarkable of the many remarkable speeches delivered by Khrushchev. It announced that the Soviet Government was defaulting on 260 billion rubles (260 million dollars) borrowed from the people. This was the amount of money Russians had spent to purchase government bonds, on the promise that their money would be returned in twenty years. Khrushchev said, in effect, that the government could not afford to redeem the bonds now and would postpone payments for twenty to twenty-five years. Russians knew this meant forever.

In Paris, in London, in Washington, in Rome, in Tokyo, probably in Warsaw too, such an announcement might have produced street riots, a fall of government, at least vociferous protests. But whatever was in the hearts of Khrushchev's listeners at an agricultural conference in the city of Gorki, they applauded.

Khrushchev was well aware of the bizarre quality of his text. The people were told to stage a marionette ritual of *asking* the government to renege on its payments to them. Always sensitive to criticism and taunts from the non-Communist world, Khrushchev indicated the re-action he anticipated when he told his audience:

"Comrades, a capitalist, a trader who, for half a penny, can cut the throat of his own father if it is profitable to him, will never understand the soul of our Soviet man. He will never believe that you are doing this voluntarily. He will read the papers and say: 'They have intimidated the workers and peasants, that is why they agree. . . .'"

There was, in fact, intimidation, but intimidation of a subtle sort. It was not intimidation of the clenched fist. It was rather the intimidation of social pressure. With the right of dissent long since destroyed, all the instruments, organs, and organizations of government spoke as with a single voice. The government leaders, the government's trade unions, the government's newspapers and radio echoed Khrushchev's words. The man who might have the courage to take exception outside of his trusted circle might not be talked to *death,* but at least into silence. In his shop or office, in his home, he would be lectured at by Communist Party "activists." If he tried to persuade others to his views his treatment would be less charitable and he might eventually face a court as an enemy of the state.

This sort of intimidation was inherent in Khrushchev's suggestion that the workers feign having initiated the idea of the bond default themselves. Several days previously Khrushchev had spoken at a factory in Gorki where, at his suggestion, the workers had voted a resolution in favor of renouncing any claim on their loans to the government.

Now Khrushchev told the agricultural conference:

"If you agree and support us you will perhaps adopt a corresponding call (resolution). We would then publish your call; and in your call it should be stated, however, that the initiative springs from the workers."

Seldom has insight been so brazenly offered into the workings of "spontaneous unanimity" in the Soviet system.

Intimidation of a similar design caused Russians to buy bonds in the first place.

An individualist might resist purchasing bonds for a time, but constant persuasion at his workbench by union officials and "enlightened" fellow workers would likely bring him around. I can recall a not entirely dissimilar experience during army infantry training at Camp Fanin, Texas, when our captain decided that subscription to war bonds was to be unanimous in our company. He made a speech about the patriotism and thrift involved in consigning a portion of one's salary to installment purchase of bonds. The speech was delivered late one hot August afternoon after a day of close-order drill and running an obstacle course wearing a full field pack. Our company of recruits was seated out in the blazing Texas sun on bleachers used for outdoor classes. The captain had cards passed around for each man's signature. The signed cards were checked off against a list on a table set out in front of the bleachers. No one was compelled to sign. But it soon became evident that we would not be marched back to the comparative coolness of the barracks, to the oasis of a shower, to the welcome shout of "company dismissed" so that a man could get a cold beer or orangeade at the post exchange, until each of us had signed. The reluctant were goaded by less resistant bone-weary comrades-in-arms, increasingly irritated by the delay. Needless to say, everyone signed. The subscription was 100 per cent. And it was 100 per cent "voluntary."

Soviet civilian society has perfected its particular modification of this system.

Each year the government announced the sum it intended to raise through loans from the populace for which bonds would be issued. It was indicated how much of his salary each worker was expected to invest, usually one month's salary annually. This was apportioned over a ten-month period and withheld from wages. The numbered bonds that were issued on completion of payment bore the inscription "Obligation for the sum of . . ." and then the denomination of the bond, 10, 25, 50, 100, 200, or 500 rubles ($1.00 to $50).

However, it was evident in the very arrangement for redeeming bonds that the obligation was at best lightly regarded by the government. There were three annual drawings—national lotteries, to be precise. Twice a year the holders of the lucky bond numbers drawn received cash prizes upon surrender of their bonds. The prizes were several times the price they had paid for the bond and up to 5000 rubles ($500) for a 100-ruble ($10) bond. The third drawing each year was the significant one. It exposed the government's attitude. The winners of this lottery were granted the privilege of cashing in their winning bond for the price they had paid for it. These bonds paid no interest, either annually or at maturity. All that a lucky-number bondholder won was the privilege of being able to cash in his bond at the price he had paid for it. This was considered a windfall.

The government's rationale for not paying interest on money borrowed from the people was that the money lent would be worth more when it was repaid because each year goods were becoming more plentiful and prices were being systematically reduced.

Over the years the Soviet Government had incurred an obligation of 260 billion rubles (26 million dollars) in sale of bonds. As bonds were falling due the government had postponed redemption. The amount of money that was due to be paid back each year for matured bonds was fast approaching the sum being borrowed from the populace in new bonds.

Khrushchev broke the profitless cycle.

There was a bright side to the confiscation of the 260 billion rubles borrowed from Soviet citizens. After 1958 no new bond loans were to be floated.

A young Russian announcer at Radio Moscow privately expressed delight. "I don't care about the few thousand rubles I've lost in bonds. Anyway, one of my bonds won in the lottery. The thing I'm happy about is that I don't have to give any more of my salary to buy *new* bonds. That's like getting a 10 per cent raise in pay."

The attitude of older Russians who, unlike newcomers to the rank of wage earners, had been obliged to invest a portion of their salary for twenty or more years, felt quite differently. For them, the default on the government loan meant the loss of money which would have augmented their meager retirement pensions.

Besides these "compulsory purchase" bonds on which the government defaulted, there is another type of bond in Russia, called the 3-per-cent bond." These are not purchased by payroll deduction, nor are the certificates received at the place of work. Rather these are bought at banks. They get their name from the fact that 3-per-cent interest on the total sum invested in them each year is paid out in lottery winnings. There are six regular drawings scheduled each year, and since 1948 there's been a seventh extra drawing.

No interest accrues over the years on these bonds, any more than on the compulsory purchase bonds. However, the 3-per-cent bonds may be cashed in at any time.

The cash prizes are large. A 200-ruble ($20) bond may win from 400 rubles ($40) to 100,000 rubles ($10,000).

The winning numbers for these 3-per-cent bonds, as for the compulsory purchase bonds, are published in newspapers, and citizens eagerly scan the lists for their numbers.

These bonds are accepted by banks for deposit in savings accounts. Posters on buildings and neon signs advertise the bonds as a means of savings.

The government floats the bond issues in amounts of one billion rubles (100 million dollars). As soon as one issue is bought up the government puts out another series, totaling another billion rubles. The basic bond is in a 200-ruble ($20) denomination, but "half bonds" in the amount of 100 rubles ($10) are also available.

The first issue of 3-per-cent bonds came out in 1947. Its term is twenty years. However, the time to maturity is entirely academic because, as already mentioned, the bonds may be cashed in at any time and pay no interest.

According to Soviet statistics a significant sum of money has been invested. A Soviet statement makes this claim:

"The public interest in this loan is mounting with every year. Whereas from 1947 to 1952 the annual intake of the loan was only 600 million rubles (60 million dollars), in 1954–55 it brought in more than one billion rubles (100 million dollars), and in 1956 one and a half billion rubles (150 million dollars). In the first quarter of this year (1957) more than 700 billion rubles' (70 million dollars) worth of bonds were sold."

The latitude permitted in the purchase and sale of this type of bond has led to abuses. I know a Russian who regularly buys a number of the 3-per-cent bonds just before lottery time. If he wins he collects. If he doesn't win and he has need of money, he simply cashes in his bonds, with payment of a small service charge. The 3-per-cent bonds were not intended for this sort of gambling, but apparently it's fairly widely practiced.

There are more serious manipulations in bonds. Soviet newspapers reported the case of a gentleman who traveled around the country with a list of winning bond numbers. He represented himself as a government inspector with the mission of advising citizens as to whether they had overlooked winning numbers. At every home he genially assured the bondholder that his bonds were not winners. However, in cases where he found that a winning bond had, in fact, been overlooked by its owner he adroitly replaced it with a genuine loser from a sheaf he carried with him. Before being caught in the act, the enterprising crook had cashed in quite a bundle of winning bonds (which, incidentally, bear only a number, no name). The man was sentenced to ten years at corrective labor for his crime.

In the payment of taxes, in the confiscation of bonds, and even in the loss of winning bonds to a swindler, the Soviet citizen has one small solace. He knows that in his old age he will receive a government pension, small and usually insufficient though it may be.

CHAPTER 18

SALT PORK, CORN PONE, WHISKY, AND SNUFF

On his 122d birthday, Arshba Suleiman was asked about the condition of his teeth.

"They're in a bad way," replied the gardener, formerly soldier and blacksmith. "One is quite loose."

The Russians are obsessed with the subject of old age. There's an institute in Moscow devoted to the study of longevity. Newspapers frequently carry pictures of Soviet citizens who have surpassed the age of 100. Their formulae for ripe old age are assiduously recounted.

Like Arshba Suleiman, many of the centenarians come from Georgia or other Caucasian mountain regions, or from Soviet Asia where climate, wine, or capriciousness of birth records seem to contribute to long life.

Various regions of the U.S.S.R. vie in claiming to produce the most old people. A census conducted by the Tbilisi (capital of the Georgia Republic) Scientific Research Institute of Labor Hygiene and Occupational Diseases found no less than 10,000 people of 100 and older in Georgia.

This claim far outdistanced that of Armenia, which, granted, is more conservative in size, numbers, and perhaps imagination. There, in the same year, 1956, only 2600 people of over 90 years of age could be registered. Of these only 340 were over 100.

In the Azerbaidzhan Republic, on the southern slopes of the Caucasus mountains and bordering on Iran, a team of physiologists, neuropathologists, and surgeons undertook a survey of the geographic location of old people where, in 1957, there were said to be 420 over the age of 90 and some even more than 150 years old. The scientists, in their quest for the key to longevity, wanted to draw a "longevity map" of Azerbaidzhan by plotting data on diet and other living conditions in areas native to the nonagenarians. They hope that sufficient maps of a wide enough area will eventually establish a perceptible clue to those elements of environment which encourage longevity.

In 1956, in the Russian Republic alone—the largest and most populous of the fifteen republics that comprise the Soviet Union—there were supposed to be 120,000 citizens over 90 years of age. The Georgian Republic, which bred Stalin and which seems generally to produce a ferocious type of individual, was said to have 10,500 persons over 90 with more than 600 of them in the capital of Tbilisi. In 1952, Soviet government figures listed 30,000 centenarians living in the U.S.S.R. By comparison, the U.S. census of 1950 showed only 2850 females and 1625 males over 100 years old in the United States.

Whatever other reasons Soviet old folk may give, hard work is almost always included in their prescriptions. This may indicate that age brings wisdom in Russia, for it is good judgement to declare yourself in favor of work in a country where the government, in its drives for industrialization and farm produce, has set work as the prime virtue.

Soviet articles on longevity in urging work in old age often quote Russian physiologist, Ivan Petrovich Pavlov, whose reflex theories are applied to many branches of Soviet medicine. A typical article read:

"Work plays a decisive role in the prolongation of life. It is known that with well-arranged work a man during his lifetime evolves a definite rhythm or 'stereotype,' as the great Russian physiologist, Academician Pavlov, called it.

" 'A clerk,' Pavlov used to say, 'carries on until seventy with his not-too-difficult work, but as soon as he retires and thereby throws his usual stereotype out of gear the organism proves to be unable to carry on and perishes quickly.'

"This is usually the case with anyone who in old age gives up every kind of work completely. We know many cases when comparatively energetic, cheerful, and able-bodied people who retire on pension suddenly become feeble and ill. This is why upon retiring a man should by no means give up work completely. It is better to take up some lighter work or some favorite hobby, such as gardening or even physical exercise, but in no way should the organism be deprived of the invigorating effect of movement.

"Hence, one of the main prerequisites of longevity, as has been proved by the lives of many thousands of old people, is work. Work has created man, it is inseparable from our life, and is our support in old age."

Writers for Soviet newspapers try to perpetuate this thought. "Specialists regard it as an established fact," writes one propagandist, "that those who reach a ripe old age are all people who have worked all their lives. Many centenarians continue to work even now."

But like the 100-year-old Los Angeles lady who gave "black-eyed peas, turnip greens, salt pork, corn pone, whisky, and snuff" as her recipe, many of the Soviet aged have novel suggestions too.

A cold bath every morning, a daily mountain walk, drinking deeply of a beverage of honey mixed with either milk or water—these were the ingredients of longevity offered by Makmud Eivazov, an Azerbaidzhan peasant. Eivazov reached the age of 150 without ever drinking liquor, but he did take up smoking at the age of 70 "to look more respectable in talking with the other old men in our village." On Eivazov's 150th birthday, Radio Moscow quoted him as declaring that "for the first time in my life I shall drink a glass of wine on November 7, the fortieth anniversary of Soviet power." Eivazov had 200 descendants, and his oldest daughter, a milkmaid on a collective farm, was 110 years old.

Abdulla Magomedov, at the age of 117, was still taking his rain-or-shine, summer-or-winter swim from the shores of the city of Madhachkala on the Caspian Sea. Sporting a thick beard, good hearing and eyesight, Abdulla was a hunter whose aim at 114 was steady enough to down an enormous bear.

Like many others of the Soviet old, Abdulla—whose pre-Soviet upbringing manifested itself in his worship of Allah—retained fertility late in life. His youngest son Ismail was born when Abdulla's wife was 60 and Abdulla himself 93. At least, that's what Abdulla claimed and he swore it true by Allah.

This was a minor feat compared to that of Gadzhi Murtazaliev who died at the age of 136 in the village of Akush in the Abkhazia region of the Caucasus.

Gadzhi, a physician, married for the third time at the age of 90 and had thirteen children by this marriage. His youngest child was born when his eldest, a daughter Khatun by a previous marriage, was 103. Khatun lived to be 121 and worked to the end on a collective farm.

Whoever the oldest person in the world may have been, he or she probably lived in the Soviet Union, if one is to accept Soviet statistics on the subject. In 1957 a rare one hundredth wedding anniversary was celebrated by a couple in the Caucasus Mountains region of Dagestan. Akhmet Adamov was 121 years old at the time, and his wife Manna was three years his senior.

At the age of 154, Lubov Puzhack of Moscow traveled regularly around the Soviet Union, visiting relatives in Minsk, Leningrad, Rostov, and her brother Luka (age 123) in Sevastopol, another brother (age 118) and a sister (age 112) in Kiev. Lubov, a vegetarian, favored fish, potatoes, noodles, and honey. She always went to sleep at midnight and arose at six.

One hundred and sixty-six years was the most I could find claimed by a Soviet citizen: a farmer from Osetia in the Caucasus, named I. Geziev.

Some Russians regard the claims of ultra-longevity with skepticism, judging from a yarn related to me by a Russian friend:

It seems that a group of scientists were investigating the reasons for old age in Georgia. They interviewed a 120-year-old man in a remote village, who told them that he worked every day, avoided liquor, never smoked, and had been monogamous all his adult life. Regularity, moderation, and model conduct seemed to be his explanation for unusual age.

Suddenly there was heard a clamor from the floor above. Swearing, shattering of wine glasses, and young female laughter could be heard.

"Please excuse the noise," apologized the old Georgian, "but it's been that way all his life—women, wine, carousing——That's my father upstairs."

Soda baths were the prescription for prolonged life offered by 81-year-old Professor Olga B. Lepeshinskaya who, in 1950, was awarded a Stalin prize for her work at the Institute of Experimental Biology. After trying the solutions of soda carbonate on tadpoles and chicken eggs, Professor Lepeshinskaya tried it on herself with what she reported to be rejuvenating results.

Whatever other explanations are given, the phenomenon of exceptional longevity seems never to be attributed to ample sleep. Yet, in a fascinating scientific study carried out by Russian doctors, sleep is the very element that seems to play a paramount role in long life.

After preliminary experiments with rats and monkeys, the Soviet scientists chose a dog of fifteen who had just about reached the end of his life span. The animal was totally senile. His energy was low, muscle tone had waned, there were spots where hair had fallen out, and his sexual instinct had long since disappeared.

The dog was put to sleep and fed artificially for a period of three months. When awakened, the animal yawned, shuddered several times, and gradually began to show signs of new youthfulness. Many of the symptoms of senility had disappeared. He barked with new vigor and again enjoyed frolicking. Fuzz appeared in spots where hair had fallen out. Most interesting, his sexual instinct was gradually restored and remained active six more years, to the phenomenal dog's age of twenty-one.

In evaluating the experiment, Dr. S. N. Braines, who directed the work at the Soviet Academy of Medical Sciences, wrote: "Personal hygiene and special prophylactic measures are of great importance for the health of man and the prolongation of his life. If the significance of food for the organism is sufficiently clear, the importance of sleep has been underestimated so far. Yet it has been proved by experiments that an animal can endure hunger even for thirty days, while the lack of sleep for ten days results in death.

"It is known that elderly people often suffer from insomnia. Disturbed sleep does not ensure restorative processes, and this, in combination with other unfavorable factors, leads to far-reaching disturbances of physiological processes."

A conclusion of the continuing experiments was that it may be possible to prolong human life far beyond present expectations by regulating and extending the amount of an individual's sleep. It would be ironic indeed if the Soviet state, whose purges have shortened many lives, should be the nation to open the secret door to longer life.

Although people of some regions of the Soviet Union may live longer than inhabitants of other countries, they receive old-age pensions earlier in life than citizens of many other lands.

At the age of sixty men who have worked in a factory or office for twenty-five years or more are entitled to a pension. Women with twenty years' employment are eligible for old-age pensions at the age of fifty-five.

In the case of persons who work in "underground jobs, on jobs with harmful conditions of labor, or in heat-treatment shops," the law provides that they are to receive pensions earlier—at fifty for men and forty-five for women, with twenty and fifteen years, respectively, on the job.

Persons reaching retirement age who have not put in the required years of service for full pensions are granted old-age pensions in proportion to their years of work.

Soviet pensions, which are exempt from taxes, depend on the salary the person was receiving, but, under a pension law passed by the Supreme Soviet parliament in July 1956, it may not be less than 300 rubles ($30) a month or more than 1200 rubles ($120) per month.

Pension funds are provided for in the nation's budget by taxation and other income. There is no payroll deduction plan, as in the United States' social-security system, by which the worker contributes to his own future pension.

Soviet authorities take pride in this. The preamble to the pension law takes special note of the fact that Soviet workers do not have to contribute directly from their wages to their future pensions:

"Maintenance through the payment of pensions is guaranteed by the socialist system created in the U.S.S.R., under which exploitation of man by man, unemployment and uncertainty of the working people in the morrow have been abolished for all time. Pensions are paid in the Soviet Union completely from the state and public funds."

When the latest pension revision was under discussion in the Council of Nationalities, one of the two chambers of the Supreme Soviet, a gentleman by the name of Goroshkin, who was deputy chairman of the labor and wages committee, dwelt at length on the advantages of the Soviet retirement system:

In Britain, the age for retirement was 65 for men and 60 for women.

In the United States, 65 for both men and women.

In Sweden, 67 for men and women.

However, the speakers did not mention that the average pension in Russia is between 400 and 500 rubles ($40 to $50) per month, which is scarcely a subsistence income.

Also, there are cases of interminable delays in receiving pensions. A cartoon in a Soviet publication showed a young man in full vigor submitting his old-age pension application at the appropriate government office. "I want to get this application in now," read the caption, "so it will be ready by the time I reach 60."

There are cases, too, of fraud. The newspaper *Dawn of the East* published in Tbilisi ran an article in its issue of May 14, 1957, scolding some factories and office heads for "carelessly issuing documentation that incorrectly reports the length of service and the amount of wages" earned by pension applicants. Apparently some enterprising officials were receiving "kickbacks" from pensions for certifying more than the correct length of service.

There is a special Government monthly grant for unmarried mothers to help them care for their offspring. There are those who take advantage of this state beneficence. As a way of augmenting family income, some less scrupulous couples no not bother to register their marriage, and then the wife files a claim for each child, pretending that she is unwed. The newspaper *Soviet Russia* exposed one such fraudulent claimant, Maria Fyodorovna, and reported that in her village alone there are more than fifty such "single" mothers drawing monthly grants.

The woman's lot is hard in Russia. She must often perform double duty. Not only do many women work, but they are also expected to act as homemakers, cooking for the family and keeping house. Although it is possible for a Russian to hire another Russian to come in for a couple of hours a day as a chore maid, such domestic help is difficult to find. Even in comparatively non-manual labor, working conditions are often less than ideal. It's possible to walk on main streets like Gertsena and Gorki and look through windows at night into State dressmaking shops where women sew under dim, bare bulbs in circumstances that resemble the sweat shops of another era in the U.S.A.

In an effort to encourage a high birth rate there is a special pension provision for prolific mothers. Article 10 of Section II of the Soviet pension law reads:

"Women who gave birth to five or more children and who have brought them up to the age of eight are entitled to an old-age pension at the age of fifty. . . ."

Besides old-age pensions there are Soviet state pensions awarded for injury which inflicts disability on a worker. There are no statistics for on-the-job injuries. However, American industrial experts who visit Russia are often shocked by the lack of safety precautions. For example, at the construction site of a hydroelectric dam not a single "hard hat" or helmet is to be seen. This would be unthinkable at a similar site in the U.S.A. Pensions are paid to non-ablebodied dependents of a worker or of a pensioner who dies. These dependents may be wife, mother, father, husband, grandparents, or children. Disabled servicemen comprise one of the largest groups of Soviet citizens receiving pensions because of the heavy casualties suffered during the war. The decision whether a person is entitled to a disability pension falls on the medical profession. A board of Soviet doctors, all of whom are employed by the government, examine the applicant to determine his eligibility for a government pension.

CHAPTER 19

TEN RUBLES PER TOOTH

Tomatoes and buttermilk are recommended in Russia for sunburn. This is not taken internally. No, rather it is spread on the skin as a paste. It makes one somewhat disagreeable to live with but apparently works. At least that's the account of a young American tourist who spent too long in the sun at Sochi on the Black Sea. That evening he felt as if he were frying and he appealed in fragmentary Russian to the hotel maids for ointment. They knew precisely what to do. They cut several tomatoes in half and squeezed them onto his back. Then they applied a coating of *kafir,* Russian buttermilk.

It smelled awful. It brought no relief—at least, not for two hours. Then, all at once, the pain was gone.

In the morning a shower easily removed the tomato-buttermilk crust, and the American's sunburn soon turned to tan. No peeling either.

If there are no tomatoes available, cucumbers are supposed to do as well. Don't lay the slices on the skin in a jigsaw pattern. Squeeze the cucumbers and spread the juice and seeds over the sunburn.

The Russians are staunch believers in such home-grown remedies. In a country which prides itself on its scientific achievements, herb concoctions are widely used and herb "doctors" respected.

Take this prescription, for example. It comes from a Russian teacher, who seems in all respects to be an entirely serious woman not given to practical jokes. She swears by it as a lotion for clearing skin discolorations, sometimes known as "liver spots," that often come with old age.

Take white lilies. Boil them in water, making a concentrated solution. Take equal portions of mustard seeds and honey and, if you dare, spread the mixture over your skin. If there are no bumblebees around it probably can't hurt you, although the stickiness may be unpleasant. My Russian friend claims it clears the skin.

Some aspects of *serious* Soviet medicine seem equally far fetched. Experiments at the Railroad Workers' Hospital in Kursk, 280 miles south of Moscow, might be cited. Following a procedure that had been first tried in a Chinese institute, Dr. S. N. Polikarpov, chief physician of the Kursk hospital, applied a minute electric current to his upper eyelids by means of delicate wires. For ten minutes a day, twenty days in a row, Dr. Polikarpov, who had been afflicted with extreme nearsightedness for forty years, subjected his upper eyelids to the light electric current. On the twentieth day Dr. Polikarpov threw his glasses away.

This treatment was claimed to be effective in nearsightedness, farsightedness and various astigmatisms. After trying it out on a mere fifteen patients the Kursk Railroad Workers' Hospital announced rather ambiguously that "normal vision has been restored in a *number* of cases."

Radical treatment is a characteristic of Soviet medicine. This may be a consequence of the fact that all Soviet medicine is government medicine, intended to treat the masses rather than to cater to individuals. Doctors, dentists, nurses, all persons in health services in Russia are employed by the government and paid by the state. That means that literally everyone in Russia is able to receive treatment. Article 120 of the Constitution guarantees free medical service to the entire population. Lack of money is not a barrier to medical care. (There are exceptions. For example, even though the prices of drugs for combating tuberculosis have been lowered, they still strain the purse of some Soviet sufferers.)

Free medicine has meant sacrifice of the personal touch in medicine. The drastic treatment is preferred over the protracted cure.

Stomach ulcers are sometimes treated by putting the patient to sleep for two weeks and feeding him intravenously. Extreme, perhaps, but the complete rest is said to produce remarkable cures.

Unlike American physicians, who proudly display diplomas on their office walls, Soviet doctors never hang up their accreditations. One reason may be that a Soviet doctor's graduating marks in each college course are imprinted on his diploma. However, Dr. Rachael Julievna Sandler had quite another explanation for it when I spoke with her at the polyclinic of City Hospital Number 57 in the Stalinsky District of Moscow.

"When a patient walks into a private doctor's office in the United States," she said, "he has no way of knowing whether the doctor is really qualified. The certificates on his wall are intended to instill in the patient a feeling of confidence for the doctor.

"Our Soviet patients need no such assurance. They know when they walk into a polyclinic that the doctors there are fully qualified by government training."

Although Dr. Sandler's hypothesis on diplomas (she keeps hers in a drawer at home) may be unique, her pride in Soviet medicine is typical of physicians in the Soviet Union.

Medical attention in Russia is free. A patient is treated by a doctor at his neighborhood clinic without charge. There's no charge for hospital care. There is a fee, though, for the services of a specialist if the patient refuses to accept the diagnosis of the assigned doctor. A visit to a specialist usually costs 25 rubles ($2.50) and a home visit by a physician costs the same. There is a charge, too, for most medicines and drugs, and for eyeglasses and false teeth. A full set of false teeth costs between 250 and 300 rubles ($25 to $30) and single teeth 10 rubles ($1.00) each. Cosmetically speaking, Soviet dentistry is retarded. It is not unusual for a silver or gold-colored cap to be placed on a front tooth. Some members of the Kremlin leadership show gleaming metal teeth when they speak; an aluminum tooth in ballerina Ulanova's smile reflects the footlights when she takes curtain calls.

Neighborhood polyclinics are divided into various sections—gynecology, dentistry, eye, ear, nose, and throat—for specific types of treatment, and Dr. Sandler is one of the two doctors in the section treating eye complaints.

Like other physicians in the Soviet Union, Dr. Sandler attended government medical school for five years (in her case in the city of Voronezh, about 200 miles from Moscow), where she studied general medicine. Then for a year she did practical work in eye medicine, thus qualifying for her specialty.

When I spoke with Dr. Sandler in her small, whitewashed office she was fifty-six years old, and although she had been a doctor for thirty years, her salary was only 1300 rubles a month ($130). Beginning doctors at the clinic earn 850 rubles per month ($85).

A doctor assigned to a clinic usually works five to six hours a day, six days a week. Unlike factory workers, a physician in Russia has no opportunity to supplement meager salary with bonuses for fulfillment or overfulfillment of production targets. To compensate for their low pay some doctors work a double shift, being employed in two clinics. It's not unknown for doctors to treat patients privately at home during off-hours.

Most doctors, about 80 per cent, in the U.S.S.R. are women. The nation's Minister of Health has been a woman—Maria Kovrigina, a large, gray-haired woman, in her late fifties, herself a doctor, married, with two children.

The Soviet Government has made great progress in combating disease, but the tuberculosis rate, as disclosed by Dr. Kovrigina at a session of the Supreme Soviet parliament, is several times that of England, the United States, and France. Mrs. Kovrigina said that there were 46.3 deaths in 100,000 from tuberculosis in 1953, whereas the corresponding figures she gave for the United States were 12.3 persons, for Britain 19 persons, and for France 32.

Children are inoculated against tuberculosis at birth. It is not very effective. There are also vaccines or serums used in Russia for immunization against such diseases as smallpox, cholera, typhus, and typhoid. However, Russia began inoculating against poliomyelitis later than the United States and England. Mass inoculations with the vaccine produced by Dr. Jonas Salk and his associates began in the United States in 1955; it was not done until 1958 in Russia. A group of Soviet medical men traveled to the United States to learn Dr. Salk's methods, and the American experience was closely followed by the Russians.

In a country where statistics, once impossible to obtain, are even now difficult to get, health authorities are justifiably proud of producing statistics indicating progress in health standards.

In 1913, four years before the Revolution, about 30 people out of every 1000 died each year. In 1956, only somewhat more than 7 people (7.7 to be exact) out of every 1000 died annually.

A person living in Czarist Russia in 1913 could expect to live only to the age of 32. Life expectancy in 1956 was 64 years.

By comparison, in the United States in 1900 a male child could expect to reach the age of 48 and a female, 51. In 1955 the U.S. life expectancy at birth for men was 66.7 years and for women 72.9 years. Russia still has a way to go to catch up with the United States in this respect.

The most dramatic decrease has been in the death rate of mothers in childbirth. In 1953 one woman out of 100 died in childbirth. In 1957 the rate had dropped to one in 1500.

A factor in lowering death in pregnancy was the legalizing of abortions by a decree of the Soviet leaders in November 1955.

A Soviet woman, wed or unwed, may have an abortion simply by requesting it at her neighborhood clinic where arrangements are initiated for the operation to be performed at a hospital. The doctor may try to persuade the applicant of the joy and duty of motherhood, but no embarrassing questions are asked and no official stigma is attached to abortion.

Abortions were originally legalized early in the history of the Soviet state, then were made illegal for several decades until the latest decree. Apparently abortions were being widely practiced against the law. Many women died or suffered injury. This was reflected in a news conference comment by Dr. Kovrigina in August 1957, when she estimated that 1700 lives had been saved during the past twelve months by the elimination of "quack" abortions. This was also reflected in the abortion decree, which said that the purpose of the new law was "to provide women with the opportunity of deciding for themselves about motherhood and also to avert the danger to women's health by abortions outside hospitals."

Although the Kremlin decree provided the opportunity for safe abortions, it did not by any means *encourage* abortion. A high birth rate remained the aim of the government. The decree made this clear, adding the hope that "abortions may be averted by further extension of state measures to encourage motherhood." As a matter of fact, moralized the decree, it was the very growth of consciousness among Soviet women of their responsibility to bear children that made it possible to repeal the measures outlawing abortions.

This may have been more pious hope than fact because, soon after abortions became legal, applicants became so numerous that some hospitals were unable to cope with them and at the same time treat other patients. The waiting list grew so long at some hospitals that not a few women reached their turn when it was already too late to perform the abortion safely.

The plentitude of applicants for abortions may be explained in several ways: crowded housing conditions may make an expectant mother willing to go to any lengths to prevent an increase in the size of her family; with several families sharing a bathroom the practice of some forms of birth control becomes difficult or embarrassing; and, finally, there is rather an uninhibited attitude toward intercourse among unmarried couples in many segments of the populace despite a severe *official* code of morals.

A Russian who goes to a neighborhood clinic for medical care— whether for a common cold or an abortion—fills out a small slip of paper in a waiting room and, unless it's an emergency, is given an appointment for later that day or several days hence.

The clinic where Dr. Sandler works is a new, yellow-stucco building, with a series of waiting rooms—all crowded with patients awaiting their turn—from which lead doors to doctors' offices. There is a staff of fifty-eight doctors. Other clinics I've visited are in old, drafty buildings which seem to provide anything but hygienic conditions.

The polyclinic of City Hospital Number 57 serves a neighborhood of 60,000 people, which is a larger number than most. The medical record of each person treated is kept on file, and Dr. Sandler would receive this medical dossier prior to examining a patient's eyes.

The eye chart in Dr. Sandler's office is identical in form with that used by optometrists in America and other Western countries. However, instead of the big letter E at the top, there are the Cyrillic letters Б and Ш. Below are lines of Cyrillic-alphabet letters of decreasing size.

In many countries optometrists—who deal with correction of faults in vision only by means of lenses—receive less training than physicians. However, in Russia the length of training is the same for all doctors. There's no difference in medical-school training for an optometrist who chooses spectacle lenses, or for an eye surgeon who performs a delicate operation. It's only after schooling is completed that specialization begins. To the Russians, they are all eye doctors. An optometrist is simply an eye doctor who happens to be selecting glasses to correct vision. An oculist is an eye doctor who has been assigned to treating eye diseases. Although a doctor like Dr. Sandler has been practicing optometry exclusively for three decades, presumably her additional training qualifies her to recognize symptoms that a practitioner trained only in optometry might overlook. An argument might be made, though, that a great deal of training is wasted in qualifying a person in general medicine and then assigning him to the comparatively limited field of optometry.

Having examined the patient's eyes, Dr. Sandler writes a prescription, if needed. There's no charge for this. The Russian then takes the prescription to an optical shop or to an *Apteka,* or drugstore. Russian drugstores differ greatly from those in the United States. There is no soda fountain, no greeting-card display, no toys, no cosmetics, no cigars and cigarettes, no chrome. Soviet drugstores are gloomy, ill-lit rooms that sell drugs, herbs, hot-water bags, and eyeglasses.

The commoner types of lenses are pre-ground and a prescription is filled quickly. The Russian chooses his frame from a selection of wire- and horn-rim models, and the clerk puts in the prescribed lenses. It takes several days if the prescription calls for lenses that must be specially ground.

I asked Dr. Sandler whether the benefits of the eyeglasses might not be somewhat diminished by the possible errors made by a drugstore clerk in mounting the lenses and fitting the frame to the wearer.

She expressed surprise. "Oh no," she assured me, "the clerks are trained for their jobs. Besides," she added in a typical pronouncement of inexorable Russian logic, "the prescription clearly states the measurement between the centers of the lenses and the distance from the eyes to the lenses."

Having watched clerks lean over the counter to fit a frame to a standing customer's craning head, I felt somewhat less confidence than Dr. Sandler in the efficacy of Soviet drugstore spectacles.

Also the Soviet approach to sanitation is rather whimsical and contradictory. A visitor to a hospital must don a white smock at the cloakroom when he checks his coat. The smocks are kept in a pile or hanging from a common hook, those worn by visitors to various wards are in no way separated. The same smock is worn several times by different visitors, thereby lending germs ample opportunity for circulation through the hospital.

White smocks also are worn by Russians in jobs considered to require antisepsis. The floor attendant in the hotel usually dons one when delivering the laundry, although her hands may be soiled from mopping the floor. Women selling ice cream wear white smocks, and so do those dispensing flavored drinks at outdoor stands, but the common glasses from which customers drink are rinsed in a cold-water spray that completely misses the rim of the glass. Containers for rubbish are conveniently placed at frequent intervals; yet spitting on the sidewalk is permitted. Often toilet paper is not provided in public rest rooms. When the flush system is unreliable, baskets are provided, in what must be one of the most filthy practices anywhere, for depositing the sheets of newspaper, a tissue substitute, after use.

Foreign diplomats, journalists, and tourists visiting Russia are treated at Soviet polyclinics. In Moscow, a special clinic in a freshly painted, roomy building is provided especially for the foreign colony. The foreign patient pays 10 rubles ($1.00) for a consultation or examination, and extra for X rays and treatments. The doctors are thorough in their examinations; one American who went to ask for a prescription for cough medicine was obliged to submit to a complete examination, lasting an hour, before the doctor would write a prescription.

Several American women, wives of diplomats, have had babies delivered at Moscow hospitals. The fathers, by appealing to the hospital director, obtained waivers of the rule against visits by fathers; they were permitted to see their wives only once during the nine-day stay and could not see their children. The lobby of a Moscow maternity hospital is crowded with anxious fathers during the evening visiting hours. Attendants at a counter impersonally advise the father whether it's a girl or boy. The new father may write a letter to his wife and wait in the lobby until his name is called; he is then handed a letter from his wife. Gifts are accepted for delivery also, but during her full time in the hospital the Russian mother must do without the comfort and conversation of relatives, for there are no telephones in the rooms.

Natural childbirth is almost always practiced in Russia. Expectant mothers attend classes at neighborhood clinics where they are taught various exercises and shown with dolls how natural delivery is accomplished. In the case of extreme pain a sedative is administered. Even in serious operations a general anesthetic is rarely given; Soviet medicine prefers local anesthetics, if any. Most diplomats' wives fly out to Berlin or Copenhagen to give birth. The British and American Embassies have kept a doctor on their staffs to look after the health of their personnel.

These and other Western doctors, who have witnessed Soviet medical practices, are generally favorably impressed, although they sometimes find techniques and equipment to be lagging. There is a greater tendency to undertake surgery than in many Western countries, but some Soviet surgical techniques are considered worthy of imitation. The Russians claim to have almost completely eliminated malaria and trachoma. Soviet medicine responded to an epidemic of Asian flu by developing a liquid that, instead of being administered by inoculation, was introduced through the nostrils like nose drops; it proved effective in prevention.

There are 228 scientific medical-research institutes and 76 schools for higher medical instruction. Before the Revolution there were 23,143 doctors in Russia. In 1956 there were 310,186.

Psychiatry in Russia differs considerably from the Western concept. Soviet psychiatry is a sort of counseling. There is no psychotherapy in Russia. Sigmund Freud is regarded as a fake. Freudian terms—libido, id, ego, and super-ego—are deprecated as hocus-pocus. There are no psychiatrists' couches, no psychoanalysis, no delving into the subconscious. Tranquilizing drugs are not sold to the public and are used only in mental institutions. As a matter of fact, the use of tranquilizer pills in the United States is the object of ridicule in Soviet newspapers. "One More Pill," was the title of an article which sympathized with the American workingman for having to swallow a good many pills, including the bitter pill of high taxes. But now, said the newspaper with sarcasm, the American "homeless and jobless can rejoice" because the latest "achievement of the American way of life is a pill guaranteed to eliminate worries, troubles, embarrassments, confusion, tension, and depressions." Warning that use of tranquilizers could lead to paralysis, the publication explained that: "Instability, lack of confidence in tomorrow, living on credit, eternal fear of losing one's job and facing the street—this is the much-touted American way of life that leads the American to a psychiatric ward."

Like other Soviet hospitals, those for the mentally ill are simple, unadorned, lacking in private sink or toilet facilities, but clean and heavily staffed. One Moscow institution which is affiliated with a medical school has 140 beds and 30 doctors (all but six are women).

In the words of a Russian psychiatrist, Soviet psychiatry depends on suggestion, hypnosis, and re-education, not on prolonged analysis. A Russian with high anxieties who seeks the aid of a psychiatrist may be given a Rorschach ink-blot test or a word-association test. In Western psychiatry, what a person sees in an ink blot or the word he gives in response to a test word are taken as clues to his subconscious. In

Russia the responses are simply measures of whether the person is in need of treatment or not. There are expected, conventional responses to test words; the word "chair" might be expected to evoke the response, "table." If it evoked some far-fetched response like the name "Trotsky," the Soviet psychiatrist would take this as a token of the man's abnormality. He would be examined for organic defects to be treated medically. He would have the opportunity for occasional talks with the psychiatrist, if it were considered beneficial.

The Soviet theory of psychiatry considers environment the main source of mental disturbances. The Russians claim that there is less need for psychiatric treatment in the Soviet Union than in capitalistic countries because Communism has removed the anxieties caused by fear of unemployment and economic insecurity. In the absence of Soviet statistics to be taken as evidence one way or the other there may be reason to believe that it is simply a case of less psychiatry being *available* rather than there being less need for it.

A leading Soviet psychologist, Dr. A. R. Luria of Moscow University said with disdain to a visiting American psychiatrist: "Your psychoanalysis is interested in the *depths* of the human, but we in the Soviet Union are interested in his *heights.*"

Behind this epigrammatic slogan-phraseology lie other reasons for Soviet contempt for psychoanalysis. As a materialistic concept, Communism contends that if the proper environment is provided for the individual he will not suffer crippling anxieties. Psychoanalysis treats the anxieties; Soviet effort—say the Russians—is directed toward creating an environment free of factors creating anxieties.

Furthermore, psychoanalysis is impractical in mass medicine. It takes months and years to restore a person to a state of adjustment by psychoanalysis. A psychoanalyst would probably have less than a score of patients at any one period of time. In Russia, where a doctor is expected to treat hundreds, this is unthinkable. Russian medicine tends toward the radical treatment because it is quick, even though a conservative, protracted method may be more effective. Treatment is accessible to everyone in Russia. But no one gets much specialized, personalized attention. In an effort to maintain national good health, however, the government does provide for an annual vacation for every working man and woman, and for occasional holidays scattered through the year.

CHAPTER 20

VERY DRUNK OR VERY WET

The story is told of a Moscow University professor lecturing on the possibilities of space travel following the launching of Russia's earth satellites. He told the class that the future held promise of space ships carrying passengers to the planets of the universe.

"We will be able to travel to Mars, to Pluto, to Venus," concluded the professor. "Are there any questions?"

A student in the back of the hall raised his hand.

"When," he asked, "can we travel to *Vienna*."

Only a very few Russians are permitted to leave the Soviet Union for travel to non-Communist cities. There is a reluctance on the part of the leaders to expose Russians to the plentitude and luxury of a society and system that is regularly denounced. The reluctance may be founded more on fear of pressures for changes within Russia than on the fear that some travelers may refuse to return. After Stalin's death Soviet delegations were sent to the non-Communist world for scientific and other conferences, and a Soviet ship makes month-long vacation cruises of 5000 miles around Europe, putting in at ports in Turkey, Greece, Italy, France, Belgium, Scandinavia, and Finland. Groups of Russians—never as individuals traveling alone—tour the United States.

Most Russians, though, must be satisfied with spending their vacations within the vast limits of the U.S.S.R. The very concept of traveling abroad is alien to many Russians. A foreigner is not infrequently asked, "Do you mean that you can travel to any country you wish?"

Russians are guaranteed vacation time by law (in most cases from two to four weeks), and shortly after the Revolution, in 1919, Lenin ordered that all confiscated mansions and palaces of the Czars and the rich in favorable locations be converted into vacation resorts. "Sanitoria" and "rest homes" are the rather unenticing Soviet words for describing such resorts. In a park in Yalta, one of the favorite Black Sea resorts, stands an obelisk monument with the words of Lenin's decree inscribed.

The Livadia Palace, a summer residence of the Czar on a promontory overlooking the Soviet Black Sea Riviera, has been converted into a vacation sanatorium for workers with respiratory and lung ailments other than tuberculosis. A factory or office worker suffering from such an ailment applies to his trade union for a ticket to spend vacation time in the marble, columned building of Livadia, where the famous 1945 Yalta Conference between Roosevelt, Churchill, and Stalin took place. The price is 1400 rubles ($140) per month; 65 per cent of this is paid by trade-union funds and the remainder by the individual, who receives full pay during his vacation. Four weeks is the time spent at Livadia. The main mansion and its outlying buildings consist of 68 rooms and, with dormitory sleeping (even on vacation), can accommodate 750 guests. The staff of the sanatorium is large—550 maids, waiters, waitresses, cooks, and 54 doctors. The large room where the actual Yalta meetings took place is now a dining room; square tables, seating four at each, are covered by soiled tablecloths. A small ground-floor reading room, its walls covered with deep-red damask, was Roosevelt's study. A nearby room, with a brick fireplace and walls decorated in orange, was Stalin's study; it now serves as an annex to the dining room. The room that once held the Czar's billiard tables is now a toilet. Upstairs rooms provide sleeping quarters for workers "taking the cure"; sometimes the physicians prescribe sleeping outdoors on Livadia's great porches as part of the cure. Whatever beneficial effects this may have on the respiratory system, it does contribute to easing the shortage of sleeping space indoors.

Another highly recommended vacation cure in Russia is mineral-water baths. There are a number of natural hot springs; some areas are noted for mud baths. A widely used mineral water is *Narzan,* sold in bottles throughout the country and bathed in at its source near a place called Kislovodsk. The Kislovodsk resort has not been without scandal. It seemed that the *Narzan* was losing its bubbles. The Ministry of Health's newspaper, *Medical Worker,* sent a reporter to the scene and discovered several reasons why. Baths had been built too far from the *Narzan* springs with the result that carbon dioxide was lost in the pipes. Worse, though, lazy attendants had fallen into the practice of filling the baths at night. By the time the vacationists were ready to use the baths the *Narzan* was as flat as a glass of beer left overnight.

Russians spend their vacations on the Black Sea shore or on the Baltic coast, where weather is cooler but less dependable. Some travel to Soviet lakes, the most spectacular being Lake Baykal, in Soviet Asia, the deepest lake in the world. Side-wheel ships on Russia's great rivers are crowded with vacationists. The fortunate few who own cars take motor trips. The wild Caucasus Mountains are a popular vacation place; month-long hiking parties are organized by sports clubs and trade-union officials.

Whether at beach, countryside, on shipboard or train, the accepted Soviet vacation garb for men is pajamas—ordinary bedroom pajamas, usually of bold, broad stripes. It is considered a fashionable lounging costume. But pajamas are no more surprising to the foreigner than the sight of gross Russian women sun-bathing and swimming in their underclothes and slips.

There are camps for children. For the youngest these are operated by the "Pioneer" organization, the Soviet version of Boy and Girl Scouts with strong doses of ideological training; for teenagers the camps are operated by the Komsomol clubs, the Young Communist League— a preparatory level for the Communist Party.

In winter Russians go skiing; there are few developed ski areas, no ski lifts or tows. Ice skating is popular in a land where skating is often possible seven months of the year. (Roller skates are not used by Soviet children.)

Some Russians spend their vacations at *dachas* (country homes) that they own or in *dacha* rooms they rent. Although 3000 sanatoria and rest homes have been built by the Communists there are not nearly enough to satisfy the needs of the people. Many are unable to obtain trade-union tickets that qualify them to stay at one, and there are cases reported of speculation in rest-home tickets—tickets sold illegally from person to person at a profit.

Although Russian families are usually close-knit, a husband and wife often go on vacations separately. The reasons are several: since both may work, they may get time off at different times, and also it may be impossible for both to obtain tickets for the same sanatoria.

Russia's main vacation town is called Sochi, on the Black Sea's east coast. Its resident population is 80,000, but each year one half million vacationists visit Sochi and its forty-eight sanitoria and two hotels (more are being built). The sanitoria, bearing such names as "Metalogue" and "New Sochi," are operated by the Ministry of Health. Most were built by ministries, but some of the ministries are now extinct since Khrushchev's decentralization of industry. A sanitoria vacation is a serious affair. The vacationist is examined first of all by a doctor, who prescribes a particular gain-weight or lose-weight diet, certain daily exercises, and perhaps hot sulphur baths. Lights are out each night at midnight. The object is not necessarily fun, but rather to get into shape after a hard year's work. On the uncomfortable black pebble beaches, sanitoria inmates sunbathe on wooden cots while a white-smocked attendant keeps her eye on the clock to make sure no one gets too much sun. Russians make a fetish out of being sun-tanned, and well they may, living in a latitude that enjoys so little sunshine. When I visited a Sochi sanitoria beach a bronzed Murmansk steel worker, on the sixteenth day of his twenty-eighth-day pass, regarded my white skin with good-humored contempt.

"Chorny kak smetana, (black like sour cream)," he joked sarcastically.

Buses take vacationists to the Matzesta Springs near Sochi where, in a columned building, a staff of doctors and attendants run as many as 12,000 persons a day through baths with supposedly health-giving powers. The sulphur waters of Matzesta are supposed to be good for an astounding variety of ills, including rheumatism, scalp diseases, skin infections, mouth ailments, nervous disorders, and sinus trouble. Whatever its curative powers, the water's potency is obvious—a silver coin dropped into the sulphur baths almost immediately turns black, and for that reason only plastic plugs and other fittings are used.

Besides vacation time, there are four holidays that are days off for the Soviet worker—the Revolution Anniversary on November 7, Constitution Day on December 5, May Day on the first of May, and New Year's. With two days off on both the November 7 and May Day holidays, the total number of work-free days is six. There is a plethora of other "days" that are marked on the Soviet official calendar with editorials and so-called solemn meetings where music, Communist clichés, and slogans of exhortation comprise the program. International Women's Day, for example, is marked on March 8. This is a Communist combination of Valentine's Day and Mother's Day (neither of which is acknowledged in Russia); it's considered appropriate on this day to present female acquaintances with candy, cologne, and other gifts. February 21 is the International Day of Struggle Against Colonial Regimes, there's an annual day for the army and navy, a special day for honoring the armored forces, artillerymen, another for tank crews. The date of Air Force Day varies with forecasts of clear weather and is held on a Sunday in June, July, or August. The main feature is an air show at Tushino Airport, near Moscow, with a display of low-flying Soviet aircraft, mass paratrooper jumps, stunt flying, and glider exhibitions. Rehearsals for weeks before the show, and also before May Day and Revolution Day, are marked by the reverberating, booming noise of aircraft breaking through the sound barrier.

The Soviet Union commemorates an annual Day of Athletes, a Railroadmen's Day, a Forestation Day, a Miner's Day, a Press Day, and a Radio Day, among others. These special days provide opportunity for Soviet authorities to preach to the people that they enjoy great advantages under Communism. For example, on International Children's Day on June 1, Russians are told by press and radio that capitalist countries provide less than Communism for children. A typical article appeared in the pocket-size *Agitator's Notebook*. It stated that care for children by the state was almost unheard of in the days of Czarist Russia. In 1913, the year before the Bolsheviks took power, there were only several nurseries in Russia accommodating 550 children altogether. Now, under Communism, there were 23,000 permanent nurseries caring for more than 900,000 children. (The extensive network of nurseries is necessary now, for one reason, because often both parents work.)

In Czarist Russia, went on *Agitator's Notebook* in its holiday piece, there were only 4000 youngsters attending kindergartens. In 1955 there were more than 1,700,000 Soviet children in kindergarten. In 1956 about 6,000,000 children went to summer camps or resident camps. Whereas under the Czar four fifths of all youngsters were barred from even elementary education, all children of school age are now required to go to school. The death rate for children had gone down six times since pre-revolutionary times.

By comparison, the position of the younger generation in capitalist lands was presented as being miserable because "the capitalist countries, swept by the arms drive, are pressing ahead preparing a nuclear war and exploiting the masses." There is "ruthless exploitation of 600,000 children in agricultural work in the United States of America.

Even five-year-olds have to work picking beans and tomatoes. Children work from ten to twelve hours daily for next to nothing. The day's work over, the children get beans, salt pork, and cabbage at night. No milk whatsoever. The children then fall off to sleep in an instant only to get up early at six in the morning to begin the same grind again. It goes on week after week. . . ." "From 12,000 to 15,000 children are sold each year on black markets in the United States at a price of from $300 to $3500 per child. Many child traffickers make fortunes."

The year starts off with the celebration of New Year's Eve—cause for parties, noisemaking and toasting in Russia as in other lands. The Soviet New Year's incorporates a number of the nonreligious features of Christmas in the Christian world. Just before the end of the year Russians buy pine trees which they carry or drag home on a sled. The trees are decorated with tinsel, colored balls, and a variety of small, painted metal figures and objects including snowmen, children, parachutists, clocks, vegetables, and tea kettles. Stores are gaily decorated. Colored letters spell out *Snovum Godum*—literally, "With the New Year," the Russian form greeting of "Happy New Year." There are large, bright, cutouts of Grandfather Frost, the Russian counterpart of Santa Claus or Saint Nicholas. In Russia he has a companion, *Snegurochka*— Snow Maiden—a gay, smiling, red-cheeked ten-year-old girl in white fur boots, coat, and hat.

It's a reflection of Russia's blustering climate that, unlike more moderate lands, where the New Year's child is portrayed as a babe in diapers, Russian cartoons and posters always show the New Year fully clothed in long jersey pants, turtle-necked sweater, and sock cap to protect his ears from frostbite. The literal-minded Russians know that he wouldn't last out the night in diapers.

The word for the New Year's fir tree is *yolka,* and parties held during the New Year season, which extends for ten days, are called *yolka* too. There's vacation from school during this holiday period, and *yolka* parties are conducted on a nonstop basis in the St. George's Hall of the Grand Kremlin Palace, in the Hall of Columns (where deceased Soviet political figures are usually laid in state), and in factory clubs. Parents working in a particular ministry or enterprise are sold tickets for children of a particular age group for a certain day. Parents are not allowed to accompany their offspring past the cloakroom. Teachers and playground counselors take charge inside for children's games, which include dancing around the tree, applauding rhythmically to the singing of rounds, and a blindman's buff. There are magicians, clowns, singers of children's songs, storytellers, and, afterwards, gift bags of candy. Knots of anxious-looking parents wait to help their young ones on with layers of clothing and to shepherd them home in Russia's early winter night.

Reservations must be made weeks in advance for tables in the limited number of restaurants. Workers' clubs hold parties. There are noisemakers, paper hats and Soviet champagne. There's no Russian equivalent of Times Square or Piccadilly Circus where jostling crowds gather to greet the New Year. I've watched the New Year in, in Red Square, on a blustery, cold night with the thermometer at ten degrees below zero. A cruel wind whipped stinging snow across the square. At five minutes before midnight the expanse of snow-covered cobblestones was empty except for a yellow-and-blue snowplow truck that methodically followed its course from St. Basil's toward the State Historical Museum. A few minutes before the Spasky Tower clock was to strike the change of guard—two soldiers and a sergeant of the guard began their wooden-soldier march from the Kremlin wall to the Lenin-Stalin tomb to relieve the pair on duty. Suddenly Russians, who had been seeking shelter, began approaching in pairs and small groups from the doorways of the GUM department store across the square from the tomb. We gathered before the tomb, collars turned up against the snow and wind. As the old guard began marching away from the tomb, the Kremlin clock began tolling in the New Year. Russians turned toward each other and smiled. A few shook hands. Couples held hands but did not kiss. No one cheered. The soldiers at the entrance to the tomb stood stiffly, their bayoneted rifles at parade rest. The crowd, which numbered about 150, drifted in several directions. I walked toward my car which was waiting on the hill alongside St. Basil's. The Soviet national anthem could be heard on the car's radio. The chauffeur opened the door, smiled broadly, and said *Snovum Godum*.

New Year's Eve is a particularly busy night for sobering-up stations, a unique and useful Soviet institution. Although Russia publishes no current statistics on drunkenness and alcoholism there are ample indications that it is a problem of considerable proportions. A walk down city streets on almost any evening will reveal boisterous drunks alone and in groups. Soviet authorities have found it necessary to try to discourage drunkenness by decreeing brief jail sentences for rowdy behavior in public, swearing on streets, shouting and disturbing the peace in restaurants. An attempt is made to limit people to one drink. However, this does not prevent a determined drinker from going from one drinking establishment to another. Anticipating this in proposing the one-drink rule, Khrushchev expressed the thought that the walk between restaurants might sober up the individual. The efficacy of the rule is doubtful anyway because it does not apply to wines.

Stern measures are taken against those who operate home stills. Frequent newspaper accounts tell of one-year jail sentences imposed on brewers of home vodka.

A drunk, incapable of making his way home safely or peacefully, is taken by a policeman or a friend to a neighborhood sobering-up station where attendants treat him by various methods—showers, coffee, and, usually, sleep. When sober, the patient pays a small fee and is released. No offense is involved. It is a way of keeping drunks out of trouble, and, in winter, from freezing to death by exposure.

Soviet publications also give insight into the magnitude of the problem. *Agitator's Notebook* wrote that 80 per cent of auto accidents in Russia result from drunkenness and that most cases of hooliganism and burglary involved persons under influence of alcohol. Also, warned *Agitator's Notebook,* drunken Russians are easy prey for foreign spies who are always busily seeking information.

Izvestia commented on drunkenness in the city of Ulyanovsk, Lenin's birthplace (formerly Simbirsk and renamed in 1924 for Lenin's family name at birth). Wrote *Izvestia:*

"The mushrooming growth of sobering-up-station customers in the city of Ulyanovsk is no surprise, and the blame lies on the heads of state offices, Party and Soviet leaders who wink at drunken brawls and play the liberal where they must act with a firm hand. Also, there are too many drop-in cheap drinking places in town that are built even opposite schools so that children can see with their own eyes all the niceties of drunken behavior and hear with their own ears the swearing accompanying it."

Entitled "Drunken Customers," the *Izvestia* article described a restaurant called Russia where vodka flows freely and brawls break out at frequent intervals. A huge, respectable-looking customer holds up a bulky fist under the nose of his smaller neighbor and floors him in a heap. Other customers intervene and escort both to a sobering-up station. One is named Sasha, a retired lieutenant colonel in the army engineers and now a school teacher. At the sobering-up station he calms down and soon is asleep. Not so with his colleague, reported *Izvestia*. His name is Boris, a worker at a teacher's college. It's necessary to bind him hand and foot to restrain him. He shouts and rants against the police and the attendants of the sobering-up establishment.

These are not the only occupants of the Ulyanovsk sobering-up station on the evening described by the *Izvestia* reporter. Present also is the director of a government farm where incubator chicks are raised. With him on a drunken spree was his driver—now both asleep. The Soviet writer explained that most drunkards are rather simple to handle. The average inebriate is carried in, given a bath, and falls asleep. He arises some time later, with a headache, perhaps, quietly pays 10 rubles ($1.00) for the service, and goes about his business. The *Izvestia* article castigated these Ulyanovsk citizens of reputation for falling into paths that lead them to the sobering-up station, especially on holidays.

Moscow night life is inordinately dull. There are beer halls but no bars, except for one at the Sovietskaya Hotel with bar stools that are so high that anyone who falls off could suffer a nasty injury. Soviet vintage champagne costs 47 rubles ($4.70) per bottle and caviar about $2.00 a portion. Most restaurants look alike—cavernous, high-ceilinged halls with bright chandeliers over rows of white-covered tables. There are a few exceptions, like the Peking Restaurant, done in bright red columns with Chinese peacock paintings, and the Aragvi, a marble-walled cellar with a minor-key orchestra of exotic instruments from the Middle Eastern Georgian section of the Soviet Union. Even these are glaringly lighted; there's not a single *intime* restaurant. Menus in almost all restaurants are alike. But there are specialties—Chinese food at the Peking and delicious *tabaka* chicken at the Aragvi.

Many of the restaurants—Moscow's Grand Hotel, the three-story Praga, and the Metropole Hotel Restaurant with its dribbling fountain— have orchestras and dancing until midnight. The music is several decades old with "Lullaby of Birdland" and "Istanbul, Constantinople" current favorites. Dancing, where there is no dance floor, is executed between tables or in carpeted aisles. Women sweep the floors during mealtime. Service is incredibly slow; waiters wear soiled white coats and have often forgotten to clean their fingernails.

There is very little prostitution in Russia, but the practice does linger on despite enforcement of laws against it. Prostitutes usually practice their trade in the back seats of taxis, because of the shortage of rooms. A prostitute in Russia cannot simply check into a hotel, because under the system of state ownership of hotels, rooms are assigned to bona fide travelers.

But to return to holidays, an occasion that Russians traditionally mark with cakes and gifts is the birthday of a member of the family or of a friend.

The revolution that brought the Communists to power in 1917 is commemorated on November 7. Actually, the revolution began in October, and the Russians call it the Great October or the October Revolution. However, after the revolution, the Julian calendar, then being used, was abandoned for the Gregorian calendar which most of the world had adopted in the years since Pope Gregory promulgated it in 1582. The Gregorian calendar went into effect in the Soviet Union on February 1, 1918. In a stroke, February 1 on the Julian calendar became February 14 on the Gregorian calendar. Think of the days of confusion! And the confusion continues in the October Revolution now being celebrated in November.

During the parades held May Day and Revolution Day, Red Square is cordoned off by several echelons of soldiers and militia (as Ministry of Interior troops or police are called). To gain admission to the square it's necessary to show a ticket as well as some form of identification such as a passport, residence permit, diplomat's card, or correspondent's accreditation card. The Red Square militia may well still be talking about the American who tried to get into the premises with only a cigar band for identification. The American was enterprising and brash Michael Todd, movie and show producer, later the victim of an air crash, who was in Moscow trying to persuade the Russians to lend him units of the Red Army for a film version of Leo Tolstoi's *War and Peace*. (The Russians did agree to use Red Army soldiers for extras. However, the negotiations broke down when the Russians insisted on final say in editorial content of the movie, claiming that, as Russians, they were better qualified to interpret Tolstoi than was Todd.)

Todd arrived at Red Square with a ticket but he had left his passport at the hotel. The militia officer insisted on some means of identifying Todd as the person whose name was inscribed on the ticket. Todd pulled a cigar from his pocket.

"Here, this proves it. Read this cigar band. It says 'Made especially for Mike Todd.'"

The Soviet officer was unimpressed by this evidence of American lavishness, and Todd had to go back for his passport.

There are no seats provided for the parade that lasts anywhere from eight hours (during Stalin's day) to four or five hours, now. There is a low concrete reviewing stand on either flank of the Lenin-Stalin mausoleum which accommodates about 10,000 standees.

An American correspondent who arrived at Red Square too late to gain entrance was permitted to stand with a number of other latecomers at the end of Red Square where the marchers exit. As the parade dragged on, he perched himself on a low embankment. A Soviet army major came along and ordered him to his feet.

"Why?" protested the American.

"Because," responded the major with self-righteousness, "in Red Square nobody is sitting down."

Few Russians are permitted the privilege even of standing up to see the parade. Now it is carried on television, but in earlier years it was necessary to march in the parade itself in order to see any of it at all. The main avenues along the line of march are blocked off hours ahead of the 10 A.M. starting time. Soldiers line the avenues and form human lane-markers through which the marchers pass. Red lines, painted during the weeks of preparation, mark the lanes too.

The parades are in two parts. The military portion usually lasts less than an hour and is followed by the civilian "popular demonstration." Just before the Kremlin clock strikes the starting hour, the Soviet leaders climb stairs along the exterior of the Lenin-Stalin mausoleum and take places on an upper level. The position of the Communist Party leaders used to indicate relative importance. The display of their portraits prior to May Day and Revolution Day was awaited eagerly by diplomats, journalists, and other observers of the Soviet scene as a guide to shifting fortunes. This has not been a dependable indication of the relative importance of the leaders since Stalin's death. Although the top two or three leaders occupy positions of greatest prominence, the others now seem placed rather indiscriminately.

Several thousand troops of army, navy, and air force and of the various military academies are lined up in vast Red Square across from the mausoleum. The Soviet Minister of Defense drives slowly past, standing up in the back of an open, steel-gray Zil limousine, reviewing the ranks. He greets the troops through an ingenious loudspeaker arrangement. There are no wires extending from the moving car. He wears a concealed microphone, and the car carries a transmitter. His voice is heard clearly throughout the several acres of Red Square and its approaches. In a throaty roar, the troops respond, "Greetings Comrade Marshal" to the Defense Minister's *zdrastivitza* ("good day") to them. It was the practice years ago to ride on horseback while reviewing the troops, but this colorful tradition fell, either to mechanization or to the advanced age and increased girth of defense ministers.

The elaborate review, which is accompanied by a 300-piece military band, completed, the defense minister joins his colleagues on the mausoleum reviewing balcony, where he delivers a brief speech, reciting tenets of Soviet policy at that particular juncture of history.

Then, to stirring accompaniment of martial music, troops, fifty abreast, march in a restrained goose step with bayonets pointed forward, around Red Square, turning eyes right at the mausoleum and exiting in the direction of the Moscow River past St. Basil's Cathedral. In the critical war year, 1941, when German armies threatened Moscow, Soviet soldiers continued their march through Red Square on Revolution Day directly to the fighting front.

Then, military vehicles roll slowly past over the cobblestones—starting with the Soviet version of an enlarged Jeep, followed by armored troop carriers, tracked vehicles drawing artillery of increasing size, rocket launchers, and missiles. The roar is deafening, and the acrid smoke of the exhausts of the larger-tracked prime movers briefly clouds the square.

Suddenly from the north, over the State Historical Museum, jet planes, fighters, and bombers in formation streak low over the square when the holiday weather permits. During Stalin's time the aerial fly-past was led by a fighter plane piloted by Stalin's son, Vasily. Loudspeakers would announce that he was leading the formation.

After the military come groups of men and women in brightly colored jersey uniforms, representing sports organizations of various factories and other enterprises. Sometimes young women perform on gymnastic bars carried by men as they march past the spectators. Other sports groups while on the march spin hockey sticks or long colored ribbons in unison.

In sunny weather it is a dramatic and colorful sight: the brick walls of the Kremlin, pointed green pine trees lining its length; across the square the government department store bedecked with four-story-high portraits of Lenin and other Communist great, and gigantic gold and red slogans crying *slava* (glory) to the Communist Party, the Soviet State, and the Soviet military forces.

Throngs of Russian citizens in everyday clothes, some of them carrying children on their shoulders, then plod through the square in endless ranks organized by factories, universities, Party groups and neighborhoods. Some years there are several hundred thousand, some holidays over a million, depending on how long, as officially determined beforehand, the "popular demonstration" is to last. The people start forming at six in the morning. They carry lunches and, not infrequently, bottles of vodka. On occasion a militiaman will lead a protesting drunk from the mass of humanity before he arrives at the Red Square reviewing stands. Some of the marchers carry accordions or balalaikas and others dance to their music to fend off boredom or cold winds as the stream of humanity moves sluggishly along avenues emptying into Red Square. The whole procession gives the impression of crimson because of the bright red wreaths of paper flowers, great banners half as wide as Red Square inscribed with slogans in gold, and huge placards atop poles with portraits of the leaders—all carried by the marchers.

At night, after the May Day and Revolution Day exercises, there is dancing and entertainment in the streets. It is a particularly remarkable sight on November 7. Often it is snowing; invariably it is cold. Against the backdrop of the Kremlin throngs of people, heavily wrapped in coats and fur hats, many arm in arm, wander through Menage Square and Red Square. The major buildings are floodlit and decorated with portraits of the leaders and with mammoth signs of electric-light bulbs in configurations of doves of peace, electric power dams, or slogans. There are bandstands erected in a number of city squares, and even in frigid weather a vocalist in evening gown sings to the shivering accompaniment of an orchestra. Traffic is detoured as crowds take over Gorki Street and other thoroughfares. It is as close as Moscow gets to a Mardi Gras atmosphere.

Another sort of holiday in which the Soviet leaders, if not the Soviet people, participate is the national holidays of the various countries represented by embassies in Moscow. Receptions held to mark the U.S.A.'s Fourth of July, France's Bastille Day and the independence days of other nations became, after Stalin's death, important diplomatic forums where the Kremlin leaders sometimes carried on conversations of international significance. At other times, though, they merely engaged in banter.

At one such party ambassadors were immersed in conversation with members of the Kremlin government, but at one end of the buffet table

stood Soviet Marshal Georgi Zhukov, then Defense Minister, oblivious
to the cocktail-party diplomacy. He was helping himself to portions of
sliced turkey, potatoes, and salad.

Some weeks earlier the Supreme Soviet parliament had approved a
budget providing for a reduction in funds for Marshal Zhukov's Ministry of Defense in connection with an announced demobilization of
almost two million men.

Charles E. Bohlen, then U. S. Ambassador, standing within earshot,
chatting with Premier Bulganin, asked: "Have you cut Marshal Zhukov's budget so badly that they don't feed him in the army any more?"

Zhukov barely managed to swallow a mouthful of turkey and potatoes
and chuckled appreciatively.

Although the conversation is unpredictable, National Day parties
follow a pattern in other respects. Invitations, usually printed in French
are sent out a week or ten days ahead of time, requesting the honor
of your presence. The parties usually run from six to eight in the evening. Almost the same faces come to every party. Most guests arrive
promptly at six in a variety of sinister-looking Russian Zil limousines,
European cars including the grand Rolls Royce of the British Ambassador, and American cars ranging in distinction from Chevrolets driven
by several impecunious correspondents to the Cadillacs of the American
and Afghanistan ambassadors. Each ambassador's car flies his nation's
flag from the right-hand fender. Just as a palace displays the monarch's
standard only when he is in residence, so the ambassador's chauffeur
is supposed to furl the fender flag and enclose it in a little leather cloth
when the vehicle is not transporting the envoy.

Policemen are on duty on streets leading to the Embassy and all
Russian vehicles, except those of guests, are detoured. Whenever mem-
bers of the Soviet Government attend, the familiar faces of plain-clothes
Kremlin secret police are seen outside the Embassy and in hallways.

Guests hurry through a reception line consisting of the Ambassador
and his wife and perhaps the Minister of Embassy and his wife, all
wearing fixed smiles and offering tired handshakes. Once through the
formalities of entrance, guests surge toward buffet tables spread with
cold salads, meat, fish, and drinks. The board is sometimes enlivened
by an exotic national dish. At the Afghanistan parties a delicious chicken
and rice concoction is served. The Italians offer piping-hot pizza pie.
Fresh fruit, rarely seen in Moscow during winter months, is sometimes
imported by an embassy for its party and is quickly consumed. I was

standing next to the titled wife of an ambassador, a woman who would never use a wrong spoon. She plucked several bananas from a bunch on a silver tray and stuffed them into her handbag. "For the children," she explained without the faintest trace of embarrassment. And why not? At Kremlin receptions wives of high Communist officials consider it perfectly proper to remove bunches of flowers from the centerpieces to take home.

The wives of members of the Kremlin's governing Presidium are rarely seen at public functions and only seldom accompany their husbands to parties at the Kremlin or even to state dinners for Communist digni-taries. Mrs. Andrei Gromyko, wife of the foreign minister, is an exception. Having lived in the United States during her husband's various periods of service there, she dresses well, speaks some English, and seems at ease in conversation with foreigners. However, the wives of Nikita Khrushchev, Anastas Mikoyan, Klementi Voroshilov, and others usually stay at home when their husbands go to parties.

The secret of success at these diplomatic parties is to master the art of small talk. The smaller the talk the greater the success because of the bizarre assortment of nationalities.

At one such party Charles Bohlen found himself standing at the head table next to the Chinese Ambassador, whose government is not recognized by Washington, just as the Chinese diplomat was offering a toast to friendship among all nations. Bohlen had no choice in that setting but to raise his glass, thus subscribing to the toast of a representative of virtually an enemy nation.

In wandering through the rooms at such a party the Israeli Ambassador, General Joseph Avidar, who had lost his right hand in the war against the Arabs, would inevitably encounter the Ambassador of Egypt or Syria or another of the Arab nations with which his country was still legally at war. It required some diplomatic skill to look right through a person on such occasions.

Once at a small gathering an Egyptian military attaché walked out when the host, in a moment of unaccountable gaucheness, started to introduce him to the Israeli Ambassador. The embarrassed host tried to apologize to the Ambassador.

"Oh, it's quite all right," replied General Avidar, "we're quite used to seeing the backs of Egyptians."

Walking out of diplomatic functions is not uncommon in the complicated diplomatic atmosphere of Moscow.

The American, British, and French ambassadors turned on their heels at a dinner party when their host, a young Burmese Ambassador, with misdirected effort at international *rapprochement,* invited the ambassadors of Communist China and North Korea at a time when the Korean War still was in progross. The attitude of the Western diplomats was that they had no choice in determining their fellow guests at official parties given by the Soviet Government to which they were accredited, but that their national sensitivities should be respected when private invitations were issued.

The biggest walkout occurred at a Kremlin reception in honor of Poland's leaders on November 16, 1956. As usual, there were toasts. Khrushchev preceded his toast to Soviet-Polish friendship with a twenty-minute speech that bristled with denunciation of Britain, France, and Israel for their attack on Egypt.

Capitalists, declared Khrushchev, try to exploit the Hungarian events to camouflage their Fascist schemes, their efforts to establish Fascist rule everywhere. Britain, France, and Israel, with the help of their friends, were engaged in a bandit war on Egypt.

A row of buffet tables separated us correspondents from the area at the front of Saint George's Hall reserved for the Soviet leaders and members of the diplomatic corps. As the words tumbled from Khrushchev's lips we could see the French Ambassador General Maurice Dejean, who led French troops in Indochina, edge toward Britain's lanky Sir William Hayter. Dejean did not understand Russian. Flush-faced Sir William translated a few phrases. They looked toward Bohlen, who maintained his austere expression, poker-faced, his patrician profile intent on Khrushchev's words.

When Khrushchev had finished speaking there was applause, appropriate after a toast, from the guests, mostly Russians. There were ill-concealed conferences among Bohlen, Dejean, Hayter, and other North Atlantic Treaty diplomats. The reasoning was that the Russians had ample platforms for denunciation. It was not in an ambassador's province to object to whatever *Pravda* chose to print or Radio Moscow chose to broadcast. But when invited to a reception to pay respect to a visiting foreign delegation diplomats—as guests—should be immune from insults by their hosts.

Bohlen walked over to the table separating us correspondents from the dignitaries' area, and announced quietly that the NATO ambassadors would leave the party as soon as the Polish leader Gomulka had delivered his toast. The walkout would be in protest of Khrushchev's insults; but by delaying until after Gomulka had spoken there was reason for interpreting their exodus as a protest to Gomulka. Nonetheless, this is the decision that was made.

A bell was sounded for silence. Gomulka delivered himself of a few inoffensive words preceding his toast. Then, led by Avi Cheloche, First Secretary of the Israeli Embassy (the Ambassador was in the Sinai participating in the attack on Egypt), the representatives of the North Atlantic alliance, walked out solemn-faced, single file from the Kremlin. In front of the Soviet leaders, past the plain-clothes men at the entrance between two tables to the leaders' area, down the long red carpet under the golden chandeliers, out of Saint George's Hall. The Soviet leaders ostensibly paid no attention. Conversation continued in the hall as the cream of Soviet official society continued sampling the pickled mushroom and macaroon cakes. But the unprecedented departure in protest was not unnoticed.

There was often considerable drinking by the Soviet leaders at these parties. But they seldom drank beyond their capacity—although it was an astounding capacity. It would be an error to believe that the remarks made at these parties by the leaders were the result of drunkenness. The Kremlin leaders considered these parties an excellent opportunity for making statements in an informal atmosphere. Such statements carried the weight of authority, but could be more easily altered if subsequent events demanded than would be true for a formal document on any subject. In a sense, the cocktail-party access to the leaders by diplomats and journalists was a deliberate substitute for the White House news conference, the mimeographed government "handout," the telephone call to a highly placed official, the background talk—all of which exist as outlets for leaders' views in other capitals, but not in Moscow.

A party at which the Soviet leaders did drink too much was in honor of Denmark's Prime Minister H. C. Hansen. Standing in a circle in a small Embassy parlor, Hansen, Bulganin, Khrushchev, Molotov, and several others began matching toast for toast. The perspiring Danish Ambassador tried to keep a path open amid the eavesdropping journalists and guests so that maids bearing trays could reach the inner circle. First, champagne glasses were raised to peace, to Soviet-Danish friendship, to more visits, to more drinks. Five brimful champagne glasses were downed by Hansen, Bulganin, and Khrushchev. But Molotov, longer in the diplomatic game and presumably wiser, cheated on several toasts. It was a favorite gambit of Khrushchev at these toasting bouts to swallow his drink and then hold the glass over his head upside down, challenging his toastee: "May you have as many troubles as there are drops left in this glass." Compelled to respond in kind, the visiting dignitary soon became very drunk or very wet.

Khrushchev took a martini from the tray. He recalled that it was at the Geneva Conference that President Eisenhower had introduced them to the wonderful martini.

At some point in the proceedings Bulganin vigorously hurled an empty champagne glass against the wall, narrowly missing the ear of the correspondent of the Communist *Daily Worker* of London. Soon thereafter Prime Minister Hansen broke into a rather indistinguishable Danish song about not forgetting old acquaintances.

When it came time for the Soviet guests to depart, an aide helped support Hansen to the hallway to do his duties as a host. Bulganin and Khrushchev reached the door under their own power but sought the banister in descending the stairs. They were not quite down the stairs nor out of sight when the aide escorted the weaving Prime Minister into a private room. A dinner party for members of the Danish Embassy that followed the reception was held without the presence of the guest of honor.

Even *Pravda,* which reports national day receptions attended by the leaders, ordinarily in a brief paragraph with the usual comment that the party was held in "a friendly atmosphere," extended itself on this occasion. The atmosphere at the Danish Embassy was described as "unusually warm."

CHAPTER 21

BALLET, STEREOKINO, AND KUNI

It was the third act of the ballet "The Bronze Horseman,"
adapted from Alexander Pushkin's poem:

> *Madder the weather grew, and ever*
> *Higher upswelled the roaring river*
> *And bubbled like a kettle, and whirled*
> *And like a maddened beast was hurled*
> *Swift on the city.*

By means of realistic stagecraft, winds swept the stage, lightning
flashed, St. Petersburg's Neva River rose slowly and finally overflowed
into the city's main square. The water was represented on the immense,
darkened stage of the Bolshoi Theatre by broad ribbons of cloth un-
dulating in ever mounting waves. The hero, Eugene, in search of his
sweetheart, was stranded on the steps of a building, and finally, amid
the surging debris, a boat came by and rescued him. During this
twenty-minute act there was drama, exciting music, clever stage
effects, but only about one minute of dancing.

As the curtain fell to loud applause, a sarcastic Frenchman in the
audience said quietly: *"Voilà un ballet bien dansé!"*

It's really not necessary to like or understand the dance in order
to enjoy Russia's ballet. Ballet in Russia is only part dancing. It is
also in large portion rich pantomime, pageant and panoply.

Sometimes it is also propaganda, at least in the case of new ballets
created since the advent of the Communists. The first ballet composed

after the fall of the Czars was called "The Red Poppy," now renamed "The Red Flower," because of the implications of opium in the word "poppy" that Russia's Chinese friends found objectionable. Presented originally in the 1920s, its music by R. M. Glier contains strains of the "Internationale," and it is a ballet with an ideological message. It may seem difficult to transmit Marxist-Leninist doctrine across the footlights by ballet, but "The Red Flower" tries to do so with more than a trace of the ridiculous. It overdraws such characterizations as that of Boss, the sneering, hook-nosed American who exploits Chinese coolie laborers, and of a kindly Soviet sea captain and his genial crew who inspire the coolies to revolution. Excerpts from the program notes convey the mood of the ballet:

"The scene is Kuomintang, China. . . . Exhausted by the everlasting work and hunger, coolies are unloading freight brought by an American ship as the overseers drive them on.

"A party of American and British officers, richly dressed ladies, businessmen, the owners of concessions, and banks are driven to a harbor restaurant in rickshaws. These are the foreign masters of China. One of them, an American named Boss, is welcomed with obsequious deference by the reactionary, Li Shan-Fu, a rich businessman and owner of the city's amusement halls, who carries out Boss's special assignments. Everything seems quiet in the harbor. But if one looks closely at the coolies' faces and intercepts the glances they dart at Boss and Li Shan-Fu, it is quite clear that they hate these masters. . . .

"One of the coolies falls down under his burden. The overseers run up and beat the coolie without mercy, compelling him to get up. Ma Li-chen (the revolutionary coolie hero) and his friends hurry to the rescue. Shoulder to shoulder they stand before the brutal overseers, alert and ready for action. . . .

"Ma Li-chen lifts the large box which has pinned his friend underneath it and hurls it aside. The box, which is labeled 'Cigarettes' is smashed, and American rifles fall out. The unexpected sight stuns the coolies and freezes them to the ground. So this is the kind of freight American businessmen are bringing to China! So this is what they are preparing for us!

"The angry Ma Li-chen addresses the coolies and calls upon them to strike, and all them decide to support him. . . ."

Later, a "Soviet ship moors alongside the quay. It has delivered grain, a gift of the Soviet trade unions for the striking Chinese workers. The square is deserted for the police have dispersed the people. But gradually, singly and in groups, the people crowd into the square. They are the city poor, workers and peasants who have come to see the Soviet ship and the people from the land of the Soviets. . . .

"The harbor master goes up to the Soviet captain and announces with malicious joy that the coolies are on strike and that therefore there is nobody to unload the ship.

"Boss and Li Shan-Fu look searchingly at the Soviet captain, their minds bent on provoking an incident with the unwelcome guests. But Boss and Li Shan-Fu have made a miscalculation, for the Soviet captain makes a quick decision. At his command the crew run out on the upper deck and down the gangway and start unloading the ship themselves, handing down sacks of grain. With joyous wonder, the Chinese people watch the harmonious and organized work of the Soviet sailors and they recall their own unbearable labor. More and more people gather . . . all of them are filled with joy at the generous gift from the Soviet trade unions. . . . The coolies join the Soviet sailors and brisk work is soon in full swing. . . .

"The toiling people of China and the men from the Land of the Soviets are welded into a single whole by their feeling of friendship and solidarity. . . ."

"The Red Flower" gets its name from the red blossom which the Soviet captain bestows on Tao Hoa, a dancer whose heart lies with the exploited workers. She conceals revolutionary leaflets for them. The reactionary Chinese Li Shan-Fu (who, as owner of the city's amusement halls, employs Tao Hoa) discovers the red flower, described as the "symbol of struggle."

"Like a madman, Li Shan-Fu draws his dagger and pierces the red flower, and his henchmen join in. Their act stands for a conspiracy against the people, against the Soviet captain; it is an oath of deadly struggle against the ideas of freedom and peace. . . ."

Time passes, and in the third and final act of the ideological ballet "it is nightfall in the European settlement of the city. Dancing pairs can be seen through the brightly lighted windows of a mansion and the muffled sounds of a Charleston are heard from within. A tense silence reigns in the street. A group of rickshaw drivers sit under a big tree engaged in quiet conversation. . . . Ma Li-chen (the revolutionary coolie) enters and goes up to the group, calling upon them to fight against the oppressors. The ricksha drivers and the coolies listen eagerly to Ma Li-chen, their faces expressing resolution and courage. . . .

"Ma Li-chen points to the floodlit windows of the mansion—a conspiracy against their motherland and their toiling people is being
carried on there. The rickshaw drivers and the coolies look with burning
hatred at the mansion and, at this moment, Boss appears on the
balcony. The eyes of the coolies meet his, and Boss peers down at
them with alarm. The curtains falls. In front stage, Ma Li-chen runs
along a deserted street. With a cautious glance around he pastes up a
revolutionary poster." (This is a ballet with as many glances as dances.)
Tao Hoa, the dancer, is compelled by Boss and his henchmen to
present a cup of poisoned tea at a theater performance to the Soviet
captain, whose presence in China is considered responsible for the
revolutionary fervor. At the last moment Tao Hoa takes courage and
knocks the poisoned cup from the captain's hands in the startled
presence of the workers' audience.

"Everyone rises to his feet in great excitement and prepares to hurl
himself on the criminals who attempted to take the life of a friend
of the Chinese people, a Soviet man. . . .

"Seized with fear, Boss and Li Shan-Fu run away along the street.
Their criminal intentions have been exposed, and they flee before the
people's anger. . . . A revolt has broken out in the city, and police
patrols rush by in a panic, followed by Ma Li-chen and his comrades. . . ."

At this point the Soviet captain and crew decide to sail, but dancer
Tao Hoa "runs after them, holding the captain's gift—the beautiful
red flower. Overtaking the captain, she tries to tell him, a friend from
the land of the Soviets, of her devotion and profound respect; to express
the sentiments overflowing in her heart. She is eager to tell the captain
that, for the first time in her life, she has found in him a genuinely
noble and just man, a friend of the oppressed and enslaved people.
Tao Hoa shows the captain the red flower which she will keep as a
treasured souvenir of the Soviet people, as a pledge of her people's
radiant future.

"The Soviet captain bids good-by to Tao Hoa and raises her hand
with the red flower: 'Keep it as a symbol of the people's freedom, as a
guarantee of a bright future'. . . .

"The revolt flares up with new strength in the city. The foreign
masters leave the city in panic, and officers and policemen rush away

throwing down their arms as they go. Crowds of revolutionary comrades headed by Ma Li-chen, carrying a red flag, burst into the square. . . ."

The triumphant moment is blighted by an assassin's bullet fired by the reactionary Li Shan-Fu at the revolutionary Ma Li-chen. The dancer Tao Hoa darts in the path of the bullet and sacrifices her life for the coolie leader.

The final scene dwarfs the Christmas and Easter pageants at New York's Radio City Music Hall. The victorious Chinese coolies, now garbed in white silk shirts and great red sashes march onto the stage where a backdrop of a gigantic red flag is unfurled in the breeze to the strains of the "Internationale."

The night I saw "The Red Flower" the female lead of Tao Hoa was danced by Russia's greatest dancer, Galina Ulanova. It seemed a shameful waste of talent in an unexacting and certainly embarrassing role.

Fortunately, many ballets in the repertoire of the Bolshoi Theatre are classics with which the Communist arbiters of culture have not tampered. "Giselle," "The Sleeping Beauty," and "Romeo and Juliet" are danced as they were originally. There are revisions of choreography and changes in costuming, but no injection of the class struggle into the stories.

"Romeo and Juliet" is tasteful, elaborate, and moving. It is a truly evocative piece, and Russians (who, granted, seem to enjoy shedding tears of sympathy for characters on stage or screen at the slightest excuse) often weep in the closing scene, when Romeo and Juliet die in their subterranean tomb. There are enormously exciting scenes— in one the Montagues and Capulets, one hundred fifty strong, duel ferociously across the vastness of the Bolshoi stage. At another point, there are three complete musical groups performing. The accomplished Bolshoi Symphony plays in the pit. On simulated stone steps leading to a street on stage there enters a brass band; and finally, from the wings, a mandolin group. The brass and mandolin bands perform for less than ten minutes, and few other theaters in the world could afford the budget of the government's Bolshoi to pay musicians a night's salary for so brief an appearance.

The good taste in costuming in "Swan Lake" is difficult to reconcile with the utter lack of taste in the clothes worn by the audience. Usually shown in abbreviated form in other countries, "Swan Lake" is presented in all four acts without a note of Tchaikovsky's music deleted.

It begins at 7:30 P.M. and the final curtain goes down at eleven. Often the audience remains for a quarter of an hour or more to applaud the stars who take numerous curtain calls. In a land where ballet is an obsession as well as an art, fans hurl flowers from the six tiers of the red and gold Bolshoi Theatre and the names of the favorites— Strutchkova, Plesetskaya, Ulanova—are shouted hoarsely over and over by youngsters. Leading ballerinas have their own mannerisms to delight the crowd. Olga Lepeshinskaya, a contemporary of Ulanova's, slight of build and coy in personality, dodges wide-eyed in feigned timorousness as stalks and bunches of flowers rain on the stage. Then she will take some up in her arms and toss them from her heart back to her admirers. Not a few of the fans' flowers miss the stage entirely and fall onto the heads of the retreating musicians in the orchestra pit.

The role of Odette in "Swan Lake" is danced with greatest assurance and drama by Miya Plesetskaya. Proud in bearing, long-legged, and with arms that can seem more like fluttering wings than human limbs, Plesetskaya is known in private life to be aloof and haughty. Shortly after seeing her perform in "Swan Lake," I met her at a Swedish Embassy reception. She accepted my congratulations coolly, with a nod. There were several moments of silence.

"You look taller on stage," I volunteered.

"Yes," she said. More silence. Then, as the explanation crossed my mind, I blurted, "Maybe that's because in the ballet you're dancing on your toes."

"Of course," said Plesetskaya with the trace of disdain the comment deserved, thus ending my first and only conversation with the great ballerina. When the Bolshoi company traveled to England in the autumn of 1956 Plesetskaya was conspicuously absent from the roster. There were several rumors current at the time in Moscow. One had it that she had made the careless remark that once out of Russia, she'd never return. Another version was that she had quarreled with Soviet Minister of Culture, Nikolai Mikhailov. Her name had been on the tentative advance list, but her brother, a new member of the troupe, was not. Mikhailov is supposed to have responded to Plesetskaya's intervention in her brother's behalf by explaining, as was already known to her, that the principle of seniority was closely followed, not only in assignment of roles but also for inclusion on trips. Plesetskaya was adamant. She is supposed to have replied that if her brother did not go, neither would she. "This country has only three good things," Plesetskaya is supposed to have declared in a burst of temper, "Tea, ice cream, and ballet. And the ballet won't be any good if I'm not there."

However credible this rumor may or may not be, the fact is that neither Plesetskaya nor her brother went to England, and for several months Plesetskaya was not cast in Bolshoi performances at home.

No matter who dances, the Bolshoi is sold out for every performance. The price of tickets ranges from 6 to 35 rubles (60 cents to $3.50). It is comparatively easy for foreigners to see a Bolshoi performance, but Russians wait months to buy a cherished ticket even for one of the backless, fold-down boards that are attached to aisle seats. There *are* a few tickets available for every performance—sold by state-employed agents who make the rounds of state enterprises and by vendors at special sidewalk and subway ticket booths. One of the changes since Czarist days that Communists sometimes mention is that theater is now accessible to the working man. Before the Revolution wealthy merchants sometimes bought out the whole house so that a small group of friends could enjoy a performance in the comfort and isolation of an almost empty theater. This is unthinkable now, say the Communists. However, now it is privileged government ministries rather than merchants who buy out theaters. Only a few upper-balcony seats, if any, may be available for a performance because the Ministry of Culture has appropriated all seats for visiting delegations from China, Hungary, or other Communist countries. Or selected workers in a Moscow factory may be alloted all the tickets for a theater. Typical was the case of a performance of the Moiseyev Folk Dance Troupe, a group of more than one hundred men and women who interpret folk dances with phenomenally robust leaps and whirls. Advertised for two weeks ahead of time on billboards and in a pocket-size booklet of theater schedules, the performance was suddenly closed to the public. The preceding night when I went to pick up tickets, ordered a dozen days in advance, I was told that it would be a private performance for the Red Army.

There are almost always lines at the Bolshoi Theatre box office, located in an administration building across the street from the theater itself, during the hours it is open. Most tickets, though, are issued on the basis of letters from factories, offices, and other state enterprises, and ministries which get precedence. Letters from individuals for tickets are more often ignored than not.

Tickets are easier to obtain for the *Filial,* or branch theater, of the Bolshoi, where the same company performs ballets of smaller dimensions, such as "Coppelia," "Fadetta," and "Nutcracker," and for the Stanislavsky Theatre's ballet performances. As in the case of all other theaters, the ballet theaters are operated by the Ministry of Culture. Income from tickets pays a considerable portion of the lavish production costs, and appropriations from the government's budget make up the difference.

Russians are rightly proud of their ballet. The intensive, prolonged training of Russian dancers is reflected in lifts and leaps that would be sheer acrobatics were they not done with a gracefulness that weaves them into the mood and story. A New York dance critic who visited Moscow described Soviet ballet as the "best and the worst in the world." The exuberance and verve and, above all, the skill of the dancers is without equal. But the lack of regard for "line," and especially the lack of development of modern dance techniques accounts for the negative aspect of the critic's evaluation. The long period of isolation under Stalin is reflected in Soviet ballet. Isolation provided the opportunity for intensive perfection of the classical ballet skills and techniques. But isolation cut off contact with new trends and ideas developed elsewhere.

In particular, contact with the outside world might have improved renditions of various national dances, incorporated into a number of ballets. There is a peculiar Soviet fascination with Spain. This is reflected in other forms of theater as well as in ballet. For example, "Don Quixote" has not only been rendered as a ballet but has also been made into a movie. A ballet of Communist-era origin, "Laurentsia," takes the locale of a Spanish village for the favorite theme of downtrodden, exploited peasants rising in revolt—in this case, against soldiers of a feudal lord who abuses the local señoritas. One of the violated peasant girls, Laurentsia, inspires the demoralized people to burn down the feudal palace. With red banners raised aloft, it is a Soviet ideological ballet in the true sense, but in those portions when castinets click and fans flirt, it is Spanish dancing in the worst sense.

The penchant for the Spanish motif is nothing new, and it seems to stem from the contrast between Russia and Spain. In Czarist times Spain was often the country that Russian artists and writers wanted to visit when they traveled abroad. It was the longing or curiosity of people of a cold, snowy, dreary land for a place of sunshine and bright colors.

The meticulous concern for detail was demonstrated during a four-week engagement of the old and respected Moscow Art Theatre in London. The troupe brought along its own log and axe for the offstage sound of chopping in Anton Chekhov's *The Cherry Orchard*. A Russian explained, "An English log and axe might not have had the correct ring."

Soviet artists, educated at state expense, are expected to devote several months a year to teaching others. Such illustrious stars as David Oistrakh, Emil Gillels, Galina Ulanova devote part of their time to instructing talented students. The salubrious effect this has on maintaining a steady succession of Soviet artistic talent need not be stressed.

Russians in literature and the arts are well paid. A successful playwright may make a million rubles a year ($100,000). A composer may receive 65,000 rubles ($6500) or more for an opera in addition to royalties of 9 per cent for each performance. A movie star of top rank earns 4000 rubles ($400) a month plus handsome bonuses for successful films. Theaters maintain permanent companies—whether in ballet, opera, or drama—so that an actor or singer or ballerina is on the payroll all year round, and not only when actually performing.

Ballet was born in Russia in the city of St. Petersburg, only some thirty years after Czar Peter the Great, in 1703, ordered the founding of a city as Russia's new capital. Before that, ballet companies had been brought in from abroad to perform for the court. This was very expensive, and the St. Petersburg school was founded to train a *corps de ballet* to accompany foreign guest performers. Teachers were imported from abroad until the end of the eighteenth century, when graduates of the school had gained enough competence to train others. Now there are fifteen special schools in the U.S.S.R. for training ballet dancers, the leading schools being in Moscow and Leningrad. The ballet school of the Bolshoi Theatre in Moscow occupies an old, roomy building constructed around a courtyard. More than fifteen hundred youngsters apply annually, but only fifteen girls and fifteen boys are admitted. The screening process is meticulous. First, the hopefuls must prove their scholastic aptitude, because while learning ballet the pupils also must study reading, writing, and Communist Party history. Next, an applicant must undergo a rigorous medical examination by a board of doctors to determine whether the boy or girl is likely to be able to withstand the considerable physical demands of ballet. Finally, a group of professional ballet dancers observes the applicants in elementary instruction to detect signs of natural talent.

Ballet training in Russia is begun at the age of nine or ten, and the course lasts for nine years. In other countries a ballerina often has only as much training as her family can afford. Five years of concentrated training is considered a great deal; the ballerina may continue to receive coaching intermittently after that. But nine years of ballet discipline day in and day out is almost unheard of outside Russia. Whatever may be the other limitations of ballet in the Soviet Union, it is no wonder that Russian ballet dancers perform with ease the leaps and lifts that are seldom attempted elsewhere and that the standard of dancing in the *corps de ballet* is so far above that usually seen.

For the first four years, ballet-school pupils attend classes from 9 A.M. to 4 P.M.; for higher grades from 9 A.M. to 6 P.M.—six days a week. In the first year, two or three hours a day are devoted to dancing. This period increases until in the final year five or six hours of the school day are spent in dance classes. During the summer most of the students continue their work at a camp run by the school. As is the case in other institutions of higher learning, ballet students receive a Government stipend in their last four years, varying in amount from 160 rubles ($16) to 200 rubles ($20) a month. A pair of ballet slippers and training tights are free, but girls must buy a pink costume, used in classical instruction; it costs about 120 rubles ($12).

Of the thirty pupils who begin each year, fewer than twenty-five usually graduate; the others drop out for reasons of health or lack of ability. During schooling they receive occasional practical training by appearing on stage in group roles in such ballets as "Nutcracker" and "Don Quixote." Upon graduation, starting salary for a member of the *corps de ballet* is 1000 rubles ($100) a month. Prima ballerinas receive 6000 rubles ($600) per month base pay. Like workers in any line of endeavor, from bricklaying to ballet, the prima ballerina is assigned a target. A ballerina's target is usually five or six ballets a month. If she exceeds that quota she gets paid extra.

The Bolshoi Theatre has first pick of each graduating class, and few dancers have the good fortune to begin with the Bolshoi company. Most receive assignments with less distinguished ballet troupes, but all are assured of jobs in ballet.

A graduation event each spring is the class recital. Each member performs solo and group numbers for an audience comprised of doting relatives and admiring friends in much the same nervous atmosphere of any music school recital. Parents and friends reserve their loudest applause for their own kin. These youngsters are part of a continuing tradition, uninterrupted by the Revolution, that has given Russia pre-eminence in ballet. Stars such as Ulanova were produced in this fashion, with training started early and security, if not intellectual independence, guaranteed. A job in the company is secure for as long as the dancer is able to perform. When advanced age comes on, ballerinas shed the tutus of the active roles for the gowns of the sedate palace ladies.

At a time when Ulanova was forty-eight years old and still dancing Juliet, I attended a performance with Sol Hurok, the American impresario. I asked him how long a ballerina like Ulanova might be expected to dance.

"Oh, she could dance for quite a while," replied Hurok in his heavy Russian accent. "After all, Pavlova could have danced until she was sixty——If," he added as a straight-faced afterthought, "she hadn't died when she was forty-nine."

The Bolshoi is Russia's La Scala and Metropolitan. The word *bolshoi* means "big" or "great", and the Soviet Union's main theater lives up to its name, both in the building's appearance and in the quality of many of its performances, both ballet and, to a lesser extent, opera. An imposing building of tan stucco with eight Grecian columns and a portico crowned by a heroic horse-drawn Roman chariot, the Bolshoi building was completed in 1824 but was swept by fire in 1853, leaving only the outer walls. It was rebuilt in its present form three years later.

Inside, a mammoth yet tasteful glass-tasseled chandelier is suspended from the dome, painted with the Muses, that dominates the auditorium, seating 2000. Designed along classic opera-house lines, the décor is red and gold. The only intrusion of Communist symbols is a small profile of Lenin in the center of the arch over the stage and in the curtain's repeating design of hammer and sickle and the letters "CCCP" (Cyrillic alphabet for the U.S.S.R.). The Bolshoi, despite the years that have elapsed since its construction, still has one of the largest stages in the world; it is only slightly smaller than the auditorium of the Bolshoi itself. In the ballroom scenes of the opera "Eugen Onegin" and in "Swan Lake" the vast stage conveys an impression of a regal spaciousness of Kremlin proportions.

The Bolshoi opera has more than 250 ballet dancers, 100 opera soloists, a chorus of 200, and an orchestra of 250 musicians. Five hundred other persons are employed in the Bolshoi's twenty-four auxiliary shops, including ballet-shoe makers, dressmakers, and printers who publish the theater's house organ, a newspaper called *Soviet Artist*. The printing shop also turns out the programs that are sold at the door for 40 kopecks (4 cents) and list the artists for each performance. Program notes telling the story of an opera or ballet are sold separately for the same amount. Some of the smaller theaters have standard programs for each work in its repertoire. The names of all artists capable of performing each role are printed, and on the day of a performance a pencil check is placed next to the name of the performers on that occasion. It takes considerable time for someone to go through 1000 or 1500 programs and check off perhaps 100 names on each, but neither in ballet nor in industry nor in agriculture is conservation of labor or its efficient use a compelling consideration.

In ballet or in opera, imaginative, elaborate stage effects characterize performances. In the opera "Prince Igor," for example, there are no fewer than two sunrises, one sunset, and one eclipse of the moon that lacks only the darting of chirping, frightened birds in the air to provide total realism. Animals are often used on stage. Prince Igor and his son Vladimir ride off for war against the Polovtski tribes on two powerful horses in full ancient regalia. The scene is as if taken from an old Russian painting: Russian warriors in mail and shield, the boyars —the privileged aristocracy—in brocade robes and high-crowned hats with fur trim. From a cathedral with onion-shaped domes march priests in religious robes bearing crosses to bless the expedition.

But the most remarkable scene in "Prince Igor" occurs when the Polovtski nomads set fire to Igor's fortified town. Smoke rises against the stage's reddened night sky. The log walls crumble and collapse into the vivid blaze—cloth skillfully cut, lighted in red, and blown by off-stage fans to simulate leaping flames. The Bolshoi has developed the technique of creating artificial fire to near-perfection, and they use it on every possible occasion. A palace is set afire in the ballet "Bakchis-araya Fountain," and again in the ballet "Laurentsia."

Supported by state funds, theaters of many sorts flourish in the U.S.S.R. The Moscow Art Theatre, founded by the great K. S. Stanis-lavsky in June 1898, performs Russian classics and Shakespearian drama with equal talent. There are thirty theaters offering performances in Moscow all year round with the exception of a two-month vacation period. During the height of the winter season there are as many as five hundred musical concerts and recitals per month.

There is a satirical theater, a theater of light opera, and of variety acts, not dissimilar to old-time vaudeville. The Abrasov puppet theater renders both serious drama and comedy. There is a children's theater and a permanent animal show for youngsters. The army has its theater troupe and the Red Army Chorus is a magnificent collection of male voices augmented by a robust dance troupe.

Although much energy and funds are expended in putting on works intended for indoctrination rather than art, the Soviet Union has provided its people with rich opportunities for enjoying theater. Each of Russia's fifteen Republics has a capital ballet and opera company. There are few major cities without a symphony orchestra.

Regardless of the type of theater or its location in the Soviet Union there is a special technique to theatergoing in Russia. For example, it is well to remember always to rent a pair of binoculars at the cloakroom. The cost is 3 rubles (30 cents), and the glasses are usually of inferior quality, but they entitle the holder to a priority in obtaining his coat at the end of the evening. This is no small advantage, especially in winter when most theatergoers have checked their coats, hats, boots, and possibly a sweater and a package or two. Binoculars may not improve one's view of the performance but they do save fifteen minutes or more of waiting in line. The binocular renter ignores the queue. He moves directly to the cloakroom counter, bypassing the line, simply by displaying the binoculars. No one objects, because it is accepted procedure, and the attendant, paying no attention to those waiting patiently in line, retrieves the binoculars and gives the privileged individual his coat.

Actually, it is a misnomer in Russia to call it a cloak*room*. The area for checking coats runs the full length of a theater, frequently on both sides of the lobby. With the exception of movies, it's against the rules to take outer garments into a theater. Russians wear so many thick layers of clothing in winter that crowds seem denser than during warmer seasons and fewer people can fit into elevators. This taxes the facilities of even the roomiest theater checking facilities. Sturdy metal bars fastened to stanchions are lined up row on row to bear the weight of furs. The bulk of the winter clothing is reason enough for the rule that it must be checked, but another reason is that most furs are poorly cured in Russia and exude an odor in heated rooms. Even with furs eliminated from auditoriums, Soviet theaters have an odor peculiarly their own. It emanates from the red bars of sweetly perfumed government-produced soap used by spectators and used, too, for scrubbing theater floors. The strong and immediately recognizable scent is one of the hazards of going to the theater in Russia. Another is the practice of Russians to appropriate unoccupied seats. This is done in a spirit of good-natured competition rather than out of any intention to deny the rightful occupant his place permanently. Just before curtain time doors are shut and late-comers are ushered to back rows of balconies in order to cause as little disturbance as possible. Russians with balcony tickets often arrive early and lurk near the sides of the orchestra section until the strategic moment when the house lights dim and then they rush to commandeer empty places. Russians occupying inferior seats in the orchestra also join in the last-minute rush for preferable places. The crisis occurs when the legitimate ticket holder arrives to claim his seat, usually during intermission. The interloper will stare innocently straight ahead. Then the appropriate procedure calls for him to register mild surprise when confronted with the proper ticket. Finally, with a shrug of indifference, the man or woman will quietly retire from the scene. It is all very much in the spirit of tradition; neither party is expected to express indignation and usually neither does.

When the curtain rings down there is a problem about getting out of the theater. Even with the foresight of renting binoculars one cannot be sure of swift exit from the auditorium. In order to avoid too great a crush at the cloakrooms, ushers periodically close the doors leading into the corridors. This may be one reason for the sustained, often rhythmic, applause at the conclusion of most performances. The captive audience may as well applaud for the entertainment, limited though it is, of watching performers take curtain calls.

There are several ways of passing the intermissions. Smoking is usually permitted only in the foyer leading to the street. Seldom is there a smoking room. Many members of the audience spend the time in promenade around a main lobby. The word "around" is used advisedly, because it is a rigid custom for couples to stroll clockwise, usually arm in arm, in a circle determined by the size of the lobby. This orderly, self-disciplined walking roundelay eliminates confusion and jostling and there's a certain communal appearance to this intermission ritual.

There is no lack of jostling, though, in theater buffets (never called restaurants or anything but buffets) during intermissions as people hurry to get a table. Since most theater performances begin at 7:30 P.M., and many in the audience get out of work at six or later, there's seldom time to eat beforehand. Many wait for the first intermission. The Bolshoi has two buffets. One is small, with only three tables and no chairs. The larger buffet contains several dozen tables with soiled white cloths *and* chairs. Champagne is sold by the bottle or glass. Bottles of soda of various fruit flavors stand in the center of tables along with dishes of pastry. Hot tea costs 1 ruble (10 cents) a glass, and a slice of bread spread with black caviar, as thick as peanut butter might be spread in other countries, costs only several pennies more. Coffee is seldom sold at these buffets; tea is the national beverage, and coffee, when used at all, is usually taken after a meal. Russian coffee is usually watery. Ice cream is sold by weight rather than by the scoop or dish. Usually there's a line at the ice-cream counter waiting for the attendant to weigh the proper number of grams on a scale against metal counterweights. Seldom are flavors other than vanilla available, and then only strawberry, chocolate, and coffee. I've never seen sherbert served anywhere in Russia except at Kremlin receptions. Whatever the flavor available in the theater buffet, it is usually well melted by the time the server has scraped a bit here and added a chunk there for proper weight and handed it to the customer.

Understandably, this practice of weighing ice cream startled a certain visiting British young lady. She accepted a Russian's invitation for an evening out, and everything went swimmingly until they sat down in a Gorki Street ice-cream parlor. "How many grams would you like?" he asked.

"How many *what?*" she echoed, her voice cracking.

In relating the incident afterwards she said that the question would have seemed perfectly proper phrased any other way—"Large or small?" "Two scoops or one?"—but "Imagine a man asking you how many *grams* of ice cream you want!"

The last type of entertainment Russians might be expected to attend would be a mind-reading act. In a land where people keep their political thoughts to themselves, they might well feel squeamish about being in the presence of anyone who claims powers of telepathy. Yet Mikhail Kuni was advertised as a mind reader specializing in "Psychological Experiments," and the Central House of Culture of Railroad Workers was sold out to its 1000-seat capacity at 15 rubles ($1.50) each. Comrade Kuni, employed by the Ministry of Culture, as is every other performer in the Soviet Union, turned out to be a gray-haired man in his late forties. (In response to a question handed up on a slip of paper at the end of the two-and-a-half-hour program when questions were solicited, Kuni refused to give his age. "I never answer that question," he smiled.)

Unusual though Kuni's performance was, the gold and red sign above the stage was similar to those found in a number of variations in practically every theater, office, railroad station and factory in the U.S.S.R. It read: "Under the Banner of Marxism-Leninism. Under the Leadership of the Communist Party. Forward to the Victory of Communism." Except for the sign there was only one other aspect of the performance which characterized it as strictly Soviet. Otherwise, change the language, the appearance of the audience, the setting—and Mikhail Kuni was a performer who might be seen in Hollywood, Hong Kong, or Hamburg. The other typically Soviet aspect came when Kuni, toward the end of the first act, blindfolded himself and then, for good measure, slipped a black hood over his head, and thus sightless proceeded to draw a face in charcoal on a big white cardboard. When he stepped aside, a perfectly recognizable portrait of Lenin was revealed. The Russian audience burst into sustained applause—whether at Kuni's blind drawing skill or, reflexively, at the portrait of the saint of Communist saints, it was impossible to determine. It was, on second thought, not entirely an exclusive Soviet device. How many American vaudeville performers have wound up a mediocre act with a bit of juggling or tap dancing or acrobatics with the Stars and Stripes somehow incorporated to assure themselves of applause?

As it turned out Kuni's act was as much sheer memory as "mind reading." He commenced by having a volunteer from the audience write sixteen numbers at random in squares on a blackboard while Kuni's back was turned. Kuni spun around, stared at the blackboard for three seconds, spun again to face the audience, and recited row by row the numbers in each square, from top to bottom and then to top again.

Kuni asked for other volunteers throughout the program to assist in his stunts, and each time there was a near stampede of Russians, anxious to get into the act. He instructed volunteers to hang eleven discs of different colors in random order on a wire stretched across the stage. Kuni faced the discs for a few fleeting seconds and spun toward the audience to recite the colors forwards and backwards. To shouts from the audience calling out the colors of various discs, Kuni responded by recalling the colors of the discs on either side of each. Several members of the audience came to the stage to inscribe in turn any number of circles of random size on a blackboard so that he might try to tell at a glance how many each had drawn. Forty-two circles, guessed Kuni: and 42 circles there proved to be by a more deliberate count by the volunteer who drew them. The same unerring precision was displayed by Kuni after members of the audience had drawn 25, 63, and 51 circles, respectively.

At this point a skeptic in the audience, of which there seemed to be quite a few, shouted that Kuni was counting the number of circles while his back was turned by the scratching of the chalk against the blackboard. Kuni invited the heckler to come to the stage. He refused to come. The audience took sides, some shouting support for Kuni, others for the heckler. Comrade Kuni, a man of obvious energy and rugged build, sprang down the steps from the stage, seized the heckler, a short, unshaven young man in a railroad worker's blue uniform, escorting him by the arm to the stage. Kuni ordered him to draw circles quietly. Obviously intimidated by the course events had taken, the heckler lightly applied chalk to blackboard. Those on Kuni's side in the audience took up the cries of "draw your circles more neatly," and "write more quietly."

When the heckler said he had drawn all the circles he wished, Kuni whipped about, poised on his toes for a moment of concentrated attention, and said, "50 circles." Apparently the encounter had somewhat unnerved or distracted Kuni, because when he checked his estimate by counting off the circles one at a time there turned out to be 51. It was Kuni's only slip of the two-hour performance, and anyway his tormenter seemed satisfied that Kuni was not counting the circles by ear.

Other hecklers were less easily silenced. It was a rowdy crowd. At one point Kuni was introducing a number by saying: "As you've seen, I've demonstrated a few experiments in visual, auditory, and mathematical memory . . ." A voice from the balcony interrupted, "I haven't seen anything yet."

Frequently Kuni would sip from a glass on a small table near the curtain. "People often ask me," he explained, as a sort of stage patter, "what marvelous elixir this glass contains. Well, I'll confide in you. It's only water." One volunteer who came to the stage, stumbling on the way in the aisle, proceeded to sample the elixir for himself. Obviously inebriated, the man disgustedly spat the liquid to the stage, exclaiming in disgust, "It *is* water!" Kuni ordered him to leave the stage.

Catering to the Russian penchant for chess, a huge board was produced and volunteers were asked to place twelve chessmen at random on any of the seventy-two numbered squares. While Kuni faced the audience, an assistant recited the chess symbol—king, knight, pawn —and the number of its square. Then, demonstrating his auditory memory, Kuni proceeded to respond to shouted numbers from the audience by naming the corresponding chess symbol for that square.

Kuni's most impressive trick of concentrated attention and memory was to add up the grand total of numbers written on four blackboards while the blackboards were being spun around. Those of us in the audience could hardly read the numbers as the blackboards were spun, let alone add them. Members of the audience had been invited to inscribe four numbers of two digits each in three columns on each blackboard while Kuni's back was turned. Then all four blackboards, each mounted in the center of an easel, were spun by assistants. In his characteristic crouched position, like a poised animal about to leap, Kuni darted from spinning blackboard to blackboard. In a few minutes he shouted the grand total of the forty-eight numbers. A volunteer carefully added the figures on an abacus and, as everyone by this time expected, Kuni was right.

By intermission time Kuni had most of the hecklers on his side, and knots of people in the buffet and lobby could be heard earnestly debating how he did it. "Cover your wrist watch with your hand," suggested a Russian at the next table to mine in the buffet, explaining to his lady friend that it was all a matter of concentration. "Now, describe the face of the watch, what kind of numbers are on it?" The woman guessed Roman numerals and was wrong. There were Arabic numbers alternating with dots. The woman admitted with some embarrassment that she'd had the watch for eight years. "See," exclaimed her escort, who wore no watch, "that's how you're different from Tovarich Kuni. He puts his mind to things, and you don't." By that time the intermission was over, and the second hour was devoted to a demonstration of "mind reading." An Air Force captain selected a single word at random from a thick volume he had with him. He wrote the word (*moloko*, meaning milk) and the page (469) on a slate for the audience to see. Then, having the captain hold his wrist and alternating an intent gaze between the captain's face and the book, Kuni proceeded to riffle the pages, back and forth, fewer pages each time, and finally to run his finger up and down a page. In a matter of minutes he announced the correct page and word.

At the end of the program Kuni replied to questions. He explained this skill in terms of attention to a person's reactions. It was as if Kuni were acting as a human lie-detecting machine and depending on the pulse beat, palm perspiration, and eye flicker of the captain to direct him toward the appropriate page and word.

This same technique of reading physical and nervous reactions rather than mind reading, enabled Kuni to find a pocketbook that a young lady volunteer had left with someone in the hall. Blindfolded and with the girl's hand grasping his wrist, Kuni made his way from the stage, moving slowly up and down the aisles, and then like some sort of a human radar system, gradually narrowing down his target.

Similarly Kuni was able to discover the name of a famous historical figure chosen by three persons in the crowd and written on a slate for the audience to see. Again, with one of the volunteer's hands on his wrist, Kuni ran his finger across a printed Cyrillic alphabet, pausing momentarily at letters when his subject reacted. In some minutes Kuni spoke up—"Garibaldi." And Garibaldi, indeed, was the name that had been written down beforehand.

It was simply a matter of practice, Kuni assured the now respectful crowd during the explanation period. It was just like training muscles for weight lifting; he had trained himself to concentrate. "Your will pulls you in many directions," expounded Kuni, "and just as you must train a child to pay attention of the most elementary form, so you can by will power train your mind to register what it sees and to detect reactions that others miss."

Kuni opened slips of paper with questions sent up. "Does he sleep more than most people?" No, seven or eight hours a night. "Why does he dart about so on the stage?" Habit and force of concentration. "When will I get married?" asked a note from a girl in the audience, a question that a girl anywhere in the world might ask. Kuni didn't attempt to answer.

The most popular entertainment is the movies. Most movies shown in Soviet theaters are produced at one of the government studios in Moscow, Leningrad, and other major cities. Films produced in other Communist lands and occasional movies of acceptable ideological tone from non-Communist countries are exhibited. A Mexican movie, *Wet-*

backs, for example, depicted exploitation of Mexican laborers in America after they had swum the Rio Grande. A French film *If All the Fellows in the World,* favorably portrayed the role played by Russians in the rescue of a ship in distress.

Until the conclusion of a U.S-U.S.S.R. cultural agreement in 1958 very few American movies were shown. The Soviet army had captured prints of three Hollywood movies in Germany, and by virtue of these Deanna Durbin became one of the best known Americans to Russians. Her film *100 Men and a Girl* gave her a greater popularity in Russia than in the U.S. It is still not unusual for a Russian to mention her name when the conversation turns to historic, great Americans. Walt Disney's *Snow White and the Seven Dwarfs,* one of the captured films, apparently made somewhat less of an impression, but the third film, a Tarzan movie, is said to have given rise to a brief fad of schoolboys trying their prowess by swinging on the limbs of park trees.

Films purchased by the Russians under the cultural agreement included *Marty, An American in Paris, Roman Holiday,* and *The Great Caruso.*

On visits to Moscow, Cary Grant and Elizabeth Taylor found themselves in the unusual situation of not being recognized on the streets. No more heads turned to look at either of them than at less notable foreign tourists.

Russia moved more slowly than the United States into the age of wide-screen processes that give the illusion of a third dimension. A theater for showing "Cinerama-type" or, as the Russians labeled it, "panoramic" movies was scheduled for opening in time for the fortieth anniversary of the Revolution, November 7, 1957. However, it was not until three months later, in February 1958, that the glass-front, domed building next door to Moscow's circus and the central "free market" was completed. Called "Mir," which in Russian can mean either "peace" or "world," it was Moscow's most modernistic edifice. It seated 1226 spectators in a circular, paneled hall. The great screen, 90 feet wide by 36 feet high, was said to be the largest in Europe, and 120 loudspeakers placed around the auditorium regaled the audience with sound from all directions.

The panoramic film, called *How Broad Is My Country,* consisted of a travelogue of Moscow, Leningrad, the Caucasus Mountains, the Black Sea Coast, brief glimpses of Magnitogorsk and Sochi.

The film bore a striking resemblance in content and technique to the original Cinerama film made a half-dozen years earlier in America.

Instead of a roller-coaster ride there was a drive at high speed around curves of a mountain highway on the Black Sea coast. A Soviet airplane trip through valleys of the Caucasus replaced the flight through the Grand Canyon. A ride on a raft through river rapids in Carpathia recalled the smoother water ride through Venice's canals. There was a bumpy speedboat ride, an airplane landing on a runway, a speeding train trip. Even this travelogue did not totally eliminate indoctrination. The color film of the Winter Palace in Leningrad faded into black and white to show three different scenes from old Russian historical films on the panels of the "panoramic" screen. In the center panel V. I. Lenin was addressing a crowd. In the two side panels hordes of workers, peasants, and soldiers were storming the Winter Palace.

Prior to the construction of the Mir movie, at a time when American movie theaters were showing a variety of wide-screen and three-dimensional processes, there were only two theaters in Moscow with wider-than-ordinary screens and one house projecting something known as Stereokino, the Russian version of 3-D.

The Stereokino movie house is near the center of Moscow, across Sverdlovsk Square from the Bolshoi Theatre. Like most Soviet movie theaters, it is a small, bare hall with straight-backed wooden chairs without upholstery. The Stereokino's narrow rectangular hall is up one flight of stairs and seats about 200 persons.

Although the Stereokino's seats are as uncomfortable as most Soviet movie houses, there is one advantage. The seats are staggered so that you can see between the heads of spectators in front of you.

This is something more than a *convenience* at the Stereokino. It's a necessity. The Stereokino process requires that you hold your head rigidly in a fixed position for the movie to acquire a third dimension or, for that matter, to have any dimension at all. As soon as you shift your head or your eyes the picture shifts out of focus. It's a most unusual 3-D process.

The screen is small—about eight feet square. It appears to be a furled or ruffled white cloth covered with glass. It's not unlike store-window displays seen occasionally in the United States which take on a picture with the illusion of depth when viewed from just the right position. The sensation of depth at the Stereokino is very much like that achieved by stereopticon-viewers that children once used.

Judging from the remarks of Russians near me, I wasn't the only one with difficulty keeping in focus. One robust-voiced Russian lady remarked: "I must be losing my sight." A Soviet officer in the row in front of me kept chuckling and whispering to his wife: "I can't see a thing."

It required so much concentration to hold one's head in proper relation to the screen that it wasn't possible to pay much attention to the content of the movie, which was a light Ukrainian operetta with young peasants in native costume cavorting up and down hills to take maximum scenic advantage of the 3-D effect.

The Stereokino movie, *One Night in May,* was intended as pure entertainment without a moral or ideological message. This has been rare in Soviet films. Most Soviet films are intended for indoctrination rather than for entertainment.

This was evident in a contest for movie scenarios announced by the Ministry of Culture. "On historic topics," read the announcement, "the scenarios should depict the heroism of the Russian proletariat and of Lenin's party in the period of the preparation and the carrying out of the Great October Socialist Revolution. . . .

"In the scenarios on modern topics it is necessary to depict the truthful and vivid characters of our contemporaries, showing the rich spiritual world of the laborers of Socialism, and the variety of the working and private life."

Typical was the movie *Lesson of Life* at Moscow's Hermitage movie house, with larger seating capacity but the same uncomfortable furnishings as at the Stereokino theater.

Briefly, it was the story of a proper Communist Party member, Sergei by name, with an attractive wife Natasha and a responsible job as chief engineer of a big construction project on the Volga River. As Sergei's responsibilities grew so did his vanity. He starts to favor subordinates who flatter him. He treats with contempt those who offer him valid criticism. Also, unhappy to say, Sergei's unsocialist behavior extends to participation in occasional parties which feature wine and women other than Natasha.

Sergei soon gets his comeuppance. He is summoned before the regional committee of the Communist Party which has got wind of his conduct unbecoming a Party member. In an interminable scene, Party officials make impassioned speeches about the wise, paternal leadership of the Party whose members must lead exemplary lives.

Sergei is expelled from the Party. He loses his job. Wife Natasha, who has long since left Sergei and is teaching school at a nearby town, learns of his disgrace when she picks up her morning copy of *Pravda,* which documents the case of Sergei on the front page as a lesson to other Communists. Natasha's first impulse is to hasten to her husband's side, but her friends dissuade her, pointing out that, having proven himself a bad Communist, Sergei is unworthy of her love.

However, Sergei is made of sterner stuff. He accepts his punishment in the proper spirit, indulging in self-confession before his fellow Party members and agreeing to start again at the bottom of the ladder. We find Sergei working as a common laborer on the Volga dam project which he once supervised.

Eventually Natasha does return to Sergei, and in the last scene we find Natasha assuring Sergei of her faith in his ability to redeem himself and prove to be an estimable Communist. They embrace.

Only recently has kissing been shown in Soviet movies. It was not considered good taste or proper screen morals, but now this is changing. As a matter of fact, in the first part of the movie trilogy of the novel *Quiet Flows the Don,* a seduction scene not only shows the couple kissing but also focuses on the young man holding his partner in a grasp that would never pass American film moral standards.

There are certain standards of conduct for those who *watch* Soviet movie screens as well as for those who perform on them.

It's all right to wear one's coat in a movie house, although this is forbidden in other Soviet theaters. Any conversation during the movie is angrily hushed by neighboring spectators. Soviet movie audiences are quiet, but during one movie I attended when the screen went black at a crucial moment in the film, the audience stamped and whistled and shouted. It sounded like a rowdy soldier audience at an army camp.

Feature films are often preceded by a Soviet newsreel which conveys mostly news of hydroelectric dams under construction, coal miners and lathe operators who have exceeded production quotas, and harvesting successes. The Soviet leaders are shown at signing ceremonies which culminate visits by various dignitaries. I've never heard a Russian audience applaud its leaders on the screen. Once when John Foster Dulles was at an international conference in London, I applauded briefly as a jest; heads turned in amusement rather than in animosity.

It's considered abominable taste to walk out in the middle of a movie. In fact, in smaller communities people simply are not permitted to leave the theater before the movie is over.

Once a movie has begun, doors are closed. A ticket entitles you to one showing of the film. There's no such privilege as staying to see a movie over. Tickets are sold in advance for showings on any particular day or for the next day, but never farther in advance. Daytime prices are usually from 2 rubles 50 kopecks (25 cents) to 5 rubles (50 cents). Tickets are slightly more expensive at night, from 3 to 6 rubles (30 to 60 cents). The cheapest seats are closest to the screen and at the rear of the hall. Few movie theaters have balconies. Tickets are for numbered, reserved seats.

There are almost always lines in front of movie ticket windows. There are not enough movies in Moscow and other communities to accommodate the public. It's said that there were no more movie houses in Moscow in 1957 than there were in 1917. Whether this particular statistic is real or imagined, the fact is that Soviet authorities have seen fit to give priority to factories rather than to buildings for entertainment. Some churches no longer used for worship have been converted to movies. There are no drive-ins, probably because there are not enough privately owned cars to provide an audience. However, Moscow developed a Saturday night "walk-in" movie. This began during the Sixth World Festival of Students and Youth for Peace and Friendship in July and August 1957. Along with multitudinous other preparations to lend Moscow a festive, carnival air, outdoor movie screens were erected on a number of buildings. The festival over, the screens remained, and Moscow municipal authorities provided movies every Saturday night. Crowds would gather for the free three hours of movies, standing up for the entire time. Moscow boys and girls would go on dates to the "walk-ins" in Manege Square, near the Central Telegraph Office, and at Pushkin Square. When it got too cold to hold hands, even with gloves on, the outdoor "walk-ins" ceased.

As part of the emergence from isolation after Stalin's death, the Russians began to enter films in international competitions such as the Cannes Festival. Some films were departures from the Soviet mold of propaganda and indoctrination. *The Cranes Are Flying* and *The Forty-first* are only two of a number of outstanding post-Stalin films that care more about conveying human emotions than an ideological message. Another was *Don Quixote,* with Russia's talented Nikolai Cherkassov. The color photography was restrained and artistic. The acting was robust. However, even in *Don Quixote* it was the moralistic side of Cervantes that was stressed; when Sancho is mistreated by royalty's soldiers he tells them, in effect, just to wait until the Revolution comes.

The Central Documentary Film Studio in Moscow and its affiliates in other major Soviet cities turn out dozens of documentary films each year, ranging in subject from the construction of a new Siberian power dam to a day-by-day report on the Soviet tour of a group of American farm experts. This latter film was produced much faster than most, and the Americans were presented with a copy of the twenty-minute film as a farewell gift. A rather unusual documentary entitled *San Francisco, Chicago, New York* was produced from footage taken by a Russian journalist named Kalitsan on a brief summer trip through the United States. The movie was not intentionally anti-American, nor were the scenes chosen to prejudice the viewer against the United States, but there were ample opportunities for a movie-goer to leave with incorrect impressions. There was a scene of a typical low-rent shopping district in Chicago. Signs that advertise perennial fire and bankruptcy sales were plastered across windows. "Liquidation Sale, Bargains." "Save—50 per cent on all goods." "Must Sell."

To Russians who never see a sign in Soviet store windows beyond occasional price tags, this must have looked like a catastrophic situation. The narration added to this impression by declaring, "These signs show how difficult it is to attract a buyer in America."

Another scene showed a street in Harlem in New York. Youngsters were playing stickball in the street. This was depicted as a typical American condition. The voice accompanying the film intoned: "Childhood and youth spent in the streets." There were shots of San Francisco's charming old cable cars. No attempt was made to explain the sentiments of nostalgia that these old streetcars evoke in many Americans.

"These streetcars," explained the Russian voice, "are very similar to Moscow's old discarded streetcars."

During the half-hour color film, which had ten showings a day, there were several scenes of heavy traffic on Manhattan's Broadway, on San Francisco's Market Street, in the Chicago Loop. Each time a murmur of amazement ran through the audience. But the most audible buzz of disbelief could be heard when a used-car lot was shown. The Russian photographer was obviously bemused by American customs. "I was told," he explained with a tone of faint skepticism, "that many Americans use a car only a year or two and then sell it to buy a new one."

A story known to Russians compares a Soviet and an American factory. The Soviet plant has a few limousines parked nearby. By contrast, the American plant is surrounded by thousands of automobiles in parking spaces. The difference between the Soviet and American factories, so the story goes, is that in Russia the workers own the factory and the bosses own the cars, whereas in the United States the bosses own the factory and the workers own the cars. Many Russians, it may safely be said, would prefer the latter arrangement. Unintentionally, the travelogue of the U.S.A. may have contributed to this preference. The unfulfilled demand for cars and for the minor niceties and essentials of life is a painful fact of life, especially evident when the Russian goes shopping and not easily forgotten even in the make-believe world of the theater.

CHAPTER 22

NO CHARGE ACCOUNTS

An unusually frank cartoon published in a Soviet magazine depicts a Russian woman examining a bolt of cloth on a store counter. "I like the fabric," she is saying, "but somehow I don't care for the pattern."

"Oh, don't worry about that," the salesgirl reassures her. "It will come out in the first washing."

In the same vein, a three-panel cartoon in a Soviet page-a-day calendar shows a man trying on a baggy suit that is many sizes too large for him. The second panel shows the salesman pouring water on him with a sprinkling can. In the final panel the suit has shrunk to a perfect fit. The caption reads: "It doesn't quite fit? Don't worry. We can fix it."

These commentaries on the quality of Soviet fabrics can be extended to many products manufactured in Russia. Faucets leak. Electric bulbs and heater coils burn out quickly. Pots and pans peel and corrode. Shoes squeak. Carbon paper is useless for more than two copies. Fountain pens leak.

The emphasis on heavy industry at the expense of consumer products has enabled Russia to create enviable sputniks, but when foreigners stationed in Moscow go abroad on trips they are asked by Russian friends to bring back the most commonplace items, that are either unavailable or poorly made in Russia. A Russian maid asks for a color-fast dress for her baby, a camera fan asks for color film that can be processed at home, a table-tennis devotee asks for a cork-covered racket. A hotel waiter wanted "Rock and Roll" (or "Shake and Shiver" as it's translated into Russian) phonograph records, a minor Health Ministry official was ready to pay any price for a portable typewriter, and a shabbily dressed interpreter shyly requested copies of fashion magazines. Others ask for sheer nylon stockings, sweaters, and fine perfumes.

A Russian friend, perhaps alert for an opportunity to escape in any direction, asked for a book on *Esperanto Self-Taught*.

The opening of Russia to tourists shortly after Stalin's death created a black market where none had existed. Russia had been rather refreshing in that respect, at least. The sort of shady characters who sidle up to a tourist in Place de l'Opéra in Paris and offer to exchange French francs for dollars at an illegal rate were missing in Moscow. However, soon after the foreign tourists from the West made their appearance in the streets of Moscow and Leningrad, this all changed. It became not at all uncommon for a foreigner to be approached and asked whether he had anything to sell. Russians learned enough English to suggest doing "business." Some even offered to trade rubles for dollars at an illegal rate of about twenty rubles to the dollar—twice the official rate. They would then use the dollars to buy clothes and other items from foreigners who had no use for rubles. An American student visitor said just before his departure that the only clothes he had left were those he was wearing. "I've sold everything else; there isn't a thing Russians won't buy, no matter how old."

The unavailability for so many years of goods from foreign countries has resulted in many Russians placing a premium on items of foreign origin. A certain set of Russian women, for example, preferred inferior coats of artificial fur, made in the U.S.A., to the genuine product made in Russia. This desire for foreign goods provided some embassies and a few correspondents with a lucrative source of income for a period of time until it was declared illegal in 1956. The Soviet equivalent of the second-hand store is the government Commission Store. There are Commission Stores for clothes, others for photographic equipment, others for art and antiques. A Soviet citizen who wants to dispose of a second-hand coat or camera or religious icon may take it to the appropriate Commission Store where an employee, supposedly expert in the field, appraises the item. If the owner accepts the price set, he deposits his possession at the store, receives a receipt, and returns in several days to check whether it has been sold. If it has, he receives the amount, minus the store's commission of 7 per cent. Foreigners were permitted to sell at the Commission Stores until personnel of certain embassies began to take advantage of the commercial opportunities. It is said that they shipped in crates of dresses and, without even going through the pretense of rumpling them to lend them the appearance of having been worn, trucked the goods directly from railroad station to Commission Store. The profit was great, because even a somewhat worn second-hand men's suit that cost $75 brand-new was appraised at 1500 rubles ($150) at the Commission Store and was sold in two days.

Some foreigners in Moscow found bargains at the antique Commission Store. An American Embassy wife saw an attractive Russian cup to add to her demitasse collection. Later she discovered in an American catalogue of antique china that the cup, which cost her six rubles (60 cents), was made in 1880 and was valued now at $25. Another American bought a religious icon of seventeenth-century origin for the ruble equivalent of $40, and—although Soviet authorities try to prevent the export of any art objects dating back before 1917—she took it back to New York where a dealer offered her $750 for it.

More often than not, Russians are proudly sensitive about shortages and inferiority of the quality of consumer products. The story is told of an American visitor who was trying out reception on his midget transistor radio while riding on a Soviet train. Russians watched with curiosity as he held it up to his ear. Finally a Russian, unable to contain himself any longer, blurted: "We have those too. What is it?"

Although all rationing was abandoned in 1947, shortages are frequent. Soviet publications concede both the inferior quality and the shortages. An article in *Soviet Latvia* on the subject of children's garments is typical. It complains that when congratulations on the birth of a child in a family are over, the problem of finding clothing for the baby has only just begun. The author of the piece takes us to the children's section of a department store, where a customer is complaining:

" 'I won't take this shirt,' says a young woman returning a shirt to the girl at the counter. 'What a way to sew things for newly born babies: the seams are so thick—as if it were the outfit of a fire-brigade man.' "

The newspaper blames a children's-wear factory in Riga for products "sloppily made and unfit for children to wear."

Now the scene shifts to the office of the head of the store's children's department.

" 'Our daily profit is about 12,000 rubles ($1200),' says the head of the department, 'and it could be that much more again. The trouble is we don't have enough clothes. Just have a look at our empty shelves. The demand is so great. People are even buying these shirts, unfit as they are. And mind you, we haven't even got enough of these.' "

The Riga newspaper complains of a lack of swaddling clothes, sheets, nightcaps, and children's blankets. Gloves for pre-school-age children are too expensive, about 25 rubles ($2.50) "considering that children are known for losing gloves frequently." Children's furniture is described as "ugly and expensive," and toys are "expensive, dull, and colorless; a child's good toy still remains a parent's dream and that of the child."

Similarly, an article in *Trud* bemoaned shortages in the city of Rostov-on-Don. The piece complained that Rostov housewives find it next to impossible to buy electric irons, electric switches, snaps for their clothes, shaving brushes for their husbands, and, perhaps worst of all in a country that eats vast quantities of potatoes, there are almost never any potato peelers to be found.

It often takes weeks of shopping to find a simple household article. A Russian acquaintance told of looking for two years for an hourglass egg timer. An American shopped for days for a pair of warm bedroom slippers before giving up and ordering them from abroad. I visited phonograph-record shops on and off for months to try to find a recording of the Soviet National Anthem without success. In November at the outset of one cold winter a main Moscow hat store closed its doors for protracted redecorating. Fur-lined gloves and warm boots are often impossible to find in winter.

Lines in front of stores are a common sight. Lines form for a variety of reasons. Most stores close for one hour for lunch, but the hour may be any from 11 A.M. to 4 P.M. It is difficult to keep track of which shops close when. Shoppers, often on their own lunch hour, congregate in front of a store to await its reopening. Lines also form quickly whenever scarce goods of any sort appear.

There is a unique Soviet system in forming lines, a queue etiquette. When word gets around that a store has received a stock of an item in short supply that will go on sale the following morning, knots of people begin to gather. However, because the police will not tolerate lines forming overnight, a sort of line "pool" is sometimes organized. Instead of people remaining in front of the store all night, a system of shoppers' guard duty is set up. By drawing lots, one person is assigned to "stand guard" at the store for each hour of the night. The names of would-be shoppers are written on a list in the order in which they arrived at the scene. Each succeeding shopping sentry is entrusted with the list that has been compiled and he, in turn, passes it on to the person who relieves him on duty. The custodian of the list enters the names of others who subsequently come to the store, having heard late of the sale, or with the intention of being the first in line. As the hour of the store's opening approaches, crowds of shoppers arrive, names are called out, and the line forms in a more or less orderly fashion, according to the list.

Russians have become accustomed to the sight of lines. It used to be worse. In the months immediately following the war, when Soviet factories were slowly returning to peaceful production there was a gigantic chasm between supply and the accumlated consumer needs to fill. As fast as articles of clothing and household utensils were put on the counter they were sold. Salespeople spent much of their time simply serving out hours in front of empty shelves. Now there are fewer and fewer lines. For example, fresh fruit was only rarely seen in Moscow stores and never during winter months. Gradually it became more plentiful. Now the appearance of oranges and apples no longer creates queues. Grapes, peaches, and plums still do.

The supply of manufactured consumer goods is rapidly increasing too. Before World War II the Soviet Union did not manufacture any washing machines, vacuum cleaners, or household refrigerators. Russia's industrialization began late, and it is in that context that the Soviet Minister of Trade boasted in 1957 that one in every three families in the Soviet Union owned a bicycle. In backward, prerevolutionary Russia there was often only one bicycle to an entire village. The Minister added with some pride that the U.S.S.R. now produces 3,400,000 bicycles annually, "or more than are produced in the United States, France, and Italy, combined." For clarity's sake the Minister should have added that in Russia, unlike the United States, the bicycle is not primarily a pleasure vehicle but a serious means of transport.

Not only short supply, but, especially in the case of perishable fruits and other produce, inadequate transportation, and especially a dearth of refrigerator cars, are sources of shortages in stores. Also poor sales organization results in waiting lines. A shopper in a *Gastronom,* a food store, for example, must work her way through a line to the counter selling, say, sausages. A clerk tells the shopper the price, and she walks across the store to the appropriate cashier's window, tells the cashier the type and price of her purchase, pays, and receives a receipt slip. Then back to the sausage counter to stand in line again, receipt in hand, to receive the wrapped sausages. Few Russians have adequate refrigeration space, so that shopping and waiting in line for daily provisions is an endless chore.

Soviet trade authorities speak and write a great deal about the need to introduce self-service systems to eliminate the constant waiting, but only comparatively few stores have converted to any form of self-service. The campaign for greater efficiency through self-service began in 1954, and four years later the Minister of Trade was able to report the establishment of only 3500 self- or partially self-service enterprises in the whole country. Minister D. Pavlov's report raises a mental picture of Soviet efficiency experts timing customers with a stop watch. He declared: "Stores selling packaged goods are increasingly gaining in popularity. The per-purchase time spent by a customer in the packaged-goods stores has been reduced by 15 to 30 per cent, compared with the conventional stores, and in the self-service stores, by nearly 50 per cent."

Lines at Soviet stores grow especially long in moments of panic buying. Such was the case during the Israeli-French-British attack on Egypt in October 1956. Russians read war into the course events were taking. They began to stock up on canned goods, sugar, flour. Trying not to attract additional scare buyers by calling their attention to the situation, and yet wanting to discourage those engaged in scare buying, Soviet newspapers adopted the course of ridiculing the practice.

An article entitled "Soap Bubble," appeared in *Soviet Latvia* with this imaginary conversation among scare buyers:

" 'Have you laid in salt?'

" 'No.'

" 'And matches, what about matches?'

" 'No. What's the matter anyway?'

"Maria Antonova (this name is the equivalent of America's Jane Doe) gave her friend a confidential wink and whispered mysteriously:

" 'Store up on matches, soap, and salt. Just look around. See what's going on?'

"Everything was exceptionally quiet. Just as usual trolley cars were speeding down the street, cars driving by, innocent-looking passersby carrying bags and bundles.

" 'Tell me in all frankness what has happened?' Bertha Augustinova pleaded.

" 'Have you got eyes or not? What do you think these people are carrying in their bags and bundles? Well, salt, soap, and matches. Go ahead and buy everything you can before it's too late.'

"Bertha Augustinova hesitated for but a moment and then rushed into a nearby store.

" 'Any salt?' she asked the clerk.

" 'Take all you want.'

" 'Soap?'

" 'Go ahead and take it.'

" 'Well, anyway, wrap 10 bars of soap and 10 kilos of salt for me.'

"While the worrying Bertha was busy packing her purchases she was approached by Ivan Donatovich," and the cycle began anew with Bertha urging him to store up for an emergency.

The newspaper then went on to reassure readers that "reactionaries in Hungary" were being suppressed and affairs in Egypt were returning "to an even keel." However, rumor mongers such as Maria Antonova and Bertha Augustinova were spreading panic. There had been an unusually great demand for salt, soap, and matches in Riga's stores. There was no need for such quantity purchases because in Riga storehouses were crates upon crates of these articles.

"The artificial shortages of these goods that narrow and speculative-minded people are trying to create is only a soap bubble. And a soap bubble is known to be a short-lived thing that bursts easily. Look around and be sure there is no Maria Antonova near you! Listen and make sure there are no rumors spread by her! And if she happens to be near, show her up!"

Stores in the Soviet Union are owned by the government, and come under the Ministry of Trade, from the big department stores down to the ice-cream cart where a woman vendor sells ice-cream bars and cup-shaped cones, summer and winter. Most stores simply have numbers—*Apteka* (drugstore) number 11 or Gastronom number 2, for example—except for some restaurants and some of the larger stores such as *Detski Mir* (Children's World), situated across a Moscow square from secret police headquarters. Russia's biggest store is called GUM from the initials of its name, State Department Store (Gosudarstveny Universalny Magazin). Flanking one side of Red Square directly opposite the Kremlin and the Lenin-Stalin tomb, it was built under the Czar in

1893 and was then the largest department store in Europe. Under Stalin it was converted into state offices, and one of the first gestures of Georgi Malenkov's administration as premier was to order the reconversion of the elaborately steepled edifice. This was intended as a symbol of the needs of the people and to alter the brutal character of the regime. This gesture suffered considerably by an unfortunate coincidence. GUM re-opened its doors on the very day that the announcement was made that Laurentia Beria, Stalin's secret-police boss, had been secretly tried and shot by his colleagues in the very manner by which Stalin himself used to get rid of his enemies. The two events were related by irreverent foreigners in a bit of doggerel: "The people got GUM. Beria got boom."

GUM is an unusual-looking store with an arched, glass roof running the full length of its center artery and lending it the appearance of a railroad terminal. Small shops open from a series of corridors and balconies, and other counters are recessed in alcoves. In the center of the store a water fountain provides a convenient and popular meeting place. When children stray from their parents, they are brought to the fountain to be claimed.

A convenience offered by GUM and other large Moscow department stores are telephones attached high out of children's reach on walls in strategic spots. The shopper picks up the phone, tells a GUM operator the article she is looking for, and is told in what part of the store it can be found, if at all.

Although there are separate government stores in Moscow for furs, phonograph records, kitchen utensils, books, toys, clothes, shoes, silk stockings, fruits, meats, and canned goods, all of these and more can be bought, when available, at GUM. The store also holds daily fashion shows, as does the Dom Modele, the Ministry of Trade's House of Fashion. At both places, attractive models, although a bit fleshy by Western mannequin standards, parade house dresses and formal gowns, ski and beach wear, depending on the season, and work clothes. A male model struts up and down the runway to demonstrate the latest Soviet fashions in double-breasted suits and sports jackets. Several foreign fashion shows—Czechoslovakian, Hungarian, British—have attracted large audiences.

The garments, recommended by government designers, at the Soviet showings are not available ready-made. As the models show each garment a woman narrator briefly describes its features and recites a pattern number. Downstairs at the Dom Modele, patterns corresponding to the various numbers are sold for 4 rubles 20 kopecks (42 cents) each. The Russian takes the pattern home to cut and sew the dress herself, after the often difficult task of finding worth-while fabrics, or takes it to a government shop of dressmakers.

Ready-made clothing prices are high. A poorly stitched man's suit of easily creased material, cut with wide-bottomed trousers, sells for 1200 rubles ($120) and a fall coat for 2200 ($222). The windows of GUM have displayed a woman's raincoat-type spring coat for 412.80 rubles ($41.28), a man's white shirt at 129 rubles ($12.90), and a man's soft hat in a ludicrous green shade at 160 rubles ($16).

Accessories are also dear. A pair of green leather high-heeled woman's shoes sold for 525 rubles ($52.50). Other prices in the GUM window reflect the high cost of consumer goods: a small table to hold a TV set is priced at 700 rubles ($70), and a single bed with a two-inch-thick mat instead of a mattress bears a price tag of 1839 rubles ($183.90).

Many customer services, however, are inexpensive in Russia. A man's haircut, for instance, costs one ruble 90 kopecks (19 cents) in Moscow barbershops. Barbershops are organized into *artels*. These are a kind of "collective" into which various artisans such as watch repairmen are organized. The *artels* elect a chairman and pay a portion of income to the state.) The price for a spray of eau de cologne has been one ruble and 40 kopecks (14 cents), but it may be lowered if the important newspaper *Trud* has its way. A front-page editorial considered it outrageous to charge one-fourth the price of a *full* bottle for a single whiff. Barbershop sprays which, like perfumes, come in a variety of government-produced scents, sell for 6 rubles (60 cents) per bottle.

It's considered perfectly proper for men to get permanent waves in Russia. Especially in the countryside, barbershops advertise six-month guaranteed permanents for men as well as for women.

Barbers are trained in government schools and receive practical training in apprentice barbershops not recommended to the discerning customer, although haircuts are cheaper there. Upon graduation, a barber may advance through three stages from barber first-class, to second-class, to the highest rank, third-class. The salary for a third-class barber is 500 rubles ($50) a month plus a commission of 70 kopecks (7 cents) for each haircut. A committee of veteran barbers occasionally drops in from the Ministry of Trade to observe a barber at his work to determine whether he is ready for promotion to a higher rank. Barbers, more than half of whom are women, usually accept tips. As a matter of fact, they have been known to help themselves to gratuities to which they were not entitled.

Such was the case in the Siberian city of Novosibirsk where barbers in shops number 1, 11, and 92 (like many other Soviet institutions, barbershops are not identified by name) were pilfering from the till money rightfully belonging to the state. Barbers keep a record sheet of the money they've earned for the shop. The cashier keeps a similar record. By collusion, the barbers and the cashier would enter the proper amount charged the patron. As soon as the customer walked out of the shop, though, the barber and cashier would alter the number on their sheets to a smaller amount. A nine-ruble charge would be altered into a figure two. A seven to a three. The money so embezzled would be divided. The barber would get 80 per cent. The cashier would get 20 per cent. All got several months at corrective prison labor when tried by a Novosibirsk court.

Russia is a land without supermarkets, without mark-down, fire, bankruptcy, or clearance sales. There is almost no advertisement of goods in newspapers or on radio or television, and word of mouth is the main medium for conveying news of the availability of products. Only a few stores deliver goods and fewer accept telephone orders. Although heavy items like furniture are usually delivered, it is not unusual to see a man making his way home down a main street with parts of a bed on his back or a tricycle in his arms.

Although Soviet Ministry of Trade officials have indicated in public statements that it might be introduced for certain high-price products, there has been no installment buying in Russia. It is cash at time of purchase. Credit buying is a device of an economy of plenty. When there are goods in abundance for sale, made by competing manufacturers, various sales devices are contrived to encourage purchases. This has not been the case in Russia. In an economy where consumer demand for many products, including such simple things as shoes and good quality fabrics, remains unfulfilled, credit buying would only serve to increase consumer pressures. Under the prevailing circumstances, Soviet propagandists have seen fit to take a critical attitude toward credit buying and have described it as an evil of the capitalist system designed to lure money from underpaid workers to keep them in constant bondage to monopolists. With no installment buying and no private ownership of business there is no need for a bankruptcy law in Russia.

Russian husbands may be envied by men in other countries in one respect; there are no charge accounts to tempt a woman's whims.

Foreigners in Moscow have certain shopping advantages over Russians. Besides shopping in state stores and the "free market," they have alternate sources of supply. The American Embassy maintains a commissary in a narrow, whitewashed corridor of its cellar where unpainted board shelves stock a variety of canned goods. Prices are necessarily high because of the distance of transportation. In addition, the personnel of almost all embassies in Russia order from several mail-order firms in Copenhagen, Denmark, that do a thriving business keeping foreigners stationed in Moscow, 1200 sea and rail miles away, supplied with groceries. Except during the winter months when Soviet Baltic Sea ports are icebound, it takes about five weeks for an order to arrive at Moscow's Leningradskaya Railroad Station. The customs office phones, and the foreigner or a Russian assistant spends several hours at the warehouse while the crates are pried open and a customs official checks off each item against a book of customs regulations. The duty, together with freight charges, adds about 40 per cent to the otherwise reasonable prices in the mail-order catalogues.

CHAPTER 23

THE BIG RED SCHOOLHOUSE

Russia may seem like the Promised Land in one respect to school children of other countries: homework is forbidden on weekends and holidays.

However, before packing up to run away to Russia, it might be well for the schoolboy or girl to realize, too, that children in the Soviet Union go to school six days a week. There is school on Saturday, and Sunday is the only free day.

The order forbidding teachers to assign homework on Saturday or before a holiday was issued by the Ministry of Enlightenment, which is the Soviet equivalent of a Ministry of Education. The restriction on homework followed a letter published by a Communist newspaper in 1956 from a group of doctors who complained that overfatigue, headaches, and eyestrain were alarmingly frequent among children of lower grades. Less homework was the physicians' prescription. Soon after, the Ministry of Enlightenment made it a rule for the first three grades of school, and a year later the rule was extended to all school grades.

Youngsters begin school at the age of seven in the U.S.S.R.; education is compulsory for ten years in cities and many other areas, and for seven years in some villages and farm districts where space and staff are inadequate. Many schools are on a two-shift basis. The plan has been to make ten-year schooling nationwide before long.

In all grades except the ninth and tenth children are required to wear uniforms. Girls wear plain brown dresses with big white collars and black aprons. Their hair is almost always worn in long braids which end in red ribbons bows. Boys wear a military type of uniform with grayish-blue pants and high-collared hip-length tunic gathered in folds at the back by a broad leather belt. The cap is a stiff-visored officers' type, and in the lower grades, at least, boys have their heads shaven.

Uniforms have been worn on and off and now on again in Russian schools. Children in Czarist pre-Revolutionary days wore uniforms, and in the zealous determination to change all things, the Communists did away with them, just as they did with braid on military uniforms. But the braid eventually came back, and so did the school uniforms after Stalin's death. The Communist argument in support of uniforms is that no child is better or worse dressed than any other; all are thus equal in quality of clothes. Some schools are on a three-shift basis.

Despite insufficient school space an effort is made to keep classes small, and thirty-five to a class is the average of schools in Moscow and other cities I've visited. Boys and girls sit on benches at rows of old-fashioned double desks with inkwells sunk in recesses at the front edge. Classrooms are sparsely decorated, with large blackboards covering most of the front and side walls, and a portrait of Marx, Lenin, or one of the current leaders benignly watching the youngsters. On window sills, there are often ungainly, giant-leafed plants of the sort Russians favor for their homes. It seems incongruous, because they take up so much space in crowded quarters.

As is the case in most Soviet state stores, barbershops and other enterprises, grade schools rarely are endowed with a name but rather are numbered. Moscow School Number 720 is a four-story stone building in a new section of Moscow that is considered a show place for visitors. Pictures of Lenin and Stalin greet the youngsters as they leave their coats minded by an attendant in the entrance lobby. There are 28 teachers for the 500 pupils. A bell signals the end of fifty-minute classes and there is a ten-minute interval between the classes which are from 8 A.M. to 2:30 P.M. on the morning shift. (Newspaper criticism of boys' uniforms for being uncomfortable and unattractive may indicate that the pendulum is due for another swing. It has become permissible for boys not to wear uniforms to school, pending possible design of a new model.)

The state begins its education early in the life of its citizens and it continues through adulthood. There are 1000 kindergartens in Moscow where working mothers leave their pre-school-age children, ages three to seven, for the day.

There are adult classes in factories and daily lectures for the public in halls in every city and hamlet. The state's Society for Dissemination of Political Knowledge provides speakers for the astounding total of 4,000,000 lectures a year throughout the country. The topics offered on a typical day in Moscow included: "Criticism of Revisionism in Modern Aesthetics," "The Role of the Arts in Communist Education," "General Crisis of Imperialism," and "Wages Under Capitalism." A second breakfast is served to the youngsters in a dining room at 10 A.M.: free of charge, it usually consists of a warm cereal or pancakes with sour cream, bread, and tea.

The course of study includes Russian language, literature and grammar, mathematics, penmanship, spelling, history in which ideological indoctrination is interwoven, and a foreign language, usually English or German.

Since 85 per cent of the children in School 720 come from families in which both parents work, many eat lunch in school and stay on for hobby clubs of various sorts until 6 P.M. when their parents have returned home from work.

There are also specialized schools for handicapped children. I visited one of Moscow's three schools for deaf and dumb children, a substantial brick, three-story building on a dirt alley near an edge-of-town subway station. In the lobby stood the usual statue of Lenin against a background of red plush drapes. A very young-looking director of the school (she said she was thirty-four) explained that the deaf-mute youngsters receive the equivalent of a seven-year education. However, because so much time is needed to teach the handicapped children lip-reading and sign language, it takes twelve years to accomplish the seven-year curriculum of history, mathematics, geography, and all the rest. The school had just undertaken a new method of teaching deaf children, who had never heard the sounds of speech, to utter sounds themselves. This system was devised by a teacher in the school who reduced the thirty-two sounds previously taught to sixteen sounds. Substitutions were found for the eliminated sounds from among the remaining sixteen. For example, the *b* sound was eliminated and *p* taught instead. Thus, a deaf Russian child would learn to say *spasipa* for "thank you" instead of the correctly pronounced version, *spasiba*. The theory is that when the sixteen basic sounds are mastered, inaccurate sounds can be gradually refined and corrected.

Of the 350 children attending this school, largest of the three in Moscow, about half go home after school every day, and the rest, whose homes are distant, live there. The director claimed that most of the parents do not pay to board their children at the school, but those who can afford to, do pay something. The director maintained that there is not a single deaf or deaf-mute child in Moscow who is not attending one of these special government schools.

An unusual Soviet school is the State School of Circus Arts, a small white building with a low green dome, situated not far from the offices of *Pravda*. Final examinations were in progress when I visited the school. A diminutive young lady in a form-fitting blue leotard was performing stretching exercises. A boy in his teens, dressed in a red silk suit, was juggling five tin plates. Another was walking on his hands in the center of the one-ring arena, while a colleague stood nearby taping his wrists. All wore appropriately worried looks of students before end-of-term examinations. Members of the committee of teachers and retired circus performers, who would judge the students' competence, gathered at a table near the rim of the ring. At each place on the table lay a folder with sheets of paper on which to grade the students.

In most countries circus performers learn their art from other circus performers or at usually privately owned schools. The circus school in Moscow, like all educational institutions in Russia, is operated by the government. Whereas most circus schools teach only circus skills, the Moscow school gives its pupils an all-around education including mathematics, physics, a foreign language, history, principles of Marxism and Leninism, and history of the Communist Party.

Soon the circus-school director, Alexander Voloshin, appeared to usher me into his office. There was no conspicuous bust or portrait of Lenin confronting me when I entered, an unusual circumstance for a Soviet office of any sort. In fact, though cramped, it was the most gaily decorated I'd seen in the Soviet Union. Offices of almost every enterprise in Russia have a depressing uniformity. There is a broad desk with a thick pane of glass to protect the surface, several deep, brown-leather seats, overstuffed but stiff, set at a small table near the desk. There's invariably a polished wood cabinet with curtained glass doors, a couple of spare straight-backed chairs, and usually a hat stand. The walls are almost always painted two shades; a dark brown from the floor to about three quarters of the height, and lighter brown to the ceiling. But the office of the circus-school director was painted two shades of bright, cheerful blue. Circus posters were gaily arranged on the walls. One lettered in French, another in Polish, and one in English —mementos of the Soviet circus's trips abroad. The wall opposite the desk was covered with a happy collection of paintings and sketches of circus acts. There were lively drawings of bareback riders, and in the center a painting of two youngsters trying to crawl through a loose plank in a circus barn. It was a Russian version of children sneaking under the American circus tent. Hung behind Comrade Voloshin was a photograph of Vladimir Mayakovsky, the renowned Russian dramatist and poet who died by suicide in 1930; before getting into circus work, Voloshin, a sad-eyed, soft-voiced person in his forties, had worked as a theater director. On his cluttered desk stood a number of small figures: a china piece of a lion and his tamer, a black plaster figure of Karand'ash, Russia's most famous clown, and a bear pawing an inkwell tree stump. Amid this collection and almost concealed by it was a small white bust of Lenin—the only nod to Communist conformity in the circus man's office.

Voloshin seemed pleased when I admired the circus drawings. Collecting them was his hobby, he said, which was one of the few facts about himself he volunteered. He did say that he had traveled to Warsaw with the circus and had spent some time in Mongolia, organizing a circus school there—which did not seem precisely the sort of assistance that backward, primitive country needed most from the Soviet Union. However reticent Voloshin was about his own career, he spoke freely and enthusiastically about the school.

It was founded in 1926 so that, unlike Russia's ballet schools for instance, it is a creation of the post-Czarist era. Each year about 700 youngsters apply. All must have completed at least seven years of schooling. Fewer than 10 per cent, or about 65 applicants, are admitted. They are chosen on the basis of natural talent, proper physical equipment for the rigorous training, a suitable academic record, appealing looks, and, if there's a background of amateur circus work or perhaps family training, that helps too. Most of the applicants are boys, and of the 65 students accepted each year usually fewer than 15 are girls. Many are unable to complete the four-year course and only about 35 graduate. The graduation class preparing for final examinations on the day of my visit numbered 31, eight of them girls.

At commencement exercises in the circus ring (which I attended a week later), the graduates in their best clothes, and applauded by beaming parents seated around the ring, received small certificates in blue covers. Most important, each was assured of a job with the Soviet state circus. The circus is an old, enduring tradition in Russia as in many European countries. Few circus acts I've seen in Moscow, Leningrad, and Stalingrad are sensational, but I've never seen an incompetent circus act, although many have a tendency, as do Soviet performers of any genre, to be overly long. There are no freak shows in Russia—no tattooed lady or pinheaded man, no "giants" (although there are strongman weight-lifting acts) or bearded ladies. It is considered beneath man's dignity to capitalize on nature's misfortunes. However, midgets are employed in circus routines, and some acts consist entirely of midgets.

There are no acts of the sort where a man gets shot out of a cannon or jumps into a small tub of water from a great height. There are no high flying-trapeze stunts without safety devices. There are no high-wire bicycle-balancing acts like the famous Alanzas of Ringling fame. Soviet tightrope performers, trapeze artists, and, in fact, in any act where the performer is at a dangerous height from the ground, the participants are equipped with a safety wire attached to a belt around the performer's waist. Should the aerialist slip, the wire, run through a pulley on the ceiling, would lower him safely to the ground. The wire is omitted, and even then not always, only when nets are spread.

Director Voloshin explained the philosophy behind this:

"We believe in a full guarantee of the safety of the circus actor. In the West you often say that in the Soviet Union there are no acts that really tickle your nerves, no acts are risky enough. That's not so, we do allow risky acts, but we provide insurance of the performer's safety by belts, wires, and nets."

The hypothesis that there can be risky acts without risk to anyone is something that Voloshin did not explain and perhaps best falls into the category of inexorable Soviet logic.

Voloshin continued: "In the Soviet Union there's a law that guarantees the safety of the circus performer by requiring that all precautions be taken."

Students at the school are trained in a particular circus skill according to their talents and desires and depending on the needs of the state circus for a balanced repertoire. Acts are organized at the school, and by graduation time complete units are ready to perform in rings around the country. There are some individual acts, too, mostly clowns. The class I watched included a solo girl tightrope walker, a solo girl contortionist, a team of four muscular boys and a petite, attractive young lady in an act of chinning bar acrobats. Another team of six boys and a girl did a routine juggling act.

Immediately after graduation each of the solo artists and teams is assigned by the Central Circus Bureau of the Ministry of Culture to one of the one hundred circus units in the Soviet Union. Starting salary is 1600 rubles ($160) a month, considerably more than a doctor's or a teacher's. Circus performers, like other theatrical artists, are well paid by Soviet standards, and an experienced, popular clown like Karand'ash may earn 20,000 rubles ($2000) a month.

Circus performers do not remain with a single circus company. Rather, the combination of acts that travels from circus to circus ring is constantly reshuffled by the Circus Bureau. Besides the permanent circus buildings in cities like Moscow, Leningrad, Stalingrad, Tbilisi, Kiev, Odessa, and Omsk, there are summer circuses set up in tents or in buildings that are unsuitable in winter because of lack of heat. A completely new program plays at each ring every few months. There are no big, three-ring circuses in Russia; all are single-ring affairs in the European tradition.

Circus-school students pay no tuition, as is the case now in all Russian schools. They receive a stipend from the government which starts at 400 rubles ($40) a month and increases in the final year to 700 rubles($70). This is for meals, bus fares (there's a dormitory building for out-of-town students), movie tickets, clothes; most books and school supplies are free. The instructors are former circus stars.

When the final examinations were about to commence, Voloshin suggested we go to the arena to watch. While a woman played appropriately cadenced piano music, one team of students after another performed. The sun-tanned young contortionist twisted her backbone into a complex variety of shapes, but apparently she felt she had earned a low mark. She was downhearted as she walked out of the ring, wearing the same dejected expression seen at more conventional schools at exam time.

Admission to institutions of higher education is supposed to be strictly on the basis of merit. At the end of each school year entrance examinations are held at institutes (where a single specialty is taught) and at universities (which have a number of faculties). Those who receive the highest marks on these competitive examinations are supposed to be admitted. Some weight is given to a student's school record, and points are given also for military service or for practical work. Young people are now encouraged by Communist authorities to go to work for two years upon graduation from compulsory seven-to-ten years of schooling, particularly at a Siberian or Central Asian construction site. A fair student with two years of work behind him on a new state farm in Siberia is likely to be admitted to an institute ahead of a youngster fresh out of school with very good marks.

There are enough cases of admission by bribery documented in the Soviet press to indicate that this is not an infrequent occurrence. Usually the guilty persons are named. On one occasion the youth newspaper, *Komsomolskaya Pravda,* published an anonymous letter from a second-year student at an agricultural institute at Samarkand. "I've become a student," he wrote, "only because my mother managed to scrape together 5000 rubles ($500) which she brought to the entrance board. I was against it from the outset. I don't like agriculture. The way I was admitted was disgusting, and I am ashamed of myself. But anytime I bring it up my mother won't listen. I don't know what to do. Some of those who know how I entered the institute say that I am a lucky person to be studying and not to give my mother grief. When you have received a higher education, they say, you will like your specialty. I am not giving you my name. I don't know a way out."

When the newspaper sent a reporter to the agricultural institute, students claimed to know many cases of fellow students who gained admittance by bribes rather than by good marks. They saw nothing unusual in these cases and refused to betray their colleagues' names.

A page-a-day calendar that adorns many Soviet desks took note of the fact that nepotism is sometimes involved in admission to schools. A cartoon shows a grotesquely fat young man talking to a girl:

"Galitchka," he says to her, "congratulate me. I've just been admitted to the Institute for Physical Culture."

"But do you have the necessary qualifications?"

"Tremendous qualifications! My uncle is the Dean of Admissions."

Five is the highest mark in Soviet schools. Five is excellent, four is good, three is satisfactory, two is poor, and one is very bad. Marks are entered periodically by the teacher in a small copybook retained by each pupil, rather than on a report card. These report books are taken home at least once a week to be signed by a parent who is supposed to take note of the child's progress. Homework assignments are entered in the notebook so that the parent has a way of checking on whether the child is really doing the work assigned. If the teacher wants to see a parent to discuss a disciplinary problem, this request is written in the report book where the parent can see it when signing.

By Soviet standards teachers are well paid. A beginning salary of a sixth-grade teacher is 800 rubles ($80) per month. Academic work commands great respect. Among the most distinguished men in Russia are the members of the Academy of Sciences of the U.S.S.R., founded in 1725. It comes directly under the supervision of the Kremlin's Council of Ministers in organizational charts. The Academy, consisting of the nation's most outstanding men of science, supervises every branch of the nation's scientific life. Its various branches deal with everything from finding new vaccines to building sputniks.

It was the sputniks that alerted the attention of the outside world to Soviet science and education. Respectful attention had been paid to the Soviet claim that more than 70,000 engineers were being graduated each year. This is compared to the U.S. annual crop of 30,000 engineers. But it could rightly be argued that many Soviet engineers were really less highly skilled technicians who do not deserve the status of engineer by American standards. Furthermore, a highly developed industrialized economy like America's does not need as great an increment of scientific skill each year.

However, there is no arguing with the fact that the Soviet educational system produced scientists and engineers capable of launching a sputnik before the U.S.A. did, and then following it with sputniks of enormously greater size.

Delegations of American educators—college presidents, professors, school administrators, teachers—flocked to Russia to see what could be learned from the Soviet system. Many carried away words of praise. It was at this very juncture that devastating criticism of the Soviet educational system was heard from no less an authority than Nikita Khrushchev. With the concurrence of his Party Presidium, Khrushchev issued a lengthy memorandum, in September 1958, recommending sweeping changes. The changes were to be brought about over a period of some years in each Soviet Republic by action of the Republics' legislatures and Party organizations. The final shape of the Khrushchev plan would vary from area to area.

Khrushchev's criticisms, however, applied to the entire country's educational setup. Parental influence rather than ability, he said, was being widely used to get youngsters admitted to college. Most objectionable to Khrushchev, though, was that the Soviet educational system was preparing pupils for higher education rather than for life. Or to state it more specifically: Soviet schools were turning out graduates well qualified for higher education but not immediately qualified to take a job at a lathe or milling machine.

Unlike the educational system in most American cities, all Soviet pupils in the first ten years of school take the same courses. In the United States it is customary, by the eighth or ninth grades, to split up those students who intend to go to college (and give them college preparatory courses) and those who will go right to work (and give them commercial or trade courses). Khrushchev, in typical Russian fashion, sought to swing the pendulum violently—further than the American system—and prepare *everyone* for work. After a transition period (during which some ten-year schools would be retained in order to maintain a flow of qualified students to colleges), all schools would become seven- or eight-year schools. After decades of struggling to make ten years of schooling nationwide, Khrushchev was turning the clock back.

Under the Khrushchev system, during this abbreviated span of schooling a specified time would be spent each week at technical training. In the city this would be in factories; in the country the training would be in the fields. Opportunities for higher education would be available for those who have the energy and determination to go to night school to take correspondence courses.

The Khrushchev plan had been preceded by months of debate—some of it in the pages of the press—between the educators (who believe that an educated man can be taught any job in time) and the man-power experts (who need hands to run machines *now* in order to meet ambitious industrial targets set for them). The man-power advocates won. It was natural that they would with Khrushchev. Having worked from boyhood and achieved his position without significant formal education (and then only of a practical nature), Khrushchev had small patience for theoretical knowledge. Yet, by the revolutionary revision of the educational system, the perpetuation of the very class that made the sputniks possible is jeopardized.

The anti-intellectual nature of Khrushchev's motivation was indicated in his memorandum. He complained that a "lordly-scornful, wrong attitude toward physical labor is to be found in some families." Khrushchev complained that at Moscow colleges "children of workers and collective farmers comprise only 30 to 40 per cent of the student body. The rest are children of office employees, of the intelligentsia."

In typical Soviet fashion, the first step was to be a slogan. Said Khrushchev: "The most important thing here is to issue a slogan and make this slogan sacred for all children entering school, that all children must prepare for useful work, for participation in building the Communist society."

It is one thing, though, to issue a slogan and another to make it work.

Russia's largest institution of higher learning is Moscow State University. It is more properly called "Moscow State University in the name of Mikhail Vasilievich Lomonosov," in the Soviet fashion of appending the name of an honored individual. Lomonosov was a Russian scientist and writer who died in 1765, after writing a history of Russia, a Russian grammar, and reforming the Russian literary language. Old buildings of the university are situated on Manege Square across from one segment of the Kremlin's wall. In 1953 a thirty-two-story skyscraper was completed on a fast-growing edge of the city, known as Lenin Hills. The broad base of the edifice rises eighteen stories and only then begins tapering toward the tower which is crowned, as are most of Moscow's nine skyscrapers, with a huge hammer and sickle.

It is a splendid building with roomy classrooms, laboratories, a large auditorium, and elevators that rise faster than most manufactured in the U.S.S.R. This is probably one of the few universities in the world where a guard stands at the entrance and admits only persons presenting identification cards as students or members of the faculty. The enrollment is nearly 18,000 students in 12 faculties and there is a staff of 2000 professors.

Somewhat less imposing and more typical is the Uzbek State University dedicated to Alisher Navoyi, the founder of Tadzhik literature. A low, gray stone building on a tree-lined boulevard in Samarkand houses the administration building and some classrooms, its entrance graced by two silver-painted statues of young men, one in civilian clothes and the other in aviator's garb. Two other three-story buildings comprise the university's property besides several small dormitories scattered elsewhere in this ancient central Asian city.

The university was founded in 1927, seven years after the area, now known as the Soviet Republic of Uzbekistan, was incorporated in the U.S.S.R. This was a region of illiteracy under the despotic rule of the Emir of Bukhara, who kept more than one hundred wives and concubines, whose word was law, and who devised such excruciating systems for torture as a twenty-one-foot deep pit of scorpions and other insects native to this desert region. Victims were lowered into the pit and left there to endure a horrible death. Whatever more refined forms of oppression the Communists devised for those who resisted their rule in Central Asia, they also established universities, and more than a third of Uzbek state's teachers are Russians even now.

There are four faculties. Physics and mathematics comprise one faculty. The philological faculty consists of departments of Uzbek, Tadzhik, and Russian literature and language as well as a foreign language department where English is taught. The third faculty is for biology and geography. Finally, there is a faculty of historical studies.

Day classes in these four faculties are attended by 7200 students. There are 1900 in night classes, and 3800 adults take courses at the university. Uzbeks and Tadzhiks, the native peoples of dark skin and oriental features in this vast region bordering on China, Afghanistan, and Iran, comprise 70 per cent of the student body. There are 28 nationalities attending the university. The Rector, an Uzbek, received me in his office, and with members of the faculty we sat at a red-baize-covered table placed at right angles to his desk. It was a typically furnished Soviet office with a portrait each of Lenin and Stalin on the wall across from a painting of the Tadzhik literary hero, Navoyi, seated cross-legged on a rug, dressed in a red native robe and a turban. Except for that touch it might well have been an office in Moscow rather than in Samarkand, one of the oldest cities of the world, the proud prize of conquest of Ghengis Khan and Alexander the Great and Tamerlane. The Rector a short, dark man in his fifties, spoke intently and devotedly of his university.

As in lower grades in Central Asian schools where there are separate schools for instruction in Russian, in Uzbek (a language of Turkish root), and in Tadzhik (of Persian origin), so there are classes in each faculty in each of the three languages.

The university has 36 laboratories, three scientific museums, a library of 600,000 volumes, and a teaching staff of 300. In the first thirty years of the university's existence 5500 students have graduated. With pride, the Rector said that about 50 of these had gone on to achieve doctorates and professorships.

Now freshman classes consist of 450 students, but in the early years of the university there were only 60 admitted each year, which accounts for the relatively small number of graduates in more than a quarter of a century.

Women comprise more than a third of the student body. In a recent freshman class of 450, women accounted for 148. An increasing number of applicants admitted each year are demobilized soldiers and young people who had worked for two years after completion of ten-year primary and secondary school. Of the freshman class of 450, 26 were discharged soldiers and 92 had worked for two years. Refresher courses are offered nights for workers who intend to apply for admission, and the armed forces have similar courses. The Rector was vague about the exact point handicap enjoyed in entrance exams by the preferred soldiers and workers. The impression was that it is rather flexible, and that every benefit of the doubt is given to former servicemen and workers, regardless of their entrance-exam marks, if it is felt that they can cope with the course of study.

"If a score of 20 points on the entrance exam is needed to enter the University," explained the Rector, "a man who has worked for two years may enter with only 18 or 19 points. It varies with the competition and with the particular faculty as well as with the number and quality of applicants in any year."

Students who maintain at least a three average receive an allowance from the state known as a "stipend." The amount of the stipend varies with the students' marks and increases with each year of a student's course. Roughly it runs from 300 to 700 rubles ($30 to $70) a month. An excellent (all fives) student in the freshman year would receive 360 rubles ($36) a month, and in his final year the student, maintaining his high marks, would get 700 rubles monthly. (In the case of a student whose parents' income is less than 500 rubles or $50 a month he would receive a minimum stipend, even if his average was less than three.) All books required for courses are available in the university library, but a student may wish to use part of his stipend to purchase his own. Books are reasonably priced and seldom more than 15 rubles ($1.50) a copy. Students who live at home usually use their stipends as spending money for clothes, movies, theater, newspapers, and occasional meals eaten out. It's possible for a thrifty student living at home actually to save something each month from his stipend. The 1400 students who live in the university's three dormitories, or hostels as they are called, pay 15 rubles ($1.50) monthly for their crowded quarters.

The starting salary of a first year instructor is 2000 rubles ($200) a month and increases to 2500 rubles ($250) by the fifth year. Two hundred and twenty members of the teaching, technical, and maintenance staff of the university are members of the school's unit of the Communist Party, the largest Party unit in Samarkand. Eighty members of the unit are students, and 90 per cent of the rest of the student body are members of the Komsomol, the Young Communist League. The dominant role played by Russians in the control and management of the Central Asian Soviet Republics is reflected in the fact that one third of the members of the university's Party unit are Russians.

Like other Soviet educational institutions, the Uzbek State University sets a rigorous course of study for its student body. Classes are held six days a week, six hours a day, for all faculties. Of this, two hours a week is spent in the study of Marxism-Leninism, ideological training in the principles of Communist doctrine.

There were 180 students studying English at Uzbek State when I was there in 1958. They were divided into ten groups—five Uzbek-speaking groups and five Russian-speaking. Freshmen majoring in English spend half of the thirty-six hours per week of classes in English courses. After the freshman year the number of hours increases. Lea Rosett, a serene-faced Russian woman with graying brown hair pulled back in a bun, is head of the English department. She had never been abroad and has few opportunities to converse with English-speaking people. She was delighted with the opportunity to practice on me. She spoke slowly, as if to make absolutely sure that she used the proper tense of the verb, but her pronunciation was good and her vocabulary versatile. Mrs. Rosett had received her degree at the Leningrad Pedagogical Institute and had worked for two years in the 1930s as an Intourist guide, showing American and British tourists around the former Russian capital. When war broke out in 1941 she and her family were evacuated to Samarkand. Her husband is a professor in the university's Mathematics Department. They have a twelve-year old son who attends a Russian language school and is already well advanced in English, says his mother.

It was obvious after a brief conversation with her, that this woman of wide cultural interests and tastes found life in provincial, backwater Samarkand drab and limited. She insisted that they were free to leave any time they wished, but whenever the question came up her husband was called in by the Rector and other university administrators and told how valued his services were in Samarkand and how badly he was needed. Mrs. Rosett explained that many honors and awards had been bestowed upon him, "and he feels a responsibility to remain here." Members of the faculty are provided with small houses, better living conditions than they might find elsewhere, and this also serves as an inducement for remaining.

Three women, teachers on Mrs. Rosett's staff, said that I was the first English-speaking person they had ever met and talked with. To compensate for the disadvantage in trying to teach a language they rarely heard spoken, the teachers hold a weekly conversation circle in order to practice English among themselves. The English Department has a speech laboratory with tape-recording machines to enable students to listen to themselves, but, lamented Mrs. Rosett, there was not a single copy of a large Webster's dictionary in all of Samarkand.

Specialized training at an institute is one of the few roads to success in Russia. There are few other steps by which a young man or woman can climb the economic and prestige ladder. Unlike capitalistic countries, a young man with natural acumen does not have an opportunity to start a business on a shoestring and build it by effort and talent to a large chain of stores. A boy just out of secondary school cannot count on being taken into his father's successful enterprise because father in Russia owns no enterprise. Membership in the Communist Party, itself the main portal to success in Russia, is open largely to those who have some special talent or skill to offer the state. Thus the number of applicants each year for the Soviet version of college far exceeds the space available, and competition is keen.

There are other reasons, too, for the crush of applicants. Family financial standing plays no role in the decision to continue education. It is not a question of being able to afford it. Tuition now is free. Also, the fact that good marks and scholarship are encouraged from childhood contributes to stimulating interest in higher education among youngsters. The smart boy or girl is seldom the butt of teasing as a teacher's pet. There is no aversion to "eggheads" at any age in Russia. Unlike American schools, where the star athlete is likely to be campus hero, students in Soviet institutes have less diversion of this sort. There *are* teams, but no program of intensely competitive contests among schools with cheerleaders and pre-game bonfires. School, whether grade school, high school, or college, is intended for study, and the emphasis is on high marks in the classroom rather than on a high score on the football field. Even so, occasionally there is newspaper criticism of over-emphasis of sports in some schools.

There is, nonetheless, a perennial problem of rearing Soviet young-sters in the mold of discipline and devotion to Communist aspirations sought by Kremlin authorities. There are frequent cases of student misconduct, teen-age indolence, and outright hooliganism. Out-of-school influences are usually blamed by the authorities. For example, it is in the home that youngsters are taught religion; this influence is so great that in some villages, despite classroom instruction in atheism, the entire student body stays away from school on minor religious holidays. The decision was made to keep youngsters in school more, under proper Communist influence, and away from the home, the church, and the street. Boarding schools were introduced in 1956, and the plan, as sufficient school space becomes available, is eventually to make board-ing schools universal where youngsters will sleep, returning home only on Sundays.

The beginning was modest; 285 boarding schools were opened in 1956, and the number is growing slowly. At first, in order to evoke as little parental resentment as possible, pupils were taken from orphanages, from broken homes, and from poor parents with large families.

The preference given to former workers and soldiers is in itself intended to encourage a serious attitude in student bodies. Infringe-ments of student discipline during the early days of de-Stalinization gave fresh impetus to the program of encouraging would-be students to go to work first. So did the leading roles played by students in the October events in Hungary and Poland in 1956. It was felt by the Kremlin leadership that a person who had served three years in an army unit or two years plowing dry Siberian soil would better appreciate the opportunity offered by education to improve his station in life and would more willingly bend to ideological discipline.

Cases of breach of discipline were many, but in terms of student exuberance in other countries, the transgressions of Soviet students might seem mild indeed. Yet, seen in the Soviet context, they might well give rise to alarm in the leadership. There were instances of previously docile lecture groups in dialectic materialism, for example, being disrupted by brash students plying the instructor with questions intended to undermine Communist theses. There was a report of a Komsomol group at a Moscow institute refusing to elect a chairman presented on a single-name slate by the group's governing committee.

There was the case of an unpopular Komsomol chairman being suspended out of a fourteenth-story window of the Moscow University skyscraper by a rope around his waist. Elsewhere this might pass as normal spring-fever conduct; in Moscow it is scandalous. There were persistent reports of expulsions.

Branches of student discipline were recorded in the pages of *Dawn of the East* newspaper in Tbilisi. An article on March 24, 1956, shortly after street disorders in which students played a prominent role, reported:

"At many meetings and conferences they often tell of students showing a lack of discipline, often cutting classes. The figures from September 1 until December 31 show that 94,083 man hours have been skipped without any excuses, among them in Marxism-Leninism (2682 man hours), in dialectic materialism (2231 man hours), and in political economics (1665 man hours).

"Sometimes lectures are skipped by whole groups, who instead go for a collective review of a new movie, leaving the teacher to lecture to a virtually empty auditorium. Especially 'organized' in this way are groups in the West European language and literature faculties. Unfortunately their record is closely followed by students in the faculty of physics. In the history faculty, A. Mkheidze and M. Dzimestarhishveli were so rarely seen at lectures that their fellow students could not have recognized them. Almost half of the students cut seminars in dialectical materialism. It sometimes happens that only one or two students from an entire group are present, and once the whole fifth group of the fourth year of the philological faculty cut their seminars."

The paper told of expulsion of students for violating public order. "Can it be tolerated," asked *Dawn of the East,* "that in 1955, for instance, there were 176 cases registered of students breaking rules of socialist order, and the 41 students were detained by the militia for a total of two and a half months?

"Some old prejudices of the area are recreated and some young people, such as a student in the geographic-geological faculty, N. Moudjiry, revived the old custom of a runaway marriage. He sneaked away with a girl student from the biological faculty."

Other cases of misconduct cited were less in the virile mountaineer tradition of this Caucasus region but equally reprehensible to the authorities, such as the student who beat up a taxi driver after a drunken spree and then struck a policeman who arrested him.

There are quips about students who misbehave or do poorly in classes. A Russian friend shook her head disapprovingly as she told about a neighbor's none-too-bright child who was getting bad marks. "Well," she shrugged, "maybe he'll be able to get a job in the weather bureau if nowhere else."

This rather light-hearted attitude is not shared by Soviet officialdom. Every opportunity is taken in publications, speeches, and edicts to impress upon young people the need for a serious attitude in studies and also in free-time pursuits. This may partly explain why Soviet youngsters spend so many free hours poring over chessboards instead of chatting on the telephone. The Soviet attitude of earnestness, seen in recreation as well as in study, has its roots in the Soviet classroom.

CHAPTER 24

NE KULTURNY

The wrinkled, old woman with a shawl on her head reached for my overcoat across the counter of a cloakroom. As she tried to hang it up she noticed that the cloth tab for this purpose had been torn loose at one end. Looking at me reproachfully, she scolded, *"Ne kulturny."*

It is also considered *ne kulturny* (not cultured) for a woman to wear a coat or hat into a restaurant, however drafty it might be, but she may use her fingers to tear off pieces of meat without being criticized for bad table manners.

A visiting tourist who wears a low-cut dress or goes out in the street in the summer without stockings exposes herself to being accosted by a self-appointed arbiter of good manners and being rebuked as *ne kulturny*.

It is *ne kulturny* for a man (and unheard of for a woman) to put feet up on a desk, to cross legs, or to keep hands in pants pockets. He may put his hands in his jacket pockets, though, without breach of Soviet manners.

It's "uncultured" to drive a dirty or dented automobile. As a matter of fact, it's against the law. Traffic regulation number 120 of the city of Moscow reads: "Vehicles are forbidden to operate if they are not neat in appearance, or if they are dirty, improperly painted, or with unpainted or unchromed bumpers, bent fenders, or lacking mufflers or with nonfunctioning mufflers, or with excessive exhaust fumes, or (for passenger cars) lacking hubcaps, or with bent hubcaps, or with hubcaps rusted on the outer surface." The regulation is strictly observed. Although there are no car-washing drive-ins in Russia, drivers of state and private cars somehow manage to scrub their vehicles clean within hours after a heavy rain has created muddy puddles. The only dirty cars on Moscow's streets are those driven in by foreign tourists.

Russians' table manners are frequently atrocious. Even people of some education often hold a fork as if it were a dagger and chew around a large chunk of meat, but, when eating an apple in the street, a Russian will stop and turn toward a building in order to conceal his mouth.

Russians think nothing of shoving and elbowing each other brutally in store, street, and subway crowds, but to whistle in public will evoke cries of *ne kulturny*.

Soviet standards of manners are still in the formative stage. There is no Emily Post or Amy Vanderbilt, but now tentative suggestions appear from time to time in the columns of newspapers and on the radio that there should be a guidebook to proper manners. The growing interest in manners is a reflection of the passing of time since the Revolution. The fanaticism of a workers' revolution demanded the destruction of social standards held by the conquered upper class. This was a workers' society; it was considered retrograde for a woman to wear make-up. It became an affectation of a workers' society to go to the Bolshoi Theatre or a restaurant in soiled work clothes and without a necktie. The Kremlin leaders themselves wore plain, dark suits at formal diplomatic receptions where foreign women were resplendent in gowns and gentlemen wore full-dress uniforms or tuxedos. It was a matter of some pride for a Soviet leader not to own a tuxedo; it testified to his working-class origins and loyalties.

It served the purposes of the Communist hierarchy to encourage a contempt for cultivated tastes and manners. The Soviet economy concentrated on heavy industry. There were few resources to spare for consumer niceties. Therefore, the niceties were disparaged. Furthermore, it was necessary for women to work at all manner of manual labor. Therefore, effeminacy of any sort in men *or* women was discouraged; the official concept of the desirable Soviet woman was portrayed in Soviet paintings and sculpture—muscular, hair drawn tightly back, without make-up, able to hold her own at the plow or the lathe with any man.

However, as Soviet industry developed and especially as the general atmosphere relaxed since Stalin's time, a pronounced interest developed in the proper way to dress, to eat, to drink, to behave in groups. It's noteworthy that even after the onset of cocktail-party diplomacy, when members of the Soviet leadership began attending Embassy receptions and holding more frequent Kremlin functions for foreign dignitaries, the wives of leaders were only rarely present. An explanation offered is that while men in high position managed by gradual contact with the outside world to overcome their workers' and peasants' background and to acquire social manners, their wives—usually women of simple background—rarely enjoyed this opportunity. Not knowing how to conduct themselves graciously in society, the wives stayed home.

As time goes on there is less self-consciousness about imitating manners from abroad or even from Russia's past. This was indicated in a broadcast entitled "How To Behave At A Dance," for young listeners in Kharbarousk, Siberia:

"Ludmilla Polyatskaya asks in a letter how one should behave at a dance. Once, at a dance she attended, writes Ludmilla, a young man approached her and asked her for the next dance. When she declined to dance with him, the man brought over some of his friends and they began to threaten her. They refused to listen to her explanations until she was finally rescued by the Komsomol patrol [a vigilante group of young people charged with maintaining order at dances and other youth affairs]. Her reason for refusing to dance with him was because he was overbearing, ill-mannered, and rude. She, and a number of other radio listeners, would like to know how one should behave at a dance. Here are some rules to be followed by the well-bred person at a public dance.

"The man always asks the woman to dance. The girl can decline if she has promised the dance to another or if she is tired at the moment or for any other reason best known to herself. However, the refusal must be offered with tact, gracefully, and without arguments and ill-feelings.

"During women's-choice dances the girl should not invite the same man to dance with her repeatedly. The young man, in turn, on being refused a dance should not invite a girl standing next to the woman who refused him, nor anyone standing in the immediate vicinity. Walk away some distance and invite some other girl.

"Should a man ask a girl who arrived at the dance with a male escort, including her husband, it is proper to thank the man before dancing, and it is also proper to excuse yourself when leaving the girl at her escort's side after the dance.

"It is not proper for a girl to dance with another girl after refusing to dance with a man. The man refused will usually attempt to break up the female pair, sometimes with the help of his friends, and since this is quite proper, he will in the end force her to dance with him while one of his friends dances with her partner.

"One should dance decorously and in the style prescribed for a given dance. The man's right arm should encircle the woman's waist, while the free left arm should not be waved around in the air. Various unnatural gyrations only attract attention and reveal a person's bad manners and poor breeding.

"At the end of a dance the man escorts the girl to the place from which she was invited or to some other place at her request.

"This applies equally in cases where the girl invited the man or when one girl invited another girl. While escorting a girl off the dance floor it is not necessary to hold her arm. One can simply walk beside her.

"At a dance held in a private home the man invites only a woman to whom he has been presented or one with whom he is well acquainted. A girl never asks a man to whom she has not been introduced or with whom she is not well acquainted."

Despite such radio guidance and a weekly television program devoted to teaching the proper manners as well as steps on the dance floor, Russian men still think nothing of approaching a woman in a restaurant and, without a word to her escort, asking her to dance. Refusals are not taken lightly. I've seen more than one protracted argument ensue in Moscow's elaborate Praga and other restaurants when an invitation to a stranger to dance was refused. It's not at all unusual to see two women dance, and there's no perversion necessarily involved when two men dance together. It's also considered simple camaraderie when two husky soldiers walk down the street holding hands or when men kiss on the lips in uninhibited greeting.

Increasing attention is given, too, to proper cultural standards in language. "Let's Protect Our Mother Tongue," was the title of a piece in the youth newspaper, *Komsomolskaya Pravda,* which singled out a factory in Stalinsk where a reporter had found that workers used profane language. It proposed that a law be passed against profanity. "If you're late at a machine this is correctly considered a violation of labor discipline, but if your tongue erupts vile language no one will censure you.

Is it not also a violation of public discipline to banalize our great language?

"We reverse rivers, we plow up thousands of hectares of old virgin lands, and all of this with enthusiasm, but we not infrequently wink at this insulting practice.

"Let us stand on guard over our beautiful Russian language, our everyday conduct, and over our Soviet morals," concluded the editorial.

A monthly magazine, *Family and School,* devoted to problems of rearing children, occasionally carries articles on manners. Entitled "The Way Your Children Behave at the Table," an article written by a Professor E. Medinsky of the Academy of Pedagogical Sciences of the Russian Republic warned especially against chewing and drinking noises. Very often, conceded the etiquette expert, children protest that they cannot eat soup without a *Khlyupat,* which is the Russian onomatopoeic word for a "slurp," or more properly, a sucking noise. Russian children are cautioned to wash hands before eating and never, never to eat off the knife. It's perfectly proper to employ pieces of bread to push meat, fish or vegetables on the fork. However, Professor Medinsky's advice to keep both hands on the table differs from accepted Western manners that the left hand be kept in the lap. In fact, the professor specifically warned against this. It's often a habit with some children to keep their left arm under the table with the result that a child's posture is at an angle and his body is slumped to one side. This looks poorly and is bad for the youngster, he wrote.

Even more difficult to regulate than children's table manners is the adult practice of tipping. The Communists frown on it. Tipping is described as a disgusting vestige of capitalism; it is demeaning for one individual to accept an offering from another. Each worker's wage is supposed to be ample without the need to accept tips. All Soviet citizens are entitled to receive the same service without recourse to tipping.

However, as in the case of so many other aspects of Soviet society's ideology, there is a great gap between preaching and practice. Russians *do* customarily give tips and expect tips. A visiting foreigner may encounter an expression of injury or indignation when he offers a tip to a Russian waitress, taxi driver, barber, or chambermaid. This can, of course, be extremely deflating to the tipper. An American movie producer visiting Moscow mentioned to his Intourist guide that he had brought along some nylon stockings and would like to give her a couple of pairs in appreciation for her work. She proceeded to express shock that he would presume to make such a suggestion, she scolded, and finally burst into tears. The bewildered American fled to his hotel room.

It's not uncommon for a Russian to feel a responsibility as a self-appointed propagandist to put the best of possible faces on all things Soviet. But even this tendency toward foreigners has worn off in cities like Moscow and Leningrad, where tourists from abroad have become relatively frequent. One way to tell how far you are from Moscow is the relative receptiveness of Russians to tips. A driver to the Moscow airport cheerfully accepts a 10 ruble ($1.00) note, the waitress at the Kiev airport restaurant hesitates a moment and then slips the tip into her apron pocket with thanks, but the porter at the hotel in Samarkand seems genuinely upset when you try to hand him a tip.

Even in Moscow, where tipping is general, I've never experienced a case of a waiter or waitress or taxi driver complaining because no tip was offered or because a tip was too small, nor have I heard second-hand of such a case.

Tips often go a long way in Russia. Such was the case when an American couple living in a Moscow hotel wanted to have a set of bed lamps, purchased in Copenhagen, installed over their beds. The hotel electrician was called, he surveyed the project, and shook his head. "No, it cannot be done," he ruled, "because it requires drilling holes in the walls and that would mean damaging state property." The electrician left, but a short while later his colleague, the carpenter, appeared to inspect the bed lamps. He indicated that a 100 ruble ($10) tip might swing the decision. The electrician returned, solemnly accepted the tip. The holes were drilled in state property, and the lamps fastened in place.

Under Soviet law tipping is considered bribery. Occasionally, but only occasionally, persons caught tipping or receiving tips are brought to court and punished as an example to others.

In the Soviet economy, where there are scarcities of many sorts, bribery is often used to receive precedence. A half-dozen officials of the Moscow bureau responsible for allotting housing space were sentenced to fifteen years in prison for accepting a number of 5000-ruble ($500) bribes in return for desirable apartment space.

The briber and the bribed are considered mutually culpable. Yet bribes are offered and taken as an accepted way of getting things done in a society where fear, bureaucracy, and disinterest complicate simple transactions. The workman in a typewriter shop estimated it would take two weeks to replace a broken key. Told that the typewriter was needed in a hurry, the mechanic suggested, "If you do not require a receipt I can do it during my lunch period today." Subsequent typewriter repair jobs were handled in the same manner; the mechanic apparently pocketed the money as private income. The soliciting of bribes can be conscienceless.

The newspaper *Izvestia* related the dolorous story of an old woman, victimized by the cemetery bribe racket. The woman, Nadezda Grigiorevna Dyakova, was bereft at the death of her grandaughter. As regulations require, the grandmother went to the district registry office and obtained a certificate of death. This she took to the cemetery where the child's parents were buried, and presented it to the manager of the municipal cemetery, asking permission to bury the child there. Heartlessly, the manager brushed the woman aside. "We have no room here," he explained. The grandmother wept, pleading with him that she wanted the youngster buried near her parents. He relented and, motioning toward a grave digger, told her to arrange it with him. The grave digger was direct. He asked for 100 rubles ($10), of which the manager apparently received a portion.

On the day of the burial, when the coffin was lowered into the grave there was no hammer or nails about for fastening the lid (it's customary to have the body exposed until the moment of burial). At that precise juncture, by prearrangement, a man appeared with nails and a hammer which he curtly offered for the price of a "quarter of vodka," (a quarter of a liter), 12 rubles ($1.20). The bribe in hand, the man nailed down the lid.

The amount of the bribe varies with the prosperity of the victim. Five hundred rubles ($50) is the customary bribe for a plot. For special requests the bribes increase steeply, although each cemetery has a schedule of prices set for all services by the government's Moscow Funeral Service Trust. However, there was the case of a woman who wanted fencing erected around her husband's grave. The cemetery manager, claiming that his staff was too busy, introduced her to a worker who arranged to do the job for 2100 rubles ($210). The workman followed the simple procedure of tearing down a fence on a neighboring grave to install hers.

The extent of bribery and the general acceptance of it is reflected in an exposé published in the newspaper, *Soviet Russia*. A Communist Party member, Alexei Fedorovich Korovin, a taxi driver, was assigned to a new place of work—the Fifth Taxi Garage of Moscow, where he immediately sensed illicit activities. On his first day of work, as Korovin's assigned car was given a customary check-up the foreman said to him, "The engine's a bit dirty. I ought to turn your car back. But I'm a human being, I am. Time is money. Okay, go ahead. I'll take the blame."

On his return to the garage that evening, Korovin discovered the price of this good will. Reports the *Soviet Russia* piece:

"The same foreman stood at the garage gates and with a kind-hearted grin collected the itinerary cards from the arriving drivers. Folded inside were three and five rubles notes.

" 'What are you staring at?' a driver asked Korovin. 'Better have a three-ruble bill ready. Or afterwards you'll have to fork out a tenner. We call these gates the "golden gates," because you won't get through without money.' "

However, Korovin was stubborn and did not submit the three-ruble bribe. The next day, in retaliation, he was assigned a place in front of the State Bank, an unpromising place to pick up fares. Besides, his departure from the garage was delayed by the foreman's inspection, which discovered faulty suction in the taxi's fuel line, and it took a few hours to find the necessary spare parts.

Korovin told the newspaper:

"I learned pretty fast that you couldn't get away from this wild system of bribes. I passed over from two to three rubles each to all the technical supervision division foremen, to Lobanev, Galkin, Belyayev, Zota, Solovyev, and Stavtsev. I paid the dispatchers, Balabanova, Medvedeva, and Yurkova. I paid column chief Cherkassov 50 rubles a month. When I needed an axle shaft, I handed over to technical supervision division chief Zolotoverskhy 75 rubles for permission to get it from the storehouse. When Zolotoverskhy became the garage manager I had to give him 100 rubles in order to replace a car that had gone out of use. . . ."

Korovin wrote a complaint of the widespread bribery to the Proletarsky district Communist Party committee. His letter went unanswered. Several other drivers placed their signatures to a joint letter. It, too, was ignored. They wrote to the Moscow Soviet, the city hall. Again, the practice seemed too much taken for granted to warrant a response.

Finally, a letter to the police evoked official interest. The bribe-takers were investigated but all eighty-six of them pleaded innocent.

The question was raised why Comrade Semenov, chairman of the Party unit at the garage, failed to take action against the bribery. The answer was that he was more interested in fulfilling the garage targets—a certain number of miles without repairs and a certain income per taxi—than in observing Party morals. To conduct a campaign against bribes might have lowered the initiative of the key personnel receiving the bribes with a consequent failure to meet the Plan and a possibility that Comrade Semenov would lose his post as Party unit chairman.

Intoned *Soviet Russia's* writer:

"It is to be expected that Soviet justice will thoroughly examine the 'system' that prevailed at the Fifth Taxi Garage and sternly punish the culprits. The bribe-takers must be tried before the general public.

"Graft is dangerous and must be done away with, once and for all."

The day this is done seems a long way off in Russia.

A type of individual that is particularly criticized (in editorials and cartoons) for his "uncultured" morals, tastes, and behavior is the *stilyaga*. The name derives from the Russian word for "style." The *stilyaga* combines characteristics of the "zoot suiter" (a taste for loud-hued clothing with extreme shoulders and pegged trousers), the teen-age jazz fan (with his enthusiasm for various forms of jazz), and the "beat generation" (with its disinterest in productive work). Foreign-made clothes and imported phonograph records are especially sought by the *stilyaga*. The stress laid by cartoons on the clothes of *stilyaga* (usually much more carefully tailored than average Soviet dress) has motivated some law-conscious Russians to demand that narrow trousers and sponge-soled shoes be outlawed! This has led the authorities to point out that clothes do not make the man, that it is incorrect to denounce a student for being a *stilyaga* because of his inclination toward letting his hair grow longer than other students or for favoring smart clothing. Rather it is "bourgeois morals" that mark the *stilyaga*. Of course, pointed out *Komsomolskaya Pravda,* the *stilyaga* trying to purchase clothes from a foreigner can jeopardize the security of the state by trading secrets to spies who are everywhere!

Posters ridiculing *stilyaga* are found along with charts indicating the increase in hydroelectric power, the targets for cotton textiles, and the goal for pork production in so-called "Parks of Culture and Rest." These public parks provide areas of grass and elaborately contrived floral designs where citizens rest on benches beneath loudspeakers that carry Radio Moscow. There are the customary statues of Lenin, Lenin and Stalin, Stalin and Maxim Gorki, and, more surprising, of thinly garbed athletes with tennis racket, shot put, javelin, or jump rope. (Some, of female athletes, are the closest thing to Soviet "cheesecake" or "leg art".) Most are painted silver.

The "Park of Culture and Rest" named after the Russian literary figure, Gorki, has rowboats for rent, a gigantic Ferris wheel (2 rubles—20 cents—for a ride consisting of four times around), and other thrill rides, including a long beam pinned to a swivel which permits the beam to describe an arc of almost 180 degrees. You pay one ruble (10 cents) for the privilege of being strapped to the free end of the pole and being flung mercilessly back and forth in a nausea-producing arc. The Russians are a hardy race! I've never seen a roller coaster in Russia—probably because too much precious steel would be required to build one, but Russians in Gorki Park seem to get as much fun as Americans do in Coney Island from a roomful of crazily distorted mirrors.

As in parks in every city and hamlet, Gorki Park has an area where chess sets are provided, and intense fans ponder pawn moves for hours. Chess is a national pastime; children learn how to play at home, and there are chess clubs when they get of school age. Chess champions are national heros, and Russians have long excelled in world championships. (Russians play cards, but not bridge.)

However, the number one spectator sport in Russia is soccer. Volley ball is the most widely played sport. Although Russia began playing ice hockey only in 1947, ten years later a Soviet team was able to beat a visiting team from Canada, where the sport is traditional. Basketball is increasingly popular, but there is no baseball (but a game called *lapta* is played by peasants and includes some of the features of baseball), no American-style football, and no golf played in Russia. And it's not likely that golf will catch on soon. It's an individual sport, and Soviet authorities prefer mass sports.

Moscow and other cities have race tracks. There is betting, although, in general, gambling is frowned on as a capitalistic vice. (There are no roulette casinos in Russia.) The explanation for having these rather shoddy race tracks at all is that they provide a means toward improving breeds of horses on collective farms. There are also trotting races. The tracks, strangely enough, come under the Ministry of Agriculture; the betting is the responsibility of the Ministry of Finance.

Russians are ardent fishermen. Licenses are not required, but there *are* fishing regulations concerning season and size of catch. Russians hunt. Surprisingly, guns are sold openly in stores. Upon purchase of a weapon a Russian must register with a hunting club. There are also dog clubs, and dog shows are held periodically. Military and hunting dogs are predominant in the shows, but there are many other breeds. Since 1943 an "All-Union Pedigree Book of Hunting Dogs" has been published, listing the best animals.

One of the favorite outdoor pastimes is collecting mushrooms. Russians are taught from childhood where to find mushrooms that are poisonous, and how to prepare edible ones.

Moscow boasts of a magnificent sports complex across the river from the heights on which Moscow University's "multistory building" (a phrase preferred instead of "skyscraper") is situated. It includes a stadium that seats 100,002 spectators (two seats were added to make it the largest stadium in the Communist world—two seats larger than one in an East European capital), tennis courts, an indoor arena, a swimming pool, and other fine facilities that would enable Moscow to play host to the Olympic Games.

The status of athletes in Russia cannot easily be compared to the United States or other Western countries where a track star is either amateur or professional. There is only one status of athletes in the Soviet Union—amateur by Soviet definition, but certainly with many of the characteristics of the paid professional. All sports in Russia come under a central sports committee whose authorities report directly to the Kremlin's Council of Ministers (Anastas Mikoyan has customarily been the Kremlin figure responsible for this besides his other duties). Under the central sports committee is a network of committees that includes every school, farm, factory, office, and military unit. These vast sports organizations have names, uniforms, and even stadiums. "Locomotive" is the railroad workers' sports club. "Dynamo" is the club of the internal security forces (the secret police). Teams are organized in each enterprise. Everyone is encouraged to participate. In so intensively organized a set-up it is difficult for a promising athlete to escape attention. As soon as a talented high jumper, for example, is discovered in a factory, his life changes. Every encouragement is offered to him—a better apartment, plenty of time away from the assembly line to practice under expert coaches, trips abroad with teams. The man continues to draw his salary— or may well be promoted to a better job, if a raise seems in order. He does not get paid for sports as such (although he receives expenses on trips). But he is paid ostensibly for doing a factory job that becomes only secondary to his main job of winning for the club's banner, and, if he's good enough, for the hammer and sickle.

Russia's remarkable record in international competition testifies to the effectiveness of this system. Women, integrated as they are into every phase of Soviet life, participate in sports more than in most countries. It's interesting that some top Soviet women athletes claim that their records improved *after* they became mothers. Whatever the connection, if any, the record book bears out this claim of at least several Soviet women stars.

A number of sports activities come under DOSAAF— the initials for the Voluntary Society for Aid to the Army, Air Force, and Fleet. DOSAAF clubs are run by the military. They include parachuting, piloting of light planes and gliders, rifle clubs, and radio ham operators. Civil defense organizations also come under DOSAAF. It's one of the more revealing contradictions of Soviet life that air-raid drills are never held, there are no arrows pointing to air-raid shelters, and no sirens visible on buildings. This despite the fact that Soviet publications and radios warn regularly of the aggressive plans of Western imperialists to attack the Soviet Union. (The answer seems to lie partly, at least, in the fact that the Soviet leaders don't believe their own warnings, and that near-hysteria might be created among a populace which has known war as intimately and tragically as Russia's if alarms were given simply to conform with external propanganda.)

As already indicated, the word "culture" in Soviet society spans a vast number of activities—physical culture, "cultured" manners, the artistic culture of ballet and opera. This survey would be incomplete without a brief glimpse, too, of other forms of Soviet culture—art, music, and literature.

The first criterion of art in the Soviet state is that it should conform with the principles of "socialist realism." The difficulty that confronts Soviet artists, however, is that concepts of Soviet realism change to fit particular policies, moods or whims of the Kremlin's occupants. Basically, "socialist realism" means that a painting or work of music contributes to the goals of Soviet society. A piece of music should inspire. A painting that merely conveys an artist's impressions or consists of an interesting arrangement of lights and shadows is censured. The painting must inspire or inform or portray. When an artist is not concerned with the content or message of his painting or musical composition, he is accused of "formalism." That is, of having greater concern for the "form" of his work than for its content. An artist's creation must be optimistic and, above all, it must be easily understood by the masses. (In other words, the men in the Kremlin must understand what the artist is trying to say.)

This imposes a strait jacket on Soviet art. Soviet-era paintings often look like calendar art. A worker stands with his arm around a fellow worker, gazing out on the construction site of a new dam. A brigade of happy collective farmers are bringing in the harvest. Nikita Khrushchev is shown in a cotton field in Uzbekistan imparting agricultural hints to the Uzbeks. Consequently, the most rewarding sections of Soviet art galleries (the fabulously rich Hermitage in Leningrad, the Pushkin and Tretyakov in Moscow) are those devoted to old masters.

One of the most striking paintings in the Tretyakov Gallery depicts the murder by Czar Ivan IV (Ivan the Terrible) of his eldest son, Czarevich Ivan, in a fit of rage on November 16, 1581. By one of the greatest of Russia's painters, Ilya Yefimovich Repin, it was painted in 1885 and is now covered by glass to protect it from viewers. This was felt to be necessary when one visitor to the museum, after looking and then glaring at the painting for long minutes, drew a knife and attempted to slash the figure of the Czar. The deranged visitor succeeded only in inflicting minor damage on the painting before he was restrained. The sight that evoked this rage is described in the Tretyakov's guide book: "Repin chose the actual moment of the murder. Horrified by what he has done, Ivan IV raises the now lifeless body, presses it to his breast, kisses it and tries to cover the gaping wound with his hand.

"The tragic, well-nigh insane state to which he is reduced is conveyed with such power that it would be difficult to find the equivalent of this picture in the whole of world art. All the furnishings of the Czar's chamber are depicted with tremendous artistic skill: the disorder of the thick, brightly colored carpet, the discarded staff with which he has killed his son, the overturned armchair, and the cushion that has fallen to the floor.

"The shrouds of time separate us from the event depicted by the artist, but it is recalled with such force that the visitor has the impression that the drama is being enacted before his eyes."

Even discounting a natural tendency toward exaggeration on the part of guide books, this is a fair description of an emotionally moving painting. It therefore seems like a remarkable redundancy when the guide taking groups through the Tretyakov's halls feels compelled to offer a word of elucidation.

"You see," she adds, after an explanation of the murder. "Ivan was a man of very bad temper."

Perhaps the most popular painting among Russians is "Morning in a Pine Wood." This canvas shows a mother bear and three cubs frolicking in a thick, old pine forest as the hazy shafts of early morning light filter through the trees. Painted in 1889 by I. I. Shishkin, one of the first artists to use the Russian landscape as subject matter, "Morning in a Pine Wood" has a photographic quality. In this respect Shishkin, although he died at his easel at the age of sixty-six in 1898, long before the Revolution, was a forerunner of socialist realism. His style can be readily understood by the masses, it leaves nothing open to interpretation. However, it lacks another prerequisite of socialist realism—social significance. Perhaps because Shishkin is closest of the old Russian masters to Communism's magazine-illustration school of art, the four bears in the woods are seen frequently on restaurant walls, airport waiting rooms, and a brightened reproduction even appears on the wrapping of a Soviet chocolate bar.

Shishkin was realist enough to concede that, although he painted landscapes effectively, he could not turn his brush to lifelike animals. So, for "Morning in a Pine Wood" Shishkin called upon his contemporary and friend, K. A. Savitsky, whose specialty was human forms at hard labor, to fill in the pine woods with the playful bears. Savitsky obliged. No secret was made of the friendly assistance. And, although it's as if Whistler had painted the rocking chair and called on W. P. W. Dana to paint in his mother, Russians seem to find nothing unusual in the collaboration.

Despite the restrictions on creative freedom, Soviet composers, including Aram Khatchaturian, Dimitri Shostakovich, and Sergei Prokofiev have written notable works. Composers of popular music are less successful in their endeavors, although lack of talent, rather than ideological restraints, seems to be at the root of the problem. A dance tune entitled "Serenade," with music by M. Tabachnikov and lyrics by V. Kharitonov, is typical of the unimaginative, moon-June-croon variety of Soviet popular music. Its lyrics run like this:

It's Spring again, the Winter's dead,
Bright clouds are sailing overhead.
And you can hear again at dawn
The cries of the returning swan.

To old homes they've found their ways,
They're bringing back the sunny days.
See them around their lake nests fuss;
From o'er the seas they've come to us,
        to us, to us, to us.

Unlike the swans you are so near,
Across the lake she lies, my dear.
There is no need to find your way,
Just stretch your hand, I'll come to stay.

The waves around so gently toss,
It takes no time to swim across.
Our pure loves, I know, survive,
So our Springs we will revive
        to us, to us, to us.

Though not a straight way but a detour
Your love has not ceased, to be sure.
The trace to heart is never lost,
Starlight will shine at any cost.

Just search about, just take a look,
See, Love is huddling in a nook.
It's never dead, it cannot wreck
And it is certain to come back
        to us, to us, to us.

Even sheet music and phonograph records of the caliber of "Serenade" sell quickly. Fewer than 100,000,000 discs (less than one for every two persons living in the U.S.S.R.) are manufactured annually. Many Russian-manufactured phonograph sets are spring-wound, and most Soviet phonograph records come only in old-fashioned 78-speed. In Moscow there are only forty-seven stores that stock phonograph discs. Understandably discs are an item most in demand from foreigners. This shortage led several enterprising students to transcribe numbers from Voice of America broadcasts onto old, exposed X-ray film, cut into circular phonograph-record shape. They found a ready market until they were arrested for engaging in private manufacture. (This ingenious scheme raises the mental image of Frank Sinatra's rendition of "I Get a Kick Out of You" recorded on an X-ray of a broken shinbone.)

Like phonograph records and sheet music, the publishing of books is an exclusive function of the Soviet state. Books are often published in tremendous editions. A first run of 200,000 copies is not unusual. By way of comparison, a first run of an average novel in the U.S.A. is seldom more than 5,000 copies. Russians read a great deal. Perhaps a more significant reason for the large printings is that, with a limited variety of interesting titles to choose from, even new printings of classics such as Shakespeare are quickly sold out. American authors published in Russian include Jack London, Upton Sinclair, Sinclair Lewis, Theodore Dreiser, Ernest Hemingway, John Steinbeck, William Saroyan, William Faulkner, and, of an earlier era, Henry Wadsworth Longfellow, Walt Whitman, and Mark Twain. To be selected for translation into Russian, an American author's work almost invariably must include passages that, in the Soviet mind, reflect badly on the American way of life. For example, *Tom Sawyer* published in huge editions, has been made into a movie (1936), and is extremely popular. A foreword included by the state publishing house tells readers that the book represents life in a typical American town—with poverty, bigotry and persecution of Negroes. To see the Russian movie version of *Tom Sawyer,* you'd never know that Mark Twain was a great American *humorist.* It is a depressing tale of outrageous racial intolerance.

At the very least a book by a foreign author must contain nothing ideologically objectionable to Soviet authorities. Strangely enough, the most popular present day American writer in Russia is Mitchel Wilson, author of *My Brother, My Enemy,* and *To Live with Lightning,* a relatively unknown person in the U.S.A. Two million copies of his works have been sold in Russia.

Having brought literacy to almost the entire population, the Communists have established a great number of bookstores in each city and at least one library in every town. The largest is the gray stone Lenin Library in Moscow, with 18 million publications on its shelves in 160 languages. Of that number, 6,700,000 are foreign publications. For admittance to rooms where certain publications are kept—including American magazines and newspapers (which, of course, are not sold on newsstands)—it is necessary to have permission as a student or functionary whose work requires such reading. Fifty thousand copies of the magazine *America,* published by the U. S. Government, are sold and distributed each month in a reciprocal arrangement which enables the Russians to sell a similiar number of their propaganda magazine, *U.S.S.R.,* in the United States. *America* is very popular and is passed from hand to hand.

With a few exceptions, American authors are not paid royalties for their works which Soviet officials choose to publish.

The yardstick that is used to decide what books by Soviet authors to publish was described in an interview with Minister of Culture Nikolai Mikhailov. "Our publishing houses," he said, "publish literature which helps to build a new world, a new society. If the work is written on a plane which is not useful for society and which has no use for our society, why should we publish anything of that nature?"

In other words, to earn a living a Soviet writer must conform with the requirements of the State and Party or remain unpublished. (An exception is poetry; purely lyrical love poems are published.)

In case you've ever wondered what Russia's Cyrillic alphabet looks like, this is it:

А	Р
Б	С
В	Т
Г	У
Д	Ф
Е	Х
Ж	Ц
З	Ы
И	Ч
Й	Ш
К	Щ
Л	
М	Ь
Н	Э
О	Ю
П	Я

The word "restaurant" in Russian and in English is pronounced pretty much the same, with the accent rearranged. In Russian, "restaurant" looks like this: *PECTOPAH*. And not a few visitors leave Russia thinking it's pronounced just the way it looks!

CHAPTER 25

WHY WAS THE ANTI-RELIGIOUS MUSEUM LIQUIDATED?

A Communist Party leader delivering a speech on plans for increasing Soviet industrial production adds a parenthetical "God willing." A young waitress, born and schooled under the Soviet flag, says to a person who has sneezed, "God bless you." "With God's help," Stalin himself is said to have murmured when discussing strategy with Western heads of state during World War II.

Although many such references to God by Russians, including devout Communists, are simply a manner of speaking inherited from the past and without any religious connotation, the fact is that religion is far from dead in the U.S.S.R. In no sense, though, does it flourish.

Moscow is said to have had 564 Russian Orthodox churches in 1917. Today there are 50, many of them small and decrepit. There are 600,000 Jews in Moscow alone, but only one synagogue in addition to two small chapels, actually apartment rooms converted for prayer. Once there were 20 synagogues. During the forty-two years from the Revolution until 1959 only 36 new Moslem priests were trained.

The Kremlin's attitude toward religion since Stalin's death has been one of tolerance but not encouragement, of granting believers a measure of right to worship while teaching atheism in the schools and through the press. Tourists are taken on a Sunday-morning tour in Moscow which includes services at the single Catholic church, just down a side street from the main iron gate that leads into the notorious Lubiyanka prison, at the only Baptist church, and at the largest Russian Orthodox

Cathedral. The visitors from abroad are often impressed to find these diverse places of worship functioning at all and startled to find them crowded. Worshippers stand shoulder to shoulder in the elaborately decorated Russian Orthodox Church; benches are provided only for the aged and infirm. The Baptists meet in a simple hall, with balconies built around three sides. It is so jammed with women in shawl-covered heads and wrinkled men standing throughout the service that it is difficult to see the center aisle between the pews.

The vast preponderance of the worshippers are old people, many over sixty. There are some under thirty, and on one usual Sunday morning in a Moscow church, a five-minute walk from the Kremlin, there were twenty babies being baptized by immersion in an engraved metal fount.

In their somewhat more tolerant attitude toward religion, Stalin's successors seem to be counting on religion gradually dying out as the old believers die out.

Actually it was under Stalin that the church in the Soviet Union renewed a measure of grip on fast-ebbing life. During World War II, hard beset by the enemy, the Kremlin sought to rally the populace by every possible device. The hierarchy of the church responded to the demands made on it by the Communist Party and the government and applied its influence behind the war effort. Declarations and proclamations were signed by church leaders and they still are today. When the Kremlin, for example, took a position on Egypt's side during the British-French-Israeli attack in 1956, Soviet rabbis signed a statement, published in all newspapers, denouncing Israel.

Such statements are dutifully issued by church leaders of every faith whenever Communist authorities consider their endorsement of value either for domestic or foreign consumption. The church hierarchy cannot rightly be condemned for such statements. It is the price of religion's survival. For example, leaders of all faiths were called upon to support the Kremlin's campaign for an end to nuclear tests. A declaration signed by "Alexius, Patriarch of Moscow and All Russia; Nicolas, Metropolitan of Krutitsky and Kolomna; John, Metropolitan of Kiev, Galicia, and Exarch of the Ukraine," and other church dignitaries stated in part:

"Whatever governments, persisting—unfathomably to our reason and conscience—in their reluctance to cease dangerous demonstrations, may say in their justification, the Russian Orthodox Church, in sharing the common alarm, believes it its sacred duty to add its voice to the demand of the World Peace Council and the Soviet Peace Committee calling for the immediate discontinuation of the testing of atomic and hydrogen weapons, and acclaims the stand of our government which has repeatedly offered and recently again affirmed its readiness to stop the testing of nuclear weapons. . . .

"In the name of the Divine Love which suffered crucifixion for the sake of human salvation, the Russian Orthodox Church urges the governments of the countries which command atomic weapons and which have still not abandoned their testing to reach agreement upon its immediate cessation and thereby earn the gratitude of all mankind."

A reward for such co-operation with the government was granted to the Moslem church in 1946 in the form of permission to open a *medresse*, a religious school for the training of priests. It was the first since the final conquest of Central Asia by Communist troops in the early 1920s. This Central Asian region encompasses an area greater in size than Texas, Oklahoma, Louisiana, Arizona, New Mexico, California, Colorado, Nevada, Utah, Montana, and Idaho. It includes what are now the Soviet Republics of Turkmenistan, Uzbekistan, Tadzhikistan, Kirghizia, and Kazakastan. Its population of more than 25 million people of mixed Mongolian, Turkish, and Persian strains are almost entirely Moslem. Cities in Soviet Central Asia were once world-famous shrine cities of Islam. Devout Moslems made pilgrimages to Samarkand and Bukhara, now Soviet cities. It was in Bukhara that the first post-Revolution medresse was opened in the crumbling shell of a deserted religious school that had been founded originally in the sixteenth century.

Built around an open, cobble-paved, square courtyard, the medresse is constructed on two levels of cloisters, the arch of each leading into a cell-like stone room. Patches of glazed blue and green tiles in mosaic designs still cling to the walls of the ancient edifice. A tall man must stoop to enter the wooden door that leads into the courtyard from the narrow Bukhara street, where turbaned men astride ridiculously small donkeys, and even veiled women wander by occasionally. The upper portion of a gently tapering minaret can be seen from within the courtyard of the medresse. Built in 1127 during a Turkish dynasty, one of the many that swept over this trade route linking China and the Arab world, the minaret had a number of uses. It was built for the primary purpose of summoning Moslems to prayer five times a day. From its cupola-summit the desert can be seen stretching in every direction, and the tower was used to send up smoke signals for guiding lost camel caravans. It also served as a watchtower to guard against the approach of enemy nomadic tribes toward Bukhara's clay wall ramparts. Finally at the end of the seventeenth century and the beginning of the eighteenth the minaret was occasionally used as an execution tower; victims were forced to leap from it to death.

The seventy-five students at the medresse live much as novices did on the same premises centuries ago. There is no running water nor flush toilets. In fact, a sewerage system is still only in the planning stage for all of Bukhara's 80,000 residents. Classes are held in the fifteen-foot square rooms, with the students crowded at narrow tables. It was a chilly early morning in March when I visited the medresse and watched a class of eighteen students, each in turn reciting the declension of the verb "to write" in Arabic. They were wearing overcoats and *tubeteika,* the black square skull caps with white thread embroidery that are the traditional hats of Uzbeks and other Central Asian men. At a worn blackboard an old, bearded teacher who resembled an ancient Chinese scholar swayed rhythmically to and fro in his chair as the students chanted the verb forms. A single, bare, electric light bulb hung from the whitewashed, vaulted ceiling, and one young Uzbek borrowed a pair of spectacles from his Tartar neighbor in order to see the blackboard better in the poor light.

Each of the medresse's six teachers and the director, Shahasidin Mominov, a *Korei,* a person who knows the entire Koran holy book by heart, has a windowless cell-like room to himself as living quarters. However, one room is shared by six students, and there is scarcely space to walk between the cots, arranged head to foot in orderly rows. The students' rooms have a narrow stone staircase in one corner leading to a sort of attic where they keep their few possessions. The rooms are clean and there is a rather pitiful effort to add a touch of cheer to the stark monastic surroundings. A calendar with a picture of a vase of flowers adorned the wall of one student room. Another wall displayed a two-page spread from a magazine, with scenes of Samarkand.

There are classes six days a week and Sunday is the day off, even though Friday is the customary Moslem holy day. Although classes were much smaller in the beginning, the school now is admitting twenty students to the first-year class and there are about seventy applicants each year. They come mostly from peasant families, but parents of the students include factory workers and Moslem clergy. Half of the candidates for Moslem priesthood are Uzbeks, and there are twenty Tadzhiks, seven Tartars, five Kazakhs, three Kirghizi, one Turk, one Balkar—representing a fair cross-section of the Moslem nationalities living in Soviet Central Asia. All have completed ten years schooling in regular government schools.

Although the students are able to leave the medresse to go home only during the summer vacation from June to September, and for emergencies, twenty are married and most of these have children. I asked the director whether wives objected to being separated from their husbands for so much of the nine-year training period. He responded that a Moslem wife must realize the need for the intensive training and be pleased at her husband's opportunity to enter the priesthood.

Unlike students at government schools, those at the medresse, run and financed by a Moslem council, do not receive any subsidy or stipend. The school's low budget of 700,000 rubles ($70,000) provides the student with a few rubles for occasional movie and theater tickets, for haircuts, for regular visits to a nearby public bath house, and for clothing. Judging from the small, neatly folded piles of clothing on shelves in each dormitory cell, the novice wears most of his clothes at once. Students may also receive money and packages from home, and because the Bukhara desert region is so poor in fruits, the students look forward to such family offerings.

In 1957 a second medresse was opened in Tashkent, capital city of the Uzbek Republic of the U.S.S.R., and, after five years, students from the Bukhara school go to Tashkent for the final four years of their religious preparation. Then they are *mullahs,* priests, usually at mosques and less frequently go to work in the council or as teachers in the religious schools.

The director of the Bukhara medresse, his bearded face rarely changing expression under his black turban, spoke with me in the small library at a table covered with Communist tracts including *Pravda* and *Dawn of the East.* The library's 4000 brown-bound volumes had been collected from mosques and individual homes when the medresse was founded. After Central Asia was incorporated into the Soviet Union, publishing of the Koran was stopped. Deprived of its own printing presses by the Communists, the Moslem church was dependent on the good will and resources of the state, and it was not until 1957 that government presses in Tashkent were made available for a new edition. It is a simple book, without any of the gold lettering for Allah's name or handpainted borders that adorn older editions. Fewer than 5000 copies were published, and the school received 100 of them.

Restoration work on the medresse's stone and tile work is being financed jointly by the Moslems and by the government program for repairing structures of historic importance. The director, a cautious man, replied to questions in a manner intended not to provoke the authorities in any way. Was there any interference by the state in the school's activities? There was no interference, replied Mominov with level gaze, and in fact the state helped a great deal by making various construction materials available for the medresse to purchase. What taxes did the school pay? None, he claimed. He said that there are four mosques in Bukhara, a city that a half century ago was the proud site of one hundred medresses and an even greater number of mosques. Friday services at each of the four mosques were now attended by 500 to 1000 worshipers.

It was a fast period when I visited Bukhara, and religious Moslems ate only after sunset. However, the director spread the small table in his room with pistachio nuts, pink and white sugar candies, a pomegranate, a native round, flat *non* bread, and green tea. It was somewhat inhibiting to eat freely with the host sitting quietly by, unable to take anything, even water. At 8 A.M. a bell outdoors rang the end of a class period, and the students gathered for a few minutes in the courtyard near a volley-ball net that seemed anachronistic in the medieval setting. Then a sound was heard that seemed even more incongruous. *"Gaverit Moskva,"* called a voice from a speaker hung under one of the cloister arches. It was Radio Moscow beginning its broadcasts for the day and penetrating even the walls of this ancient Moslem sanctuary with the official voice of indoctrination.

The council which supervises and finances the medresse and other Moslem activities in the region has its headquarters in the city of Tashkent and is called "The Spiritual Department of Moslems in Central Asia and Kazakhstan."

Other religious faiths in the Soviet Union have analagous bodies, authorized and supervised by the government. The Central Asian spiritual department has a staff of sixty and there are separate, similar Moslem councils with headquarters elsewhere for the Soviet Trans-Caucasus area, the North Caucasus, and for the eastern Siberian part of the Soviet Union. The Moslem council's functions include the opening, when feasible, of new mosques, the maintenance of existing mosques and medresses, the restoration and repair of religious shrines and monuments, the assigning of religious officials and priests and, in general, the leadership of Moslems in their religious life. Authorities of the body are also called upon by Moslems to interpret the meaning of portions of the Koran and to lend guidance in personal religious problems.

A Tartar official, Abdul Bari, explained that voluntary contributions from believers are the only source of funds. There are several forms of traditional contribution. Once a year each member of a Moslem family is supposed to donate a sum of money equivalent to the price of two kilograms (about four and one-half pounds) of wheat. In addition, Moslems with money in the bank are expected to contribute one fortieth of their savings annually. Those few remaining individual, noncollectivized farmers in isolated regions are supposed to give the money equivalent of one tenth of their crop. Bari said that almost all Moslems observe these traditional payments. He estimated that in the Soviet Republic of Uzbekistan alone, with its more than 8,000,000 people, 60 to 65 per cent were Moslems or, by his definition, people who believe in the Koran. In Tashkent, a city of 1,100,000, there were sixteen active mosques attended by as many as 4000 worshipers on a holy day. In addition, Tashkent had about one hundred neighborhood mosques, small prayer areas attended by a neighborhood-appointed old man rather than by a trained mullah. In the region supervised by "The Spiritual Department of Moslems in Central Asia and Kazakhstan" two hundred mosques were functioning. Ever conscious of the impact his words might make on sensitive Soviet authorities, anxious to give the impression of complete freedom of religion, Bari refused to estimate how many mosques there were in the same region before the Communists came to power. I asked whether there was not a measure of discrimination involved in the state's imposing Sunday as the only nonworking day on a region preponderant in Moslems to whom Friday is the holy day. Bari thought a moment. "I can't say it's discrimination," he began slowly. "No one tells us that we can't observe Friday as a religious day because it interferes with work in the state's factories." Then he spoke more briskly, with intensity. "We know what discrimination means. Under the Czars (much of Central Asia was under a weak Russian Czarist protectorate) there was talk of forcibly converting all Moslems into Christians. Some fled to Turkey. *That* was discrimination." It was a reply designed to satisfy the most critical Communist official.

The main mosque in Samarkand is entered through a wooden gate

that opens off a muddy lane. It is a square, white building, decorated
with a floral design, and stands in a yard of many gnarled trees. Carved
wooden beams jut out and upward from the roof, in the manner of a
Siamese Buddhist temple. At the 1 P.M. service I attended, Moslem men
prayed on their knees inside the mosque and on rugs spread outdoors in
the shade of the eaves. Several children played quietly nearby. A Samarkand bazaar is not far away, and traders in Uzbek striped, quilted coats
and turbans arrived during mid-service, removing their rubbers at the
edge of the outdoor carpets and taking places at the end of one of the
precise rows of kneeling worshipers. For a half hour the three hundred
aged Moslems successively rose and genuflected in unison, rubbed their
palms over their faces in a gesture indicating "amen," and touched their
foreheads to the ground from a kneeling position. The service completed,
I spoke with the mosque's handsome, bearded mullah, Nazarullah Ab-
dullayev, who said that prayers are offered five times a day, at 6 A.M.,
1 P.M., 6 P.M., 7 P.M., and 8:45 P.M. On Fridays as many as 6000
crowded the entire yard of the mosque, but usually only 300 to 500 worshipers attended. The mosque, named after a saint, Hoja Zud Murad,
has a staff of seven priests of varying rank and stands on ground owned,
as is all land in the U.S.S.R., by the government. The clergy pays 1000
rubles ($100) a year in rent. The mullah admitted that there were very
few young worshipers, estimating that less than 15 per cent are under
thirty years of age, although under Moslem custom a boy is entitled to
come to a mosque to pray when he reaches the age of twelve. However,
Moslem customs are perpetuated in the home, and circumcision, prescribed by Moslem as well as Jewish law, is universally practiced. I
asked how old the mosque was, and the wrinkled, brown-shinned men
who had formed a circle around us as we talked, argued the age among
themselves. Finally heads were turned toward a bent, aged man leaning
on a staff. He said that this particular mosque was new, only two
hundred years old, but there had been old mosques on this site for
many centuries before that.

Equally ancient among houses of worship in Soviet Central Asia is
the synagogue on the narrow Street of the Jews in Bukhara. Like the
other low, one-story buildings next to it, the synagogue is built of clay
and straw on a frame of light wood. Age has given it a dull gray appearance. There is no sign outside to indicate it is a Jewish temple. A high,
blue-painted door swings in from the street to a small courtyard and
painted on the whitewashed walls is a blue Star of David. Windows on

either side of the court look in on the rooms for prayer. I attended an early morning daily service which commenced at 5 A.M. Old men, their shoulders covered with *talisim,* tasseled white prayer shawls, inscribed on the hems in gold-lettered Biblical words of praise to God, swayed gently as they chanted the service. About sixty men were present and, in a corridor partitioned from the main room by windows, a few women sat in the place to which they are relegated.

This community of Bukhara Jews is believed to have come to Central Asia 2700 years ago as one of the ten lost tribes that once inhabited the northern Palestinian kingdom of Israel. The southern kingdom of Judah with its two tribes was left intact when Israel was conquered by Assyria. The ten tribes wandered into exile. One group is believed to have found its way through what is now Syria and Turkey into the Caucasus Mountains. The Jews living in the Soviet Georgian Republic are believed to be their descendants. Other Israel exiles wandered farther still to Baghdad, now capital of Iraq, and later were a part of an invasion from that region that moved into Central Asia. Bukhara Jews retain their Semitic features, their prayers and services are read in the traditional Hebrew. They speak no Yiddish, as do Jews of Russia and other European lands. Their native tongue is Tadzhik with its Persian origin, rather than the Uzbek language predominant in the Bukhara region.

The Jewish population of Bukhara is about 3000 and, with fifteen small neighboring communities totals about 5000. Although they encountered discrimination during Stalin's later years and were frequently the target of Uzbeks, the Jews now worship quite freely. On Rosh Hashana and Yom Kippur, the Jewish New Year holidays, 500 crowd the synagogue, and for Friday evening services, the eve of the Sabbath, 200 frequently are present. The sixty-year-old rabbi is permitted to supervise the slaughter of animals at a state butcher shop in accordance with dietary laws, and there are two stands at the outdoor market where kosher meat may be bought. The congregation pays 400 rubles ($40) rent per year for their building. The only religious training is that received at home, and when I asked whether there was any religious education at the synagogue, a young man spoke up: "They'd put us in jail if we tried to do that." His elders made no comment but turned the conversation to other subjects. Each year now there are seven or eight *bar mizvahs,* the traditional service for boys upon attaining the age of thirteen. Intermarriage is rare; only about one per cent of Bukhara Jews had intermarried, these with Uzbeks and Tadzhiks, not with Russians.

A young man has been sent to a Moscow seminary, opened since Stalin's death, to study to become the congregation's rabbi.

In the synagogue's courtyard during the service sat a ragged man selling *kashnish,* a parsley type of greens used in Tadzhik soups. Many of the worshipers bought a bunch on their way home.

There were also ragged people on the stairs of the Moscow synagogue, hands outstretched pleadingly, but they were begging rather than selling. It was a cold day in September with rain swept by stinging wind and a crowd of 2000 people milled about in the street in twilight while the Rosh Hashana service was in progress inside the synagogue. About 1200 Jews, men downstairs and women on a balcony, were compressed in the shabby auditorium. Those outside, waiting fruitlessly for a chance to enter, must have felt their presence near the synagogue was a form of participation. Tubes of neonlike lights, newly installed, lit the altar with a garish brightness where a bearded rabbi and a cantor led the service, chanting in minor key. An open curtain revealed the scrolls of the Torah, the ancient law, and high on the wall the Ten Commandments were inscribed in Hebrew. In this congregation as in all others there was only a scattering of young people born since the Revolution.

Although anti-Semitism is forbidden by Soviet law it *is* practiced, as are other forms of racial and religious discrimination. A Russan woman in Alma Ata, capital of Kazakhstan, confided in me: "We Russians consider these Asians to be below us. No self-respecting Russian would intermarry with them." It is known that institutions of higher education in the U.S.S.R. have "quotas" on the number of Jews admitted. Institutes that train people for the Soviet diplomatic service are closed to Jews and so are high posts in the military services.

Such was also the case at midnight services celebrating Easter at Moscow's Yelohovskaya Cathedral. A few minutes before twelve, members of the congregation, standing for the five-hour service, began lighting small red tapers preparatory to a procession led by the Patriarch Alexius, the "Pope" of the Russian Church. From a balcony a choir, including several voices from the government's Bolshoi Theatre, sang. As the church bells chimed midnight the procession of priests, dressed in rich religious raiment and carrying great candles and icons, walked, chanting, slowly around the Cathedral. About 3000 Russians, more than were jammed inside the building, watched from outside the iron fence for a glimpse of the procession. Many carried candles which blew out in the brisk April wind. Policemen on foot and on horseback restrained the crowd from overflowing into the Cathedral grounds.

It is, of course, difficult to obtain creditable statistics on Soviet citizens who still believe in God. In Russia no one can tell what a man believes in his heart. Nikita Khrushchev is reported to have joked that some Communists don't believe in God at Party meetings but do believe in God at home. Church authorities of the respective faiths claim there are fifty million Russian Orthodox believers, three million Jews and two and a half million Baptists in the U.S.S.R.

Although Communist authorities now permit worship, they are unrelenting in their criticism of religion and in disassociating themselves from it. This was made clear to an American correspondent who, in a friendly gesture, sent Christmas cards to members of the Communist Party Presidium. The colored drawing on the cards, sketched by the correspondent's wife, caricatured the correspondent in Russian peasant's costume, boots, and embroidered shirt. He was reeling, a bottle in hand, in the shadow of St. Basil's Cathedral at the walls of the Kremlin. Nearby, his disapproving spouse, also in Russian traditional dress but barefooted, was carrying a fir tree on her shoulder. The caricatures were unmistakable to anyone who knew the couple. The Russians saw no humor in this. The correspondent was summoned to the Foreign Ministry and told that the leaders had taken offense. The authorities apparently had seen the card as an attempt to ridicule Russians. The correspondent explained that it was intended as a good-humored greeting with no one caricatured but the senders themselves. It did no good. Whether as a result of this incident or not, several months later the correspondent was ordered to leave Russia.

Attacks on religion are frequent in Soviet neswpapers. The youth newspaper, *Komsomolskaya Pravda,* carries articles seeking to discourage young people from religious beliefs by logic, cajoling, and ridicule. A young man, considered an outstanding member of Komsomol, was portrayed by a publication as a fool for submitting to a religious wedding at the urging of his bride's mother. When a child was born to the couple the Komsomol member again submitted to his mother-in-law's pleas and had the child baptized. There's only one thing worse than a God-fearing mother-in-law, proclaimed the scornful article, and that is a mother-in-law-fearing husband.

The newspaper *Truth of Kazakhstan* has carried denunciations of congregations of Jehovah's Witnesses in the Kazakh Soviet Republic. The sect is accused of receiving tracts from the United States and of seeking to undermine the Soviet system. A confession, allegedly made by a member of the sect, was published in which he described the "secret, mysterious, and conspiratorial" atmosphere of prayer meetings. "Soon I realized," read the confession, "that the meetings were not for the purpose of praying to God, but rather for softening up people in an anti-Soviet spirit. Our state, the heads of the sect told us, does not derive its authority from God. That is why it must perish. These lunatic statements were accompanied by slander against our country and the Communist Party."

The significance of the article was its warning to all clergy that, while the state permitted worship, it would not tolerate any preaching against the state in any form. Any criticism of the state or Party from the pulpit would promptly bring down the full wrath and power of the government, plots would be contrived, trials arranged, and conviction ensured. Such was the case for the Kazakhstan Jehovah's Witnesses. Jail sentences were imposed on a number of the leaders.

The newspaper *Literary Gazette* criticized authorities in the town of Kuntsevo, a few miles from Moscow, for failure to punish leaders of a Quaker congregation. The newspaper claimed that Quaker leaders had preached that medical care was not needed by believers and as a result a woman had died of appendicitis. "The authorities quite forget," wrote the newspaper, "that the freedom of conscience guaranteed by the Constitution does not mean that public organs are free from tireless and relentless anti-religious propaganda, especially against such ugly forms of religion as this."

A letter to the editor of *Soviet Russia* from a civic-minded reader, N. Lebedev, in the city of Gorki, asked, in the words of the title, "Why Was the Anti-Religious Museum Liquidated?" Comrade Lebedev wrote: "We in Gorki used to have an anti-religious museum that was very popular. However, shortly before World War II for some reason or other it was reduced to a department of the regional historical museum and then, during the war, liquidated altogether. At present all the exhibition items and documents are kept in the archives of the historical museum.

"We don't understand this at all. An atheistic museum, given thoughtful organization and good management, could be turned into a militant center of propagating scientific atheism and natural science. It could do much in helping propagandists, schools, and cultural bodies oppose religious prejudices and superstitions.

"All the necessary conditions exist for reopening the museum. The various articles and documents are preserved. Experienced scientific workers are able to lead anti-religious work. An appropriate place for the museum is available. Why is it no one sets about this job?"

The *Truth of the Ukraine* praised the organizers of a two-month course of atheistic readings in a Ukrainian city. Attended at first by thirty people, the Sunday morning class grew to two hundred. The lecture topics included "How Was the World Created?" and "What are the Moon, the Sun, the Stars?" and presumably deviated considerably from the usual Sunday-school explanations.

There are a number of museums dedicated to atheism in the Soviet Union, and one of the largest is Leningrad's great domed Kazan Museum, once a Russian Orthodox Cathedral. It is called a Museum of the History of Religion. The exhibits are intended to evoke contempt, indignation, or rage at religion. One display of pasteboard figures shows a peasant being executed in ancient times because he refused to give up a portion of his crop to the church. In the museum's basement a realistic torture chamber had been recreated with three corpulent monks seated at a table. Branding irons of crosses are being heated in a fireplace. The wax figure of an infidel is shown suffering in a stock. Another is undergoing torture in a chair of nails. Still another is being slowly crushed under a series of weights being lowered on his head. The sign over the exhibit reads, "Headquarters of the Inquisition of the sixteenth century."

There are some paintings of leering priests, words of denunciation of the Vatican quoted on display cards, caricatures of church figures. The intent is to depict the history of religion as one of human oppression. In recent years reconstruction work has been completed by the state on a number of churches of historic or architectural interest and work is in progress on others. All of these are being restored, not for worship but as museums. There seems to be a genuine desire on the part of the Kremlin's leaders to preserve treasures of art, even though their origin may be religious. The policy of converting churches into museums serves several other purposes as well. It impresses visitors from abroad to see the brightly colored onion-shaped cupolas of old churches freshly painted in neighborhoods of shabby houses. It helps dissuade the visitor from an impression of religious repression by the state. It lends an illusion of liberality. It serves, too, to assuage the feelings of the faithful to see that church buildings are no longer being converted into movie houses, living quarters, and offices as was the case in earlier days. The *Avant-garde* movie, for example, with its low green dome, was a former church which was closed, either because worshipers feared to attend services or by the state's imposition of heavy taxes.

The most remarkable religious monuments converted into museums are within the walls of the Kremlin. The Cathedral of the Assumption, completed in 1479, is a majestic structure crowned by five golden domes. This was the cathedral for festive Czarist religious services, coronations, and ceremonies. Sharing a cobblestone square with the Cathedral of the Assumption are the Cathedrals of the Annunciation, under construction from 1484 to 1489, and the Cathedral of the Archangel, completed in 1509. The walls, columns, and ceilings of these Czarist churches are covered with magnificent paintings of awesome beauty. Many are dimmed deep brown by annual layers of varnish that were traditionally applied to preserve the artist's work. Slowly and meticulously, layer by layer, the varnish is being removed by experts and images of Christ, the Madonna, various saints and Biblical figures are revealed in colors of exciting vividness.

The burnished gold domes of Ivan the Terrible's belfry stand boldly against the leaden Moscow winter sky and shine radiantly in the summer sun. The great belfry's construction was begun in 1505 and served as a support for huge church bells, as a place of worship, and as a watch and signal tower for old Moscow. The belfry was completed in its present form during the reign of Boris Godunov at the end of the sixteenth century, and within its impressively proportioned gray towers hang 22 large bells and more than 30 small ones.

When viewed from the Moscow River, on the southern edge of the Kremlin, a golden Russian Orthodox cross tops a cupola of Ivan's belfry and is the highest point of the Kremlin's domes and steeples and ramparts. The cross rises above the five red stars of Communism that punctuate the Kremlin's walls and above the Soviet flag that flutters from a Kremlin dome. This may give solace to the faithful and even appear symbolic to some. Worship continues and probably will for a long time to come. The Communists show increasing signs of accepting and tolerating religious practices as they grow stronger and more secure in their revolution. But, withal, religion has ceased to exist as a significant force in Russia today.

CHAPTER 26

WAR OR PEACE

What does the future hold for Russia and for Soviet relations with the non-Communist world?

There's a quaint Russian proverb that notes: "There will be a holiday on our street too." This is a way of saying that "every dog has its day." There have been a good many "holidays" on Russia's street since Stalin's death and there's reason for the Russians to anticipate more.

Industrial and agricultural production surge ahead steadily. The educational system has yielded highly talented scientists. Sputniks have been launched. Space travel begun. Russia has led the world in commercial passenger jet aviation. Soviet dance troupes and concert artists win acclaim in foreign lands, Communist and non-Communist.

An old story still holds true to some degree. It seems that a refugee from Communism decided to return to Russia. He promised to write to his fellow-Russian refugees, in black ink if what he wrote were true, in red ink if censorship prevented him from writing the truth. The letter came. It was in black ink. "Everything is wonderful," he wrote. "You can buy everything in Communist Russia—food, cars, perfume, furniture, clothes. Everything, except red ink."

There still are many shortages, but the fact is that the Soviet Union is making progress not only in sputniks and jet aircraft but in the living standards of its people.

Since 1945, Communism has spread to Eastern Europe and into China, the most populous and second-largest country in the world. More than one third of the world's population lives under the banner of

Communism. This includes thirteen nations and one billion people.

It is true that the rumblings of discontent and even mutiny have been heard within the Soviet alliance, principally from Yugoslavia and Poland. In Hungary there has been revolution. The nature of Russia's alliance is never again likely to be as monolithic and easily controlled by Moscow as during Stalin's time.

But, withal, the successes have been so staggeringly great that it is with confidence that the Soviet leaders pronounce their prophecy that Communism will spread throughout the world. Various phrases have been employed by Kremlin leaders to express this aspiration. Nikita Khrushchev has declared "we will bury you" in the presence of Western ambassadors in Moscow. In a more benevolent mood, Khrushchev expressed the same fanatic confidence by assuring the ambassadors at an embassy reception that "we will re-educate you" when Communism triumphs throughout the world.

The Soviet leaders insist that they do not want or intend to win the world by war. The change to Communism will be gradual, evolutionary, coming about by the workers in capitalistic countries recognizing the "superiority" of the system.

Russians do not want war. This is as true of the men in the Kremlin as of the man on the street. There is scarcely a Russian who did not lose a member of his family or a relative in World War II. A maid in the National Hotel tells with welling tears how her brother lost the toes on both feet in freezing weather at the front and how she hid from bombings. A resident of Leningrad recounts the horrible days of German siege when hunger reduced some to cannibalism. A student says she does not remember her father very well; he was captured in the war and never returned. The scars of war on the land have only recently been erased. Soviet statisticians claim that the war caused 489 billion dollars' worth of property destruction and compare this figure with estimates by economists that the total wealth of the U.S.A. in 1949 equaled 898 billion dollars. Thus, stated an article in *Pravda,* if the money wasted in the war had been used for peaceful pursuits, the U.S.S.R. would long ago have attained the level of America's industrial production, which the Communist Party has set as the nation's main economic goal.

It is only through a prolonged period of peace that Russia can achieve a standard of living which will provide adequate housing, ample shoes, and a few of the niceties of life that have for so many years been denied the people. This is acknowledged by the men who govern the Soviet Union.

The time of danger seems not so much *now* as in the *future*. War could come by accident, by a miscalculation, by a brush-fire war, such as Korea or Suez, spreading. The chilling question of these times is: how long can Russia and the United States skate over the thin ice of repeated crises such as Lebanon and Quemoy without one of these days inadvertently plunging through into the waters of war? There is, of course, always the danger, too, under a form of government that gravitates toward one-man dictatorship as does Soviet Communism, that one individual's impulsiveness may hurl the world into war. But there are checks and balances of a sort within the Soviet state, too, in the Communist Party's Central Committee and Presidium and within the command framework of the army, that mitigates against this possibility.

The danger that lies over the horizon of the future is this: when the passing of time convinces even the most fanatic of Communist believers that the Western democracies are not in a state of inevitable decay and that the triumph of Communism is not predestined, what is their reaction to be? Will they accept the falseness of their dogma that Communism must triumph? Will their currently professed doctrine of temporary coexistence be revised to one of eternal coexistence?

Or will Communism, having failed to become universal by peaceful means, be impelled to fulfill its "destiny" by force of arms?

Only the future will answer these crucial questions.

But the perceptible trends and tendencies in Russia today give cause for optimism that Russia may choose the path of peace.

As the Soviet people acquire more goods and property they acquire, too, a vested interest in a stability that will enable them to retain what they have. A kind of Soviet bourgeois class, so roundly denounced by Communist dogmatists, has been created that is more concerned with retention of what it has than with revolution abroad. Furthermore, the passage of time has diluted the fanaticism that ignites revolution and war.

This applies to revolution at home as well as abroad. There are many Russians dissatisfied because of shortages, crowded housing, red-tape bureaucracy, lack of freedom. But dissatisfied Russians talk about *changes* in their way of life, about improvement, not about revolution. Also, I've never heard a Russian suggest that he would like the American army to liberate him. What's more, deprived of an organized opposition to rally around, Russians are quite unlike Cubans or Guatemalans in their opportunities for revolution.

In fact, what instability exists in Russia seems to be among the leadership rather than among the people. Since Stalin's death and before there has been a steady procession of purges. But these purges have not produced symptoms of disintegration of the Soviet system. In a short span of time, for example, the Soviet system survived the death of Stalin, the purges of Laurentia Beria, V. M. Molotov, Georgi Malenkov, Lazar Kaganovich, Dimitri Shepilov, Georgi Zhukov, and Nikolai Bulganin. It survived the shocks of Hungary and of a short-lived American policy of liberation of Soviet satellite states. The Soviet structure shows durability despite dislocations caused by reorganizations of industry, education, agriculture, and other phases of life.

This durability under duress manifested by the Soviet state makes it naïve to think that the West can simply sit tight and wait for Communist Russia to crumple from within. However, time may be on the side of the non-Communist world in another way.

Great changes are in motion in Russia. Education has produced sputniks; it has also created a hunger for contacts with the outside world, for more goods, for a measure of self-expression. The acquisition of property and the dimming of fanaticism act as a brake on adventurist Soviet policies. Time may be on the side of the democratic West in eventually shaping a Russia that is more moderate, more reasonable, more amenable to living and letting live.

CHAPTER CONTENTS

ACKNOWLEDGMENTS

At the start of my Soviet sojourn I was offered a friendly word of caution by a person who had spent more than a score of years in the U.S.S.R. "The greatest mistake in writing about Russia," he said, "is to think that Russian history begins the day you arrive and ends the day you leave." I have tried to keep this in mind and to take a somewhat longer and more constructive view of the Soviet Union. If the effort to produce an accurate, informative book has been successful it is due in considerable measure to many people who have given of their knowledge, experience, and time. For any failures, the responsibility is mine.

For the opportunity to represent the National Broadcasting Company as radio and television news correspondent in Moscow I am indebted to William R. McAndrew, vice-president in charge of news, and to Joseph O. Meyers, director of news. Their support and editorial principles make it possible for me to report Russia as I see it.

I have received unfailing encouragement, too, from Robert W. Sarnoff, chairman of the board of NBC, and from Robert E. Kintner, president of NBC. My thanks, too, to Davidson Taylor for his consistent help during his services as NBC's vice-president in charge of public affairs.

A special word of appreciation is due to Iverach MacDonald, foreign editor of *The Times* of London, for which I write as "Special Correspondent." My thanks, too, to editors of other publications for publishing my articles about Russia, parts of which have proved useful in this book: C. B. Roberts, article editor of *This Week* magazine; Abel Green, editor of *Variety;* John Hunt, formerly editor of North American Newspaper Alliance and now with *Look* magazine; William Stapleton, formerly of *Collier's* before the demise of that magazine; and Gordon Kester, editor of *Du Pont* magazine. Also, to Leon Daniel of Pix, Inc. for his assistance in the selection of my photographs to illustrate the book.

Edward C. Aswell, editor at Doubleday and Co., Inc., deserves grateful acknowledgment for his encouragement and patience in our correspondence and cables over a distance of five thousand miles. For his many services, I thank my friend and attorney Gerald Dickler. Although they bear no responsibility for the opinions and facts herein, members of the United States Embassy staff in Moscow were especially helpful. My many conversations with our able Ambassador, Llewellyn Thompson, were invaluable. My sincere thanks, too, to Vladimir P. Prokofieff, Harry C. Barnes, Jr., George Winters, Edward L. Kilham, and Major Harry J. Koepp, assistant Air Force attaché.

For experiences shared and views exchanged, I thank my colleagues of the radio-television and press corps in Moscow: Roy Essoyan, Harold Milks, Angelo Natale, Henry Shapiro, Max Frankel, Paul Niven, B. J. Cutler, William Jorden, and Howard Sochurek. Although a number of Russians lent immeasurable help, I know they would prefer to remain unnamed, but my appreciation to them is profound.

Finally, but foremost, for her patience, encouragement, enthusiasm, and assistance, I thank my wife, Nancy, whose presence makes life even in Moscow a delight.

Moscow, October 14, 1958